WOMEN SHAPING the WEST

Stories from Wyoming

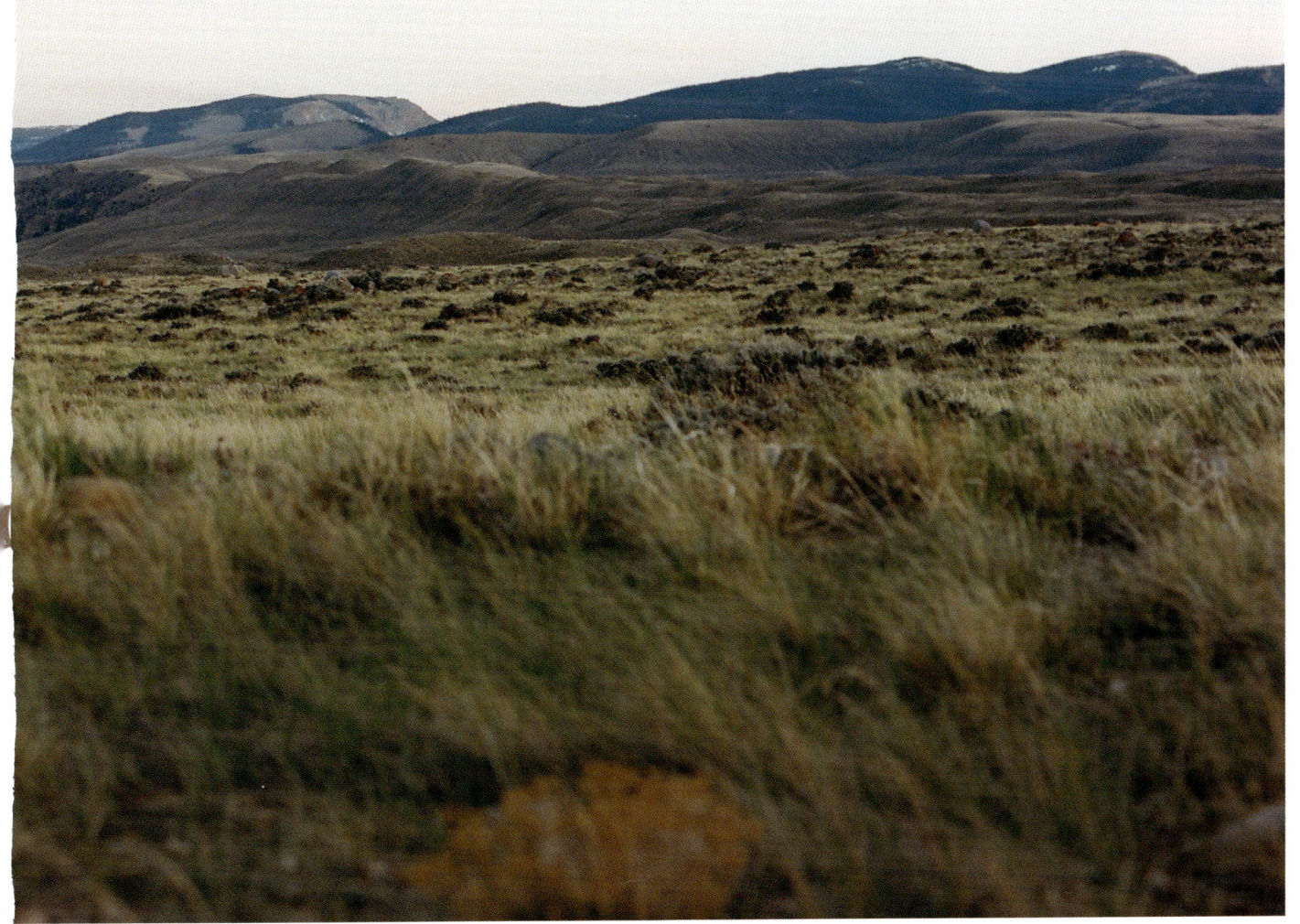

*To my parents, for believing in me,
and to my Buk boys—Dane, Hank, and Luke—
for your love and wildness*

WOMEN SHAPING the WEST

Stories from Wyoming

LINDSAY LINTON BUK

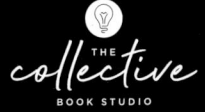

THE
collective
BOOK STUDIO

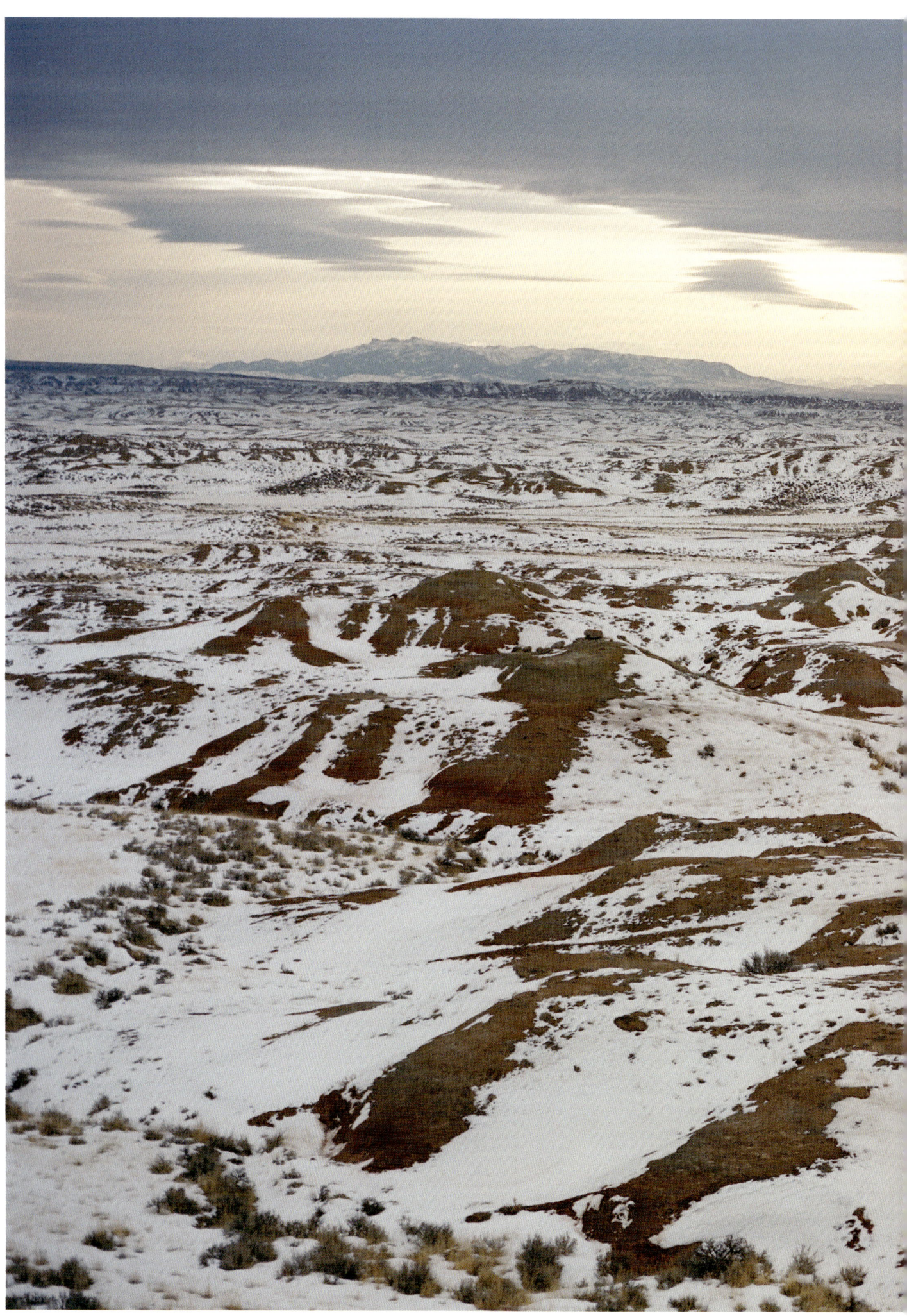

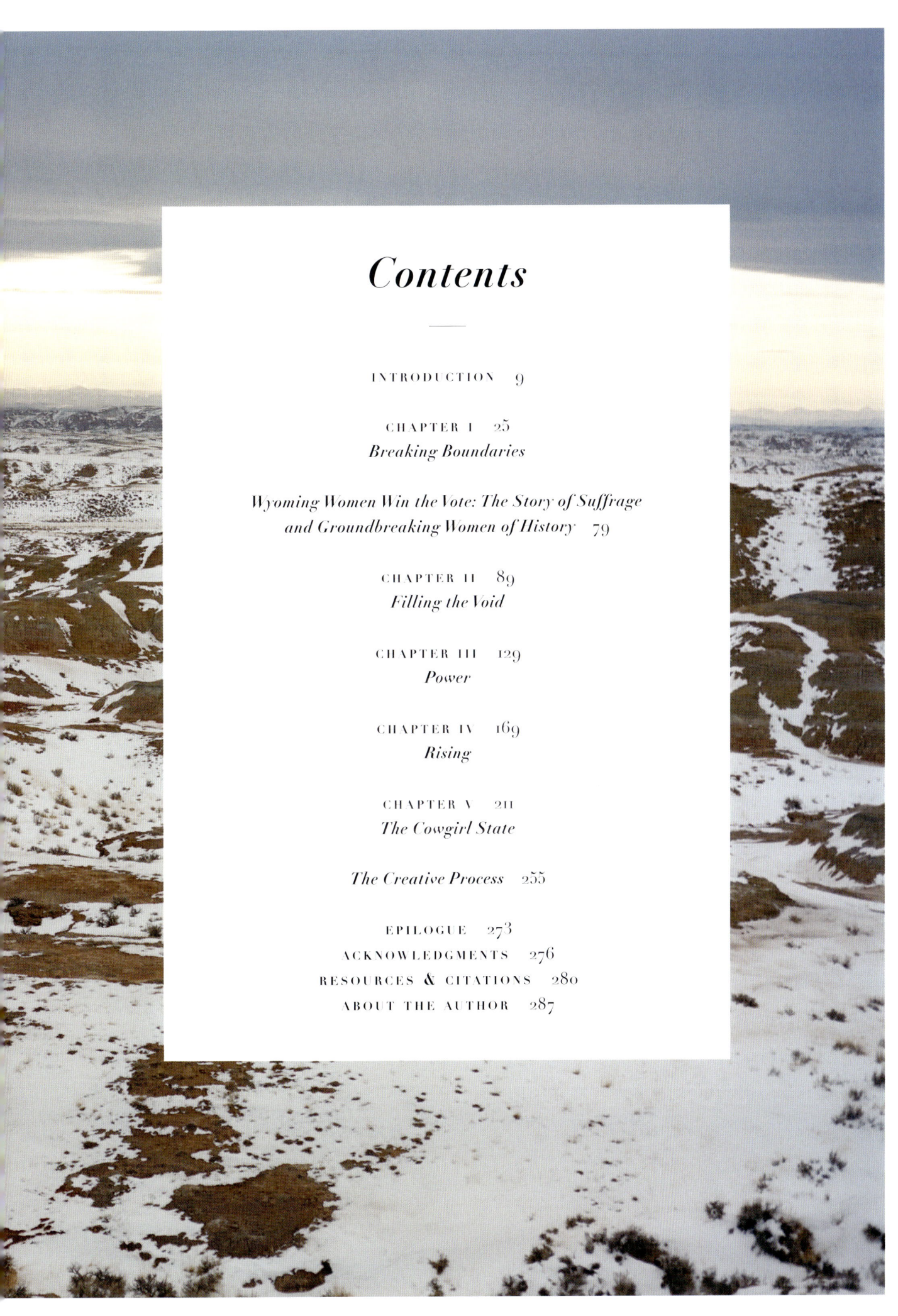

Contents

Shape:
form, create

Especially: to give a particular form or shape
to determine or direct the course or character
of events that shaped history

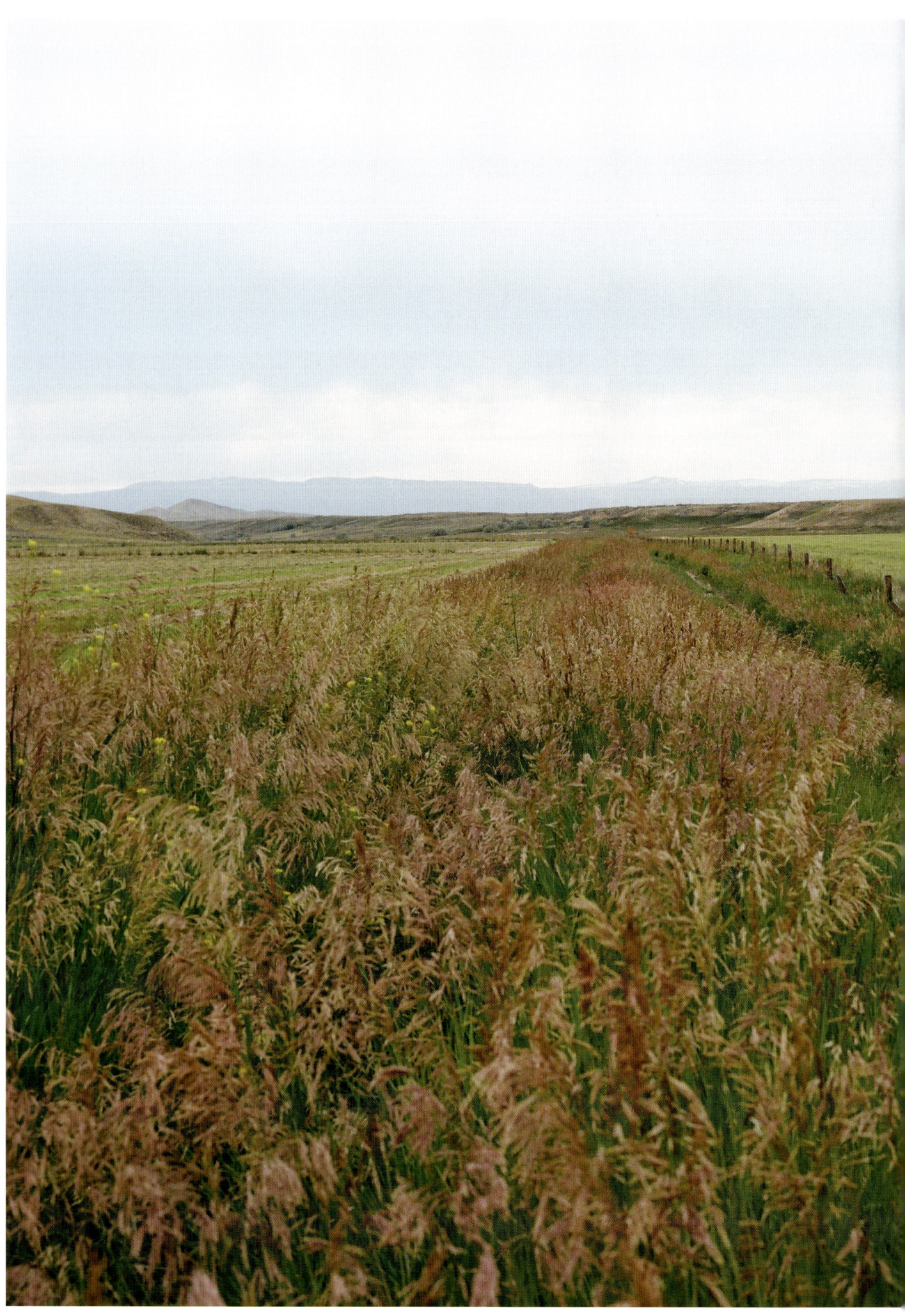

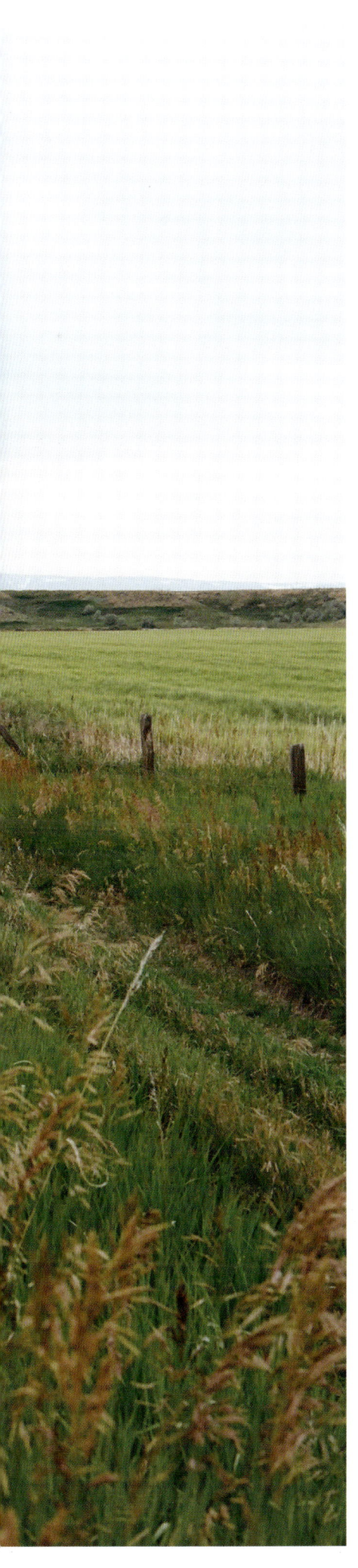

Introduction

—

THIS PLACE IS PHYSICAL. In Wyoming, expansive terrain shapes the least-populated and tenth-largest state in the country. Across 97,914 square miles, humans and organic surroundings have intertwined for centuries. At its core, Wyoming is rural and wild.

The ever-widening landscapes are awe-inspiring but can be isolating. Winter reigns half the year. Living in Wyoming means an intimate overlap with the elements. Less asphalt, fewer big-box stores, more immediacy to the natural world. Highways and neighborhoods border ancient wildlife migration routes. Three-quarters of the state are preserved grasslands or rangelands. Most of Yellowstone National Park, home to a massive underground caldera, behemoth bison, and apex predators like grizzly bears and wolves, constitutes Wyoming's northwest corridor. Interconnectedness with the land breeds resilience, no matter one's background.

What can be forged across these stark, often harsh, largely untamed landscapes?

Shaping a life in Wyoming is physical too. The act of constructing your path demands devotion, energy, and persistence. Women in Wyoming have long embraced this spirit of hands-on effort, courage, and determination. As a result, they have directed the course of American history and continue to influence the state in deeply impactful ways.

Women Shaping the West offers a guide to honoring your innate gifts, strengths, and talents—to release your dreams, visions, fears, or vulnerabilities and not keep them locked inside. Through witnessing the lives of some of Wyoming's bold, impactful women, you'll learn how to embrace an intrepid spirit, harness your power, and forge your own path. By doing so, you make your mark, illuminating the way for others to follow.

Life is a creative act.

Origins

When I was child, in the corner of our family room, next to the dinner table, was a narrow bookshelf stacked full of row upon row of *National Geographic* magazines. The iconic yellow spine, a small world of its own, became impossible to ignore as the bright blocks multiplied. Instead of one world, they became many. An entire universe lay on those shelves. Some evenings, the graphic stacks would glow amber against the light of the fireplace. During meals, my gaze would inevitably wander to that captivating corner of our home. This was when I first longed to explore the world and faraway lands, my earliest memory of being fascinated with people—how they live their lives and their connection to place. In fact, this imprint was so strong that when I went back to school to study photography, years later, my original goal was to become a *National Geographic* photographer.

I was born in Powell, a vast desert basin in northwestern Wyoming that was once an ocean, millions of years past. Pale-washed earth meets pastel peaks in Powell, home to wild mustangs who roam and attempt to survive the tough conditions and terrain. The glacially molded silhouettes of the Beartooth and Bighorn mountain ranges frame the horizon, extending a hundred miles in each direction. Heart Mountain and rocky benches are softened by endless sagebrush and fields of sugar beets, beans, barley, hay, and alfalfa. Eyes fixed on the long horizon, I'd wonder: *Who will I become? What does life have in store for me?* My visions and aspirations were nurtured here in the great expanse of the Bighorn Basin, where I felt small and boundless all at once.

My Linton ancestors first came to the region in 1878, from the Scottish Highlands and Ontario, Canada. They settled in the small ranch town of Meeteetse (population <1,000), where they served on local commissioner boards, held political offices, and founded a mercantile, bank, and insurance company. My Grandpa Bud opened Linton's Big R in 1960, a farm and ranch business in nearby Powell. My dad became an official employee by age eleven and moved home the day after he graduated from the University of Wyoming. The duty of family called, and he

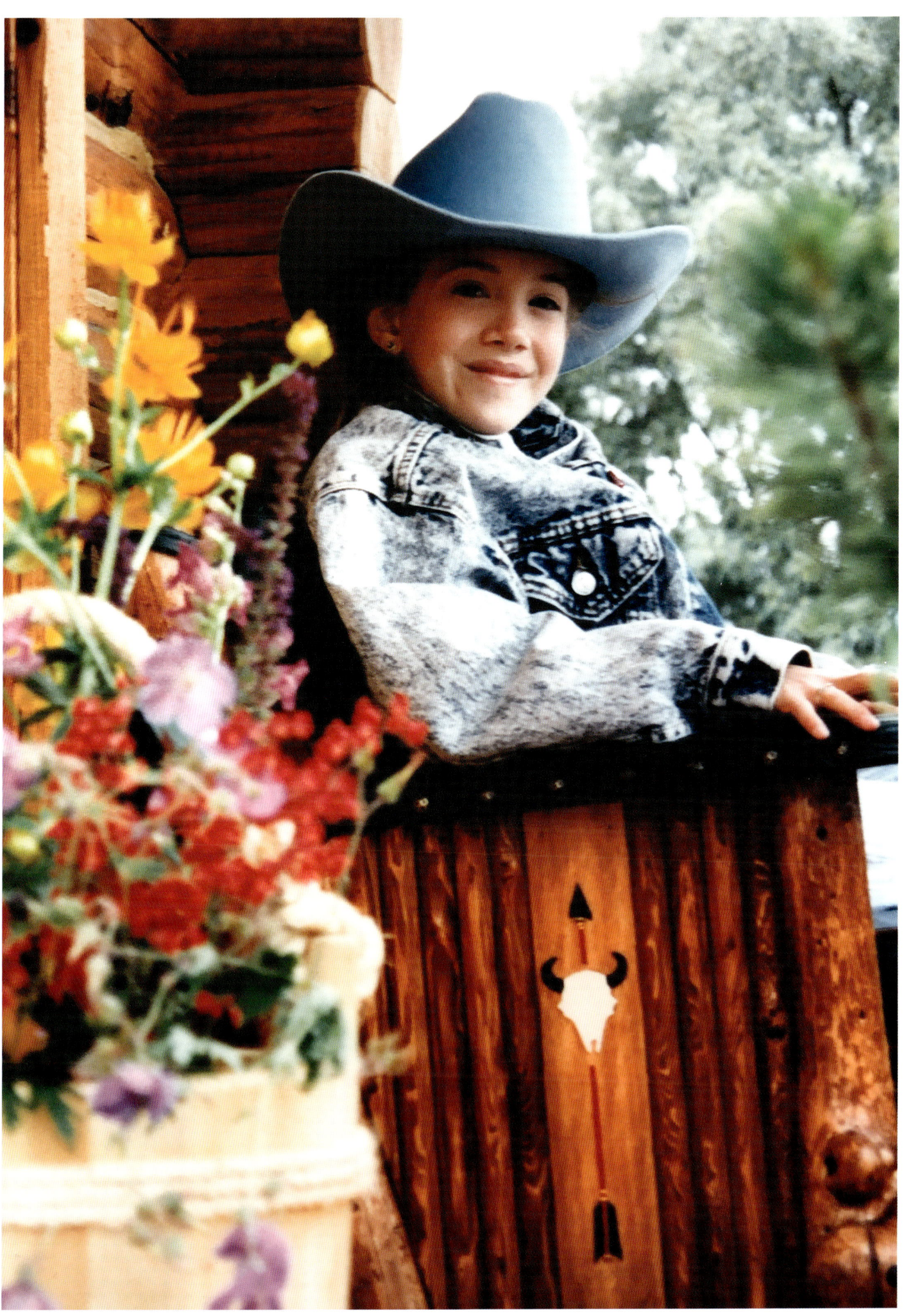

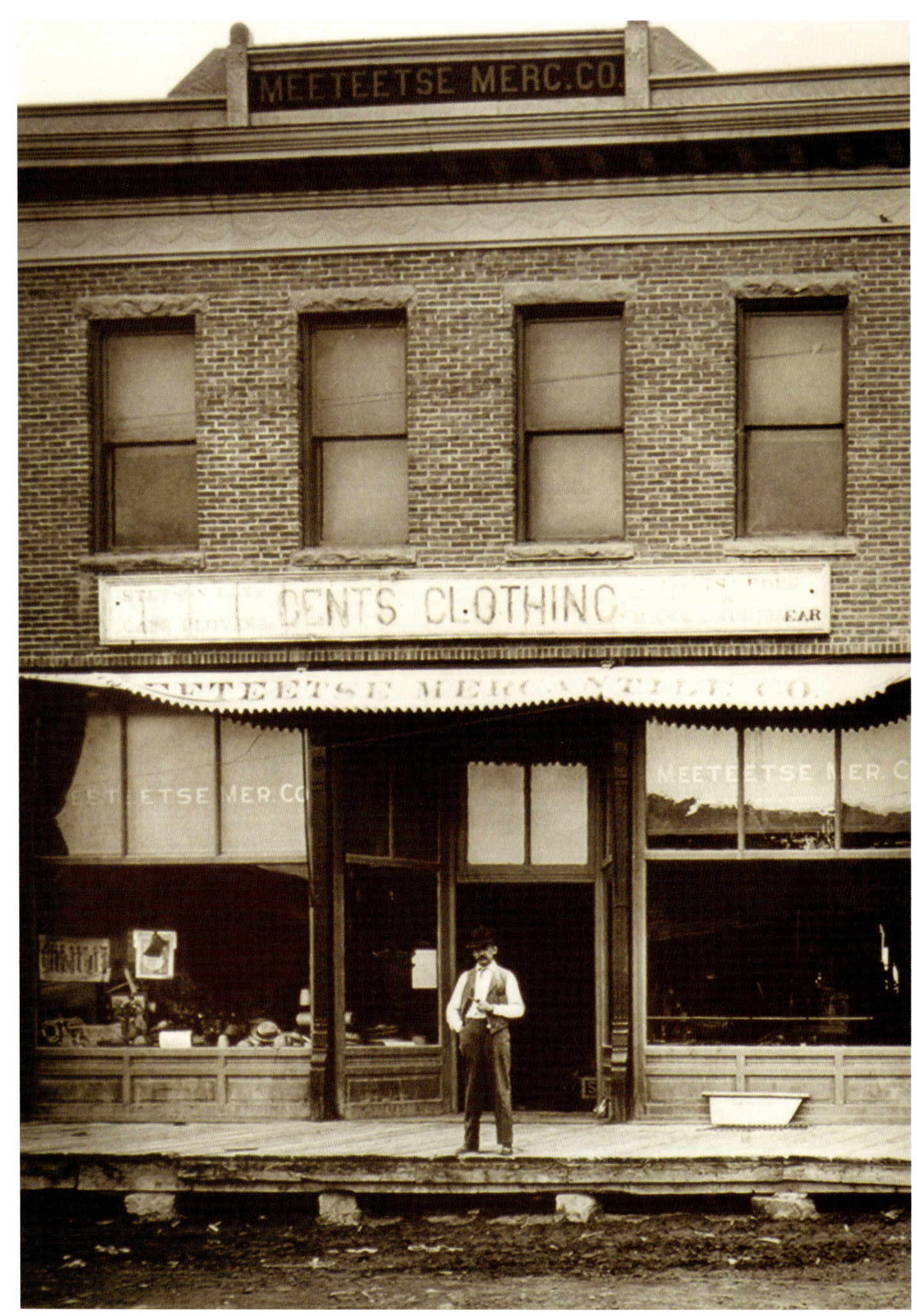

recognized an opportunity to expand the Linton legacy. He is a man with deep love for and devotion to his family and community.

Hailing from Connecticut, my mom was drawn to Wyoming's wildness. She craved the expansion and openness that only places like the West can offer. When she moved to Powell as a high school chemistry teacher, she brought exposure and perspective that opened a whole new world for my dad. Together, they gave me such a strong appreciation for community and discovery. It's a dichotomy that's never left me.

Despite my fifth-generation ties to our state, I never imagined a future for myself in Wyoming. While it provided me the freedom to roam and explore, a part of my spirit felt contained here. It seemed too small, too limiting for the scale of my dreams and my desire to make a large-scale impact on the world. What I gathered from the pages of those magazines—from strikingly honest portraits to unimaginably biodiverse rainforests and foreign wildlife—only ignited my curiosity about a larger world around me, never satiating it completely.

When I graduated from high school, I retraced my mom's footsteps and headed east. My passion for understanding diverse human experiences led me to major in history. After college, I signed up for an introductory photography class at the local community college, ready to take the world by storm and harking back to the little yellow spines that became larger than life. Eventually, I became a professional photographer, and my interest in human stories led me to specialize in portraiture.

History teaches a critical lesson: The stories we prioritize reflect our values. Thus, history is not static but continuously evolves as new stories and perspectives come to light. Photography became my means to tell stories and share them with the broader world.

FACING: My great-great-grandfather Alexander Linton in front of the Meeteetse Mercantile, which he founded with his relative Angus James McDonald in 1899. Image courtesy of the Meeteetse Museums.

The Cowboy State

They call Wyoming the Cowboy State, but women have always been at the heart of our most powerful transformations. Wyoming's official state motto is "Equal Rights," for our historic past, enfranchising women more than fifty years before the Nineteenth Amendment was ratified.

Wyoming, also known as the Equality State, is a place of firsts. In 1869, it became the first territory in the United States to recognize women's right to vote *and* hold office—though most Indigenous women would have to wait to vote until the passage of the Indian Citizenship Act in 1924. As a result of the landmark 1869 decision, Wyoming also gave the country its first female jury (Laramie, 1870), first woman bailiff (Martha Symons Boies Atkinson, 1870), first woman justice of the peace (Esther Hobart Morris, 1870), and first woman governor (Nellie Tayloe Ross, 1925 to 1927), to name a few. Additionally, more legislation furthered women's equality: Wyoming passed one of the nation's first equal pay laws, requiring that teachers be paid on the basis of their qualifications, not their gender. The state also recognized married women's rights to control their own property and wages. At the time, these freedoms were unheard of across most of the country.

Wyoming is no stranger to uplifting bold, impactful women and instigating a take-up-the-reins spirit, in a way that speaks to *both* the Cowboy State and Equality State mottoes. Yet, in the twenty-first century, Wyoming has one of the largest gender wage gaps and ranks toward the bottom for representation of women in state legislature. This is something that should concern us not only as we look to the future but also as we seek to honor our historic legacy.

In other ways, the legacy of the generations before still rings loud and clear. Wyoming is a place deeply in love with freedom, adventure, and self-determination. A place that seeks balance between self-reliance and interdependence. A place where connection and community can flourish, with less anonymity and a greater need to share resources.

One truth is certain: The future is always ours to shape.

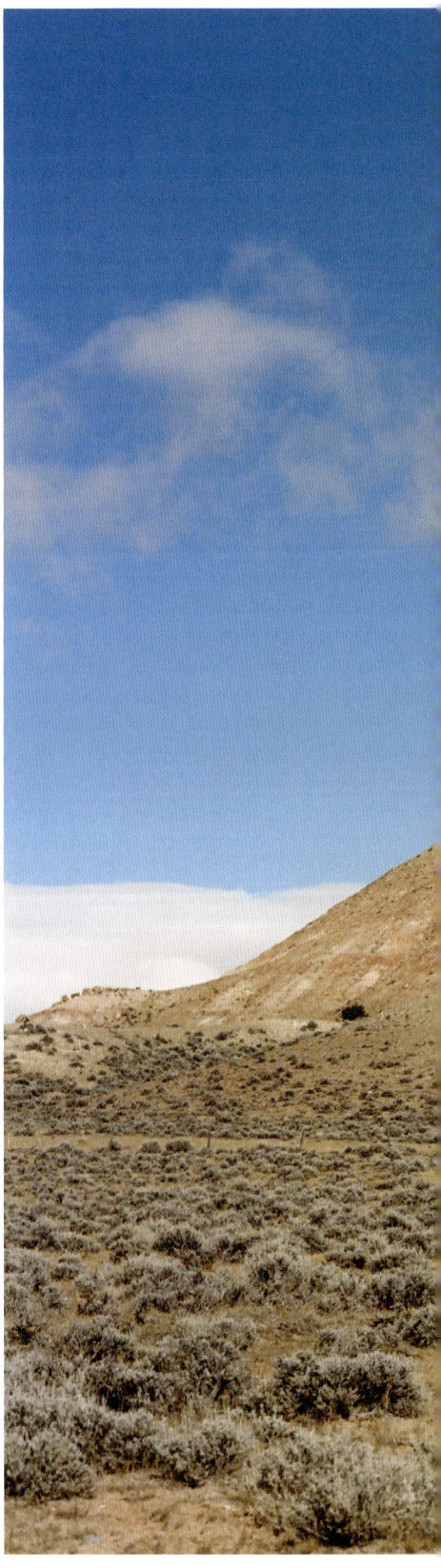

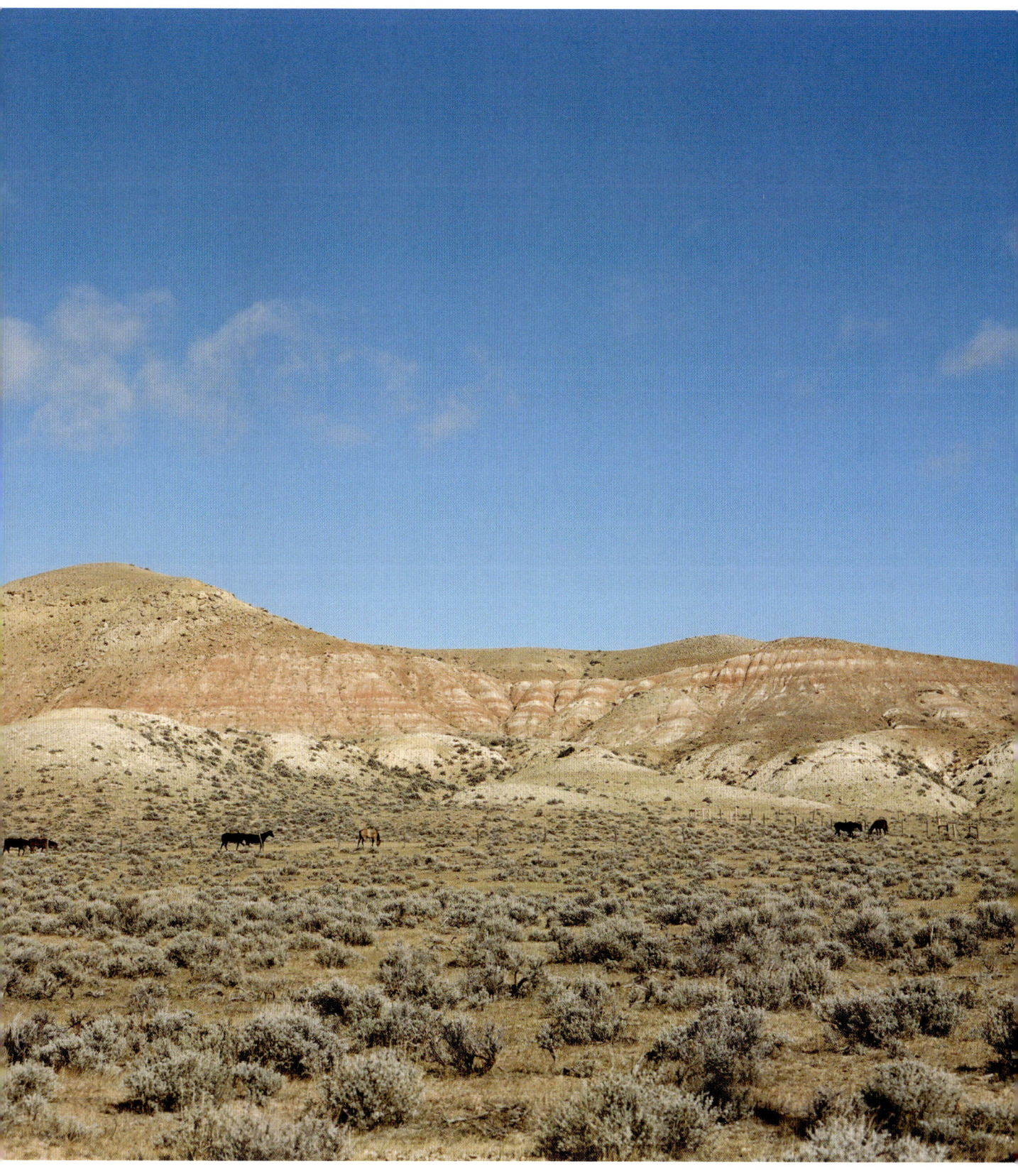

Expand, Contract

In my mid-twenties, I lived in New York City and worked as a photographer. It was one of the most exciting, difficult, and therefore transformative experiences of my life. The energy of the city was invigorating and exhausting. It was the opposite of Wyoming's extremes—filled with culture, eye-opening conversations, shopping, opportunity, density. I loved existing in a microcosm of the world, where every race, religion, attire, profession, and enigma hustled off to their respective spaces. Everyone in New York dreamed big. No dream was too large or insignificant. Living in New York finally allowed me to feel confident identifying as an artist, a creative being, someone who digests the world differently and must create in order to process and grow.

But the incredible concentration of layered worlds, along with being smashed against half a dozen strangers on my daily subway commute, often shoved beneath someone's armpit because that's where my height landed me, was a course in survival in and of itself. There were many times I wanted to give up and return to familiarity, ease, and fresher air.

I cut my teeth in the city. My primary mentorship was working for acclaimed headshot and portrait photographer, educator, and entrepreneur Peter Hurley. Peter is a force. He just did it. The pace was intense, the learning curve steep. But Peter's instruction was invaluable. He hired me as the studio manager of his very busy, very successful business. I eventually became his associate photographer, and I'd work with clients who couldn't afford Peter's rate but wanted his style. I picked up best practices and hands-on experience to photograph an actor's headshot or a yogi's portrait. From Peter, I witnessed firsthand the power of bringing a dream to life. Long-term, my sights were set on becoming a renowned editorial photographer.

The space between when I moved to NYC in 2010 and returned to Wyoming in early 2013 was monumental. I picked up as much as I could as fast as I could. I pushed against time. It was as if my spirit had been catapulted onto a sprint course. Somewhere deep down I knew that

Wyoming was the finish line and that, when I moved home, I'd plant my feet firmly into the ground, rooting myself to the land to forge my own legacy and family.

Stepping off the plane in January 2013, after a few rapid years of discovery and growth, I paused. The wind whipped my hair, taking cold, biting nips at my face. I pulled my weighted winter jacket tighter around my chest. It was a literal contraction.

The tension of my childhood returned, yet with a difference. In Wyoming, the state that champions freedom, I wanted to find my freedom to create. Having learned so much and come back home, I was ready to live on my own terms and push against the boundaries of what I believed to be possible. It was amid this permission to dream that the spark of an idea came to life.

It's been my life's work to break free from the confines. For me, it all comes down to story. The stories we tell ourselves, the stories we share with others, and the stories forgotten by history. This project became my vessel to expand, widen, stretch, and ultimately shatter the tensions holding me back.

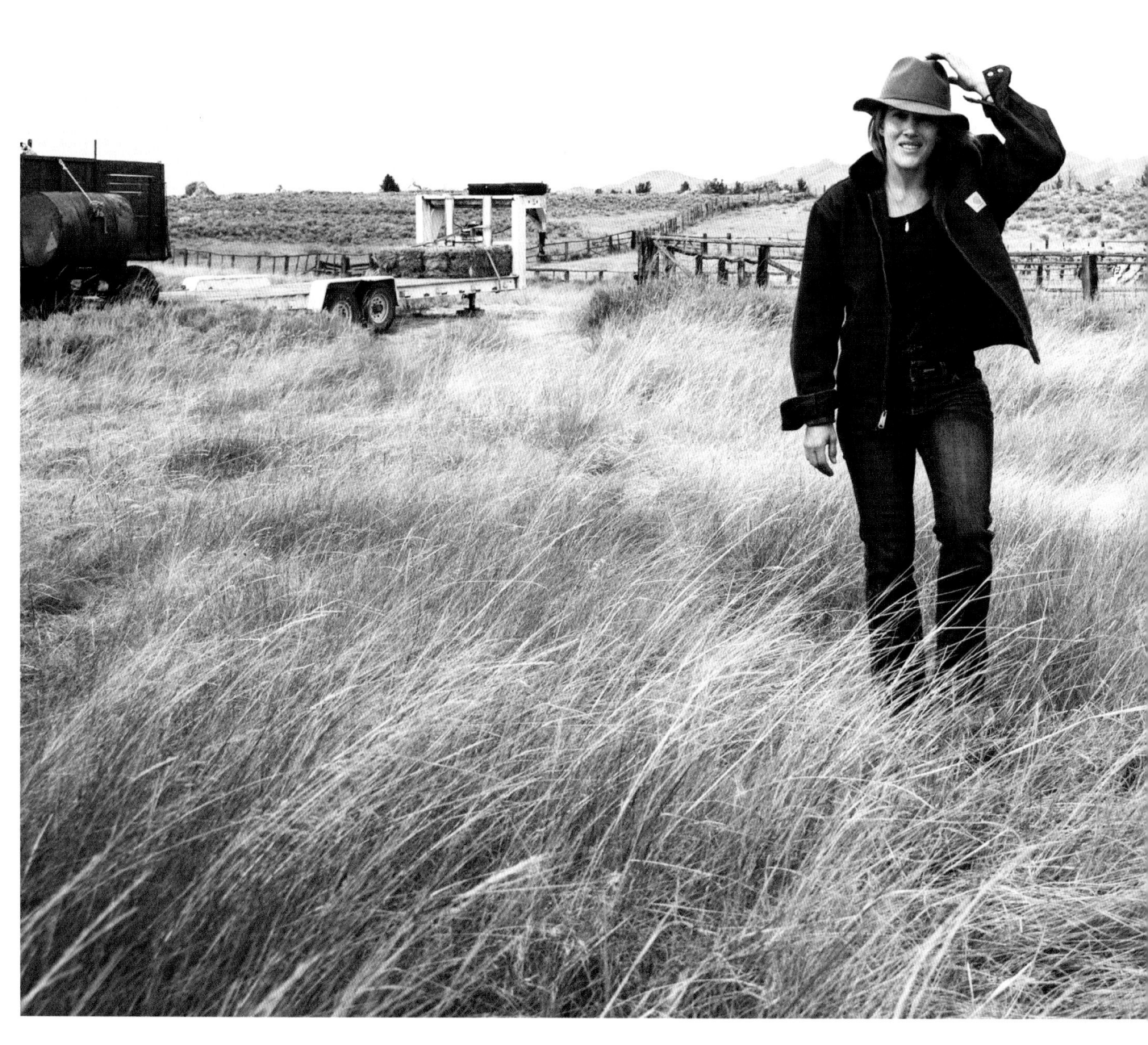

The Project

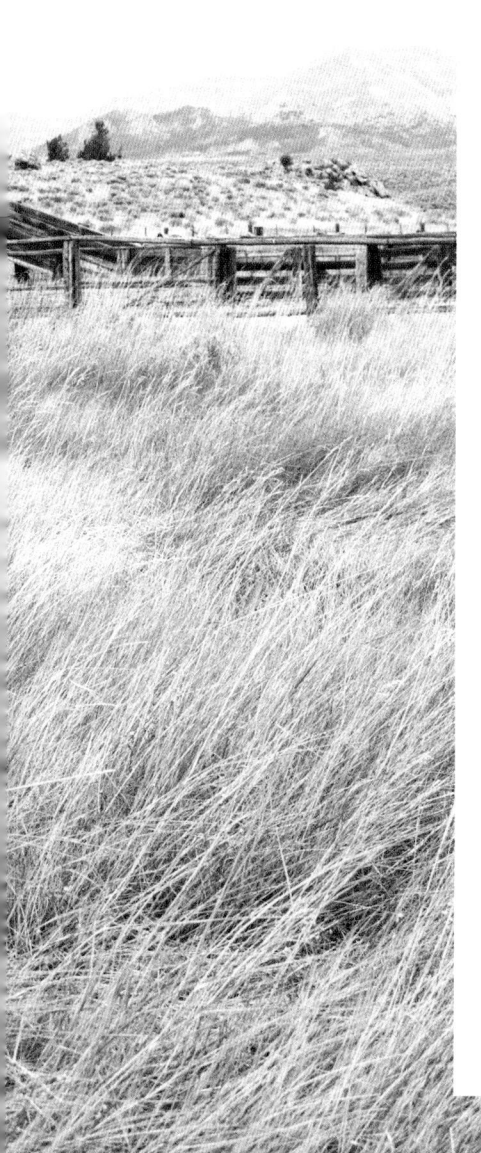

Between late 2016 and 2019, with an additional final production run in 2021 to complete the remaining three profiles of the project, I traveled thousands of miles across the state to meet with some of Wyoming's changemakers, rule breakers, and community leaders. I captured their stories through medium-format film photography using a Contax 645 camera and primarily Kodak Portra 400 color film. Additionally, I told their stories through podcast interviews, a traveling art exhibit, and, now, this book. (For more about the shooting and production process, podcast, and exhibit, see p. 255).

This project became my way to challenge my idea of Wyoming as limiting, explore unknown territory, and learn directly from my peers. The women in this project have constructed a life of great value and impact. I wanted that for myself too.

Throughout these pages, you'll meet an artist, a politician, a community advocate, a rancher, a backcountry pilot, an inventor, a regenerative farmer, and many more women. Their twenty-five stories, both decidedly individual and collectively powerful, share messages of courage, determination, and, ultimately, triumph.

In addition to my personal curiosity—my desire to better understand my home state and the women contributing to its ecosystem—another mission developed around the need to chronicle and celebrate women's narratives, adding to the cultural history of Wyoming and a broader depiction of the West. Seeing is believing. When women and girls see their stories reflected in powerful ways, it inspires them to engage in their own personal leadership, paving the way for others to follow.

From a woman herding sheep in the Wind River mountains to one flying a Black Hawk helicopter as Wyoming's only female medevac pilot, the individuals you see in this project are a mirror for how we see ourselves, our potential, and our power to be the creators of our world.

The Women

Artistically, I intentionally showcased contemporary, living, breathing, in-color figures. Traditionally, imagery of the American West has focused on monochrome nostalgia and largely been tied to a certain kind of mythology, like the cowboy or a lone figure against the landscape. This project strives for a broader representation beyond traditional portrayals, emphasizing the depth of experiences of humanity.

And, because history *is* an important part of the picture—we would not be where we are today without the people, and specifically the women, of the past—I share twenty additional historical stories here, as well as Wyoming's woman suffrage story. The goal of this book is to connect past to present and to showcase the long thread of history of women shaping our state.

Finally, during production, every woman featured in the project was actively contributing to their community or the state. Sadly, however, since 2021, two women have passed away: Neltje and Clarene Law.

Twenty-five stories about the strength, spirit, and profound legacy of Wyoming women and girls is by no means exhaustive. Far from it. I realized early on that my quest to uncover every story, every corner of the state, would be impossible. In fact, I have yet to discover and visit many parts of Wyoming. The longer I live here, the more I realize the number of women who make an impact is countless. This book should be read as a metaphor for the incredible depth of women across Wyoming, rather than a complete, finite list.

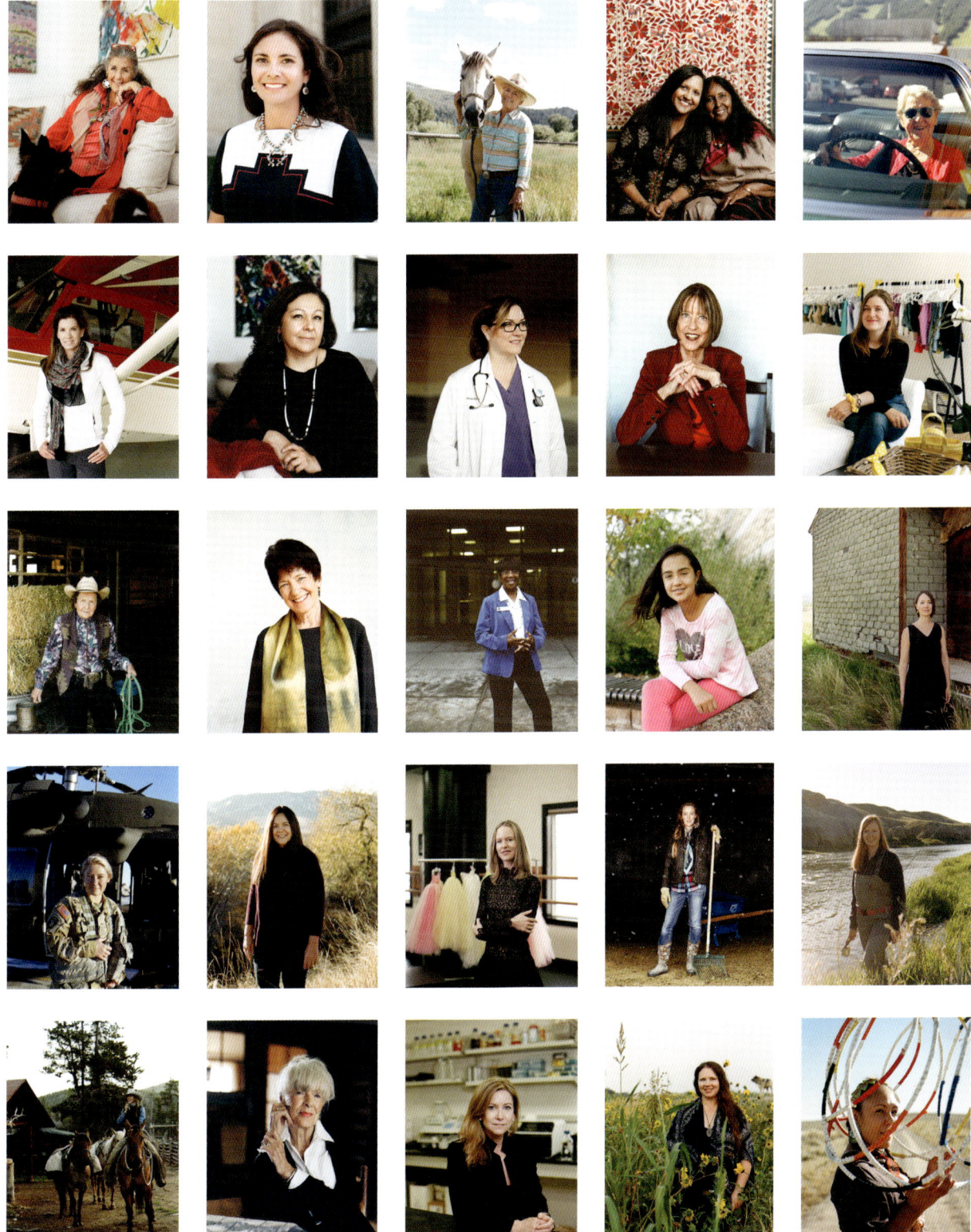

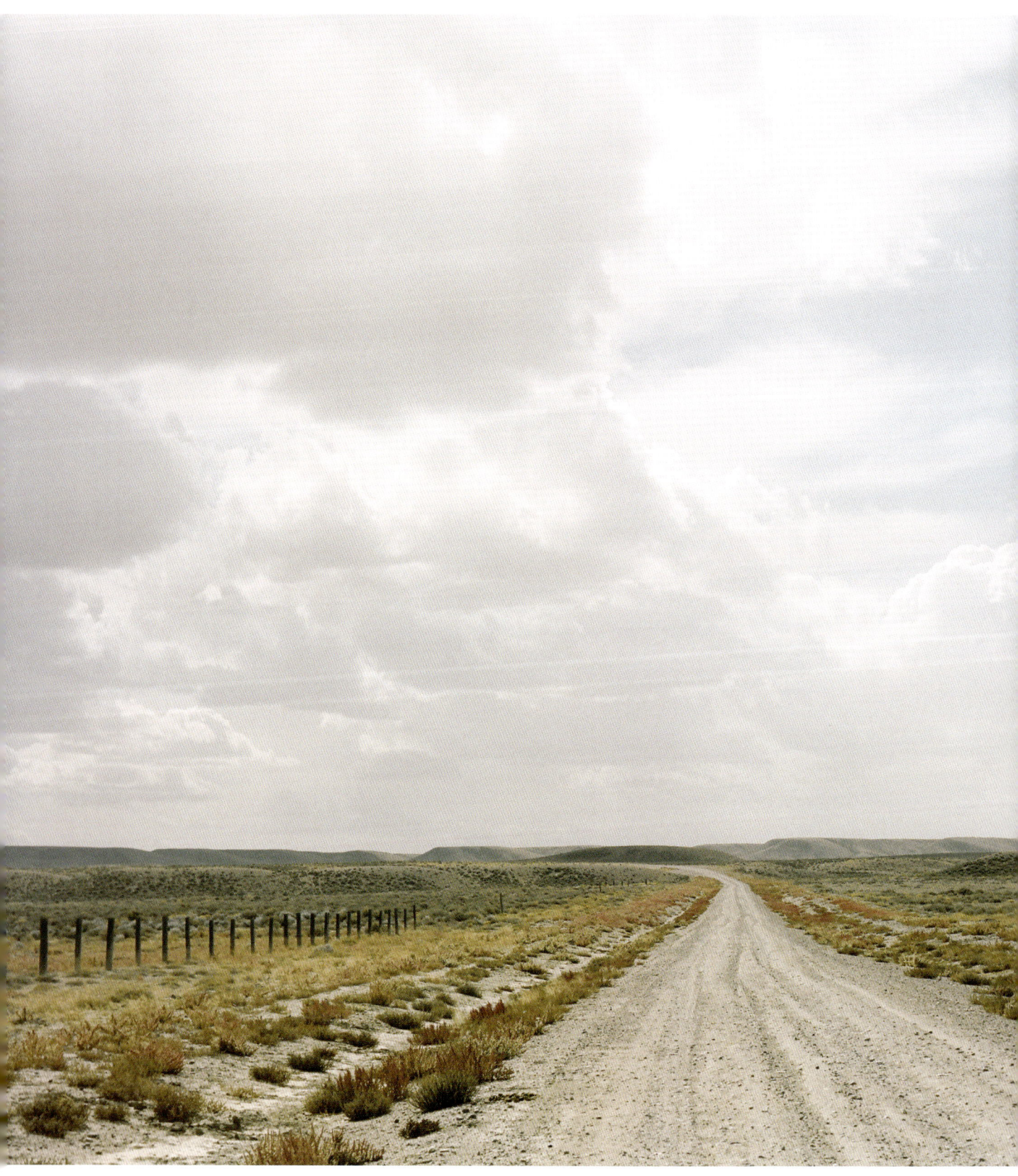

The Horizon

There is always more to uncover. Learning, exploring, and sharing the stories in this project broke down beliefs I had constructed around what my life would look like when I returned home. It became a personal quest to be more free, expansive, and alive. The more I traveled, the more my view of my home state widened. This project became my means to explore the many worlds of Wyoming; it ultimately deepened my understanding of home.

I had no idea what I would find when I first set out to tell the early stories of this project. My drive was a runaway train that couldn't be stopped. Any logistical obstacle simply became another problem to solve rather than an impenetrable barrier holding me back.

Though I have never taken a straight path, pursuing my vision and embracing creativity despite the possibility of failure has expanded my life far beyond the confines of what I believed to be possible. Life can be as open and expansive as the vast landscapes of my homeland.

Creating these stories was an absolute joy. To each woman who invited me into her home, helicopter, ranch, kitchen, business, sheep wagon, airplane hangar, farm field, and more: Thank you for being part of one of the greatest adventures of my life.

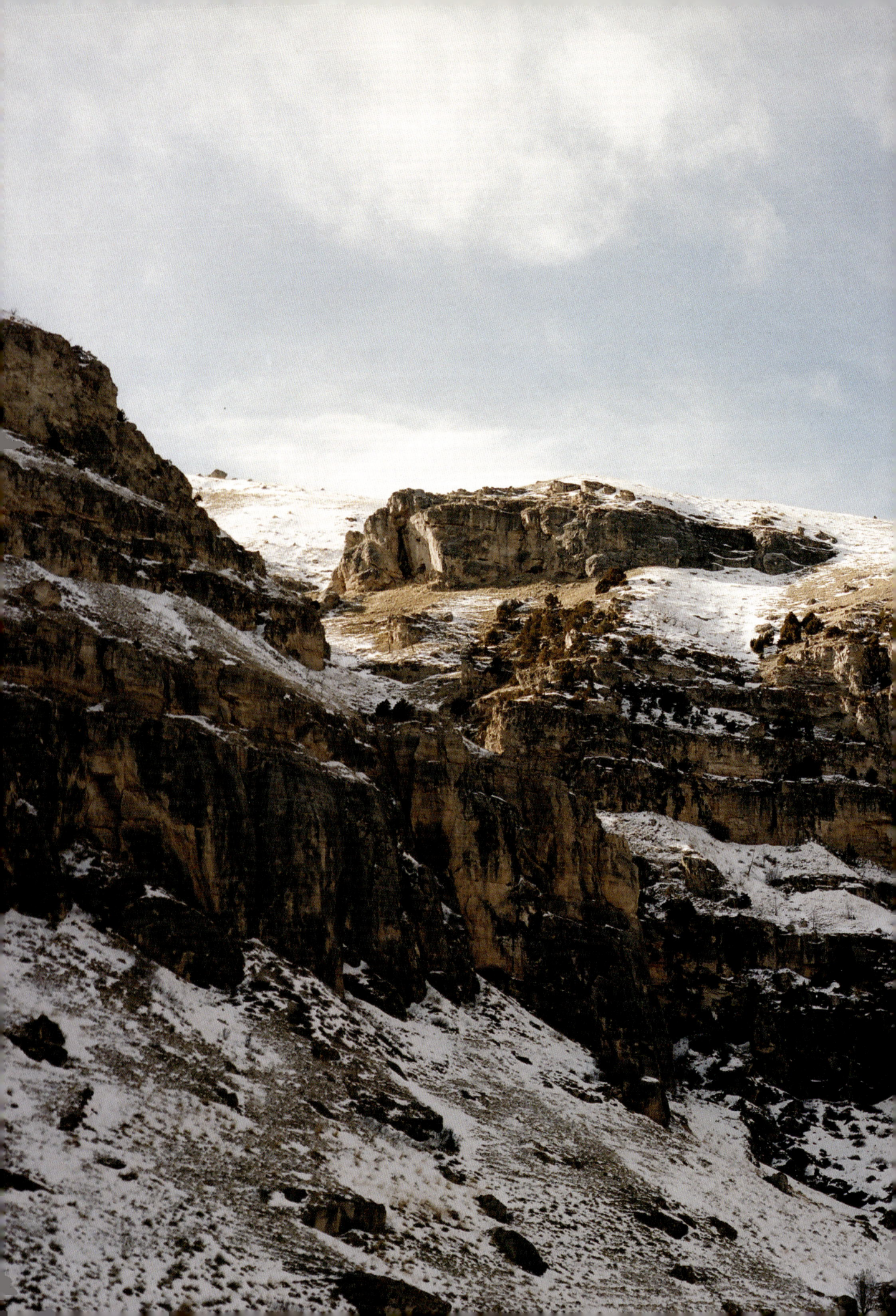

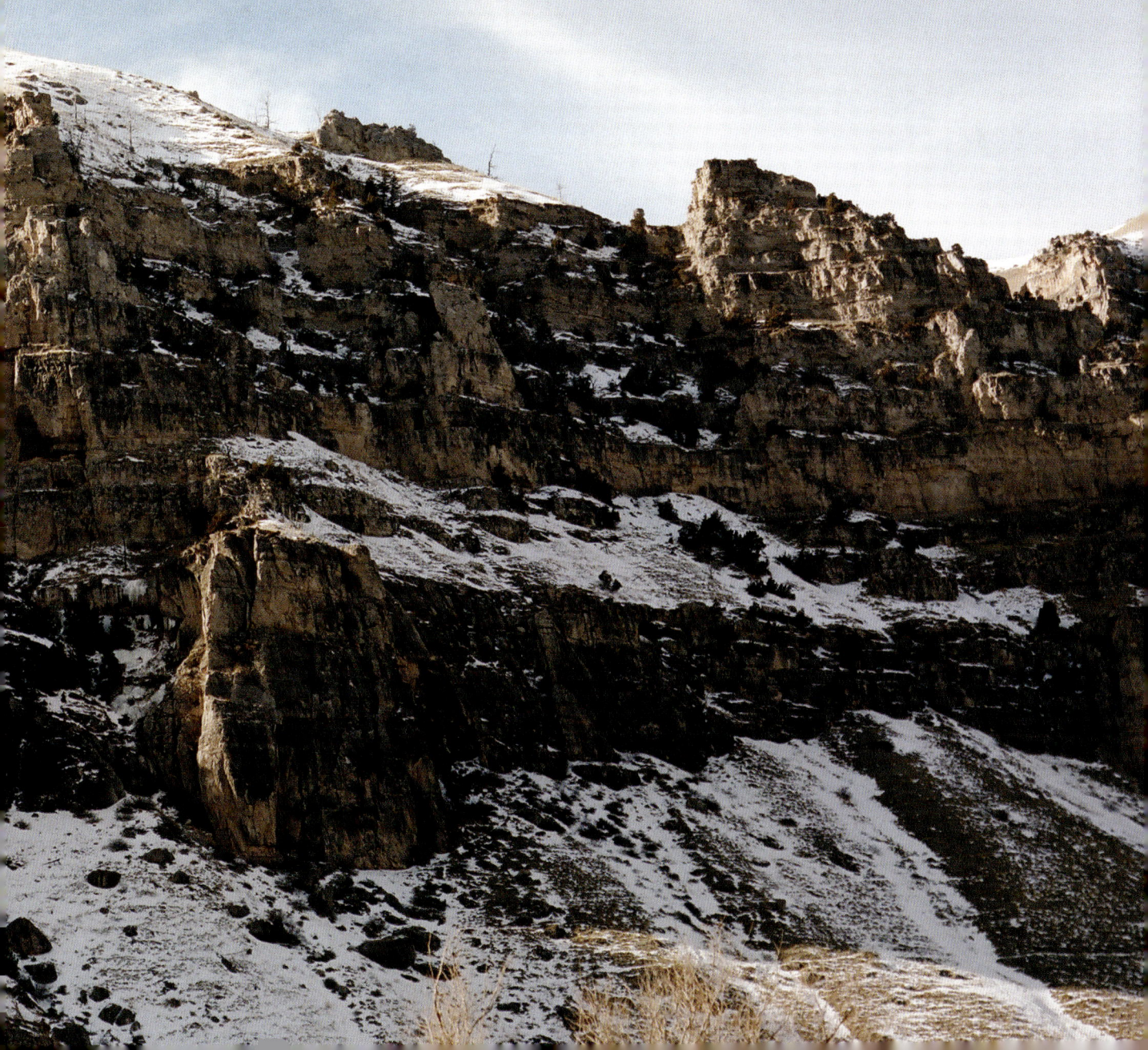

CHAPTER I
Breaking Boundaries

Who are the modern icons, rule breakers, and women shaping
the West right now? To be a boundary breaker is to be celebrated.
But the reality of being the first in one's field, or overcoming immense
personal odds and obstacles, can be challenging. Growth isn't easy.
Courage is key to go somewhere no one has been before.

Behind the Scenes:
The Road to Neltje

When I hear about a woman painting ten-by-thirty-foot abstract expressionist paintings from her Wyoming ranch, I know I must meet her.

It is December 4, 2016, and winter is fully underway, as it always is by this time of year. To go see Neltje (last name Doubleday Kings, but like many of the greats, she goes by her first name only) on her ranch in Banner, in northeastern Wyoming, I need to drive seven hours and 358 miles from where I live in Jackson, on the western border of the state near the southern entrance of Yellowstone National Park. I cross wind-whipped, hibernating tundra over a snow-covered Togwotee Pass before dropping into the red hills of Dubois and empty desert basins of Shoshoni. I continue through the steep, jarring cliffs of the Wind River Canyon and pass through Thermopolis, where winter is milder and the farm ground isn't yet completely covered in snow. This agricultural corridor continues for another thirty-five miles through Worland, where more crops hibernate beneath frozen ground. On these isolated highways, it's nonstop landscape and time. Fellow travelers are few and far between.

I don't mind these long drives. My thoughts settle and wander along the never-ending horizon. I pass through the sleepy ranch town of Ten Sleep (population 315) on Highway 16. I begin my second mountain pass over the Bighorn Mountains. The approach to the summit of Cloud Peak Skyway Scenic Byway is stunning. I ascend over 5,000 vertical feet, climbing switchback after long, stretching switchback. At 9,666 feet above sea level, I reach the road's summit. I'm on top of the world.

An hour or so later, my nerves start to fire when I begin my descent into Buffalo, the last town before I arrive at Banner. I question my preparedness, even though I packed my entire photography studio, from backdrops to lights and modifiers. I'm not completely sure what I want to capture for my first official photo shoot of the project, but I want to try everything. Plus, I'll have traveled fourteen hours total and more than 700 miles round trip for this visit, so I better make it count.

I exit the highway onto a dirt road that weaves between more ranches and burly cattle. I spot a mailbox with bold, uneven letters spelling N-E-L-T-J-E. My heart dances.

Stepping into Neltje's world is a swift transport into another dimension. I enter an environment of complete aliveness, color, and curiosity. Everywhere I look is a treat for my eyes: Hand-carved wooden sculptures from her travels decorate tabletops and shelves. Gorgeous rugs cover the floors. Tapestries and paintings adorn the walls. The structure of her home, which she designed, is a work of art in itself—expansive and playful, with long, stretching hallways that lead to a cozy nook or an overflowing library. A seemingly misplaced skylight brightens an alcove that in any other house may have felt incorrect. Her home defies traditional design rules and expectations.

I am so taken by this fantastical world that, for a moment, I lose myself in the sheer wonder of my new surroundings. *Where am I?*

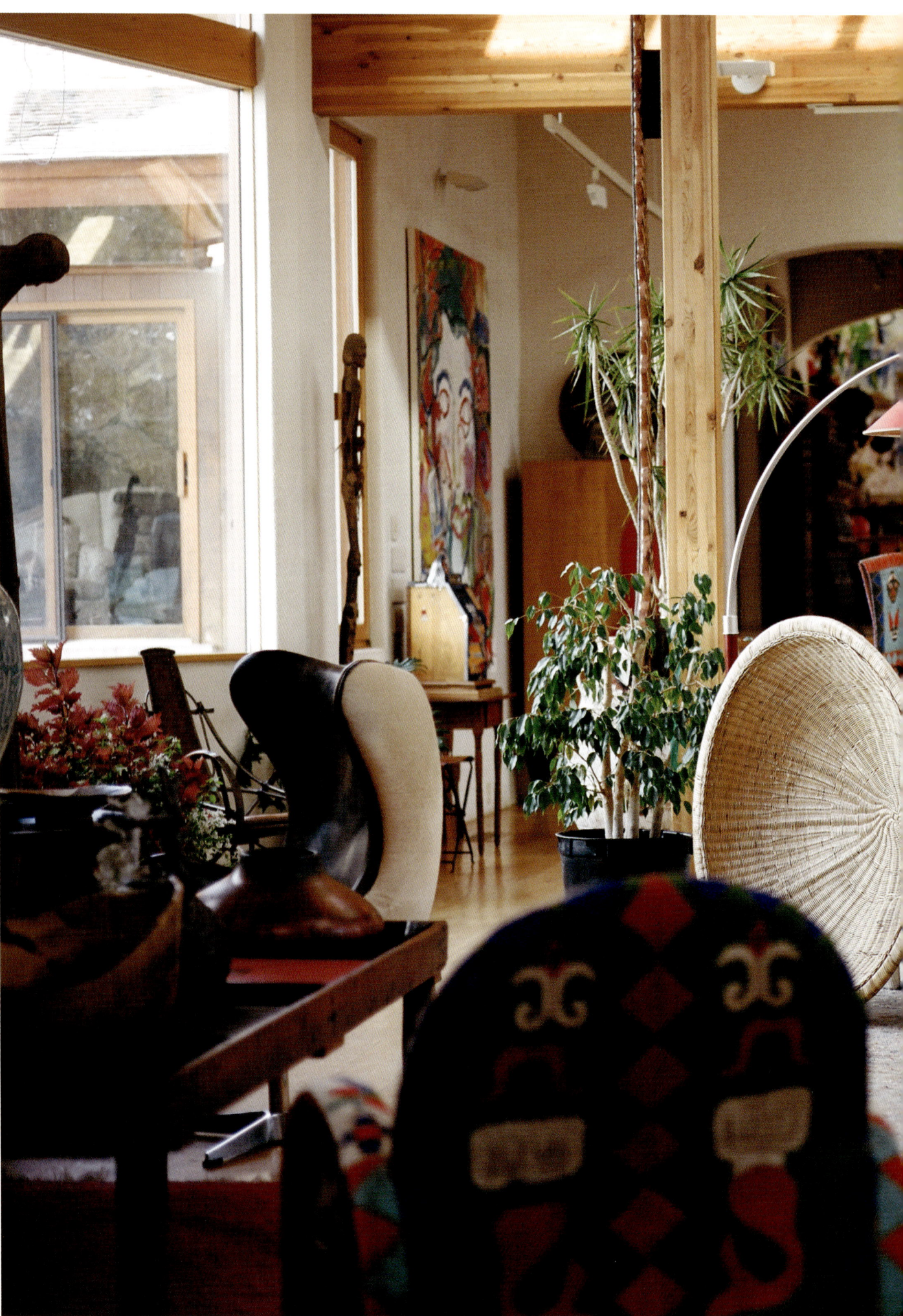

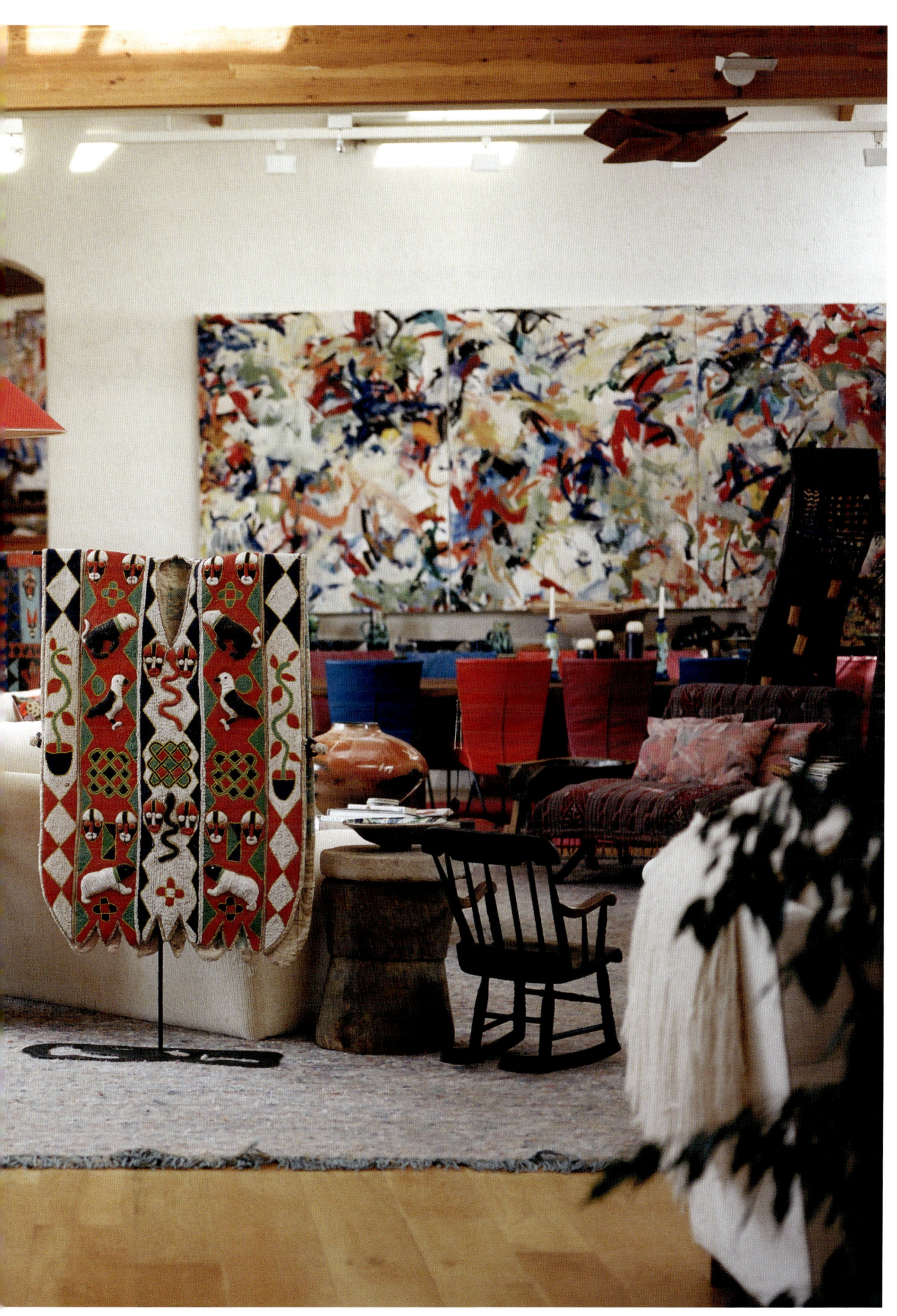

NELTJE

1934–2021

ABSTRACT EXPRESSIONIST PAINTER, PHILANTHROPIST,
AUTHOR OF *NORTH OF CRAZY*

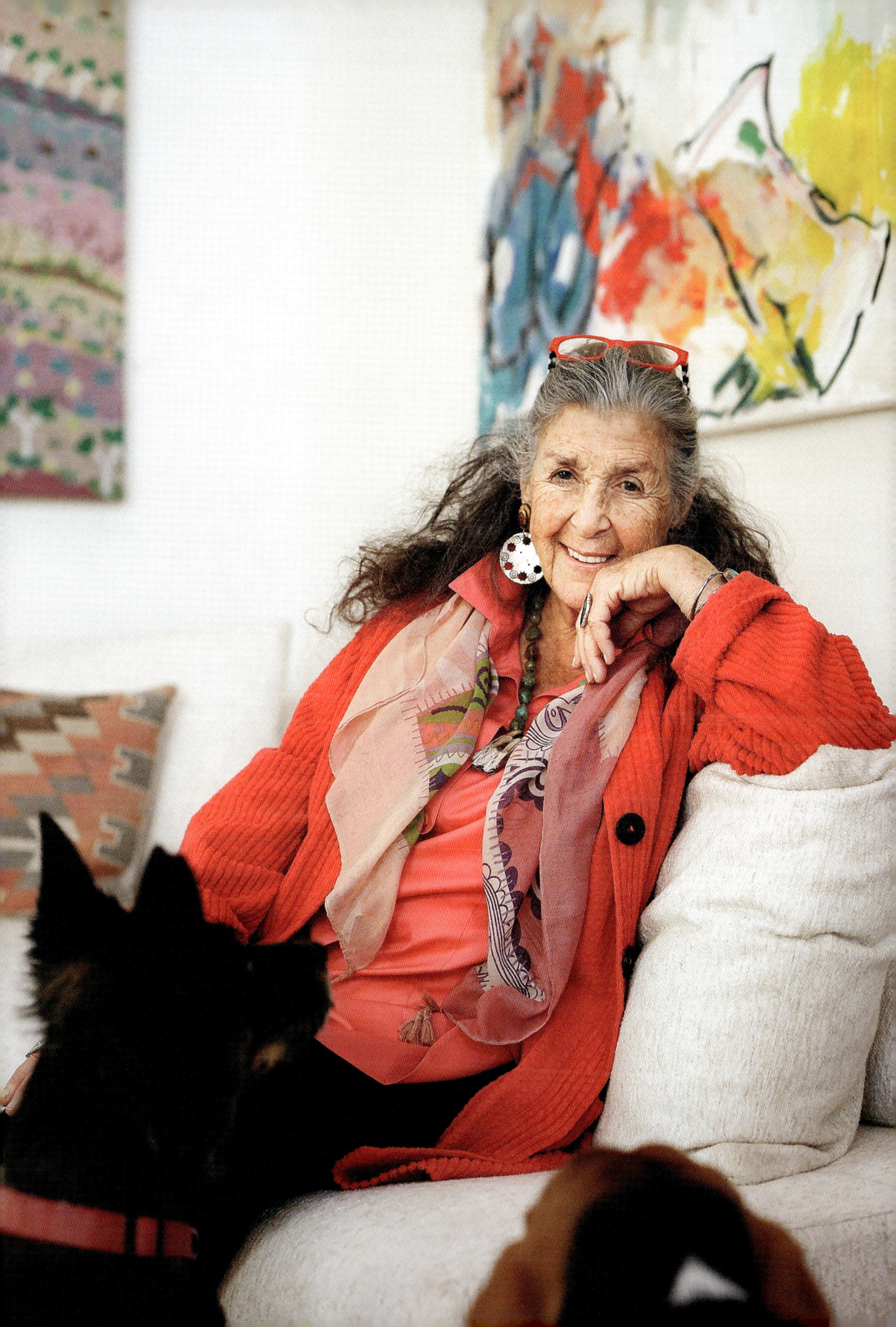

"I would say that I'm a painter of the moment. I think we are all painters of the moment. We are creators of the moment."

Neltje lived in Wyoming for more than fifty years and was unafraid to live out loud. She painted enormous abstract expressionist canvases and published a memoir, *North of Crazy*, detailing her life and her journey to become a full-time artist. Playfulness, joy, and curiosity permeated everything she touched. In Neltje's world, all was fair in art and creation. From her world travels to antique dealings, philanthropy to entrepreneurial endeavors (such as saving, restoring, and operating the historic Sheridan Inn), Neltje went full out.

On the outside, Neltje's upbringing in New York City and Long Island, as the daughter of Nelson Doubleday, the famed book publisher of the Doubleday publishing company, seemed to revolve around opulence, glamour, and affluence. But beneath the glossy surface, Neltje experienced neglect and sexual abuse by a friend of the family. Wyoming became her foundation, a place to heal, rebuild, and face what she described as her life's "boulders." Her ranch and the surrounding community became a refuge from which she could channel her strength, sense of community, and prolific creativity. Starting in 1984, Neltje's work was

featured in over 200 solo or group exhibitions across the state, region, and nation.

"Well, color. Let's start with color. I don't know what my favorite color is, probably red. Because it's outrageous. It demands courage, strength, and an unwillingness to be put down." Neltje's dynamic painting process involved quick, expressive physical movements as well as intense deliberation. Similar to a dialogue, each stroke communicated with the next. This back-and-forth guided each movement and the direction of her creations.

A generous spirit, Neltje wanted to create a place for others to unlock their voices and release their creative powers. She founded Jentel Artist Residency in 2001 on her ranch in Banner, a program for artists and writers from across the country that continues to operate and offer free residencies throughout the year. Her love for people, art, and travel led her to found Turned Antiques, a hidden gem of an antique store with pieces sourced from around the world. Her memoir served as a beacon of hope to other sexual assault survivors, offering solace and hope of healing. She received the

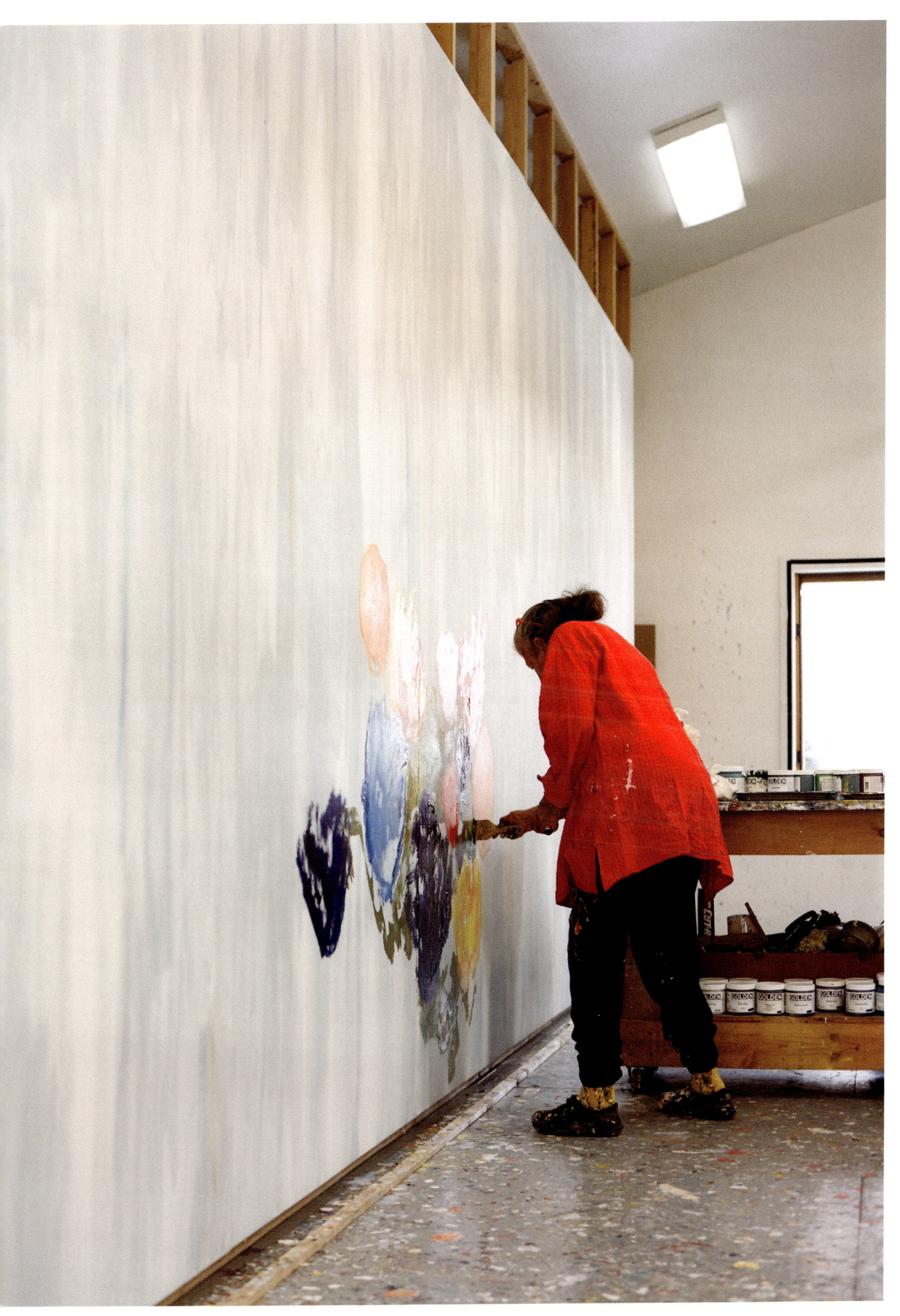

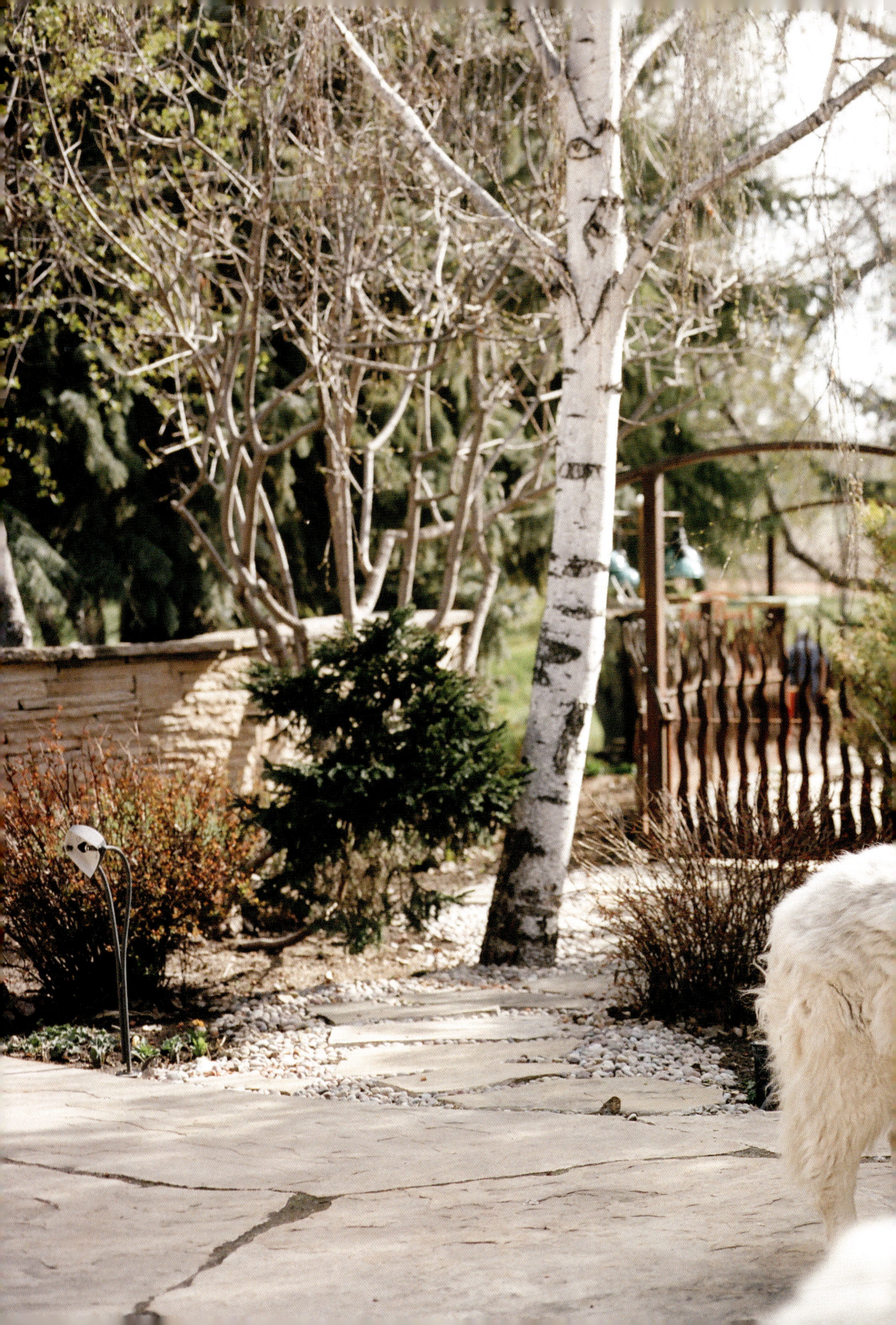

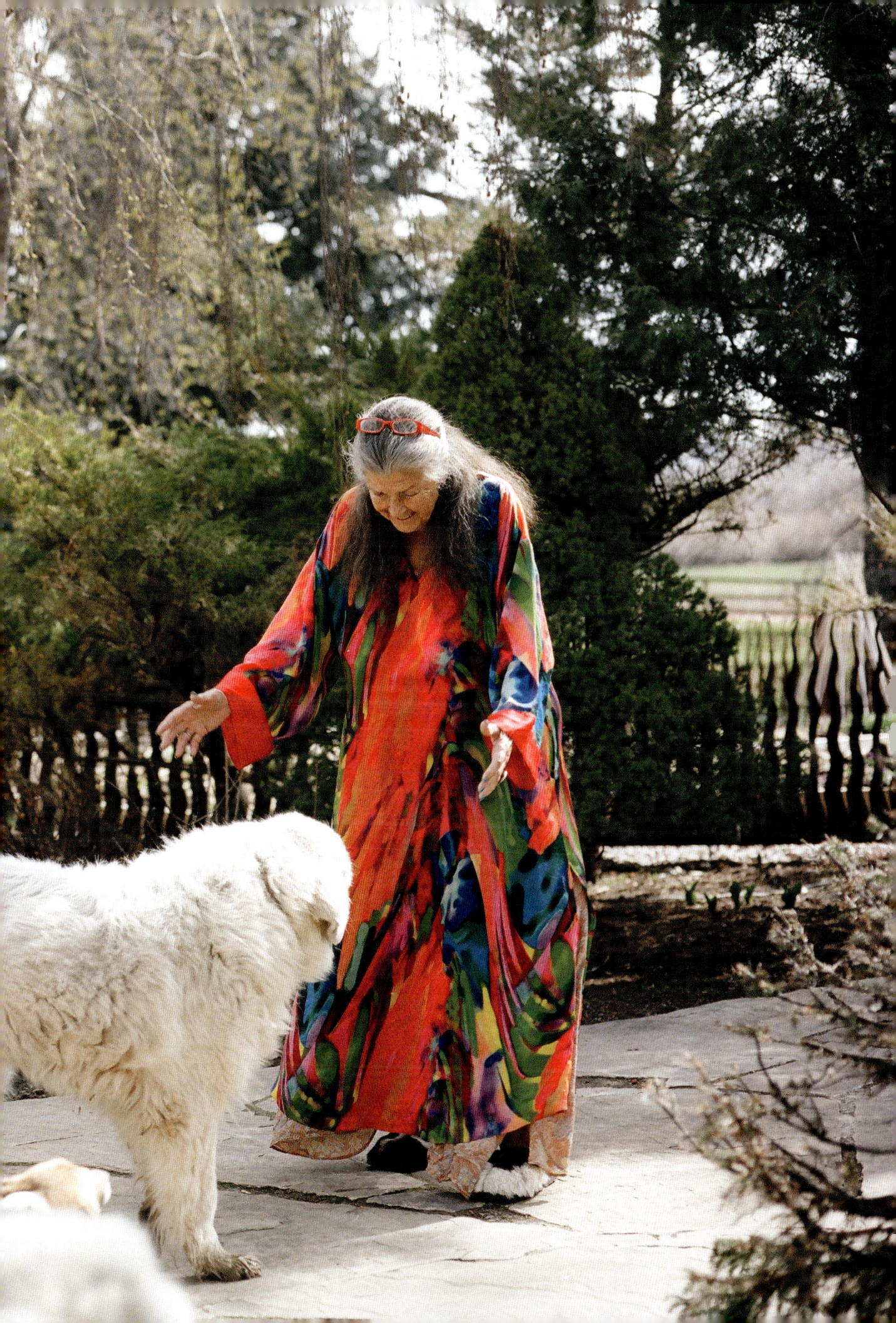

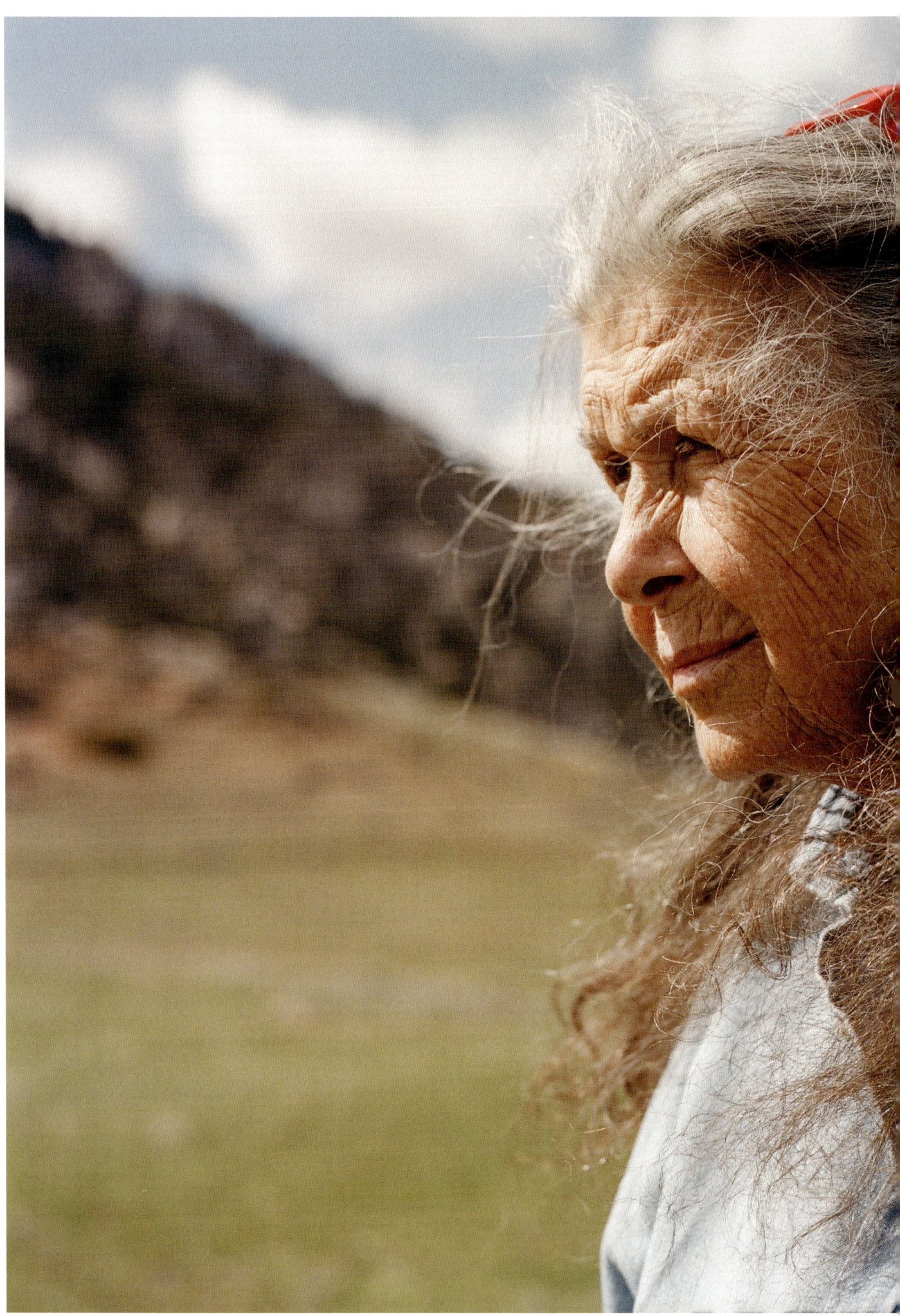

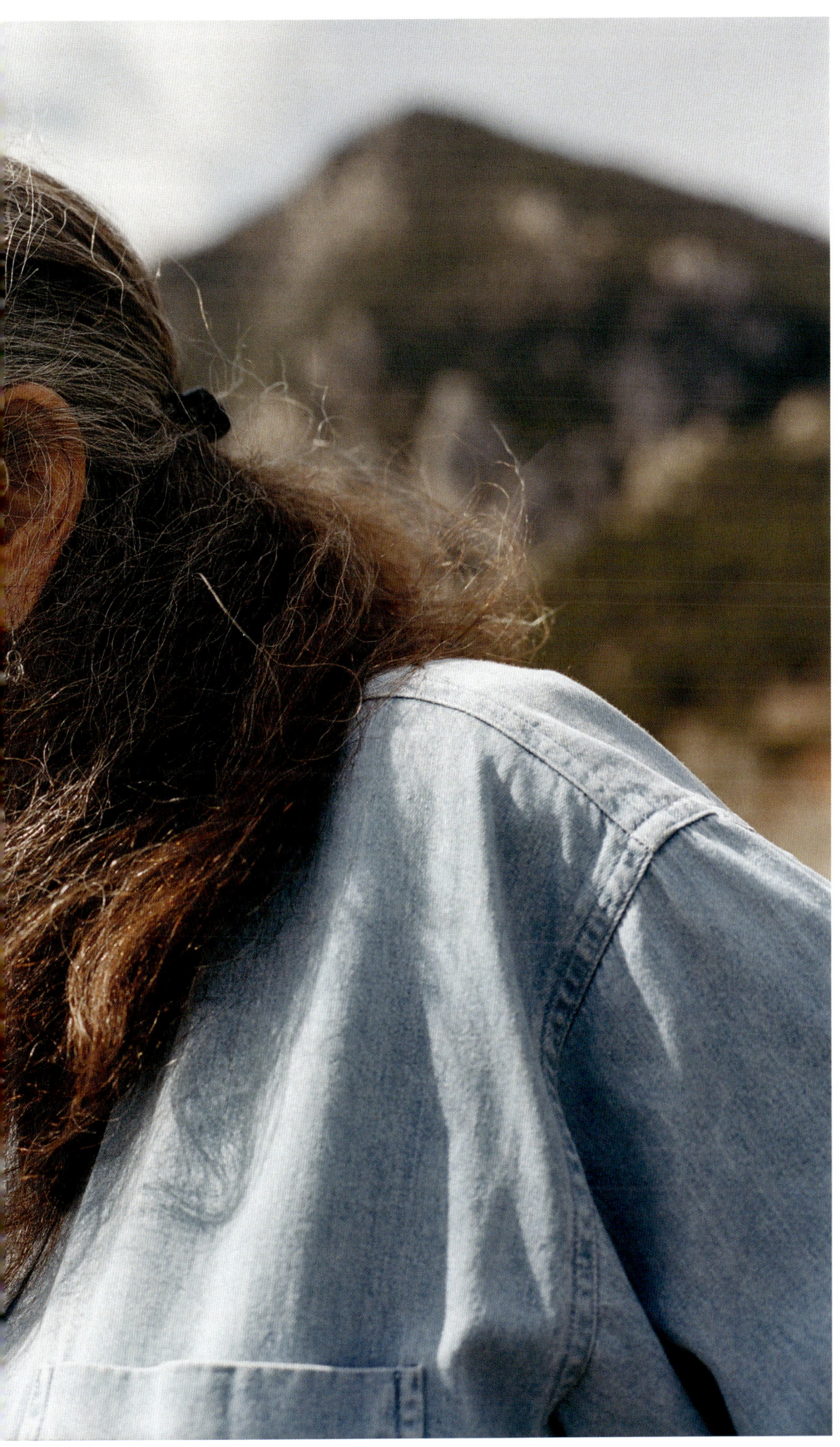

"I paint the moment, I think the moment, I feel the moment. You have this second, then BOOM! It's gone. The wind comes up, and your hat flies off. You drop your glass of champagne. It's just a moment."

Wyoming Governor's Arts Award in 2005 and an honorary doctor of arts degree from the University of Wyoming in 2018. In addition to her painting and artistry, Neltje was a loyal friend, mother, and grandmother. Those who knew her well said she was tender and kind, funny and sharp. She was unconfined in her art and life and proved that the only limits that exist are those you imagine for yourself. Neltje was the ultimate creator of her world.

Upon Neltje's death in 2021, she gifted her ranch in Banner, including her home, artist studio, gallery, and Jentel Artist Residency, to the University of Wyoming. Her home and gallery now operate as the Neltje Center for Excellence in Creativity and the Arts, a sanctuary for creators to unleash their imagination through mini-residencies, retreats, and other creative initiatives.

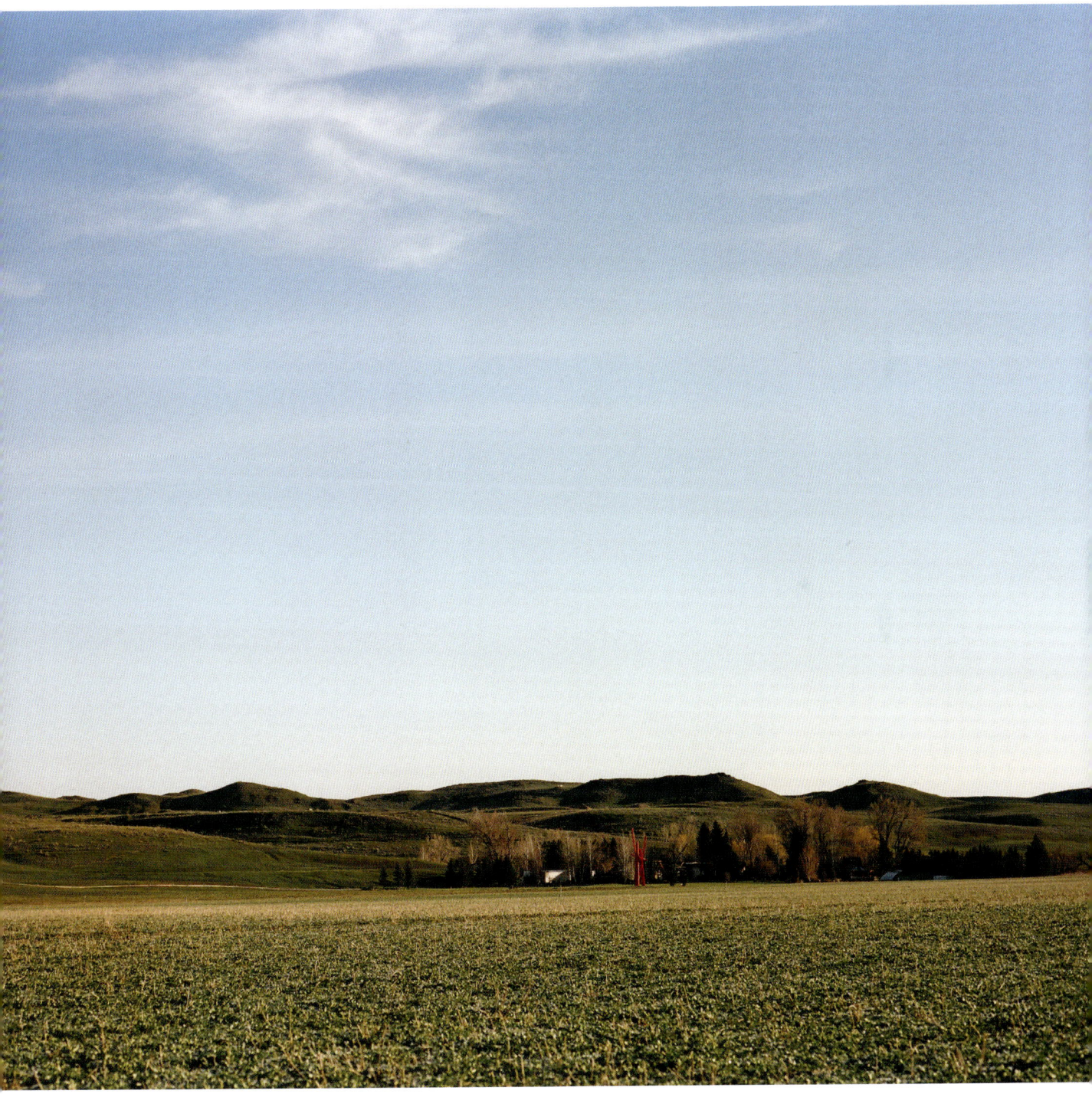

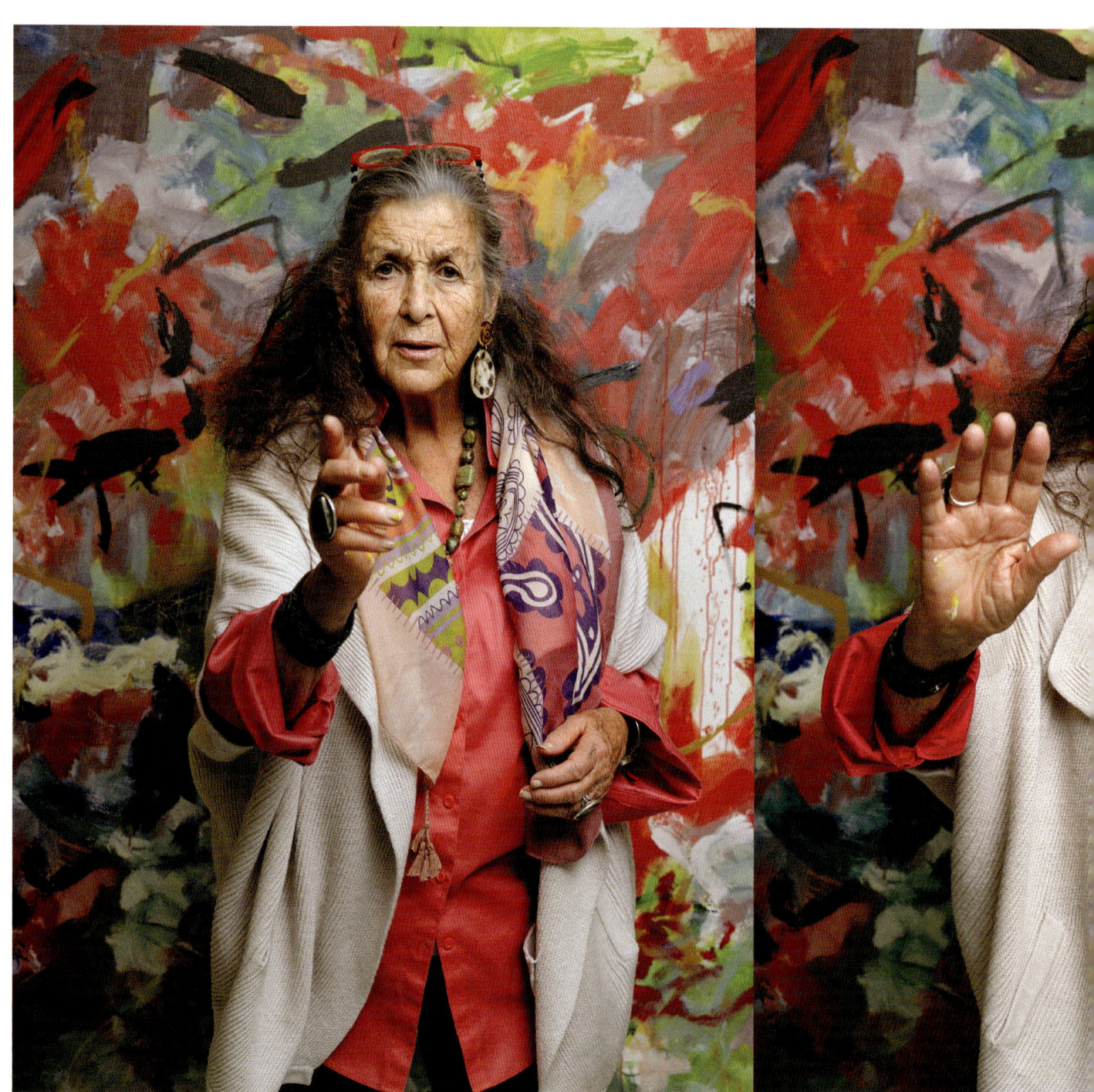

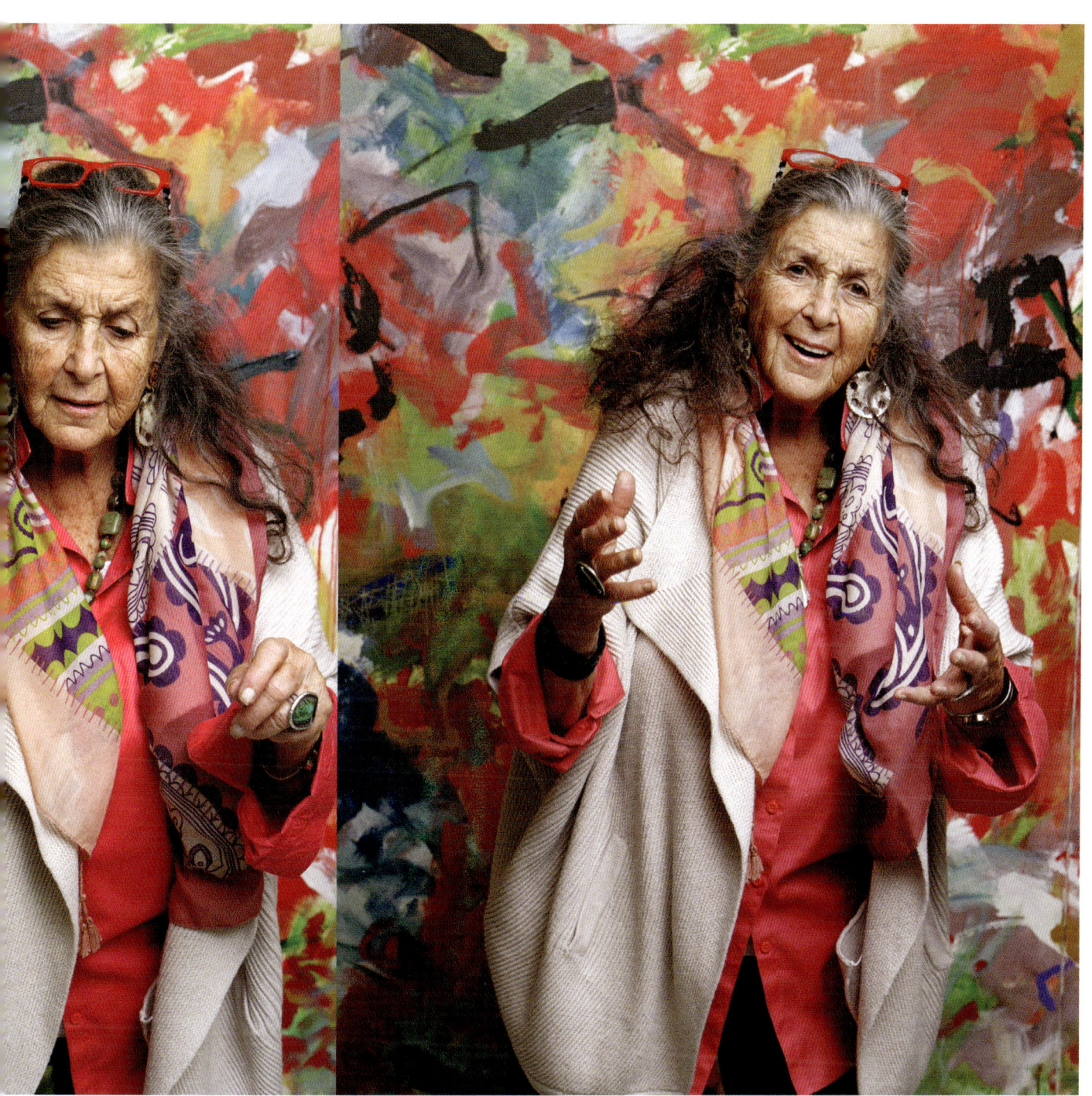

AFFIE ELLIS

WYOMING'S FIRST NATIVE (NAVAJO) FEMALE LAWMAKER

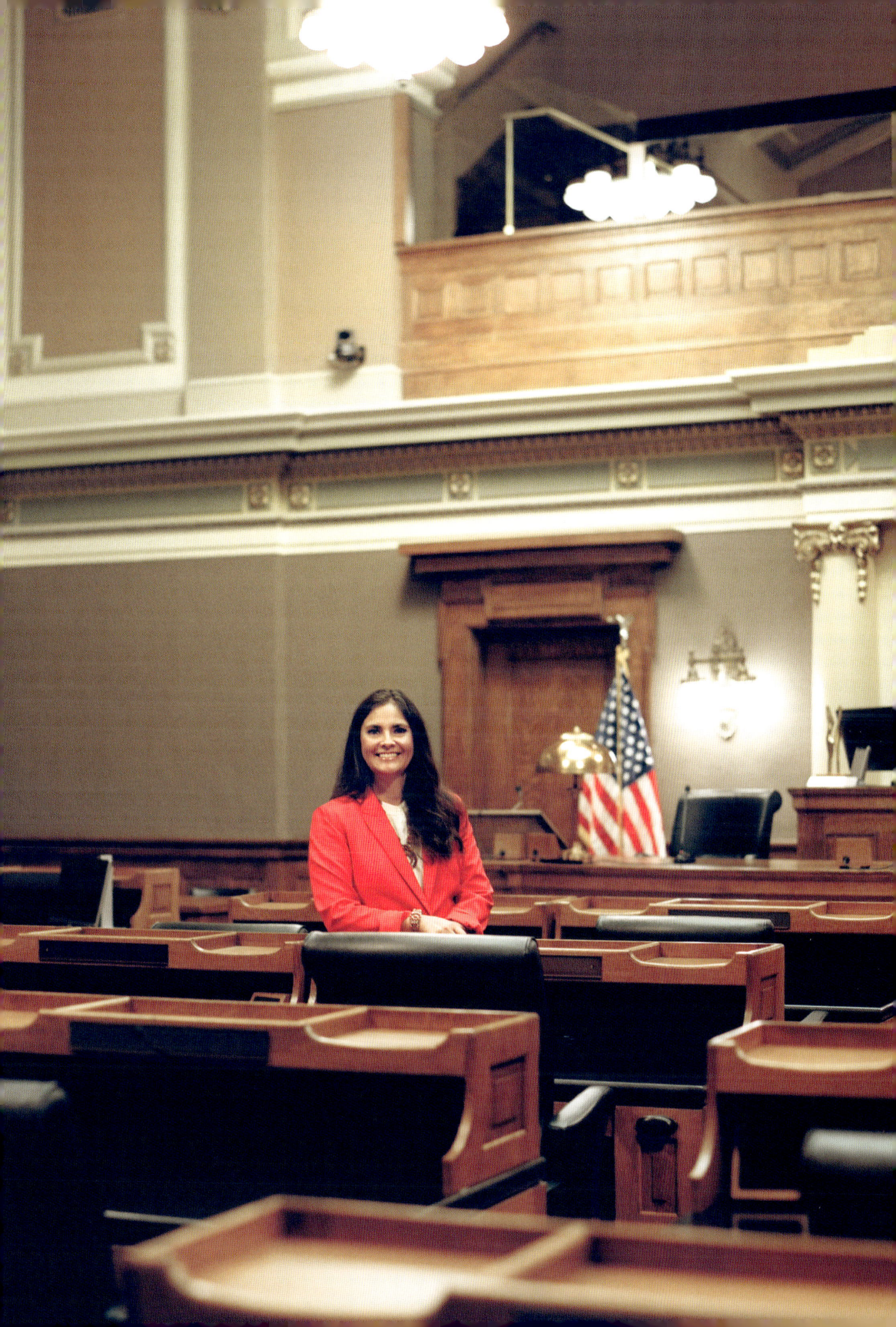

"These moments matter because when you're taking a vote, and you're thinking about how decisions affect people, you remember standing on their doorstep. I feel strongly about making that connection with folks."

"Mom, do they let girls serve in the senate?" When Affie Ellis's ten-year-old daughter, Marlo, asked this crushing question, there was only one woman serving in the Wyoming state senate, Senator Bernadine Craft, and she had just announced her retirement.

Affie knew that if no women ran and won, there would be a Wyoming state senate with zero women represented. She couldn't shake the thought and decided to do something about it.

A lawyer, mom of three, and avid quilter, Affie was born in Jackson, into a working-class family facing the often-stifling pressure of trying to make ends meet in the state's most affluent zip code. To help out, she spent weekends cleaning motel rooms with her mother, noting now that she "wouldn't trade that experience for anything." It taught her lifelong lessons of perseverance, and hard work, and instilled a desire to better herself and be in service to others. To Affie, that has always meant bettering the ecosystem around her.

She became the first person in her family to attend college, at the University of Wyoming, then pursued her JD at the University of Colorado Law School. One of her most pivotal career experiences was an opportunity to work for the late U.S. senator Craig Thomas, in Washington DC. This experience cemented one of her mantras and guiding aspirations: "For me, the metric is, and will always be, how much do I have to give?"

Affie, an enrolled member of the Navajo Nation, taught federal Indian law as an adjunct professor at the University of Wyoming and served as a commissioner of the U.S. Indian Law and Order Commission, which developed a comprehensive study of law enforcement and criminal jurisdiction in Indian Country. She has testified before the U.S. House of Representatives and Senate committees on the commission's work and findings and submitted recommendations to Congress in 2014.

In 2016, Affie was elected to her first term as a Wyoming state legislator, making her the first female Native American person to ever serve in Wyoming's state senate.

She served two consecutive terms, from 2017 to 2024, representing Wyoming's Eighth District.

FACING: Affie's squash blossom necklace was made by her grandfather, the master Navajo silversmith Tom Burnside.

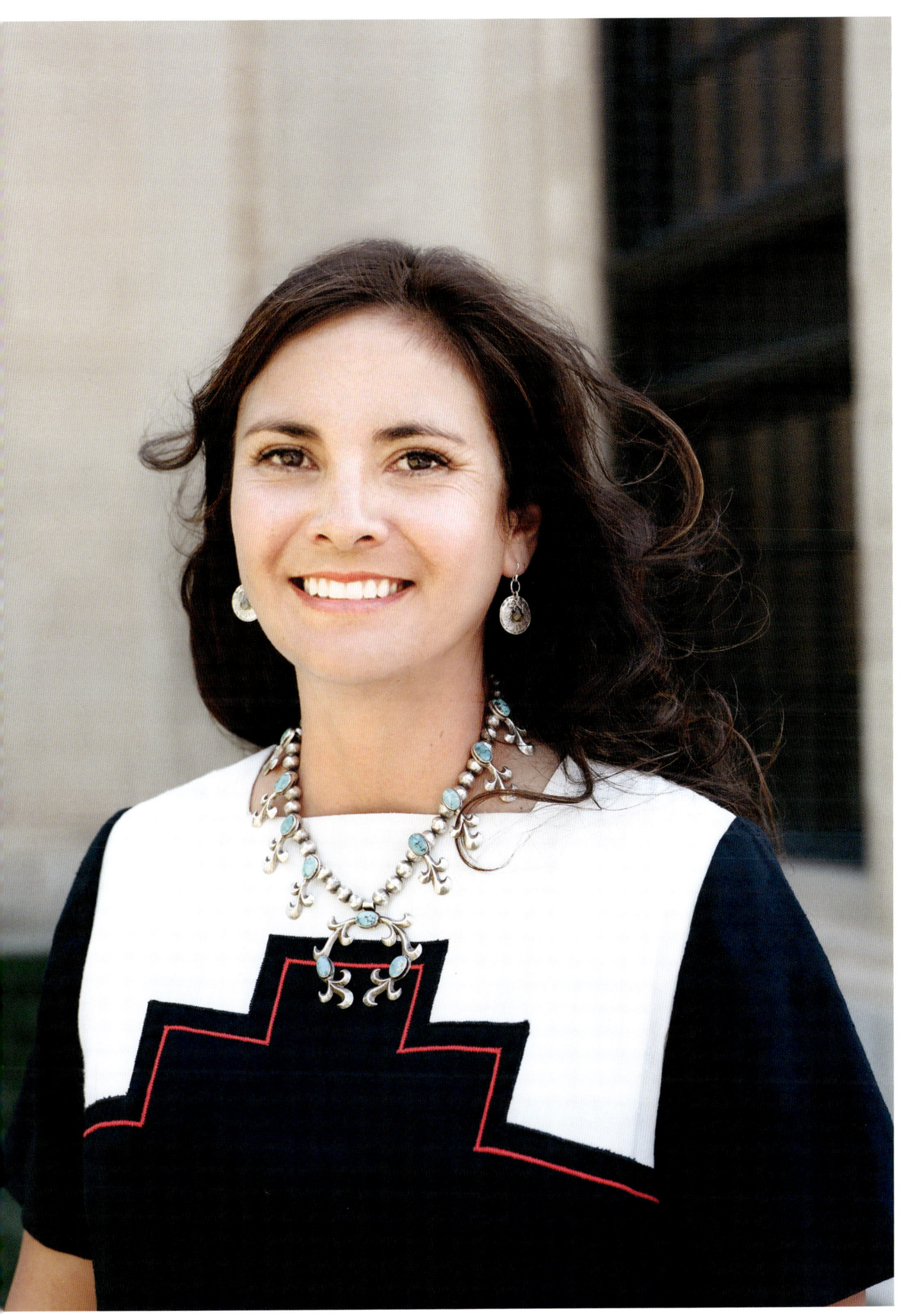

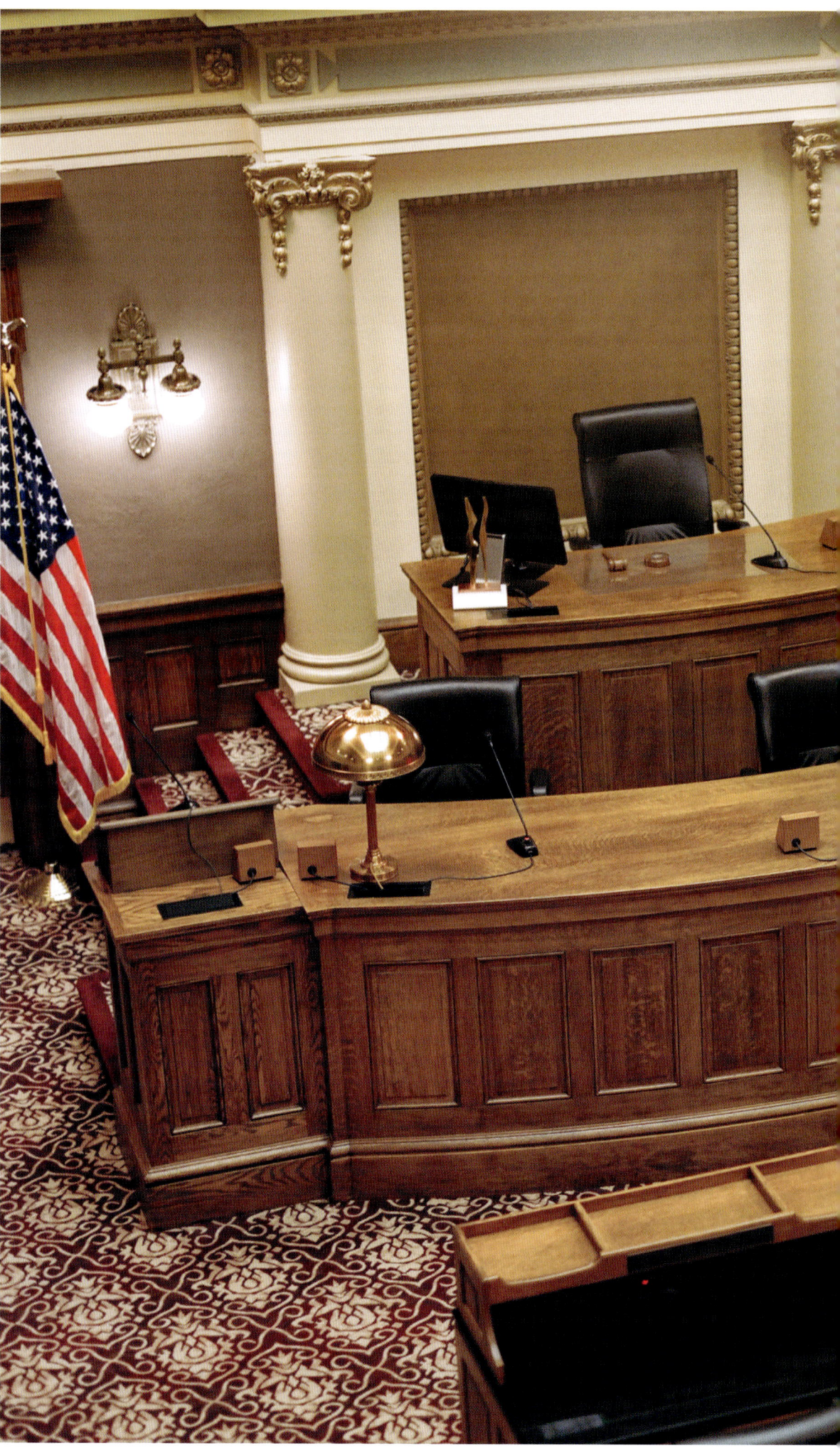

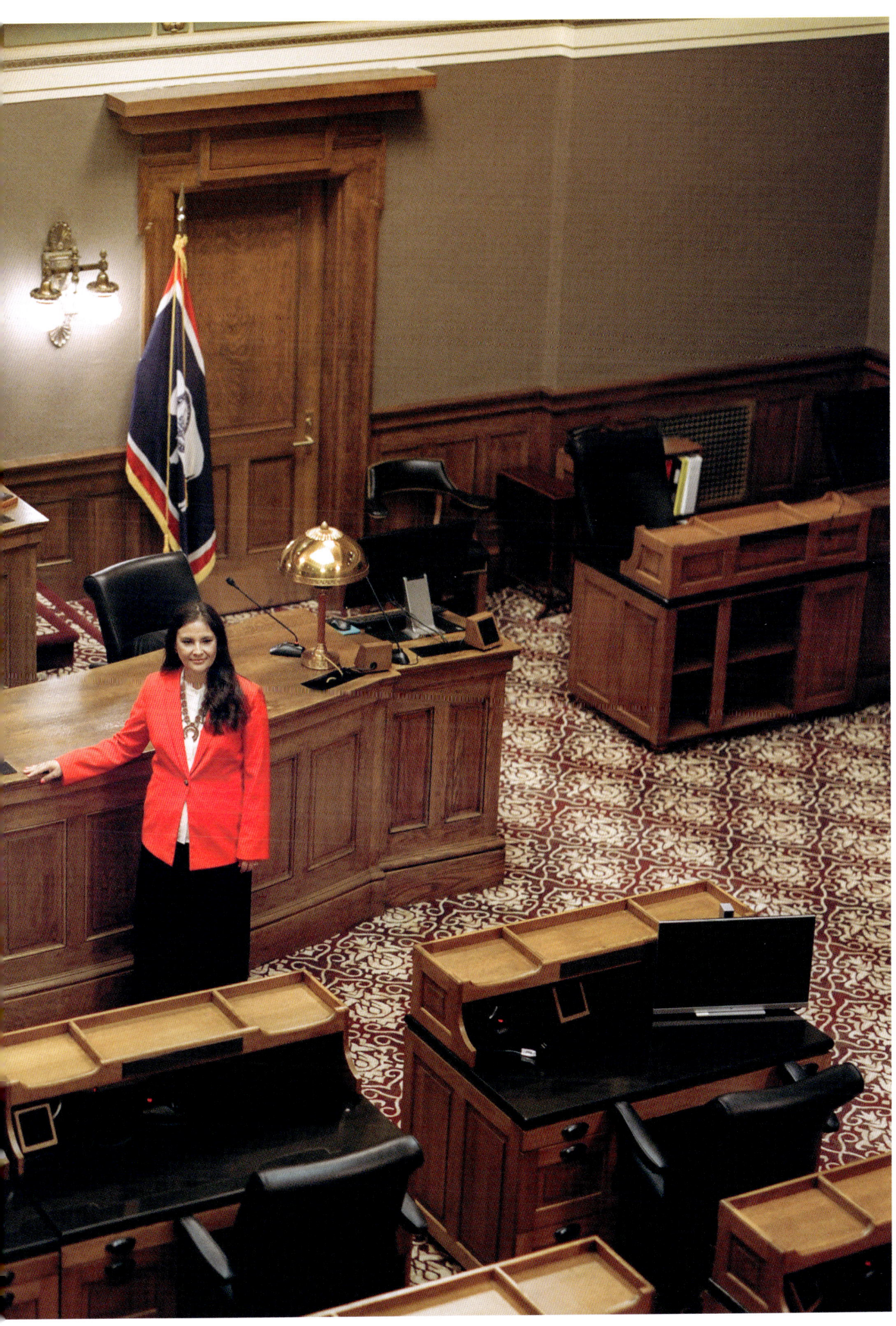

"When I ran for the legislature, I knew that it would be a journey of self-growth and becoming the person you really want to be. Which is someone who understands the severity of the decisions we make, respects the chamber we serve in, and knows that it's greater than and will long outlast me and my time on this Earth."

During that time, she worked on legislation related to a variety of Native American issues, including the enactment of laws to address the epidemic of Missing and Murdered Indigenous Women and Girls (MMIWG) and a state Indian Child Welfare Act law. Her passion for improving education in Wyoming led her to play a significant role in supporting legislation to make Wyoming the first state in the nation to require its schools to offer computer science education to all K-12 students; expand scholarship opportunities for career and technical education students; and establish a scholarship to provide financial assistance for adult learners to fill workforce needs. She also took the lead in drafting and passing laws to protect victims of sexual assault by ensuring that evidence collected during sexual assault examinations is not destroyed without a court order.

As a lawyer, she finds common ground on complex issues between government, private industry, and environmental groups. Additionally, she is a respected adviser on federal Indian law and policy. Affie serves on the board of directors for several organizations and nonprofits, including the Navajo Transitional Energy Company, Wyoming Congressional Award Council, Cheyenne Frontier Days Foundation, Grand Teton National Park Foundation, Cheyenne LEADS, and Wyoming Women's Legislative Caucus, and acts as an at-large member of the Wyoming State Bar, Federal Indian and Tribal Law Section.

Affie is not done giving.

FACING: Affie with her late parents, Jim and Lenora Burnside. Jim operated a welding shop for more than fifty years, and Lenora worked in hospitality. Lenora became a master seamstress, a connection Affie shares with her mother in the form of quilting.

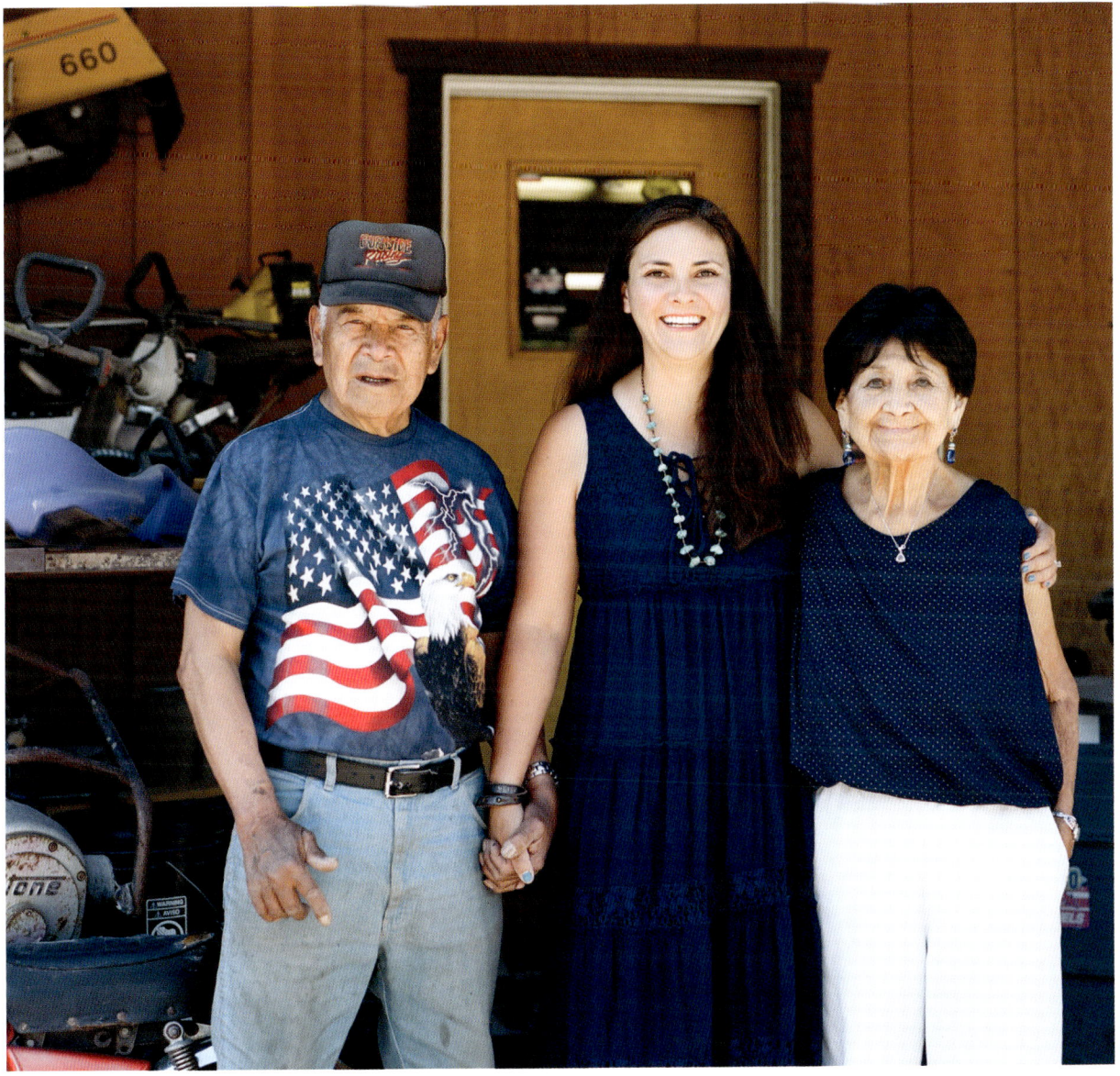

MARILYN S. KITE

FIRST FEMALE JUSTICE AND FIRST FEMALE CHIEF JUSTICE
OF THE WYOMING SUPREME COURT

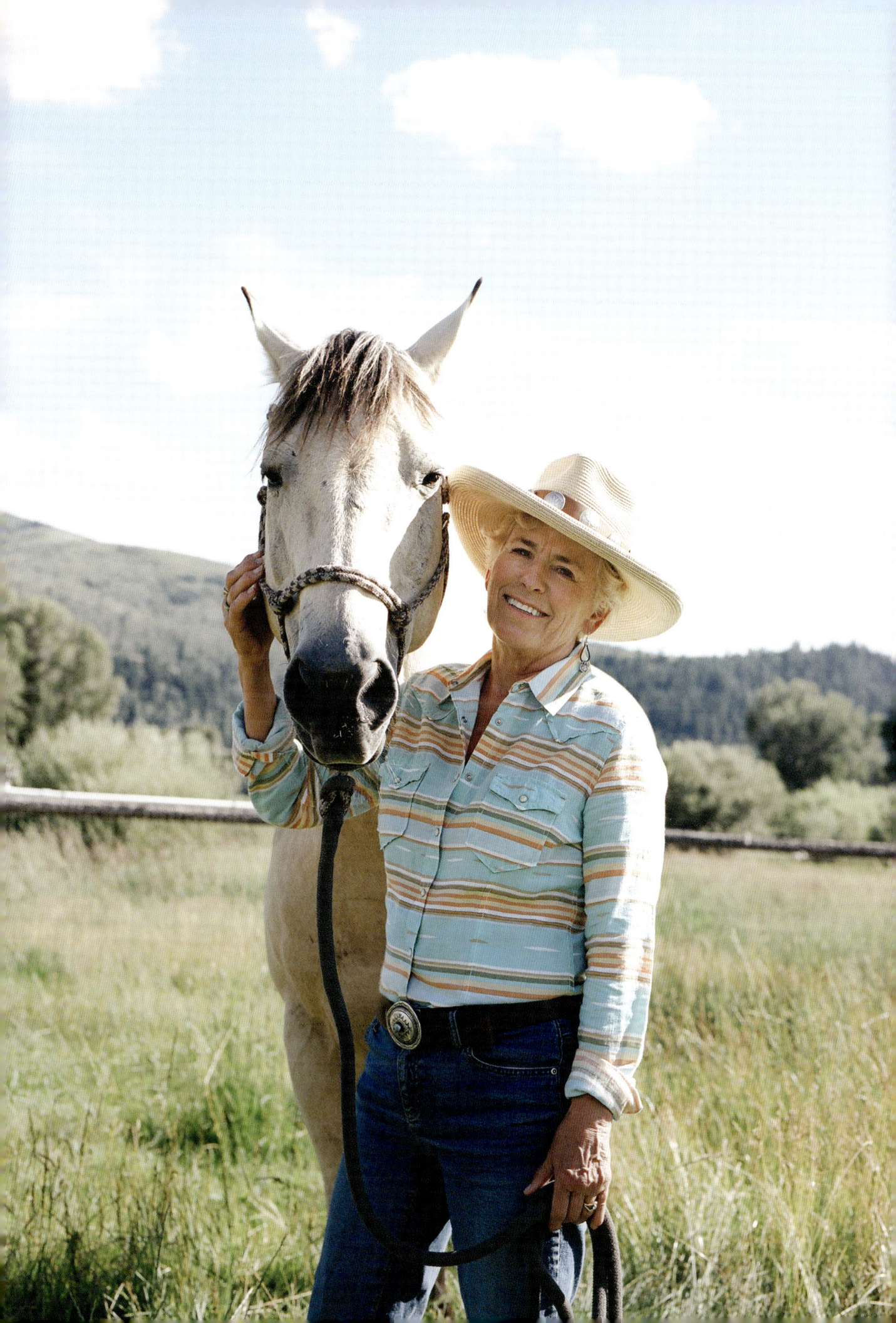

"I think you're never limited in what you can get out there and do."

In 2000, one woman—the first ever—stood among the five commanding judges to serve on the Wyoming Supreme Court.

Marilyn is a thoroughly Wyoming woman— she was born in Laramie, graduated from the University of Wyoming College of Law, and built her career in the Cowboy State. Growing up, she was significantly impacted by her father. His approach to his own life and career as a nationally respected dentist drove her to be curious, hardworking, and determined. She learned to advocate for herself and do what she thought was right.

Though first drawn to international relations as a student, Marilyn couldn't imagine moving away from the wild expansiveness of her home state. Chasing an interest in policy and government, she pivoted to law and never looked back. No stranger to breaking boundaries, she emerged as a lawyer during a time when entering the field of law as a woman was novel: Of roughly 125 law students, Marilyn was one of only seven female graduates in her class. Despite this imbalance, she thrived. One of her first breakthroughs was working for the

attorney general's office under Dave Kennedy, where she was assigned to the Department of Environmental Quality as the state's first environmental lawyer. In that capacity, she was responsible for the development and enforcement of air, water, and mining regulations. In 1978, she left state employment to join Holland & Hart, now a nationwide law firm, where she became a partner and the driving force in opening their Wyoming offices.

From 2000 to 2015, Marilyn represented Wyoming as a supreme court justice. Starting in 2010, she was the state's first female chief justice. During her fifteen years of service, she authored more than 500 opinions, including one recognizing the state constitutional requirements for public school funding. Following thirty years of court precedent, she authored the unanimous opinion requiring the state to fund public schools adequately and equally in each county. One of her proudest moments from her role as chief justice was supporting the Access to Justice Commission to uphold the Constitution's promise of equal justice for all by providing free or low-cost legal help to those in need through a state-funded

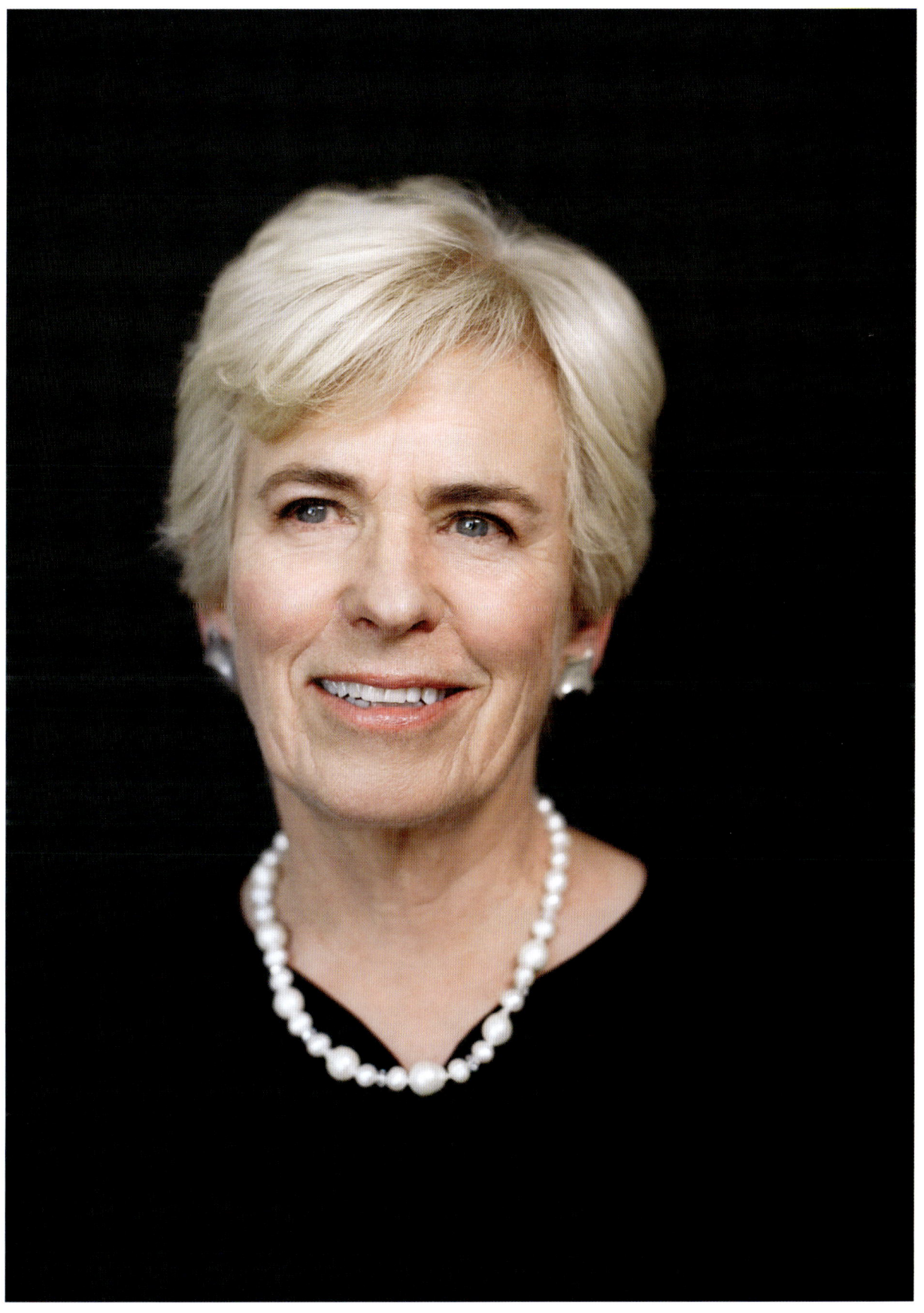

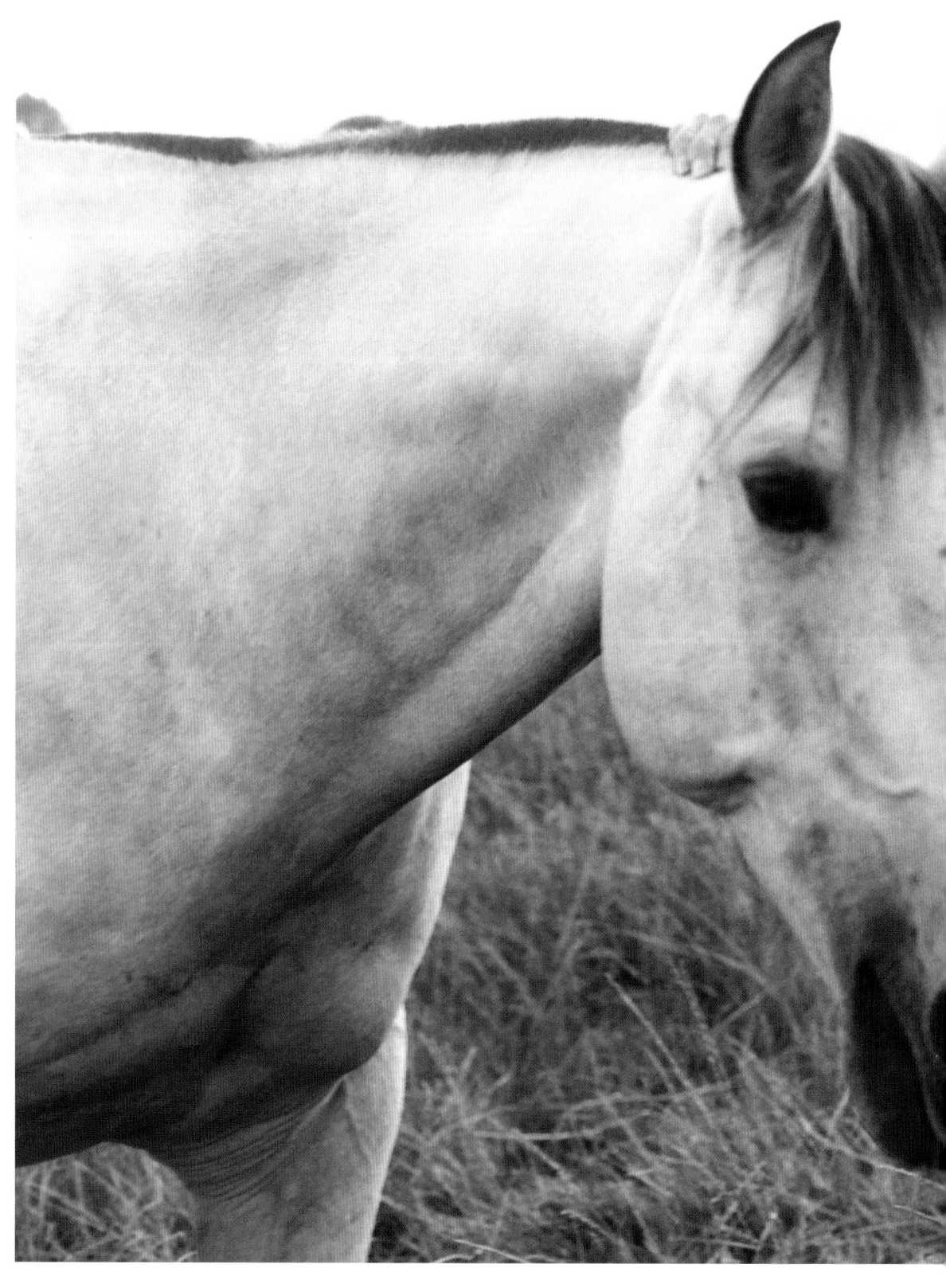

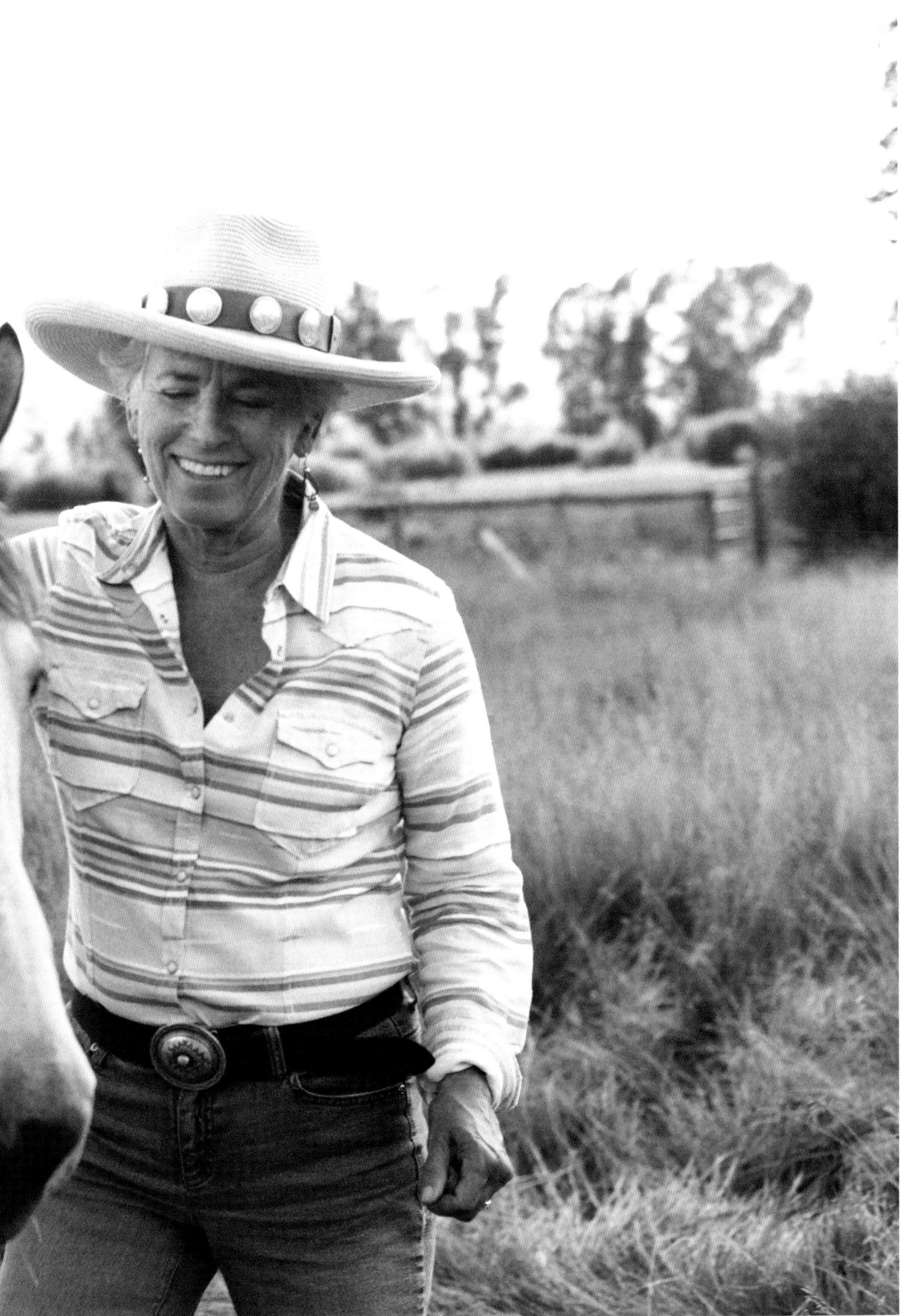

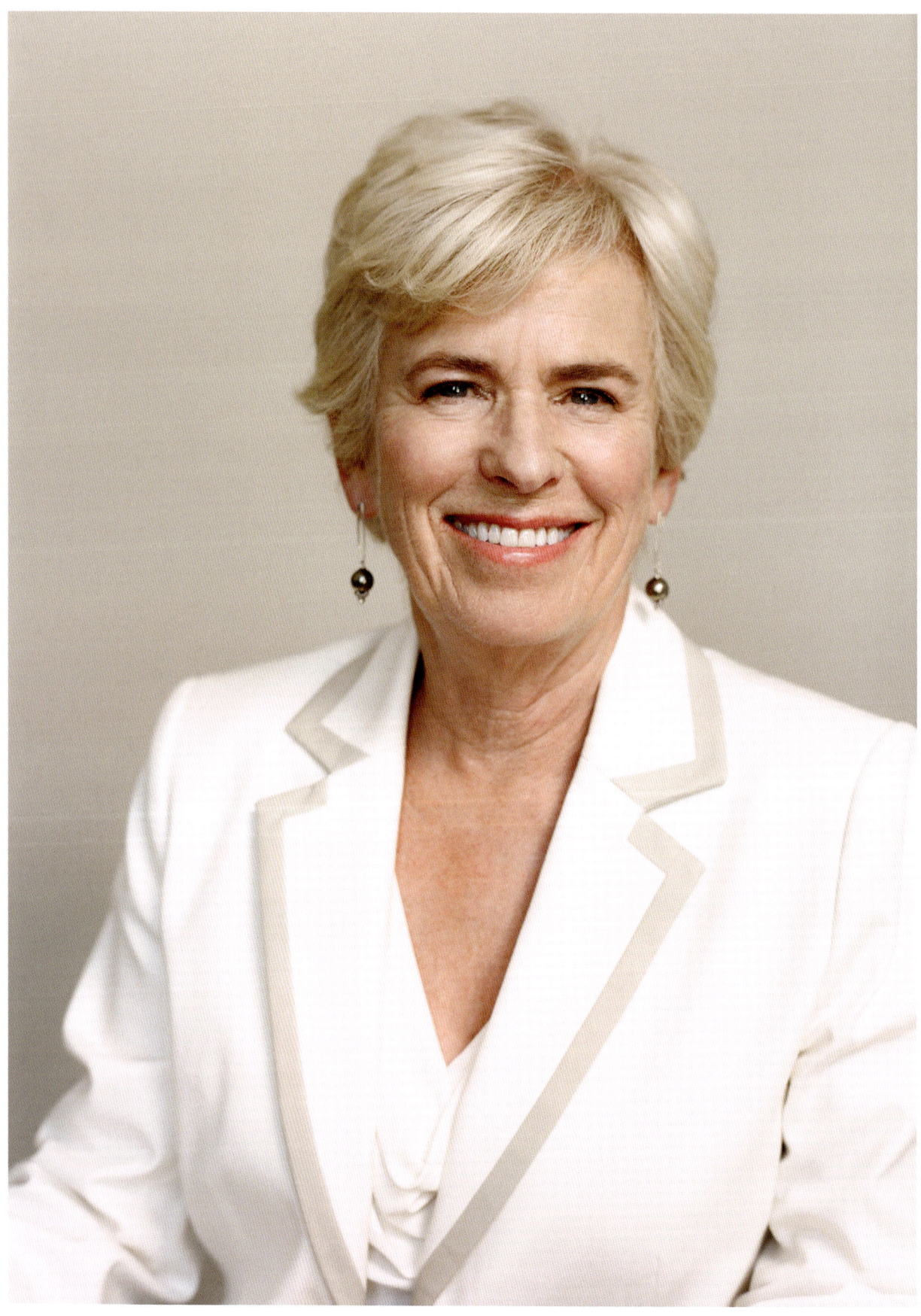

"You have to have the trust and confidence of the public for the courts to do their job. For there to be the trust and confidence of all the public, you need to have more women represented on the bench."

civil legal services program. She also worked to create the Judicial Learning Center in the Supreme Court building, aimed at students and all Wyoming citizens to explain the judicial process and its impact on their lives.

During her appointment, Justice Kite advocated for increased state funding for court security, which previously had been minimal, to protect the safety of judges, jury, family, and anyone else participating in the legal system, where stakes and emotions run high. In Marilyn's words, "Every day judges do their job, they are at risk." Increased funding helped all communities around the state, no matter their size, have secure courtrooms for all parties involved.

While Marilyn no longer issues opinions from the bench, she remains committed to ensuring Wyoming maintains an accountable, vibrant judiciary system. A healthy, functioning, independent democracy is dependent upon a healthy, functioning, independent judicial system. As chairman of the University of Wyoming College of Law Advisory Board, she and other board members advise the

dean regarding the law school's operation. In Marilyn's words, "A functioning legal system starts with ethical, competent lawyers. They're grown in law school."

Beyond law, and more personally, Marilyn is an accomplished horsewoman and was a founding "doe" of the country's first all-woman antelope hunt. The event benefits the Wyoming Women's Foundation, which works toward women's economic self-sufficiency and opportunities for girls in the state of Wyoming.

A true daughter of Wyoming and her father's teachings, Marilyn has devoted herself to mentoring the next generation and bettering the state through her work in the judicial field. As of this book's publication, four women have followed Marilyn's path to Wyoming's highest court, including Justice Kate M. Fox, Justice Lynne J. Boomgaarden, Justice Kari Jo Gray, and Justice Bridget Hill.

NIMI & NINA McCONIGLEY

NIMI *(MOTHER)*, FIRST INDIAN-BORN PERSON
IN THE UNITED STATES TO BE ELECTED TO STATE GOVERNMENT
NINA *(DAUGHTER)*, AWARD-WINNING AUTHOR
OF *COWBOYS AND EAST INDIANS*

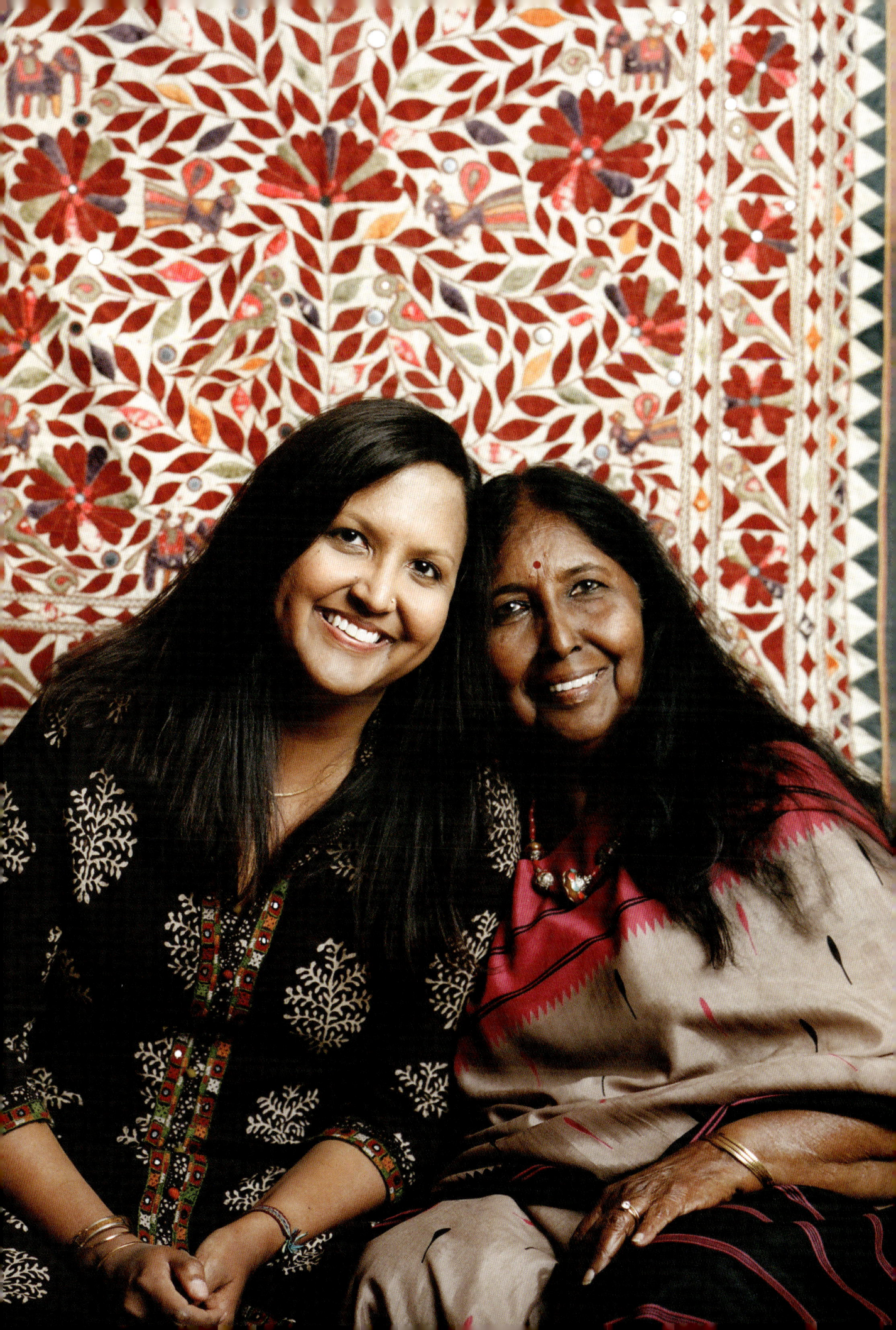

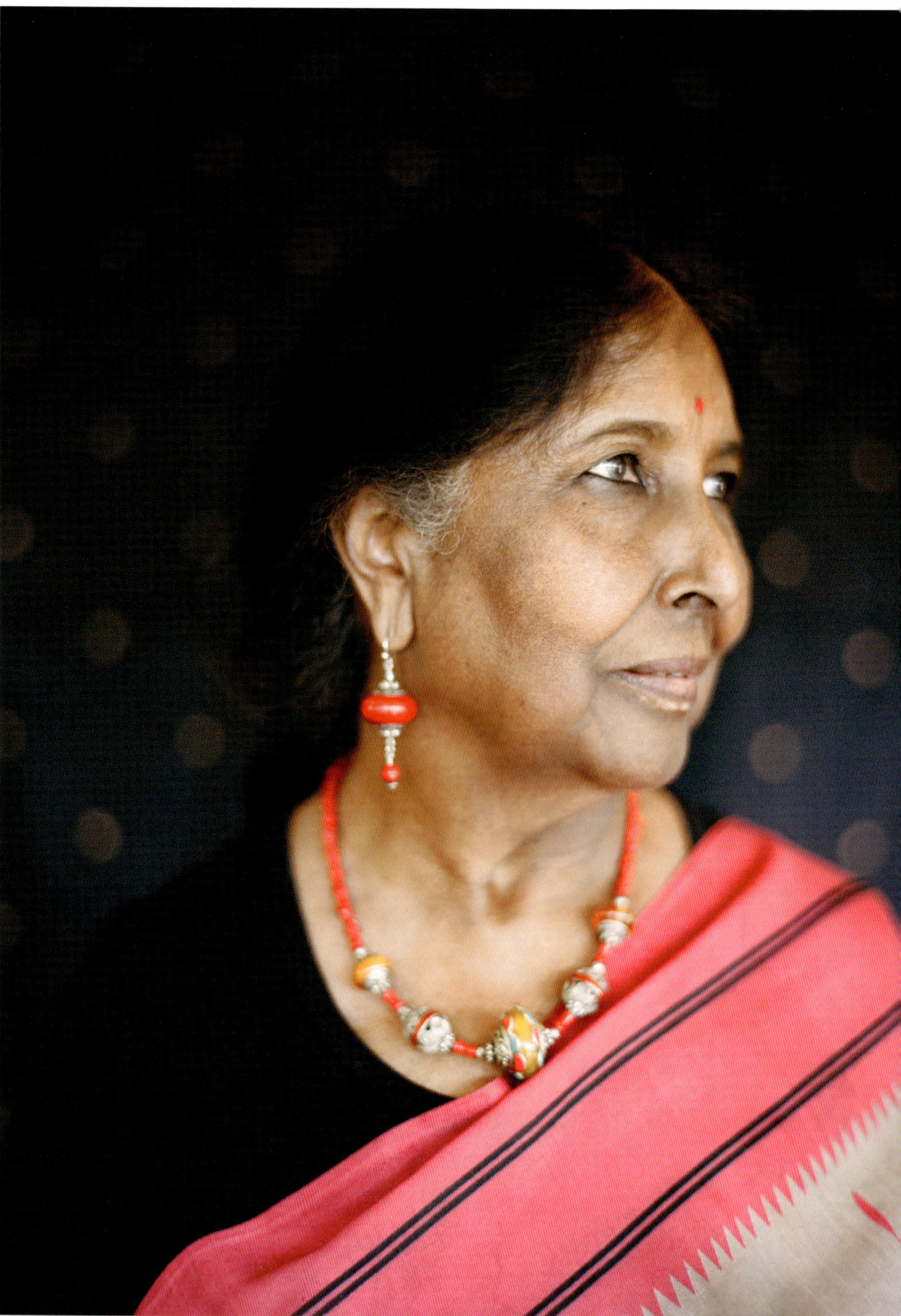

"You've got to believe in yourself. When your validation comes from inside you, and you validate yourself, that can't be taken away by anyone." —NIMI

Nimi McConigley grew up in Madras (now Chennai), India. On some hot summer nights, she would lie on the open terrace of her home, listening to the sounds of a nearby movie theater. The soundtrack of Westerns drifted through hot night air—galloping horses, yips, and yeehaws—transporting Nimi to another world. *Will I ever leave this city?* she would wonder. Decades later, when Nimi was sworn into the Wyoming State Legislature, her mind flashed back to dreaming on rooftops and how the sounds of her childhood became her future.

For most of Nimi's early life, she reflects, she felt like an outsider—first as the only Brown girl in her British school in India, then as one of four women in her graduating class from law school, and later as the only Indian woman in her graduate studies program in New York. But the experience that changed her the most was becoming a beloved member of the community in Wyoming.

With degrees in law and English literature, Nimi became a senior news writer for the All India Radio national news network in New Delhi. She studied at the Columbia University Graduate School of Journalism in New York City and was a producer trainee at WGBH, the PBS station in Boston. She returned to India to set up and direct the first youth radio station, a brainchild of Indira Gandhi, India's first and, to date, only female prime minister. Nimi met her future husband, Patrick, while he was volunteering in India with the Peace Corps. The couple moved to Singapore—where Patrick, a geologist, worked in oil and gas exploration—and afterward relocated to the United States.

Given the choice of Oklahoma City, Oklahoma; Casper, Wyoming; or Bakersfield, California, Nimi researched each location. Upon finding a picture of the Tetons, a wild, dramatic mountain range located near Jackson, Wyoming, Nimi chose Casper. She thought it looked like Switzerland. Little did she know that the picture-postcard image in the book bore no resemblance to Casper's high desert, prairie landscape. After arriving in Wyoming in 1976, Nimi spent several months trying to convince Patrick's company to transfer them elsewhere.

One moment changed all that—when her priest asked her to assist with pastoral care. Now able

Previous page:

Daughter and mother, Nina McConigley (left) and Nimi McConigley (right)

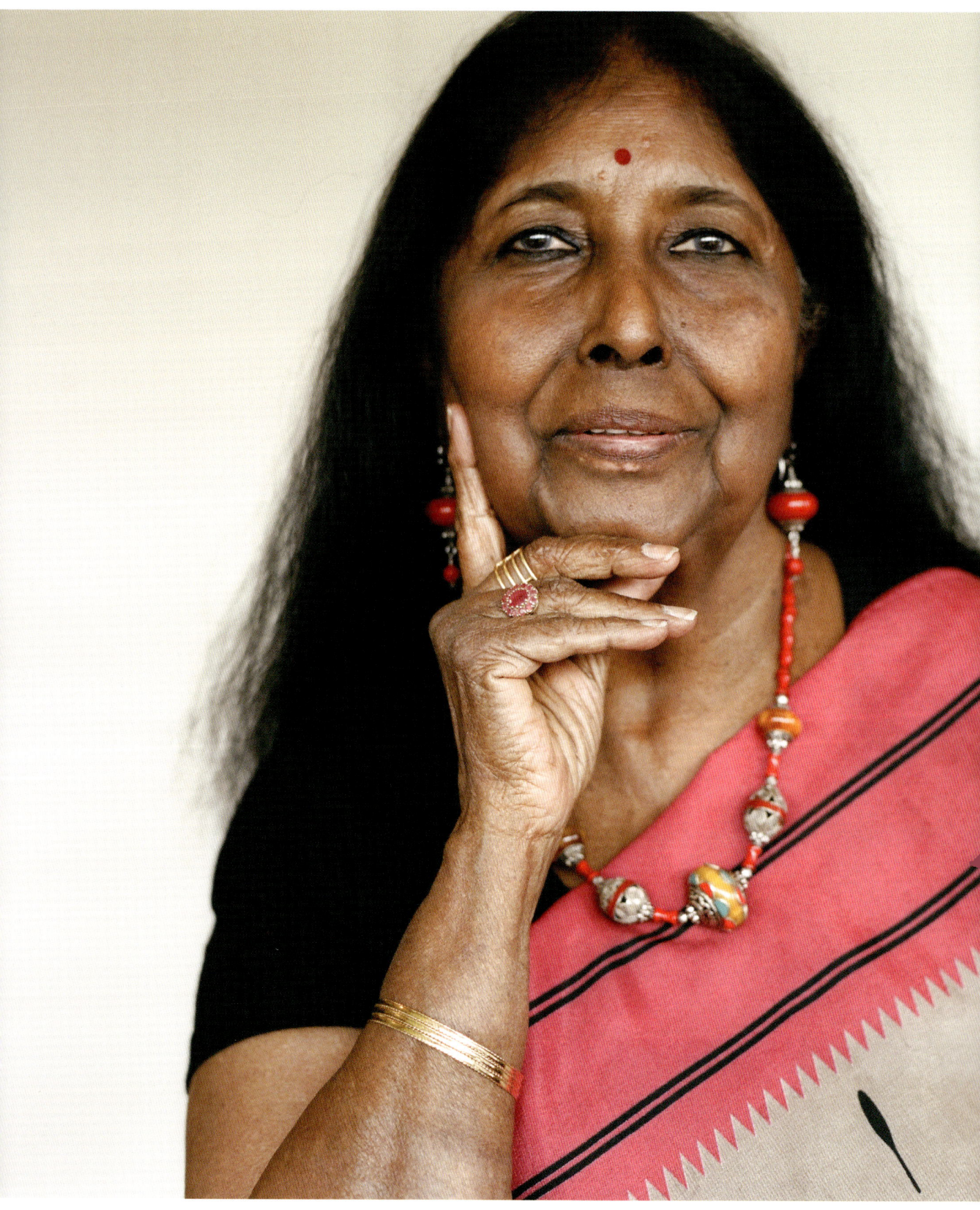

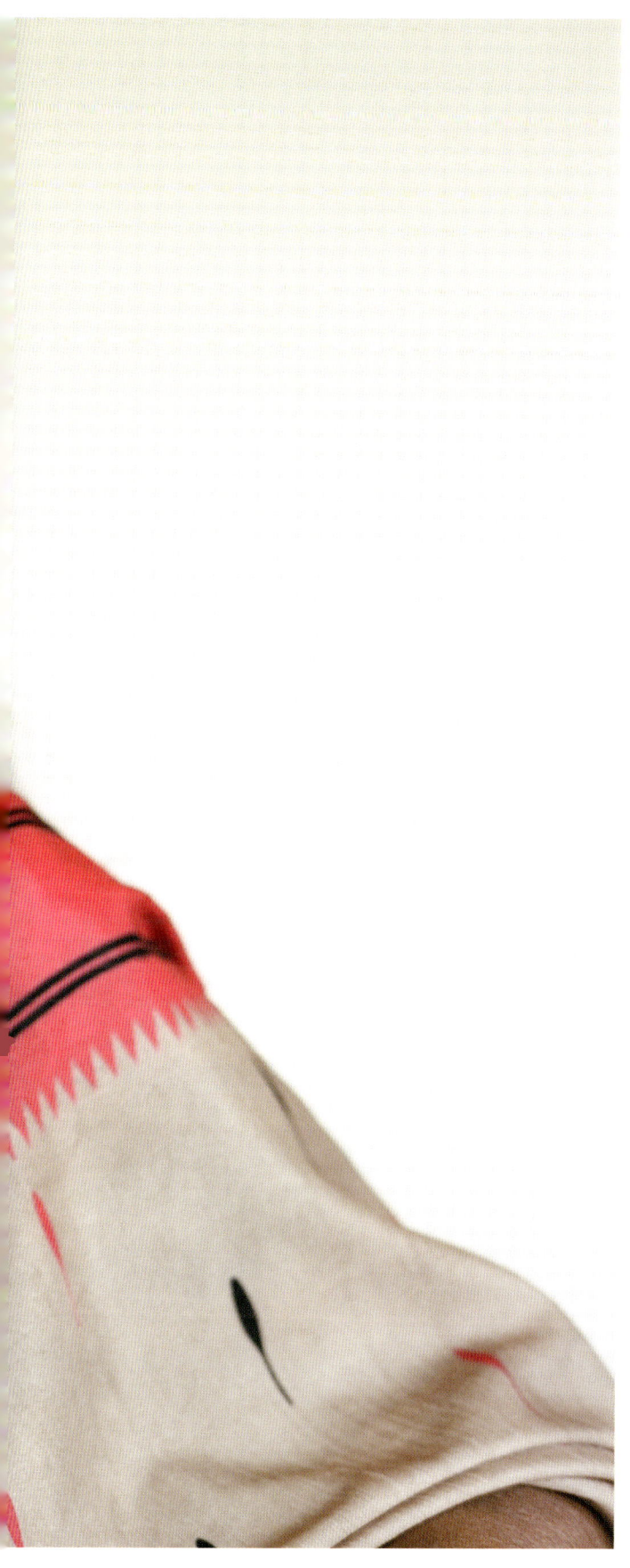

*"You can do it!
You just have to
have courage, and
trust and believe
in yourself, and not
let defeat stop you.
Keep trying!"*

to channel her talent for human connection into a meaningful purpose, a significant shift occurred. Her life took on new meaning when she recognized the opportunities around her for contributing her gifts and talents by becoming a part of, rather than separate from, the community in her Wyoming home. When the opportunity eventually came to transfer away, Nimi and Patrick decided to stay.

In Casper, Nimi worked briefly for the *Casper Star-Tribune*, a statewide daily newspaper, and then became news director of the Wyoming CBS station, KGWC-TV, where she could focus on Wyoming political coverage, local news, and human-centered stories.

After covering state politics daily for almost five years, Nimi felt compelled to run for political office herself and was elected to the Wyoming State Legislature in 1994. She became the first Indian-born person to be elected to any state legislature in the United States. Known as a community-minded person for years before running for office, Nimi had served on many local boards; spoken to schoolchildren, churches, and organizations; and volunteered wherever

she could. She was involved with establishing the first hospice program in Casper. Passionate about film, she shared her love by starting the Casper Cinema Club at the local public library, where she screened classic and foreign movies every week for more than fifteen years.

Nimi has lived in Wyoming for more than fifty years. In her words, "When I was sworn into the legislature, my mind flashed back . . . Did I ever think I'd end up in cowboy country? Here I am in the Wyoming State Legislature, being sworn in. Who would have thought this little girl from India would have ever ended up here?" Nimi has forged her way as a Wyoming woman while holding on to the rich heritage of her native country. She has embraced her difference, using it to highlight the strengths of America.

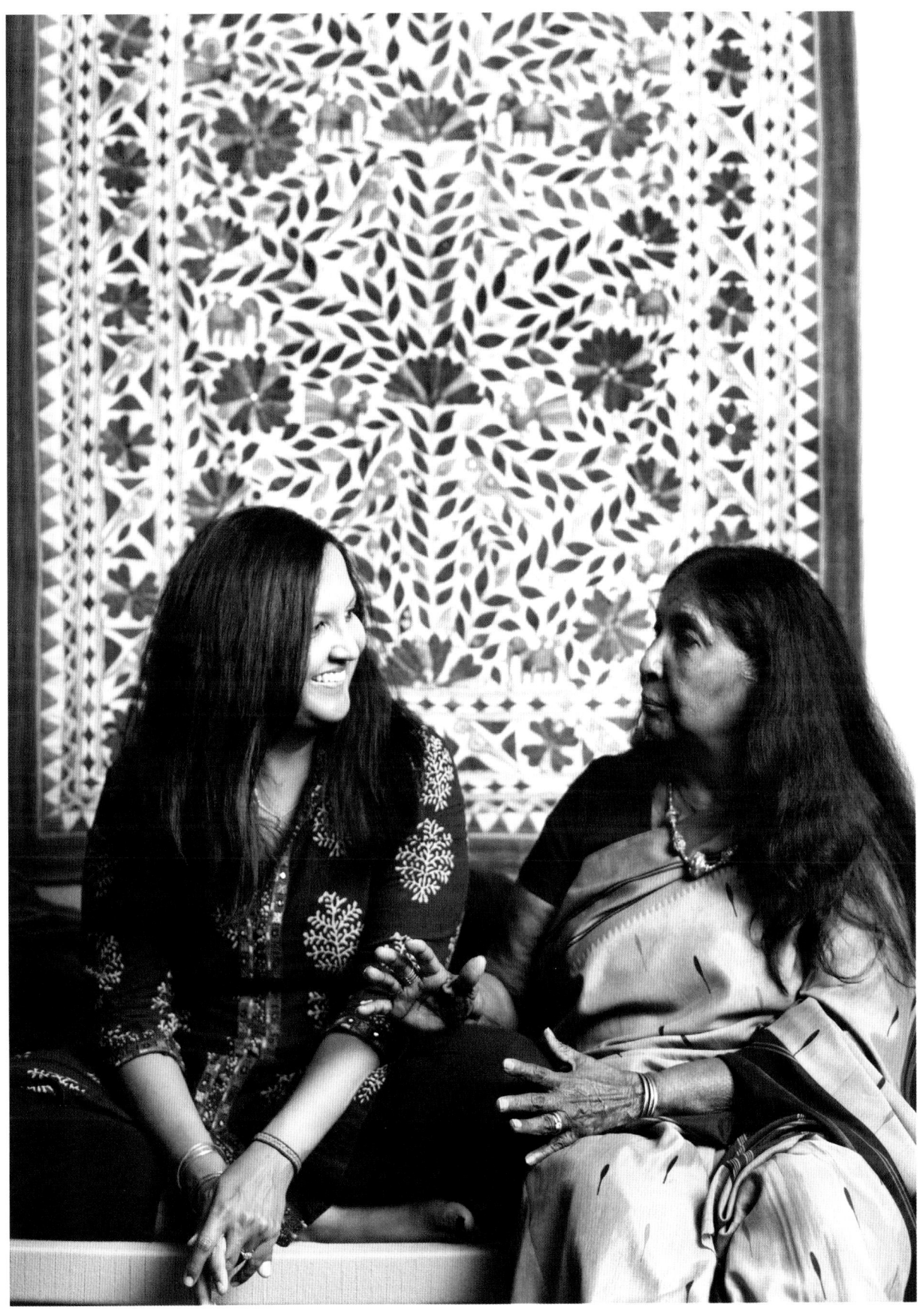

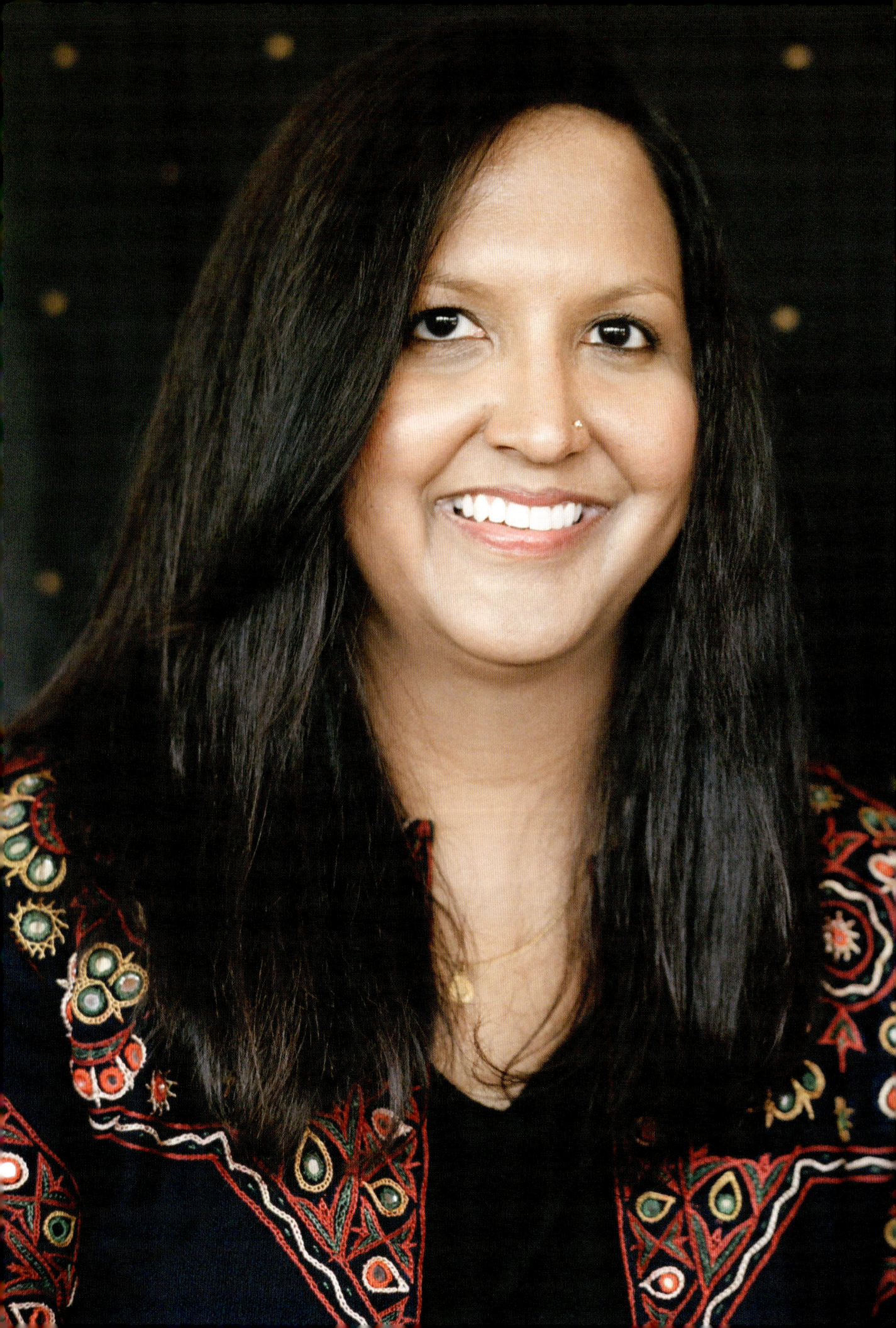

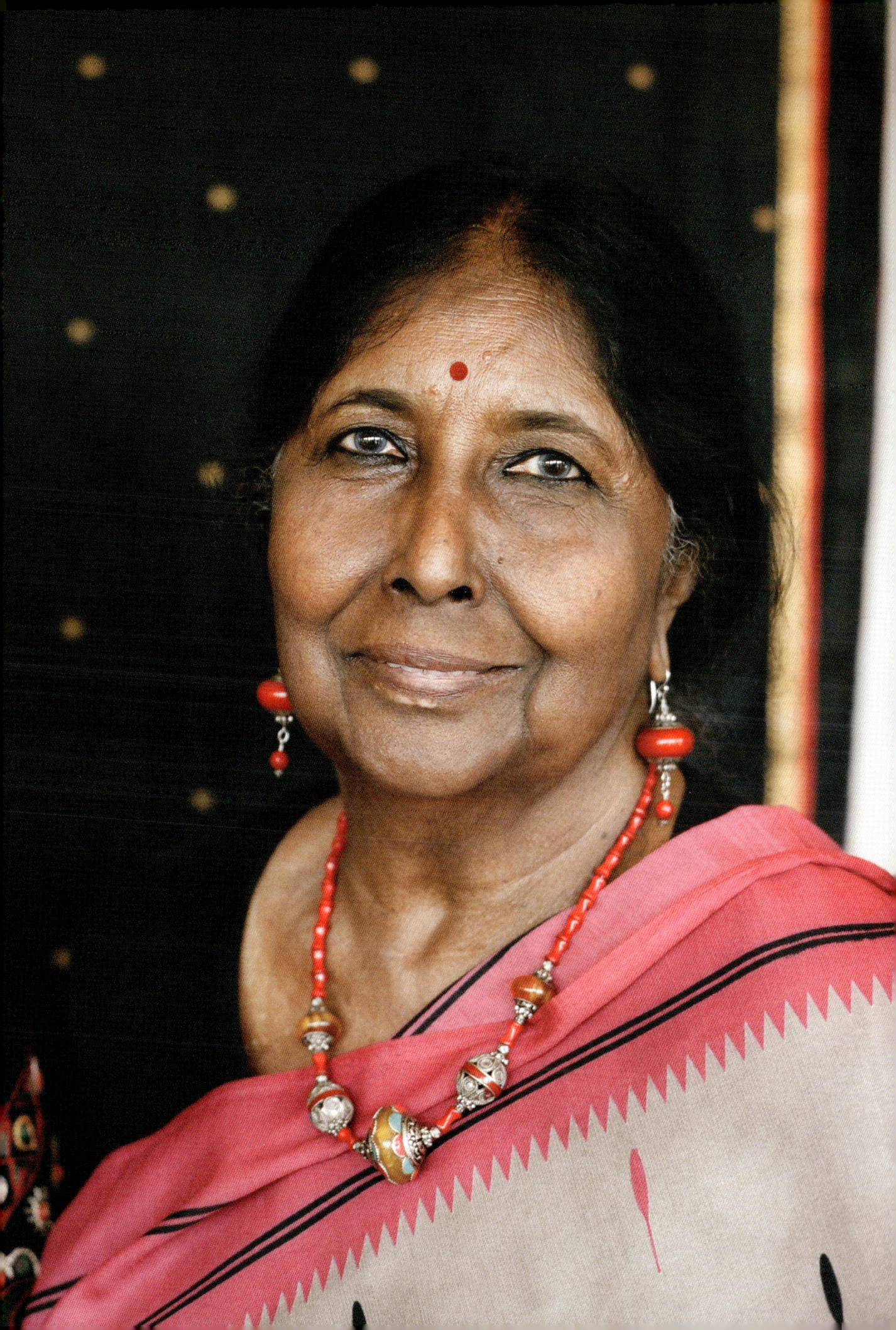

"When I sit down to write, it's that I want to tell an interesting story. It's what's in your subconscious. It just seeps onto the page." —NINA

Growing up as biracial girls in a rural American state, Nina and her sister were the only Indian-American students at their school. This difference informed her life and led her to write about the rural immigrant experience.

Nina didn't call herself a writer until she was holding her published collection of short stories, *Cowboys and East Indians*, in her hands. In her youth, she imagined herself as an archaeologist or a journalist. The career-defining moment came after she took an insurance-industry job, where she was confined to a cubicle. Looking for an escape, she took an Intro to Creative Writing night class at the local community college, which ignited a spark of inspiration. She went on to earn an MA in English from the University of Wyoming and then returned to school to get an MFA from the University of Houston, where she began writing and publishing the stories that would later become her award-winning book. Still, the process of getting her first book published took tenacity and patience—many publishers loved the collection but were wary of short stories and their capacity to sell. Nina knew she hadn't read stories like hers, which explore difference and the rural immigrant experience in the West, a not-so-common perspective. Her work explores themes of identity, migration, and the complexities of belonging through the lens of South Asians in the American West.

Nina's story collection won the PEN Open Book Award and a High Plains Book Award. From 2019 to 2020, Nina was the Walter Jackson Bate Fellow at the Radcliffe Institute for Advanced Study at Harvard University. In 2022, she was a recipient of the National Endowment for the Arts Creative Writing Fellowship. The Denver Center for the Performing Arts commissioned her to write a play based on *Cowboys and East Indians*.

Nina's writing has appeared in *The New York Times, Ploughshares, Oprah* magazine, *Virginia Quarterly Review, American Short Fiction,* and *The Asian American Literary Review,* among others. Her second book, the novel *How to Commit a Postcolonial Murder*, was published in 2026. Nina taught at the University of Wyoming for thirteen years and is currently a professor at Colorado State University.

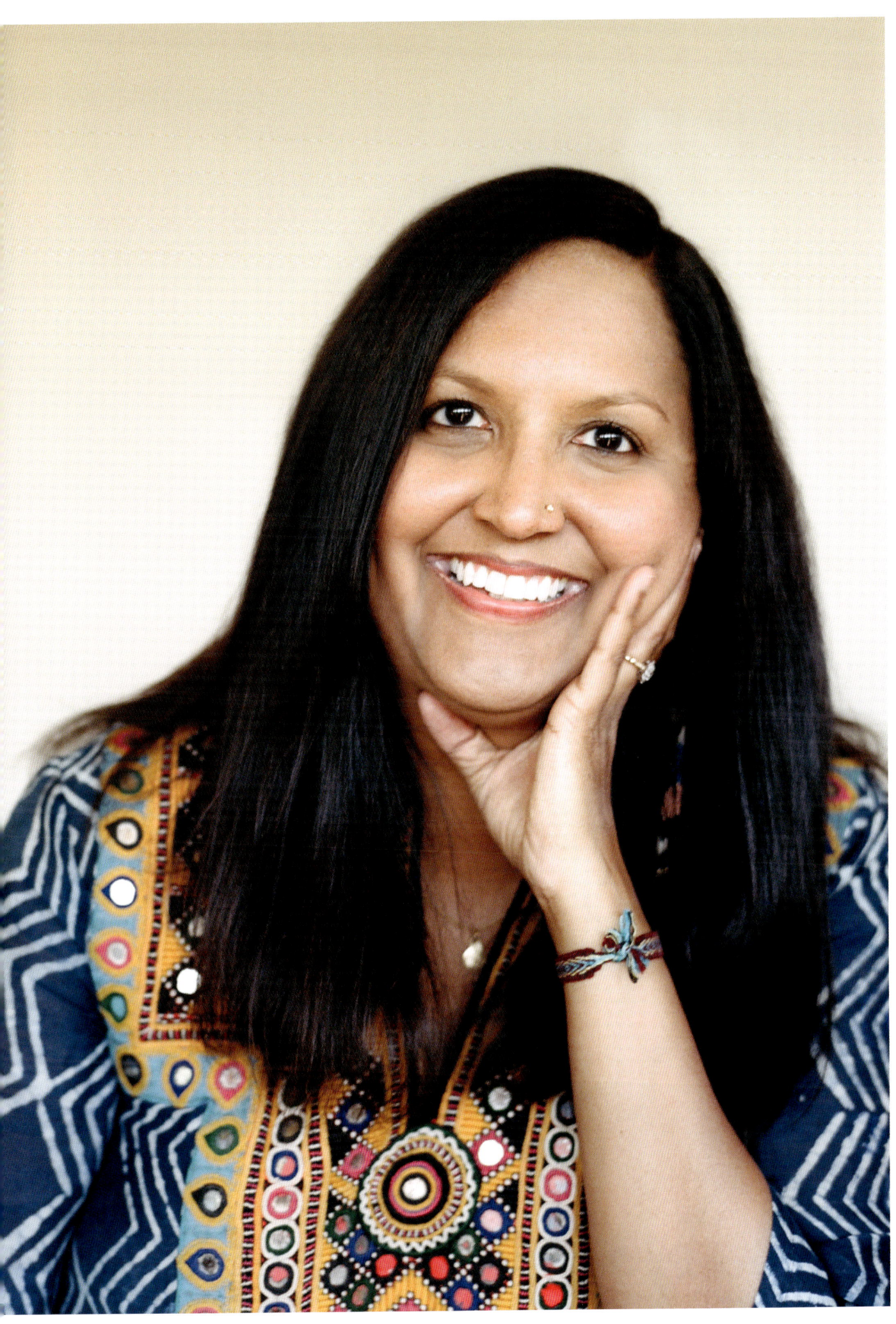

CLARENE LAW

1933–2022

SELF-MADE BUSINESSWOMAN, COMMUNITY LEADER,
LONG-TIME LEGISLATOR

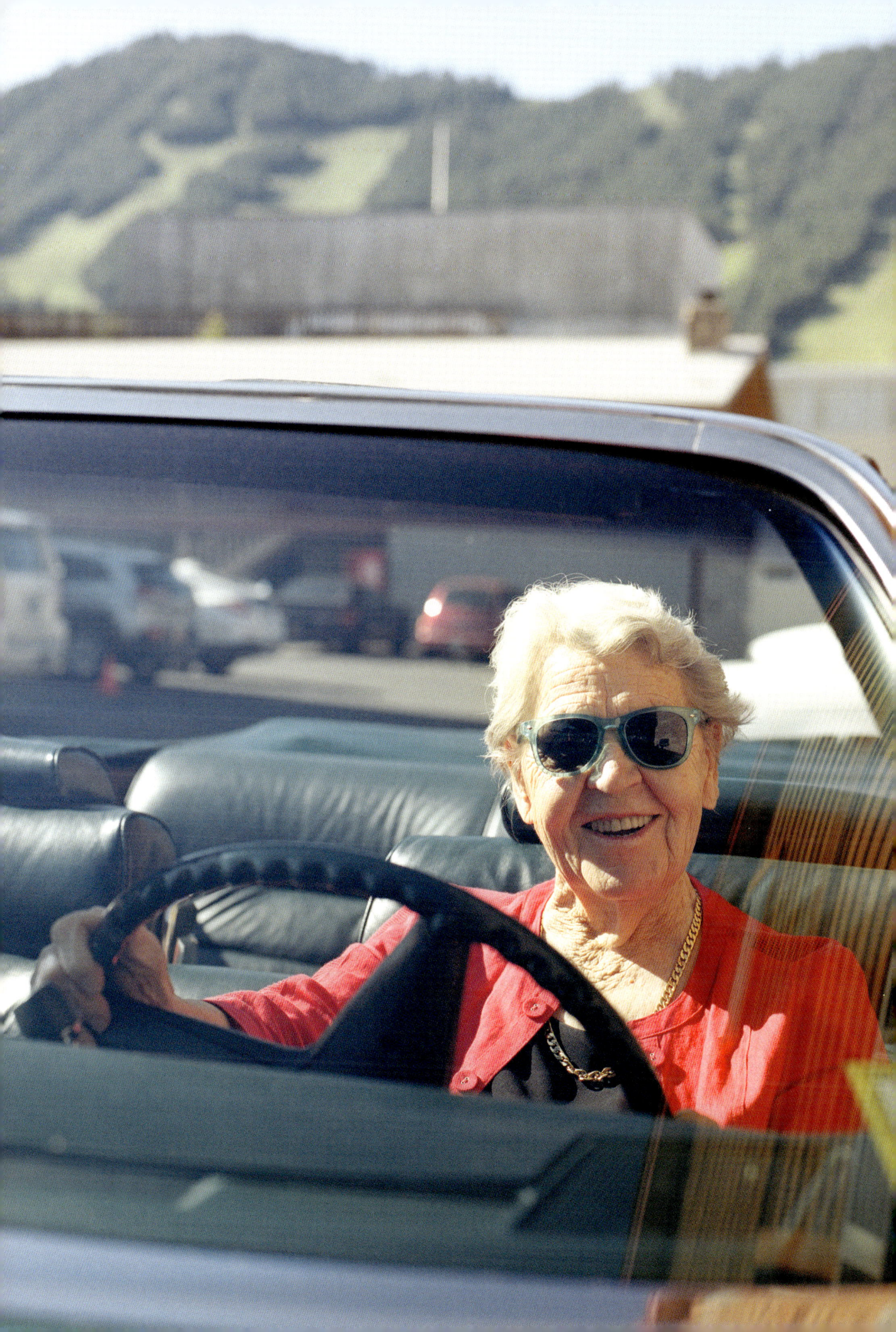

"The only way you do things, you don't do them alone. There is no such word as just me—I. It is all of us. It'd take everybody in my life to make what I am today."

Some people choose to take a cutthroat approach to business. And one can achieve great power that way, but at what cost? Clarene Law embodied a markedly different approach—"not by pushing others down, but by standing on each other's shoulders."

Clarene was a force in Wyoming's business and political communities for more than sixty years. She grew up in a blue-collar family and was well-known in the state as "the matriarch of the tourism industry," due to her success-ful hotel and business endeavors. Clarene did not think of herself this way, however. In her mind, her greatest success was her network of relationships. In her memoir, *And I Had Fun!*, she wrote, "Everybody wants to be at the top of the mountain, but you don't get there all at once, and you don't get there alone. Your strengths, your perseverance, are developed on the way up."

With her father in road construction, Clarene's childhood was largely nomadic. Her family moved twenty-one times before they settled in one place long enough for her to go to high school. This constant change developed her reliance on family as the ever-present anchor, her confidence as she was repeatedly entering someone else's domain, and her empathy as she readily put herself in another's shoes. Through difficult years of moving, sickness, and the loss of a younger sister, Clarene's mother imparted advice that ended up guiding her life: "The only contentment you'll find is in your own heart . . . The greatest gift we'll ever have is the gift of contentment. You only have what you become." Clarene credits her beloved parents for her strength, drive, and lifelong dedication to service.

After working as a clerk of court and a reporter for the *Deseret News* in her early twenties, Clarene first entered into hospitality at the historic Wort Hotel in Jackson, where she took inventory and drafted contracts. When the bookkeeper left, she stepped into new terrain, taking correspondence courses to bring her-self up to speed. In 1962, while on her lunch break one day, she overheard the proprietor mention that a nearby motel would be "hitting the block" and coming up for sale. Though Clarene had little means, loaned life savings from her parents and in-laws and an early SBA

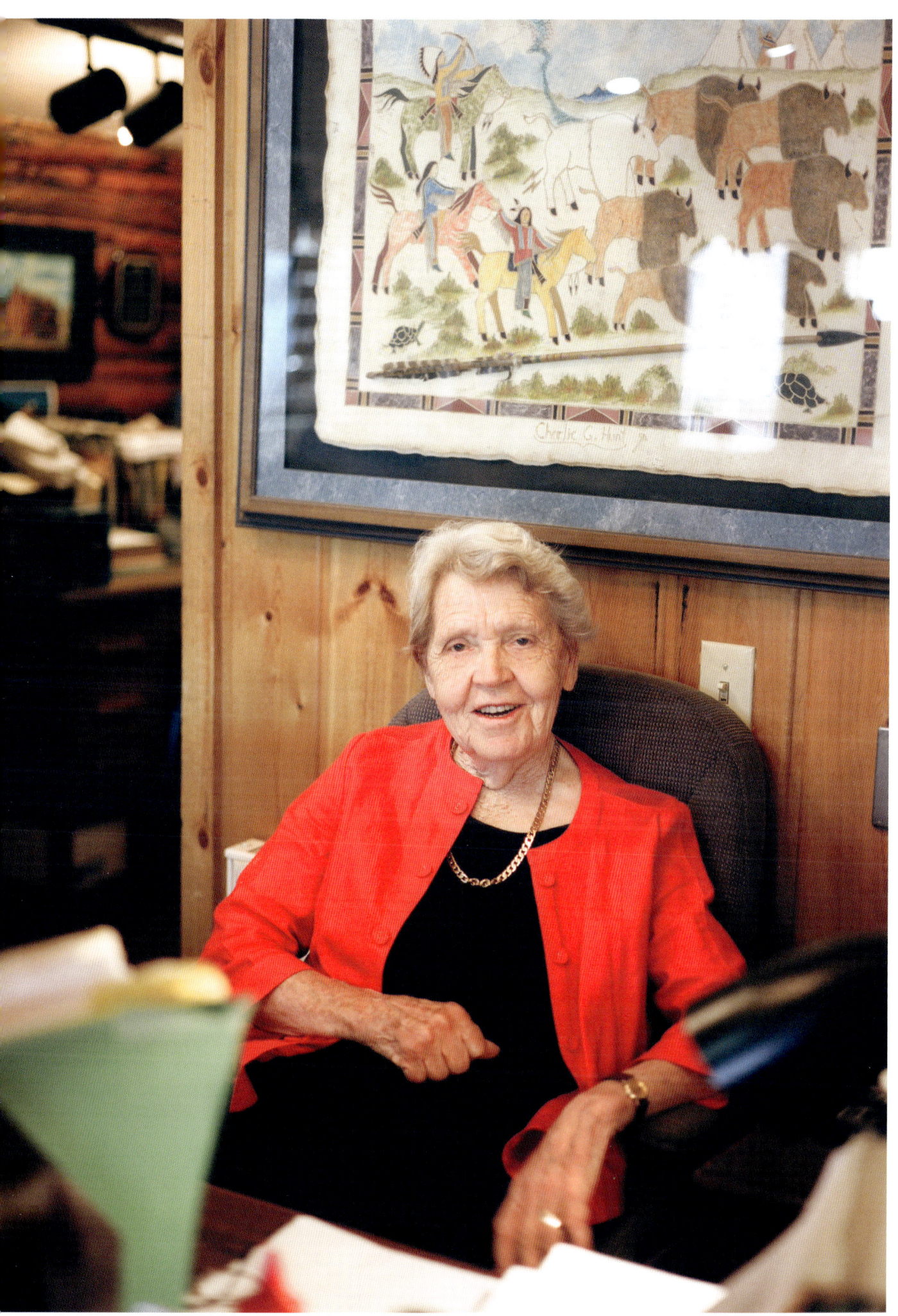

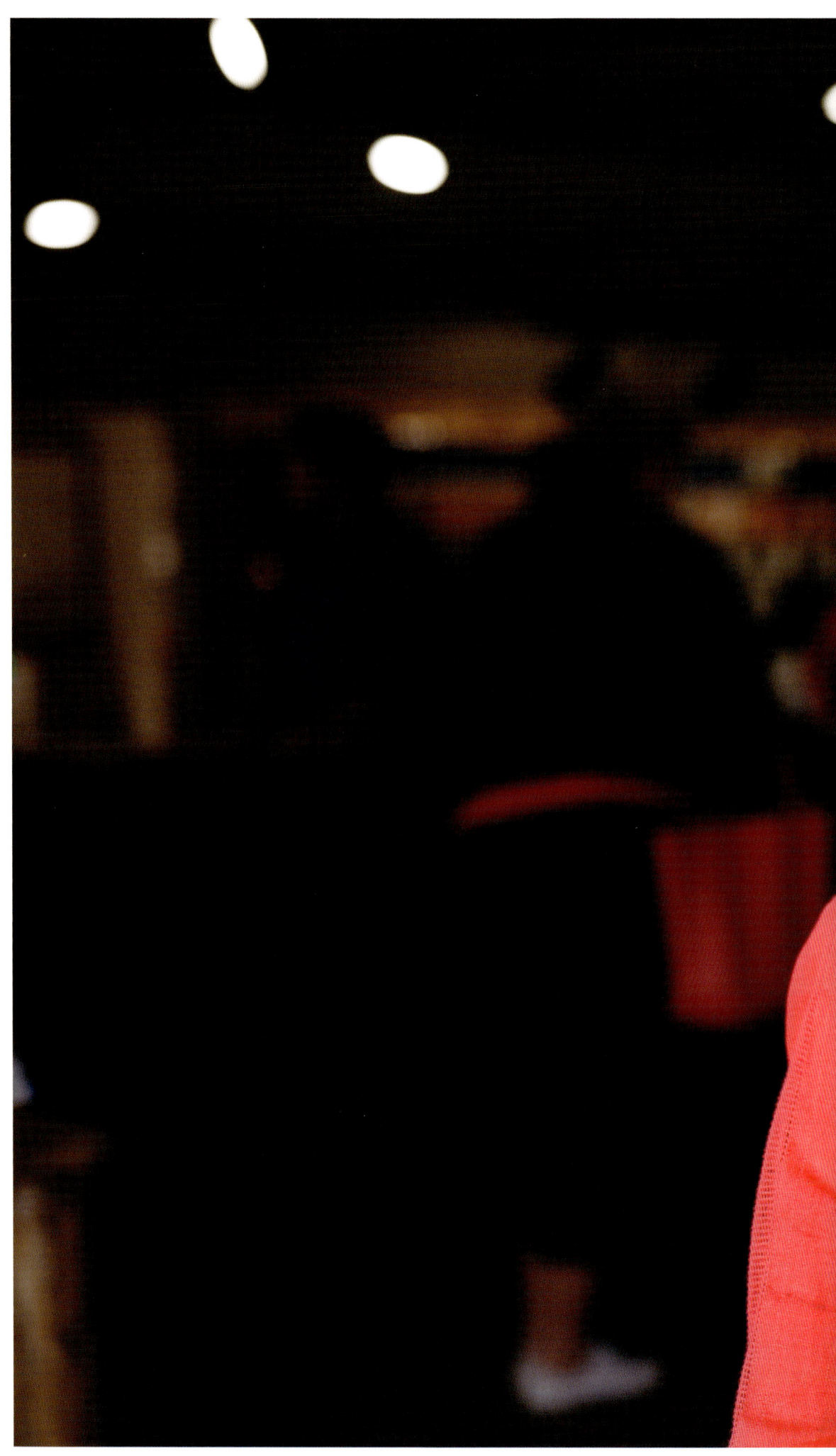

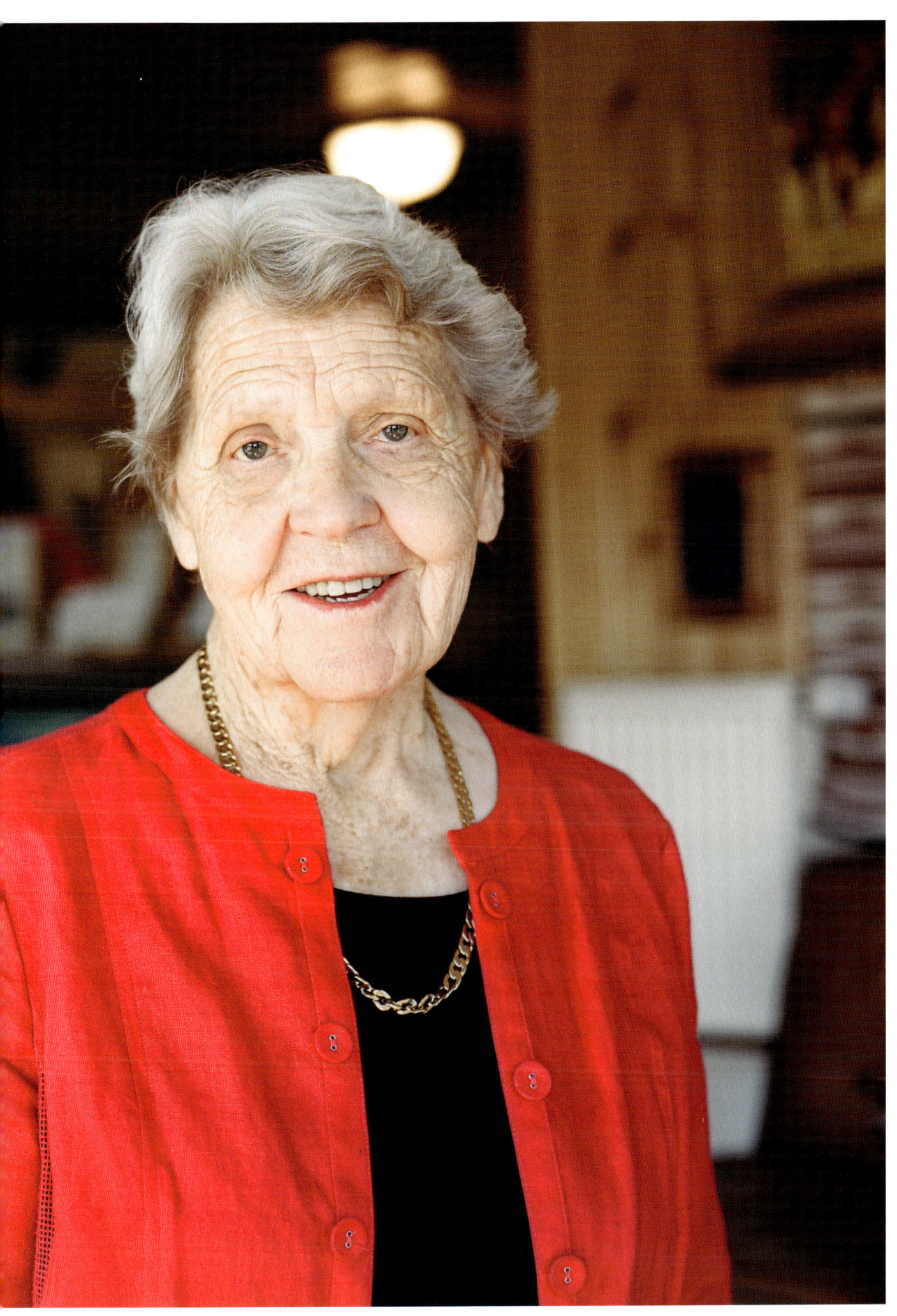

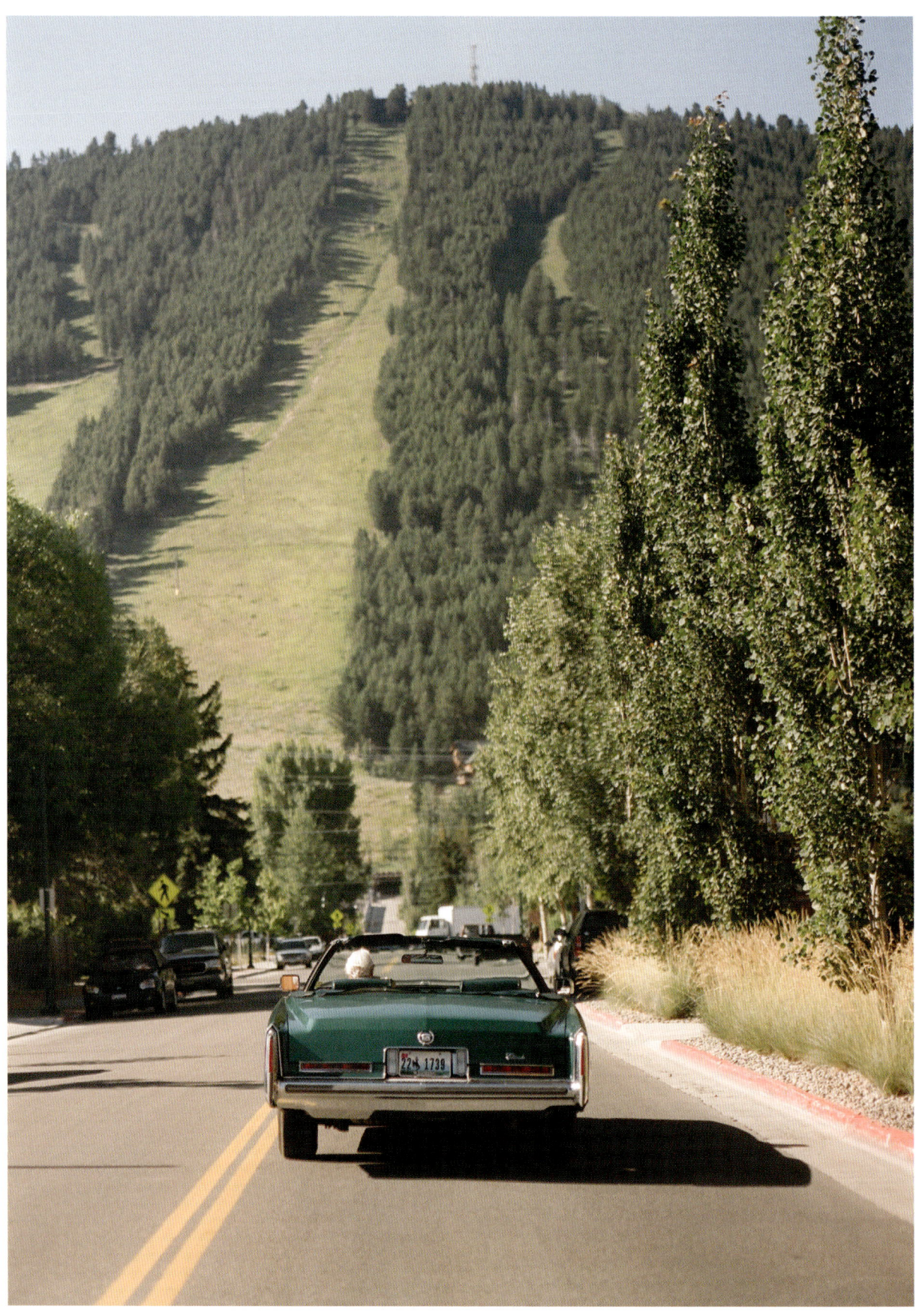

"You have to believe in yourself, and you have to be willing to take the advice of others, and you have to find an awfully good banker."

loan made the purchase possible. She acquired the Antler Inn, her flagship motel, when she was just twenty-seven years old. Over the years, and after the first particularly difficult ones of building a business while raising her young children, Clarene continued to expand and build her family's hospitality network into four hotels and multiple properties. The businesses continue to be some of the few family-owned and operated lodging properties in Jackson. Despite her own business acumen, she credited her success to employee and employer loyalty, support from loyal customers, and her family.

In addition to her business savvy, Clarene was equally known for her kindness, compassion, and public service. She served fourteen years in the Wyoming House of Representatives, where she was named chairwoman of the Minerals, Business, and Economic Development Committee and the Travel, Recreation, Wildlife, and Cultural Resources Committee. She devoted her time to numerous boards and commissions and earned accolades for her dedication, including a Lifetime Achievement Award from the Wyoming Business Report, the Wyoming Women of Influence award, the

Wyoming Business Person of the Year, and the Jackson Hole Citizen of the Year. She was inducted into the Wyoming Business Hall of Fame in 2013.

More than sixty years after buying the Antler Inn, Clarene could still be found working there most days. Why? "Because it needed to be done." And she loved it. When she was inducted into the Wyoming Business Hall of Fame, she said that her greatest wish was to be able to keep saying, "May I help you?" Clarene knew the secret to lasting success was a love of people and uplifting others. What a boss!

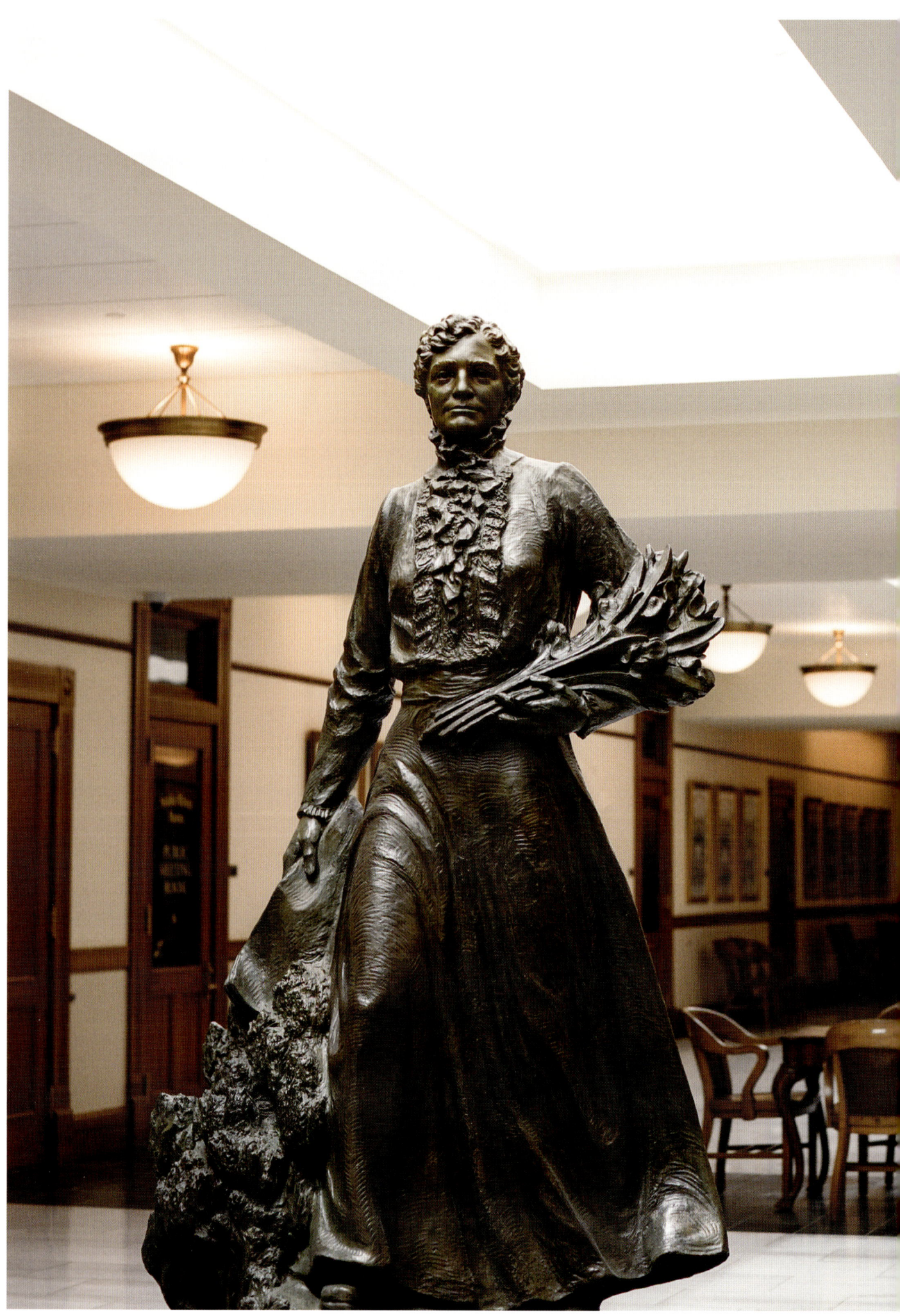

Wyoming Women Win the Vote: The Story of Suffrage and Groundbreaking Women of History

Historical advisory by Jennifer Helton. Additional support by Kylie Louise McCormick.

The passage of woman suffrage in territorial Wyoming on December 10, 1869, was revolutionary. The groundbreaking legislation enfranchised women *and* recognized their right to hold office. Additionally, Wyoming's suffrage law recognized the voting rights of all women citizens, regardless of race. While their names have not been preserved in the historical record, it is believed Wyoming supported the first female Black voters in history. Some women still had to wait. States, including Wyoming, didn't recognize the citizenship and voting rights of most Indigenous women until the passage of the Indian Citizenship Act in 1924. However, most women in Wyoming held power and positions of influence unmatched by their American contemporaries.

Additionally, more legislation was passed to protect women's economic rights. This included bills recognizing the rights of married women to control their own property and wages. Women were guaranteed the right to sue and be sued, to make their own will, and to have a share in their husband's estate. The legislature also recognized women's parental rights and their right to initiate a divorce and protect their property rights in divorce settlements. These freedoms were unheard of across most of the country. The legislature also passed one of the nation's first equal pay laws, requiring that teachers be paid based on their qualifications, not their gender.

Despite this progress, in 1871, an attempt was made to repeal woman suffrage. But Governor John Allen Campbell, a supporter of women's enfranchisement, vetoed the bill. The legislature then attempted to override his veto, but the effort failed by a single vote. Senator John Fosher, who knew firsthand how much women contributed to their communities, and who may have headed the advocacy of suffragists like Amalia Post, delivered the final, tiebreaking vote that saved the vote for women. When Wyoming officially entered the Union in 1890, it became the first state to guarantee women's freedom and equality.

Suffrage historian Jennifer Helton shares, "While men still held most elected offices, women served on election boards, on school boards, as game wardens, as justices of the peace, as mayors, as constables and county clerks. In other parts of the country, this might have been remarkable, but in Wyoming, it was routine."

In addition to political offices, women ran businesses and became doctors, professors in higher education, and more. These women shaped the evolution of Wyoming while making history around the country and globe. Here are a few of their stories.

FACING: *Mother of Suffrage,* a bronze statue of Esther Hobart Morris created by sculptor Avard Fairbanks, stands in the Wyoming State Capitol building.

First woman in Wyoming to vote:

LOUISA SWAIN (1801–1880)

A grandmother and respected elder in Laramie, Louisa Swain was Wyoming's honorary first female voter, on September 6, 1870. The occasion was celebratory and communal. An aisle parted for Louisa as she made her way to the ballot box, and the crowd continued to cheer for her as she walked home. While Louisa was not technically the first woman in U.S. history to vote—women in Utah (which had recognized woman suffrage a couple of months after Wyoming) had already voted in February of 1870, as had Indigenous women like the Haudenosaunee (Iroquois), who held enormous power in their societies and had voted for centuries—her participation on Election Day, surrounded by community support, was nevertheless revolutionary.

America's first female justice of the peace:

ESTHER HOBART MORRIS
(1814–1902)

Suffragist, abolitionist, and businesswoman Esther Hobart Morris came to Wyoming with a mission. She moved to South Pass City in the spring of 1869 and immediately began advocating for woman suffrage to William Bright, her representative for the newly created Wyoming Territorial Legislature. In Esther's words, the passage of the suffrage bill left the "gates wide open" for women to enter public life in ways that had not previously been possible. In February of 1870, she applied for the justice of the peace position for South Pass City. When a board of commissioners approved her application and acting Governor Edward M. Lee approved her appointment, Esther became the first woman in U.S. history to serve as a judge. She served for eight months and did not seek reelection. Esther remained active in the

national woman suffrage movement for the remainder of her life, attending the California Woman Suffrage Association convention in San Francisco in 1872, serving as vice president of the National American Woman Suffrage Association (NAWSA), and speaking at suffrage conventions around the country.

Suffragist and one of the first women in the United States to serve on a jury:

AMALIA POST (1826–1897)

Businesswoman, suffrage advocate, and community organizer Amalia Post led a ladies' committee that lobbied legislators to enfranchise Wyoming women. After winning the vote, she co-led the Laramie County Republican Committee, which supported two female candidates, Phoebe Pickett for county clerk and Melvina H. Arnold for superintendent of county schools, for the 1870 election. In 1871, Amalia served as a jury forewoman in a criminal case, sparking national news coverage as a result. In 1889, she presided over a gathering of around one hundred women in Cheyenne to draft resolutions in favor of woman suffrage. One of the resolutions successfully encouraged voters to elect only pro-suffrage delegates to Wyoming's Constitutional Convention. Of the fifty-five delegates in attendance, only one voiced his personal opposition to woman suffrage during the event. Like Esther Hobart Morris, Amalia was active in the national suffrage movement, serving as vice president of the NAWSA for over twenty years.

America's first female bailiff:

MARTHA SYMONS BOIES
ATKINSON (1830–1917)

In March 1870, the first grand jury in the country that included both men and women coalesced. Due to a long court session, the jury was required to spend the night in a hotel. Given the sensitivity of women being on a jury, Martha was selected to guard the women's rooms overnight. In all, she served as bailiff for three terms of court before a new judge decided to cease calling women jurors for service. After the 1870s (with the exception of an 1891 civil case in the Bighorn Basin town of Bonanza), Wyoming women did not serve on juries again until the 1950s! Martha's first husband, with whom she had two children, died a few years after they were married. With her second husband, Jeremiah Boies, she headed west to Nebraska, operating hotels and boardinghouses. The Boies family followed the work crews when the railroad came west, settling in Laramie in 1868. With her long history of working in railroad camps, Martha knew how to assert her authority and was well-suited for the role of bailiff.

America's first female prison chaplain:
MAY GORSLIN PRESTON SLOSSON, PHD (1858–1943)

Suffragist, educator, and prison chaplain May Slosson organized beloved lectures for prisoners at the Wyoming State Penitentiary and eventually was appointed the chaplain in 1899, making her the first female chaplain in the United States. One of the prisoners said of her abilities and popularity, "At the first sound of Mrs. Slosson's voice, the prison walls faded away. I forgot utterly where I was for the half hour she talked to us and then woke with a start to its realization when she ceased. The world which had been so bright grew dark again, yet not quite so dark as before." Originally from New York, May was the first woman to obtain a doctoral degree in philosophy in America and the first woman to earn a PhD from Cornell University. She moved back

to New York in 1903 and became active in the fight for woman suffrage after having voted in Wyoming for most of her adult life.

Wyoming's first female legislator:
MARY GODAT BELLAMY (1861–1955)

Mary Godat Bellamy was born in Missouri as the youngest of seven children but from the age of twelve years old was raised in Laramie. Unlike most American children of her generation, Mary had the unique experience of growing up around a community of enfranchised and politically active women. Wyoming's first female justice of the peace, Esther Hobart Morris, was a babysitter. Mary followed in her family's footsteps to become a teacher, a profession she continued after marrying surveyor Charles Bellamy and having three children. Mary, a working mother (rare for women of her era), was elected as Albany County superintendent of schools, 1902–1904, before her election to the 1911–1913 legislative session, making her the state's first elected female legislator. An advocate for public education, the University of Wyoming, and prison reform, Mary was also active in the national woman suffrage movement. She laid the groundwork for future generations of women to serve in politics and leadership positions.

First women in Wyoming to own and publish a newspaper: **THE HUNTINGTON SISTERS—GERTRUDE** (1866–1925), **LAURA** (1870–1962), AND **CAROLYN** (1879–1904)

Gertrude and Laura Huntington were the first women in Wyoming to own a newspaper. They purchased the *Platte Valley Lyre*, based in Saratoga, in 1890, and ran it until 1902. Gertrude edited the paper—the first woman in the state to do so—while Laura served as

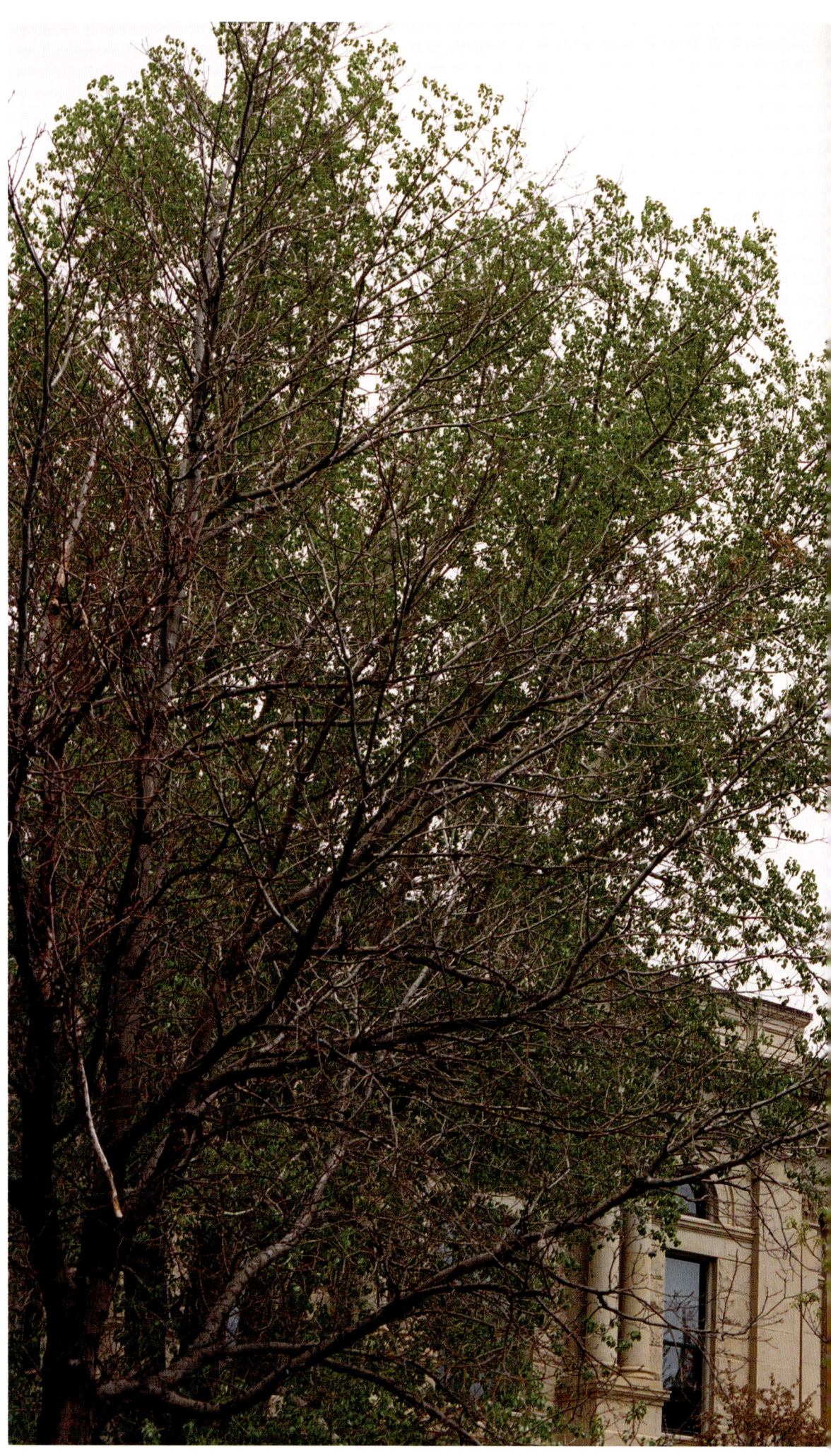

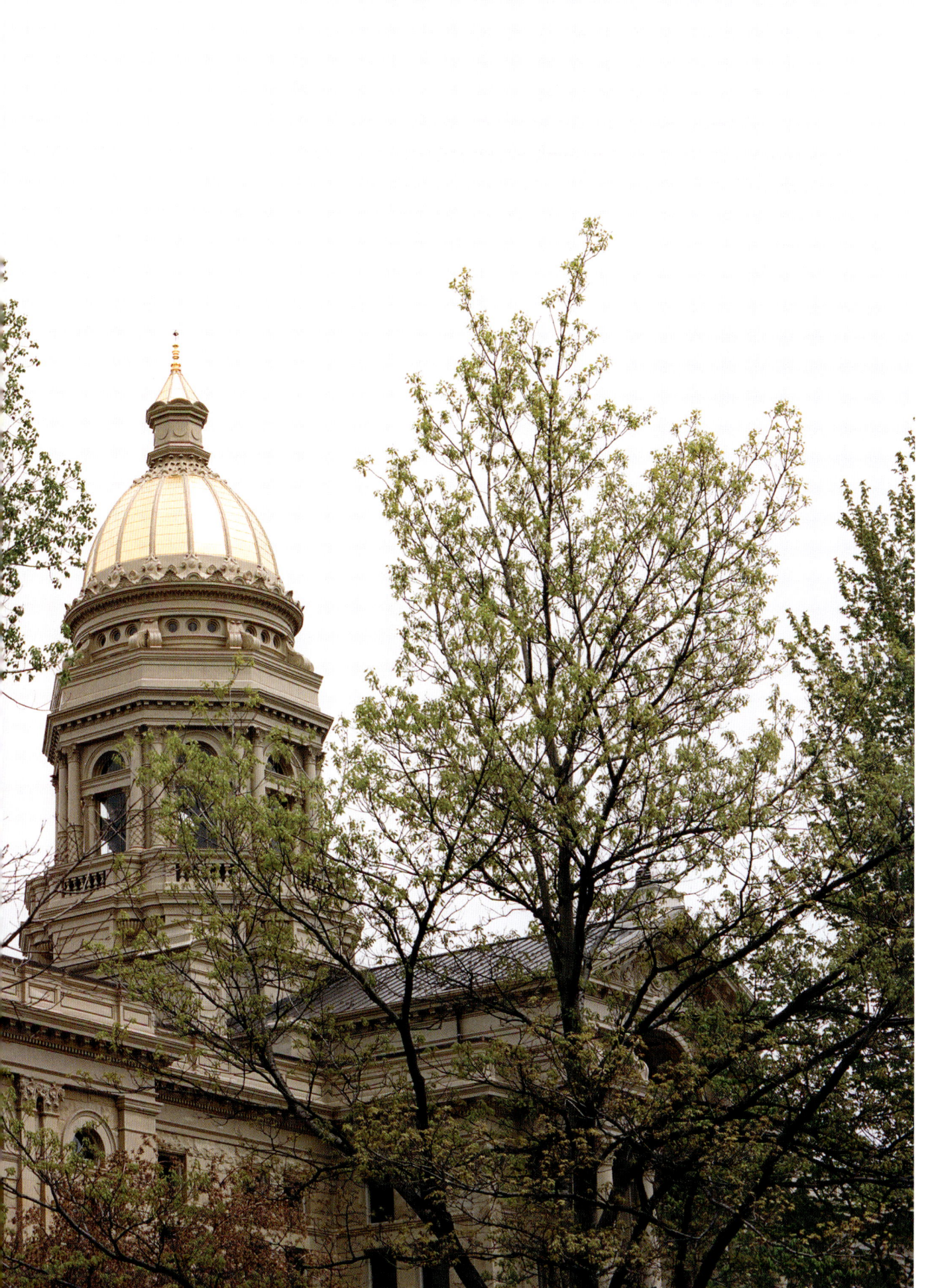

business manager. After Laura's marriage in 1898, their younger sister, Carolyn, took over the manager role. The sisters also held office and ran other businesses in southern Wyoming. Gertrude served four terms as Carbon County superintendent of schools and later ran an insurance business with her husband in Rawlins. Carolyn worked for the *Dillon Doublejack* until her early death from typhoid in 1904. Laura lived until 1962, working at various times in the offices of the Carbon County clerk and assessor, and as Carbon County treasurer.

One of Wyoming's first female physicians:
DR. LILLIAN HEATH (1865–1962)
Lillian Heath arrived in Wyoming when she was eight years old. Her first foray into medicine was in assisting Dr. Thomas Maghee, a physician and surgeon employed by the Union Pacific Railroad. At sixteen years old, Lillian assisted Dr. Maghee with the medical study of criminal Big Nose George Parrott. Maghee gifted her the top half of the skull, which was used to identify Parrott's remains in the 1950s. Lillian would wear men's clothing and carried a gun for protection when making house calls at night. She graduated from medical school in 1893, rare for women at that time. Afterward, she moved home to Rawlins to open her own practice. Her skills ran the gamut from delivering babies, treating bullet wounds, and amputating limbs to helping perform plastic surgery before that medical specialty was even named.

Influential psychologist: **DR. JUNE ETTA DOWNEY** (1875–1932)
Author, professor, and psychologist Dr. June Etta Downey led research on handwriting and personality tests. As a published author, she wrote seven books and more than seventy articles. When she was appointed head of the

Department of Psychology and Philosophy at the University of Wyoming in 1915, she was the only woman leader of a psychology department at a state university. From 1923 to 1925, she served on the council of the American Psychological Association.

Historian, geographer, and first female member of the Wyoming State Bar: **DR. GRACE RAYMOND HEBARD** (1861–1936)
Few people have had as much influence on the development of Wyoming's higher education system as Grace Raymond Hebard. Born into a family of Congregationalist missionaries, Grace came to Wyoming in 1882 after graduating with a BS from Iowa State University, the first woman ever to earn a science degree from that university. She was hired as a draftsman in the surveyor general's office in Cheyenne, helping map the territory, eventually rising to the rank of deputy state engineer. In 1891, she was appointed to the University of Wyoming Board of Trustees. She served as the board's secretary, oversaw university finances, and advocated passionately for the foundation of the university library. While engaged in this work, she also secured (via correspondence courses) a master's degree in literature from Iowa State, followed by a PhD in political science from Illinois Wesleyan University. In her spare time, she studied law and became the first woman admitted to the Wyoming State Bar. With these credentials in hand, she began teaching in UW's Department of Political Economy, becoming its chair in 1907. Over the next several decades, Grace wrote numerous books and articles about Western history and politics, with a particular emphasis on documenting the contributions of women and Indigenous peoples. She was also active in the national women's suffrage movement and the movement to abolish child labor.

Rancher, justice of the peace, game warden, and politician:

MAGGIE GILLESPIE (1861–1942)

Esther Hobart Morris was the first woman in U.S. history to serve as a judge, but several other Wyoming women followed in her footsteps. Among these was Maggie Gillespie. Born in North Carolina, Maggie and her husband, Samuel, came west in the 1880s and ran cattle in Albany County. After Samuel's death in 1907, Maggie ran the ranch on her own while simultaneously raising seven children. She was also elected justice of the peace in the small community of Lookout, as well as serving on the local election board, working as deputy game warden, and serving on the community school board.

Wyoming state flag creator:

VERNA KEAYS (1893–1982)

In 1916, the fear of World War I spreading to the Americas prompted the Daughters of the American Revolution (DAR) to spearhead state flag campaigns across the United States. Wyoming DAR State Regent Grace Raymond Hebard organized a contest with a twenty-dollar prize. The winner was voted on during the biannual DAR state conference in October 1916 in Sheridan. A recent graduate of the Art Institute of Chicago, Verna Keays, of Buffalo, Wyoming, won. On January 31, 1917, Governor John B. Kendrick signed Verna's flag into law. Before they deployed to France, every member of the Wyoming National Guard Medical Corps received a hand-size silk reprint of Verna's design to carry to the front lines.

Journalist, writer, historian:

AGNES WRIGHT SPRING (1894–1988)

Raised on a ranch on the Little Laramie River, Agnes Wright Spring served as the state librarian of Wyoming, the state historian of Colorado, and director of the Wyoming Federal Writers Project. She devoted her professional life to expanding the representation of women's contributions in history. Throughout her life, she authored twenty-two books and several hundred articles, from historical accounts to traditional Western romances, and also stock and farmer reports. Working and writing in the male-dominated history field from the 1910s to the 1960s, Agnes added another voice to the history of the West and forged a path for more women to join the profession.

JACKSON'S ALL-WOMAN GOVERNMENT (1920–1923)

In 1920, one of the first all-woman town councils in the nation was elected. Mayor Grace Miller, council members Mae Deloney, Rose Crabtree, Faustina Haight, and Genevieve Van Vleck, town clerk Marta Winger, treasurer Viola Lunbeck, health officer Edna Huff, and the town marshal, a job appointed to twenty-two-year-old Pearl Williams Hupp, won the ticket. Jackson, newly incorporated in 1914, was developing. Infrastructure was almost nonexistent, as were the funds to support its development. The council collected unpaid taxes and debts to support the town's construction. They cleaned streets, passed an ordinance to prevent people from disposing of their trash in public, and established a dump. They graded streets, built sidewalks, installed electric lights in public areas, and herded cattle off the town square. They even purchased land for a town cemetery. The women's council focused on transforming Jackson from a disorderly settlement to a livable community.

Small-town mayor:

LIZABETH WILEY (1870–1957)

Lizabeth Wiley's reputation was one of being fearless in her convictions and her ability to "get things done." Before she won her first election as mayor in Greybull, Lizabeth was a business owner and served in leadership positions. She ran a bookshop and soda fountain, which eventually became the town library. Through donations, she grew the library to a 3,000-volume collection. She served three consecutive terms as the Greybull Women's Club president, as well as a term as the reporter and another as the treasurer. When she ran for mayor in 1923, Lizabeth faced an additional challenge: the Ku Klux Klan, which was growing in popularity in the small community. The story goes that some leaders of the community were afraid to stand up to the KKK, but Wiley was not. Once elected, she faced them down, investigated bootleggers, and helped the town rebuild after a devastating flood. At the state level, she served two years as the treasurer of the Wyoming Federation of Women's Clubs. The community supported her efforts as mayor: Lizabeth served three terms.

Thrill-seeking journalist, author, and publisher:

CAROLINE LOCKHART (1871–1962)

Caroline Lockhart defied convention. As a stunt journalist, she combined dangerous feats with investigative journalism. Some of these acts included jumping out of a four-story building to test the integrity of the Boston Fire Department's safety net, interviewing convicted murderer Eli Shaw, and riding one of Buffalo Bill Cody's bucking broncos. Her fascination with the West brought her to Cody in 1904. Between 1911 and 1933, she published seven novels, and by 1920, two of them, *The Fighting Shepherdess* and *The Man from Bitter Roots*, had been adapted into films. She owned and wrote for the local newspaper, *Cody Enterprise*, from 1920 to 1925 and used the platform to take a stand against prohibition. In 1920, Caroline was elected by six prominent men in the community to serve as president of what would become one of the world's premier rodeos—the Cody Stampede. Her publicity savvy and passion for the West established the success and legacy of the stampede—an event that continues to this day.

America's first female governor and first female director of the United States Mint:

NELLIE TAYLOE ROSS (1876–1977)

From 1925 to 1927, Nellie served as Wyoming's fourteenth governor, making her the first woman in the country to hold the position of state governor and, as of today, Wyoming's only female governor. Her gubernatorial agenda, which she had only limited success in implementing, included the enforcement of prohibition laws, support for farmers and miners, and funding public schools and the University of Wyoming. From 1933 to 1953, Nellie was the first female director of the U.S. Mint, making her one of the United States' highest-ranking female civil servants of her time. In this role, she played an important part in implementing Franklin Delano Roosevelt's New Deal. Nellie served five terms as director. She died at the age of 101 in Washington, DC.

American photographer, businesswoman, and homemaker: ## LORA WEBB NICHOLS (1883–1962)

Lora's prolific 24,000-image library is one of the largest photographic archives in Wyoming. Her work includes thousands of portraits, still lifes, domestic interiors, and landscapes from her home in the rough-and-tumble mining town of Encampment. Through an intimate, personal lens, she documented life on the Wyoming frontier in the early twentieth century. She owned a commercial photography studio, which supported her family after the collapse of the copper industry and the town's mining company, and also owned and published the town newspaper, *The Encampment Echo*.

Wyoming's first female secretary of state:
THYRA THOMSON (1916–2013)
Originally elected in 1962, and sworn into office in 1963, Thyra served for twenty-four years, until 1987, making her the longest-serving statehouse official in Wyoming history. In addition to her position as secretary of state, she served on several commissions and as acting governor on many occasions. Thyra was a vocal supporter of equal pay for women and an advocate in Wyoming and nationally for the ratification of the Equal Rights Amendment. Her papers include materials related to the 1973 passage of the ERA in Wyoming.

First Black woman in Wyoming's legislature:
HARRIET ELIZABETH "LIZ" BYRD (1926–2015)
A fourth-generation Wyomingite, Liz Byrd was elected to the Wyoming State Legislature in 1981, making her Wyoming's first Black female legislator. An educator with a twenty-plus-year career, Liz loved to expose her students to state government. In fact, one of her classes lobbied the legislature to advocate Wyoming's recognition of the bison as the official state mammal in 1985. One of her most well-known feats, to which she was devoted, was the passing of legislation to make Martin Luther King Jr. Day a state holiday. It took nine introductions before the legislation was passed, in 1990, under the title "Wyoming Equality Day." In 1989, she was one of seventy-five Black women of distinction featured in Pulitzer Prize–winning photographer Brian Lanker's book *I Dream a World: Portraits of Black Women Who Changed America*.

CHAPTER II
Filling the Void

The void is not empty. The void stands for space, potential,
and energy to be harnessed. Filling the void means trusting the
unknown and having the bravery to discover what potential lives in the
spaces you may overlook, if you dare to venture beyond the edges.

LORI
MATERI

DIRECTOR OF THE UPTON MUNICIPAL AIRPORT,
BACKCOUNTRY PILOT, RURAL-AIRSTRIP ADVOCATE

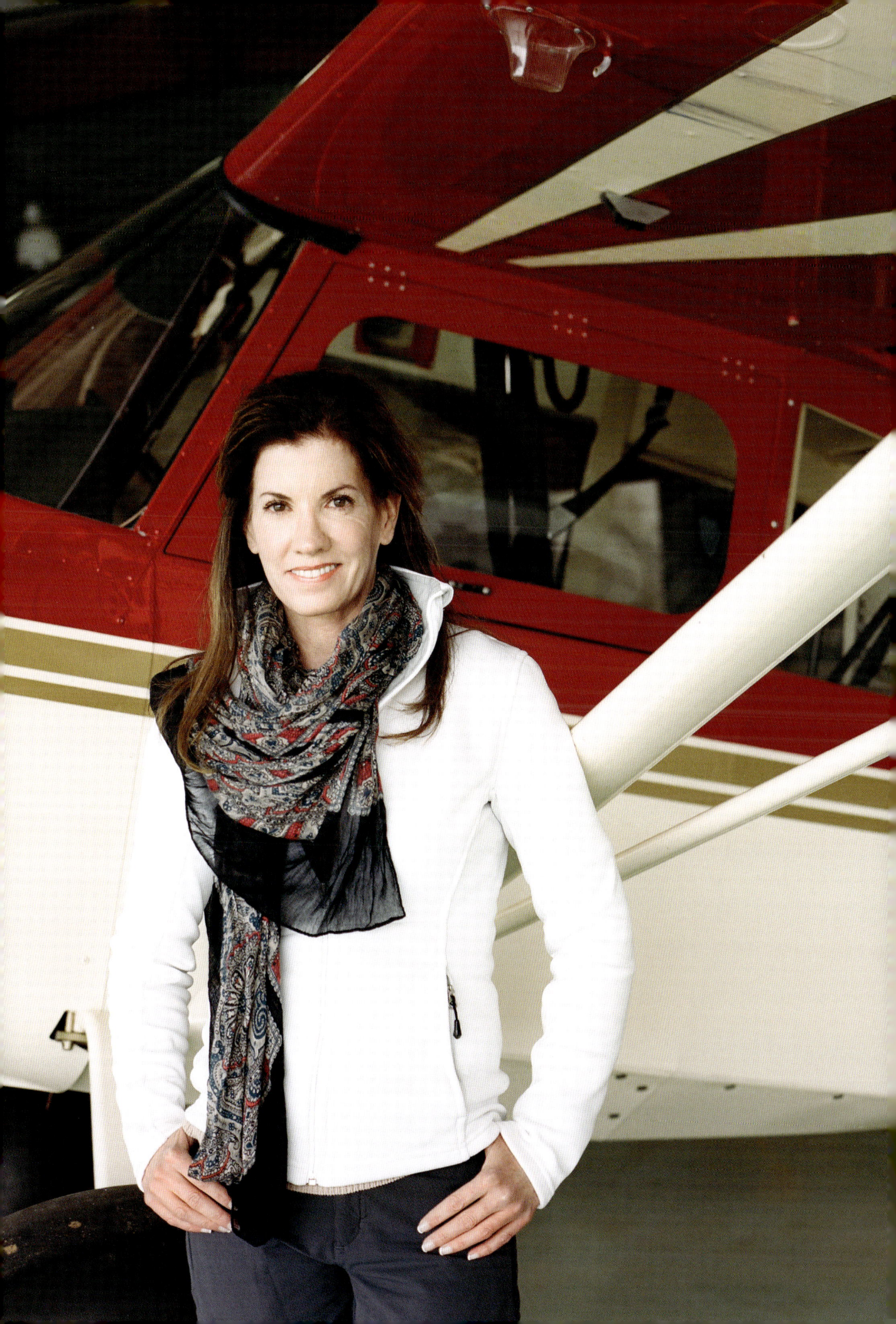

"I don't care if it's ten degrees out.
If I'm in my plane, I'm where I need to be."

Lori used to be afraid of flying. Now, it is her entire world. She came from a flying family in Upton. Her father served as a navigator on a B-29 bomber during World War II and later piloted their family in various planes—a Piper PA-11, a Piper Navajo, and a Cessna Skywagon—as their primary mode of transportation around Wyoming and the region. As the youngest children, Lori and her twin sister shared a seat in the back of the plane. The experience ignited a passion for travel, but it also terrified her. Those fears remained for years, until fate would bring her home.

While caring for her aging mother and raising her own twin teenage daughters back in Upton, Lori started to wonder what was next for her. At the same time, she found her mind being flooded with memories of flying as a child. She faced her fears, booked a discovery flight, and was hooked. Not long thereafter, news broke that the local municipal airport could be shut down and turned into the town landfill. Lori advocated, alongside a dedicated group of individuals, for its preservation.

Once a teacher and archivist at the University of Wyoming, Lori has been instrumental in keeping the Upton Airport alive as part of the statewide aviation system. As Lori notes, "Once these small municipal airports disappear, it's extremely expensive and difficult to reopen them." She now serves as director of the airport and also as the Wyoming state liaison for the Recreational Aviation Foundation (RAF). In this role, Lori leads a statewide task force that works to preserve rural airstrips around Wyoming and open new ones. She worked with the Wyoming Bureau of Land Management to allow access to a dirt landing strip along the famous "Miracle Mile" fishing area of the North Platte River. In addition to her advocacy work to preserve small, general aviation strips around the state and in the backcountry, Lori is also an instructor at Gillette College in the Adult Education program.

To some, diamonds are a girl's best friend. For Lori, it's *Papa Charlie*, her beloved American Champion Citabria plane. She feels most free and alive when she's flying to remote areas of the state and country in *Papa Charlie*, her loyal partner in adventure and discovery.

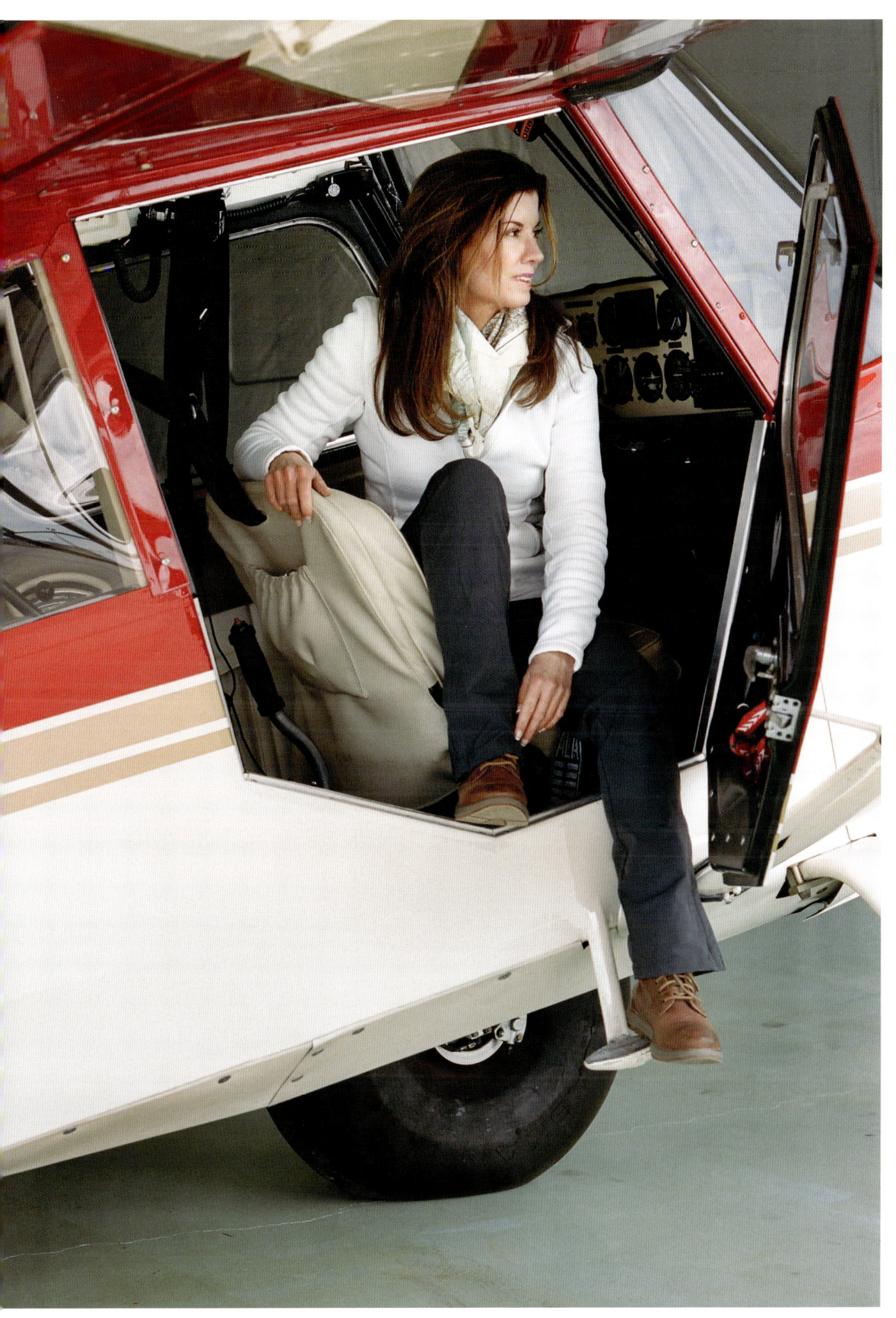

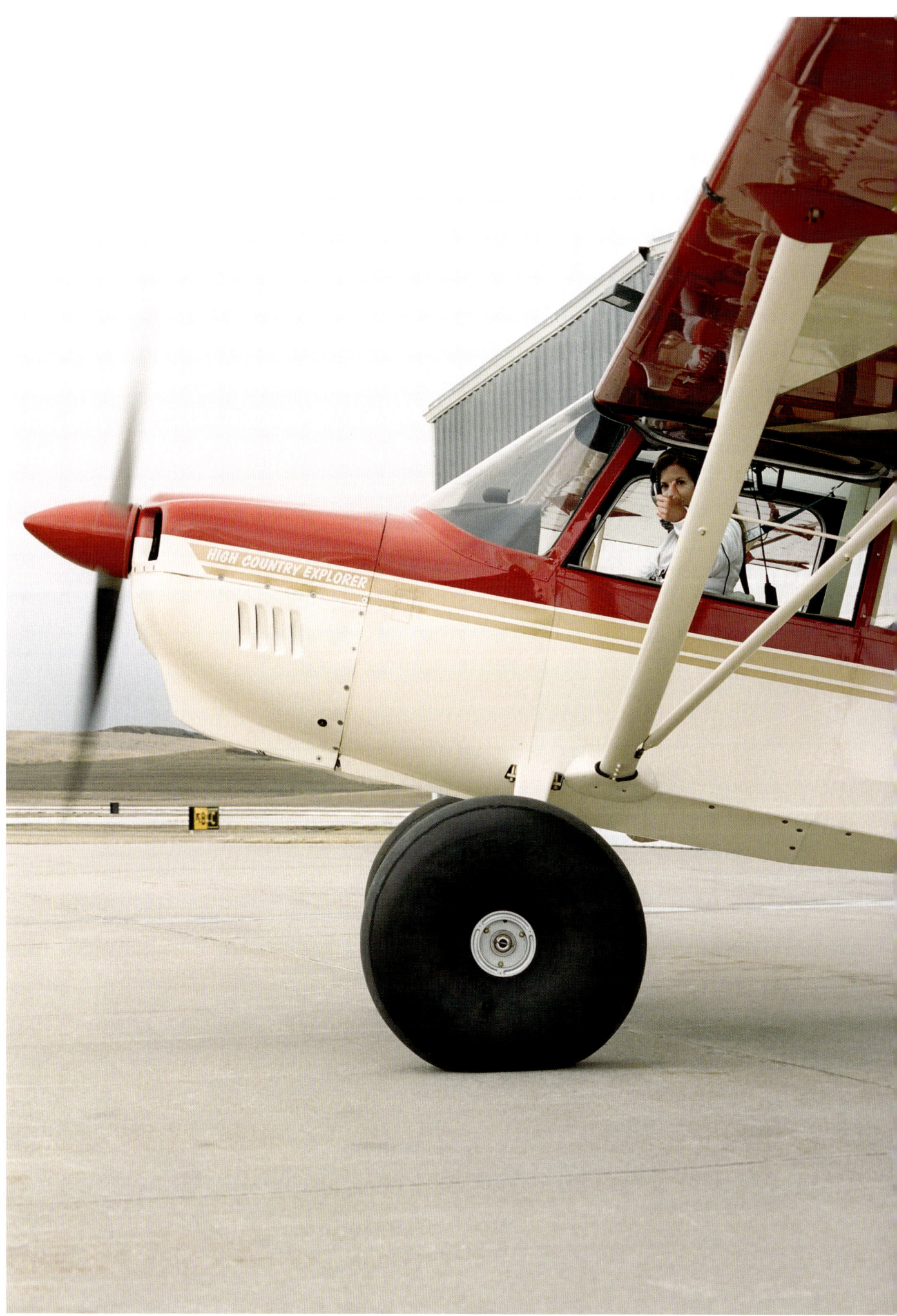

"At what point do you say, 'My life is over?'
Hopefully never! Keep going out there and
find what fulfills you and brings you joy.
Flying has done that for me."

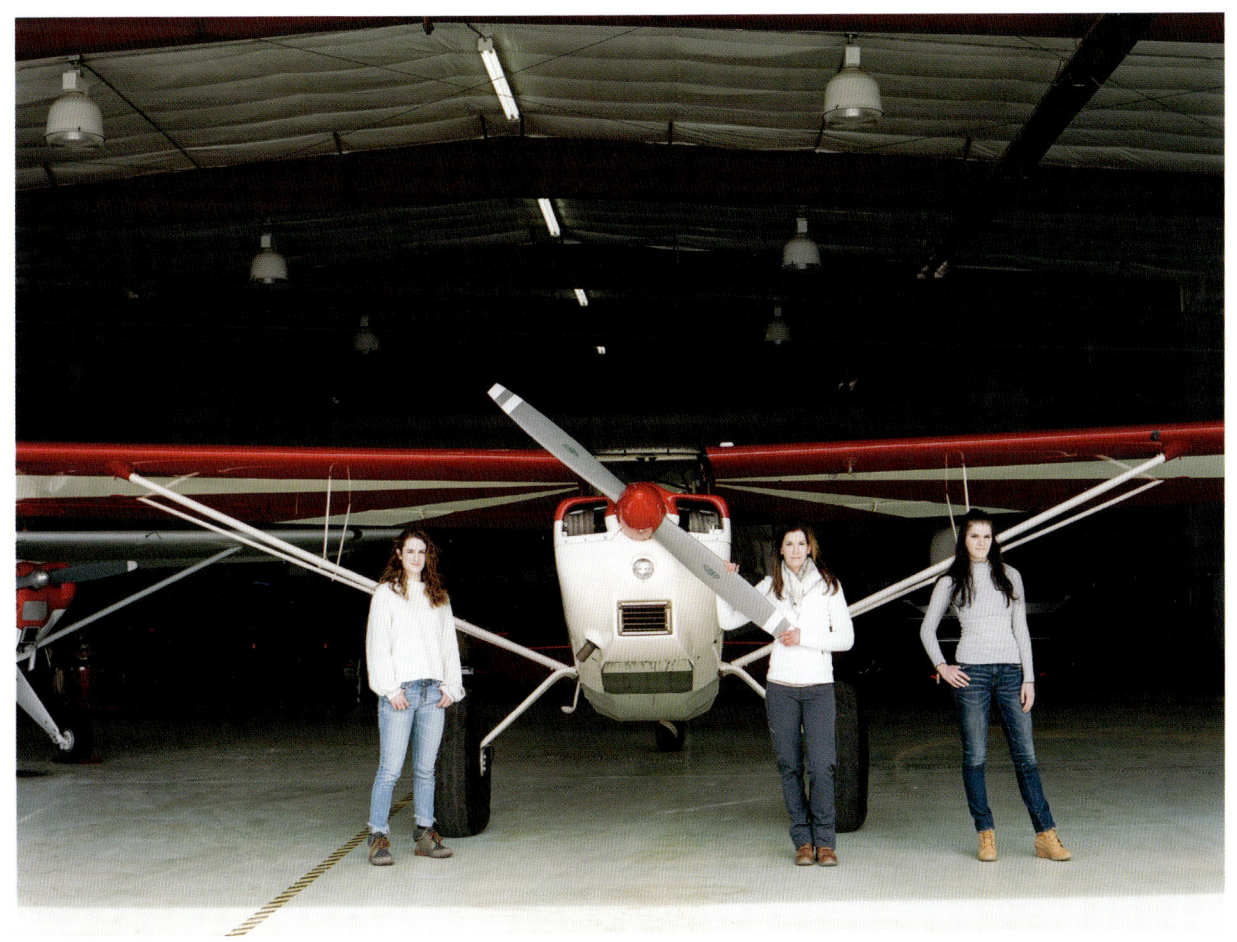

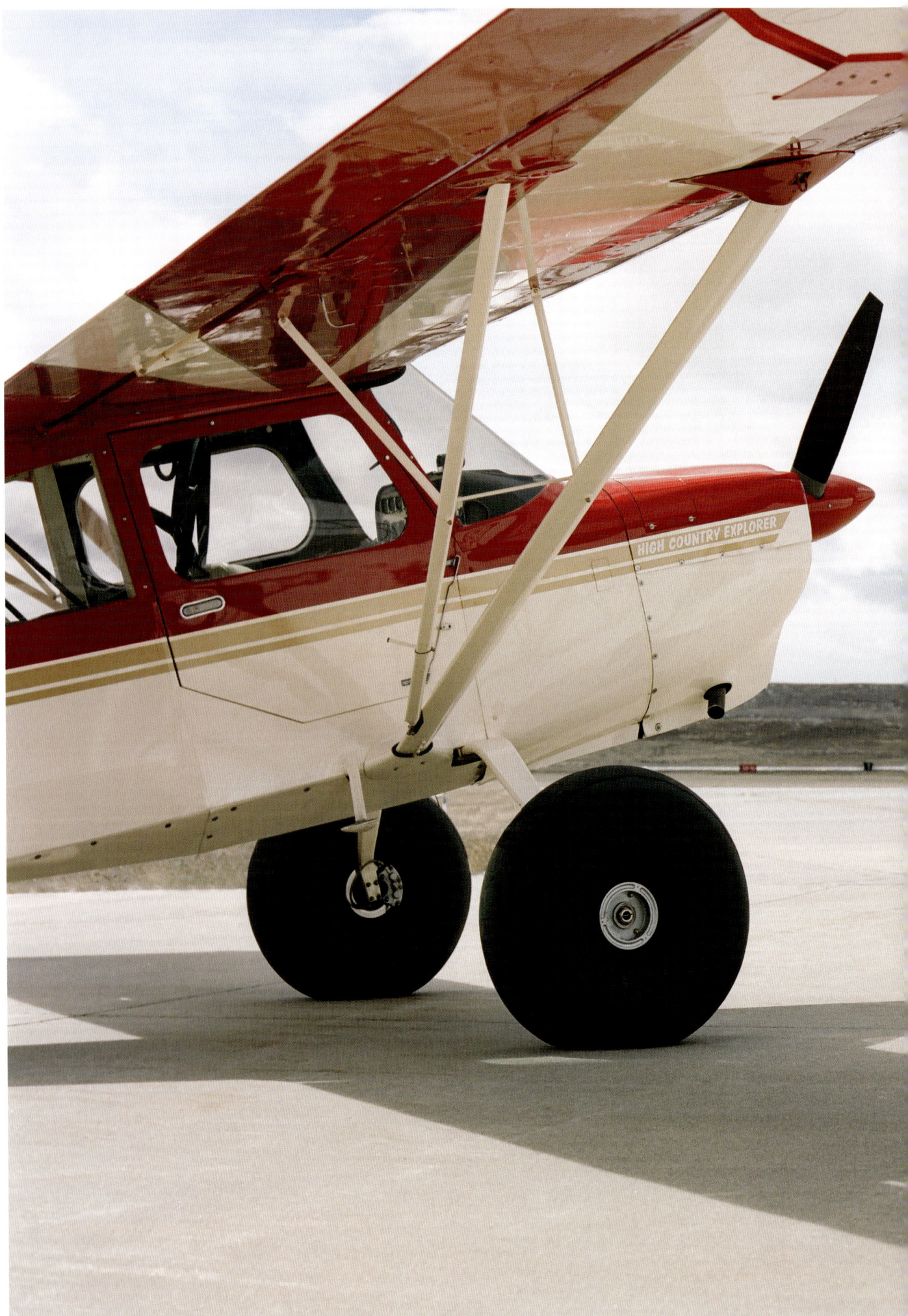

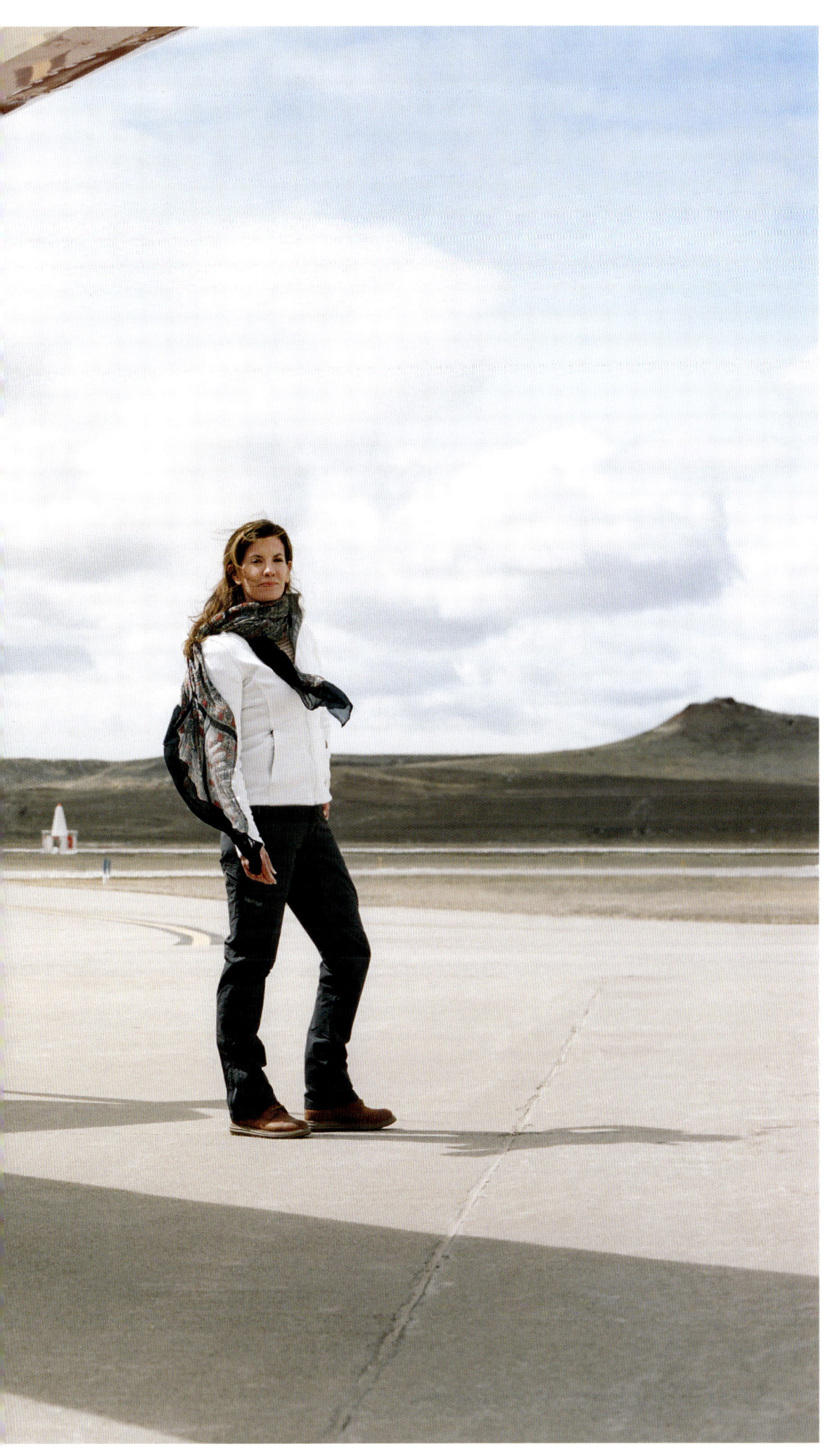

LYNETTE ST. CLAIR

EASTERN SHOSHONE LINGUIST, CULTURAL PRESERVATIONIST,
EDUCATION CONSULTANT ON THE WIND RIVER RESERVATION

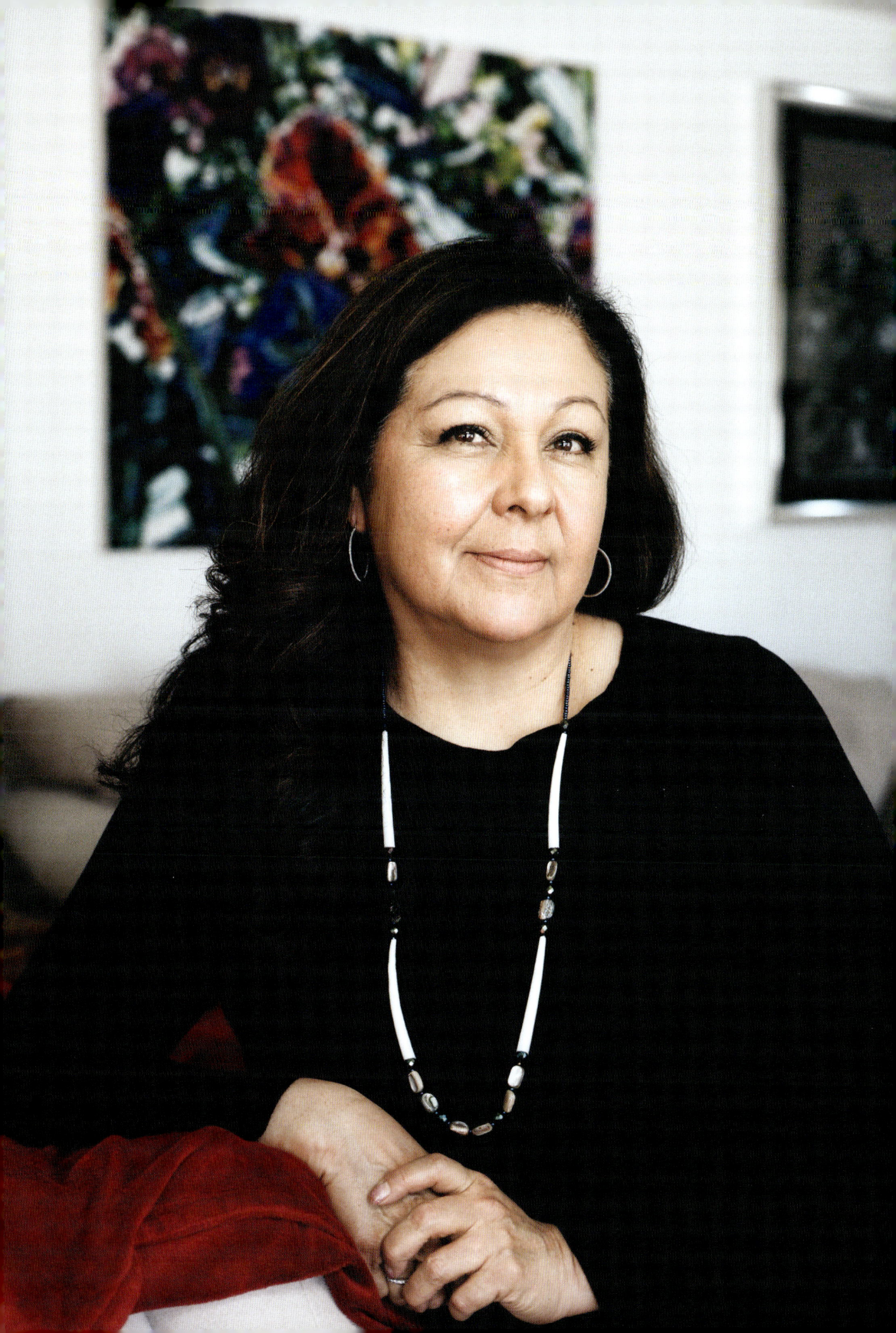

"Our language is who we are. It's in our DNA. It's synonymous with our very existence."

Language is more than words; it is a bridge between generations, carrying stories, customs, and values that define a people. It evokes emotion, connection, and identity. It is sentimental, yet essential, connecting past to present and future. For Lynette St. Clair, preserving her native Eastern Shoshone language is not just about survival—it is about ensuring that future generations inherit the strength, culture, and wisdom of their ancestors.

Language is woven into Lynette's earliest memories. She remembers falling asleep to the sound of her parents playfully teasing each other in Shoshone, a language she grew up speaking fluently. Lynette was a child in Fort Washakie on the Wind River Reservation in the 1970s. The Red Power movement was gaining momentum, and Indigenous peoples across the country were reclaiming their rights, history, and sense of self. In the midst of this cultural reawakening, Lynette's upbringing was filled with a strong connection to her heritage.

Lynette began working as a school secretary in Fort Washakie, where she became a trusted presence for students, greeting them with warmth and positivity, knowing many carried burdens from home. Eventually, she was encouraged to apply for the role of Indian education coordinator. It was a position she hadn't considered but was ultimately drawn to because it afforded the opportunity to develop a comprehensive language and cultural program, ensuring language, tribal history, and government were essential learnings.

When the position was later cut, Lynette moved into the classroom, where she thrived as a teacher, implementing firsthand the curriculums she'd developed. In 2015, she was awarded the National Johnson O'Malley Teacher of the Year distinction for her implementation of technology to enhance language instruction for the children of the Wind River Reservation. "The language isn't dead," she says. "It's just sleeping. We need to wake it up."

Lynette's impact extends far beyond the classroom. She has played a key role in developing statewide education standards to ensure the contributions of American Indians are taught in Wyoming schools. She has spearheaded cultural projects like Art for the Sky, Hopa

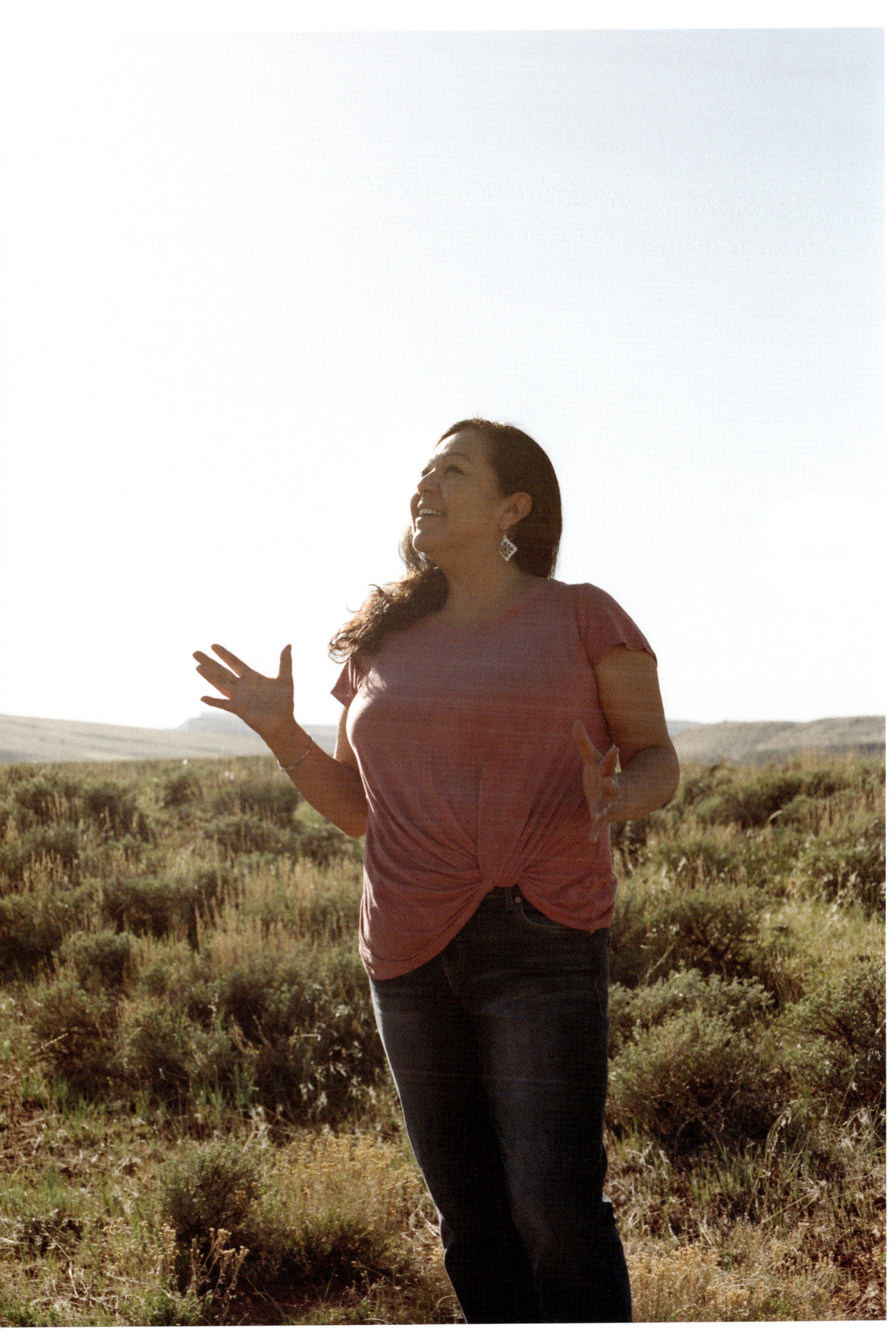

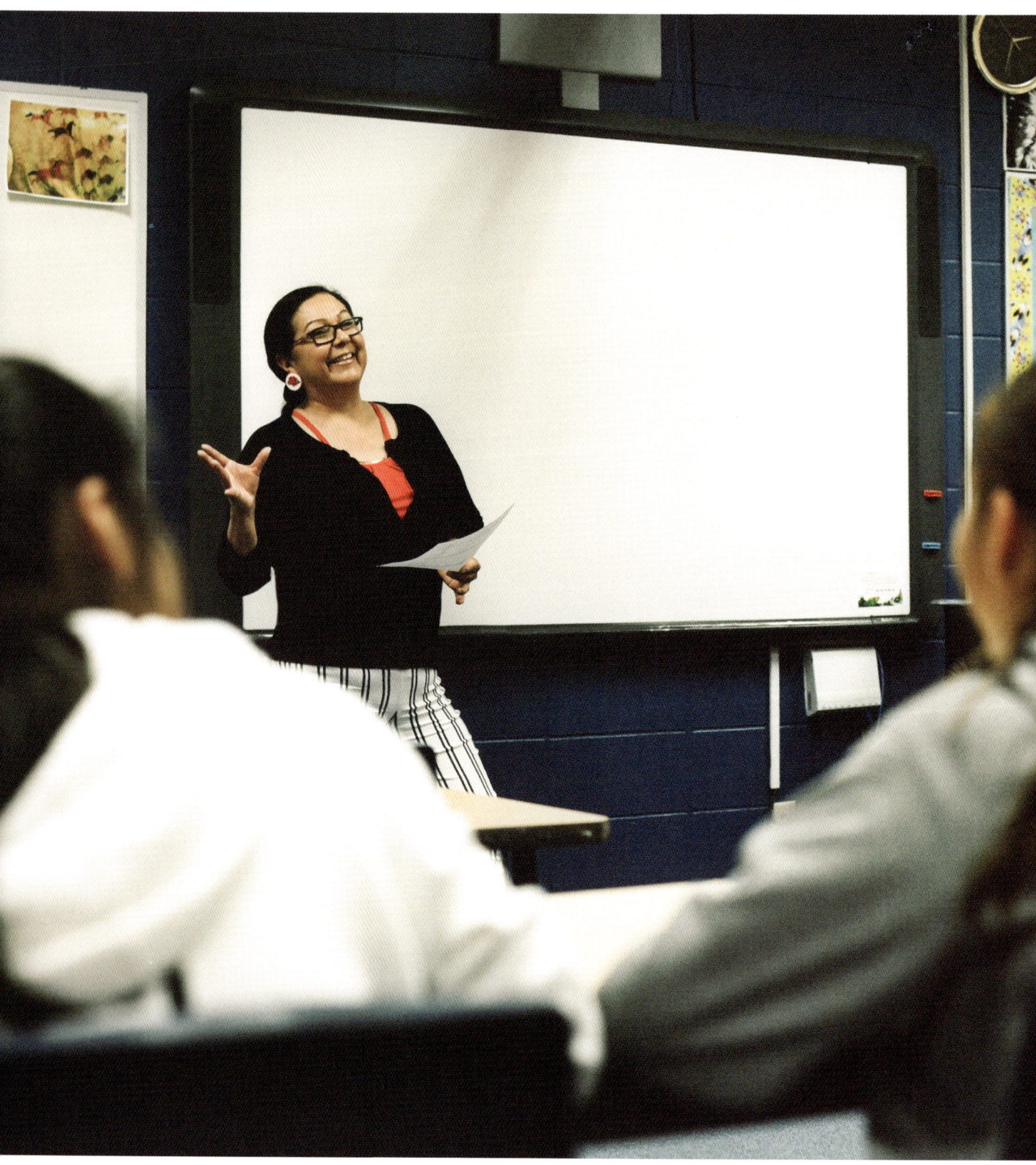

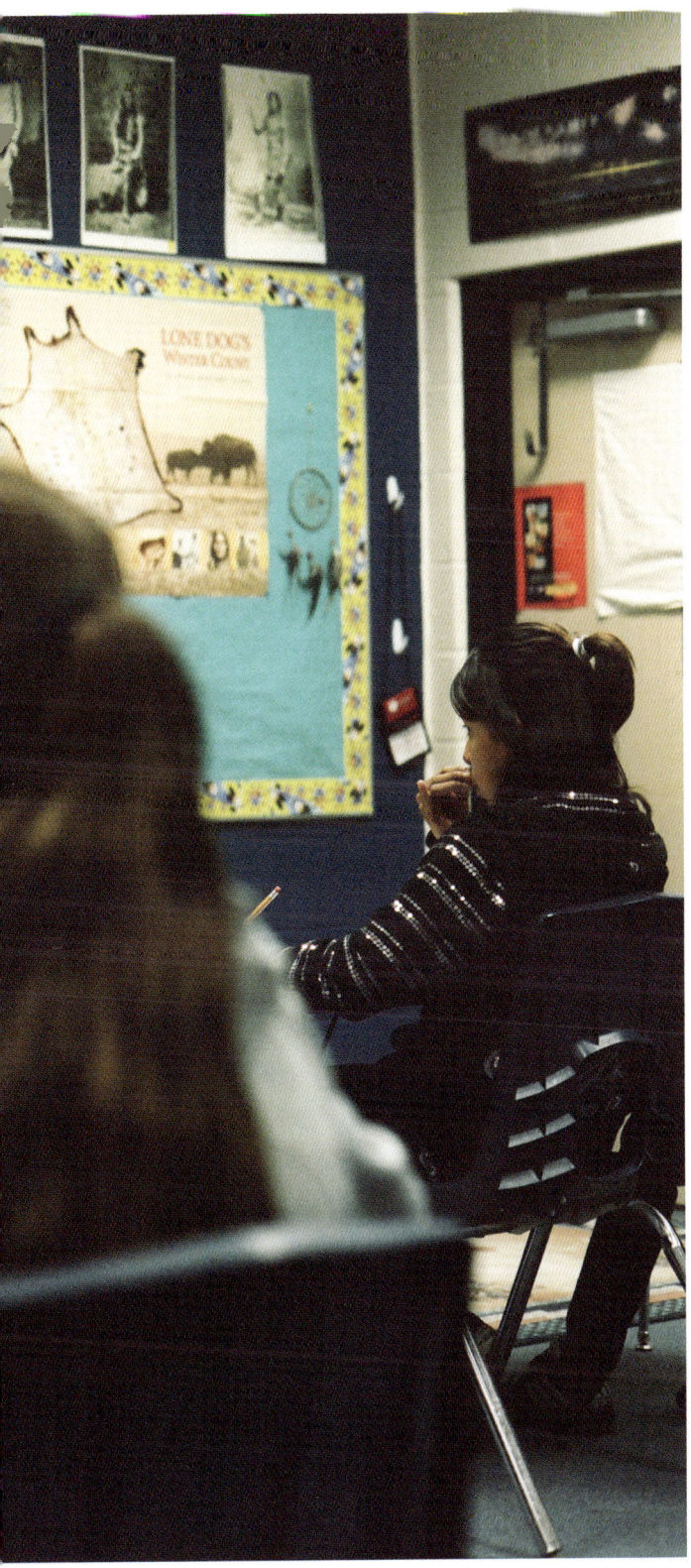

Mountain Cultural Exchange, and Five Buffalo Days. She developed the Newe Daygwap language app and worked with Fort Washakie High School students to create the first-ever mobile tour of the Wind River Reservation through the TravelStorys app. Most recently, she has expanded her influence beyond Wyoming, serving as a language coach for television series like *Outer Range* and *American Primeval*, ensuring cultural authenticity in the portrayal of the Shoshone people.

For Lynette, this work is about more than language—it is about identity, belonging, and pride. She wants her students to know where they come from. "It's in our DNA. It's our very existence. We need to remind our children of the importance of who they are."

Lynette's dedication to cultural preservation and education has not gone unnoticed. In 2019, she was named Wyoming Woman of Influence in Education, and in 2025, she was honored as one of *USA Today*'s Women of the Year.

The fight for language preservation is, at its core, a fight for existence. Many Indigenous nations today are reclaiming their languages as a means of healing, reconnecting with their roots, and reasserting their agency. Lynette St. Clair is at the forefront of that movement—ensuring that the Eastern Shoshone language, and the rich history it carries, will not only survive but thrive.

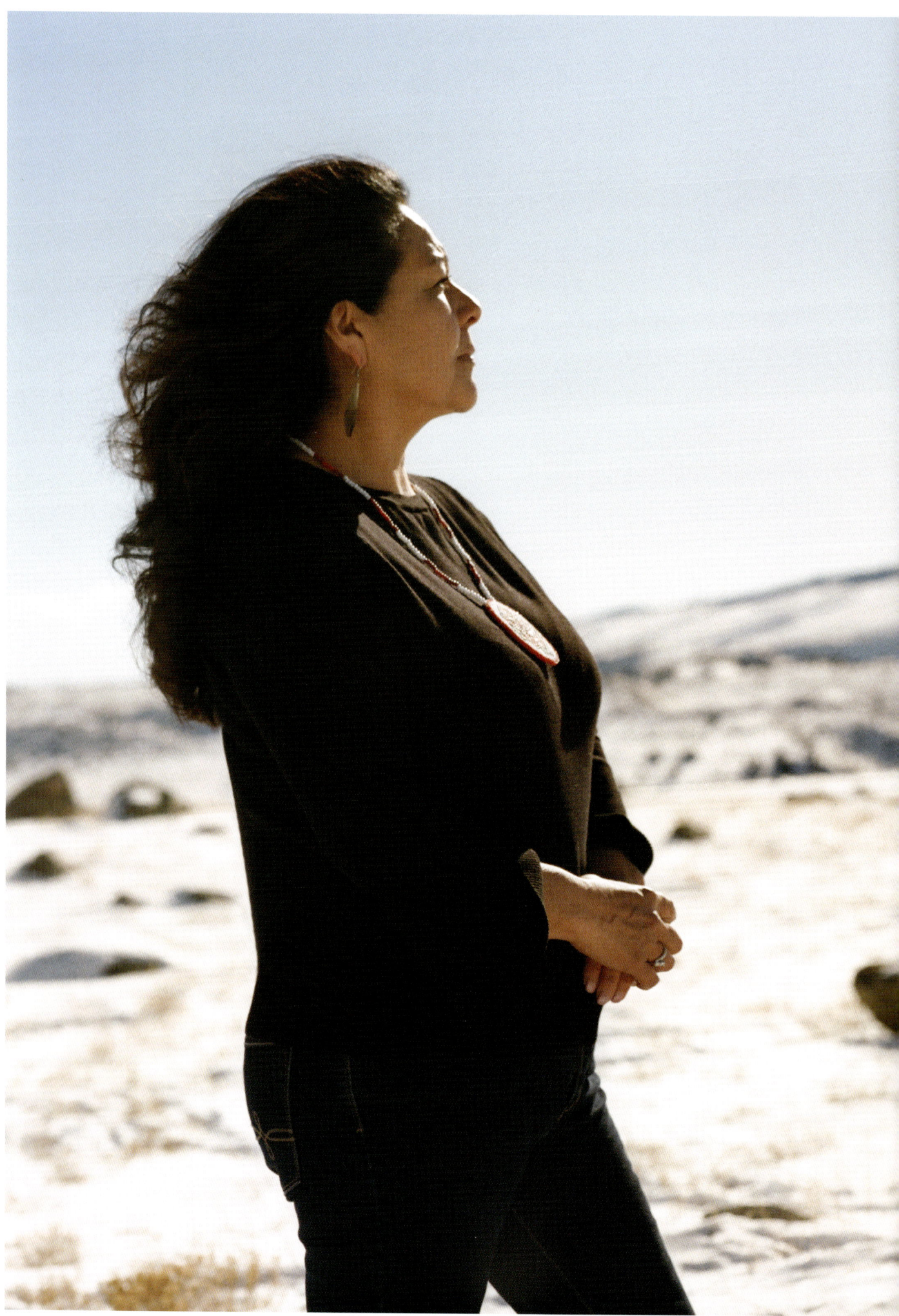

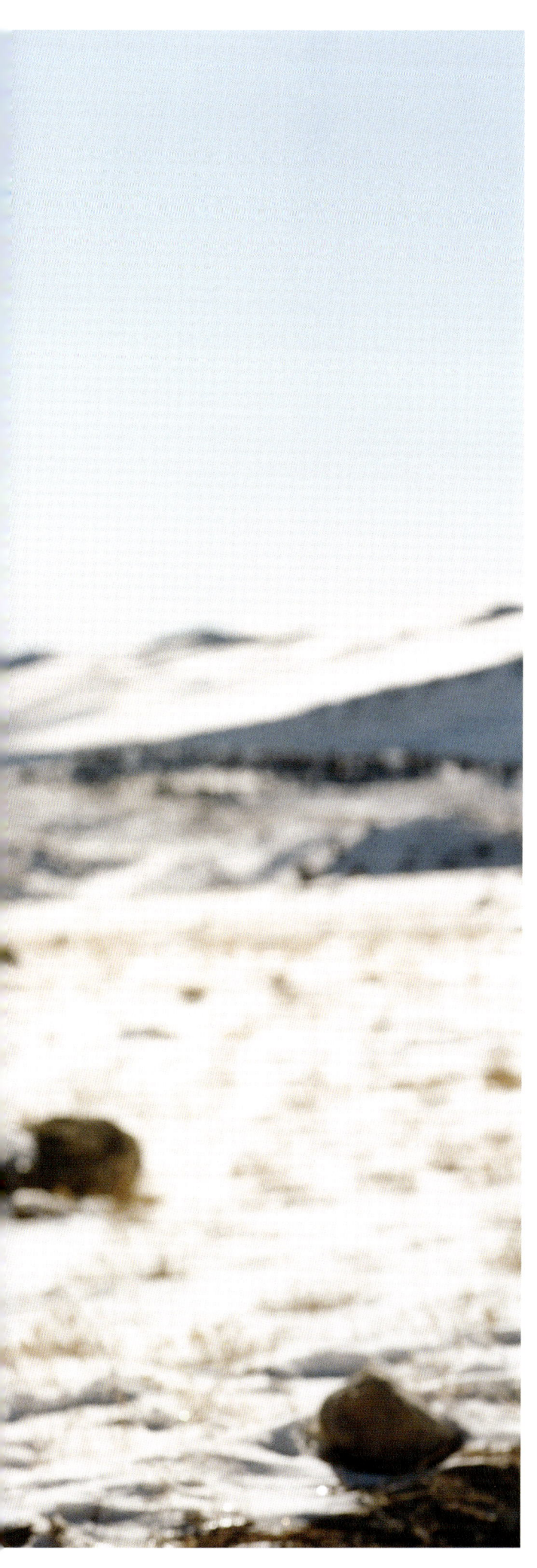

"Damme newe daygwap gay nahsoowazeet." (Never forget our language.)

DR. DIANE
NOTON COALE

EMERGENCY ROOM PHYSICIAN, RURAL DOCTOR

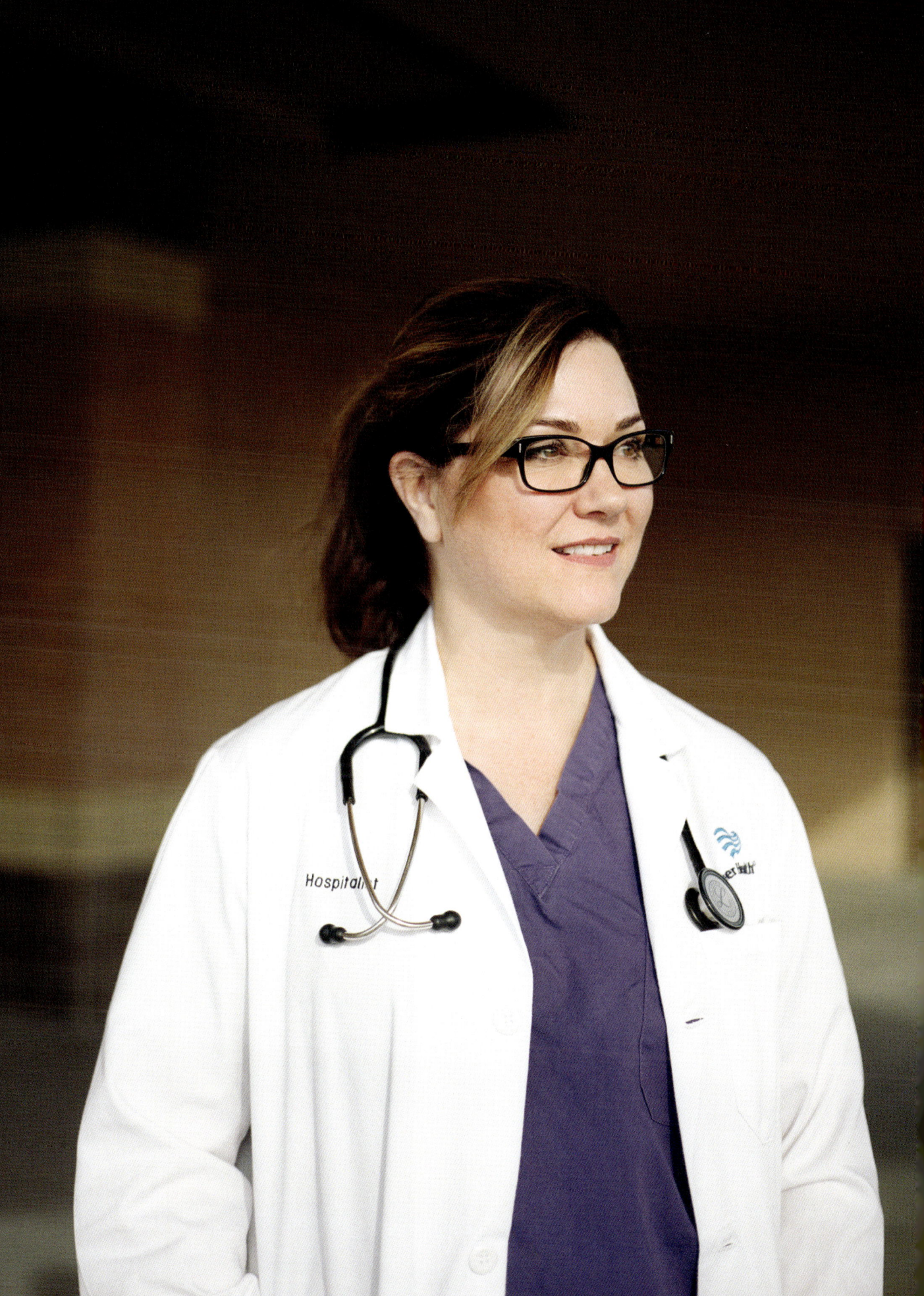

"I wanted to go there because no one was there. I like to be the person who does things when no one else is available. I'll fill that spot."

Dr. Diane Noton Coale has always cherished small towns and felt called to medicine. Though her childhood took her through cities like Chicago and Dallas for her father's work, it was the summers spent in the frontier town of Encampment—population 450—that solidified her love of rural life. Her family's roots in Encampment run five generations deep, tracing back to 1879. By high school, Diane was ready to trade city lights for small-town life full-time. She convinced her parents to let her finish school in Meeteetse—population 314—where she lived with her aunt and uncle.

Diane's desire to become a doctor started early. At five years old, during a holiday gift exchange, she broke down in tears after receiving a doll instead of a toy doctor's kit. When the doll was returned and swapped for a stethoscope, everything changed. "One night my dad was tucking me in and asked what I wanted to be when I grew up. I told him I wanted to be a doctor but that girls couldn't be doctors. He said, 'Of course you can be a doctor. You can be anything you want.' I replied, 'Then I'm going to be a doctor.' And that was the end of it."

She studied human nutrition at the University of Wyoming, then earned her medical degree from Creighton University School of Medicine. Her first job brought her to Jackson, which, though its population is modest by some standards, at 10,649 still felt too large. Not long after, she heard about a family medicine practice for sale in Saratoga, a small town with a population of 1,752, near her ancestral home. At just thirty years old, Diane purchased the practice and became the sole physician in a forty-mile radius.

Diane didn't just run her clinic—she made house calls, served as medical director for the ambulance service and nursing home, and extended care to the remote town of Medicine Bow, eighty miles away. "I have no idea how I did it all, except that I was really focused and determined," she reflects. "When I entered medical school, my goal was to return to a small town. Once I arrived, that's exactly what I did."

Over time, the intense demands of rural medicine began to take a toll. More than 50 percent of health-care providers experience burnout,

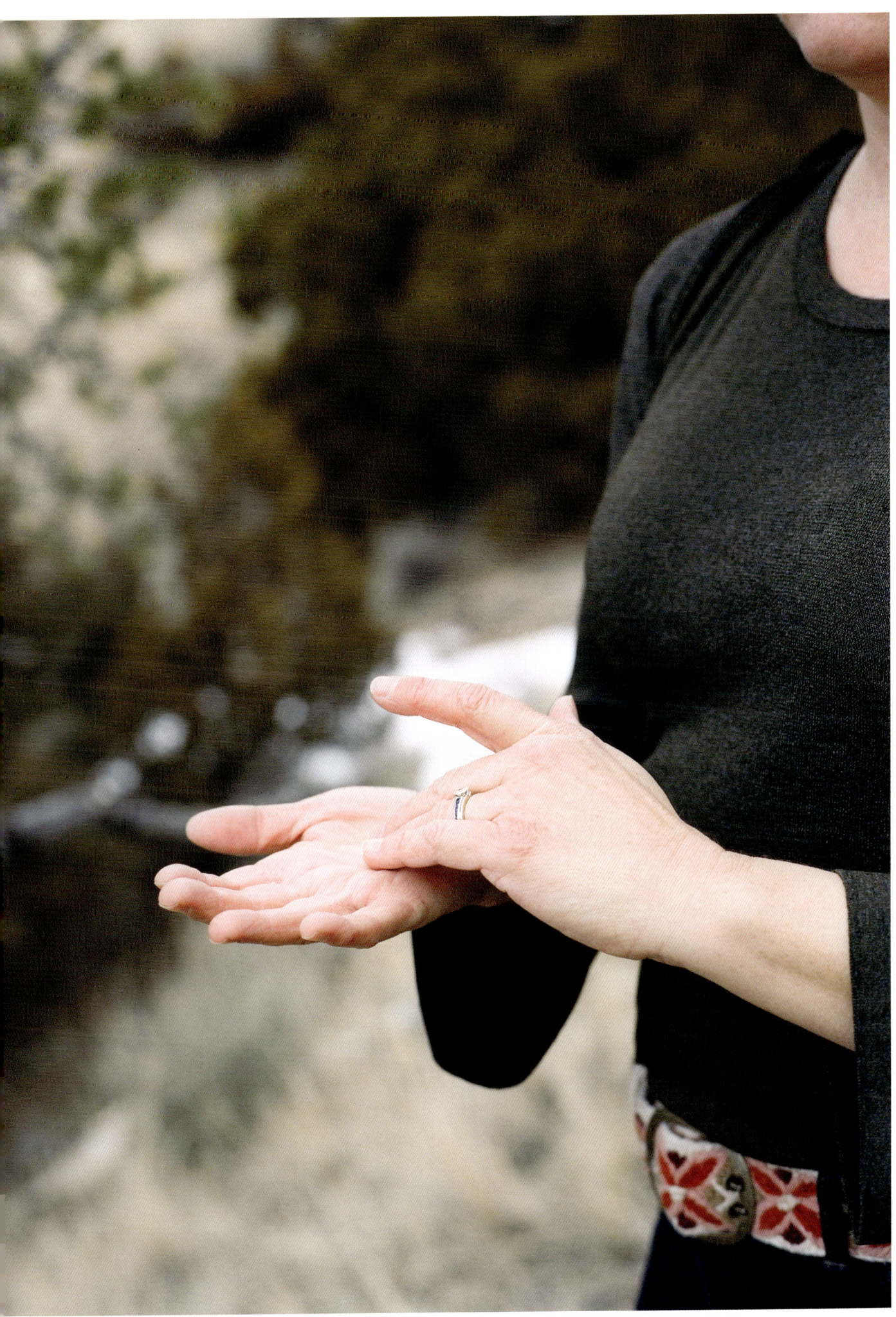

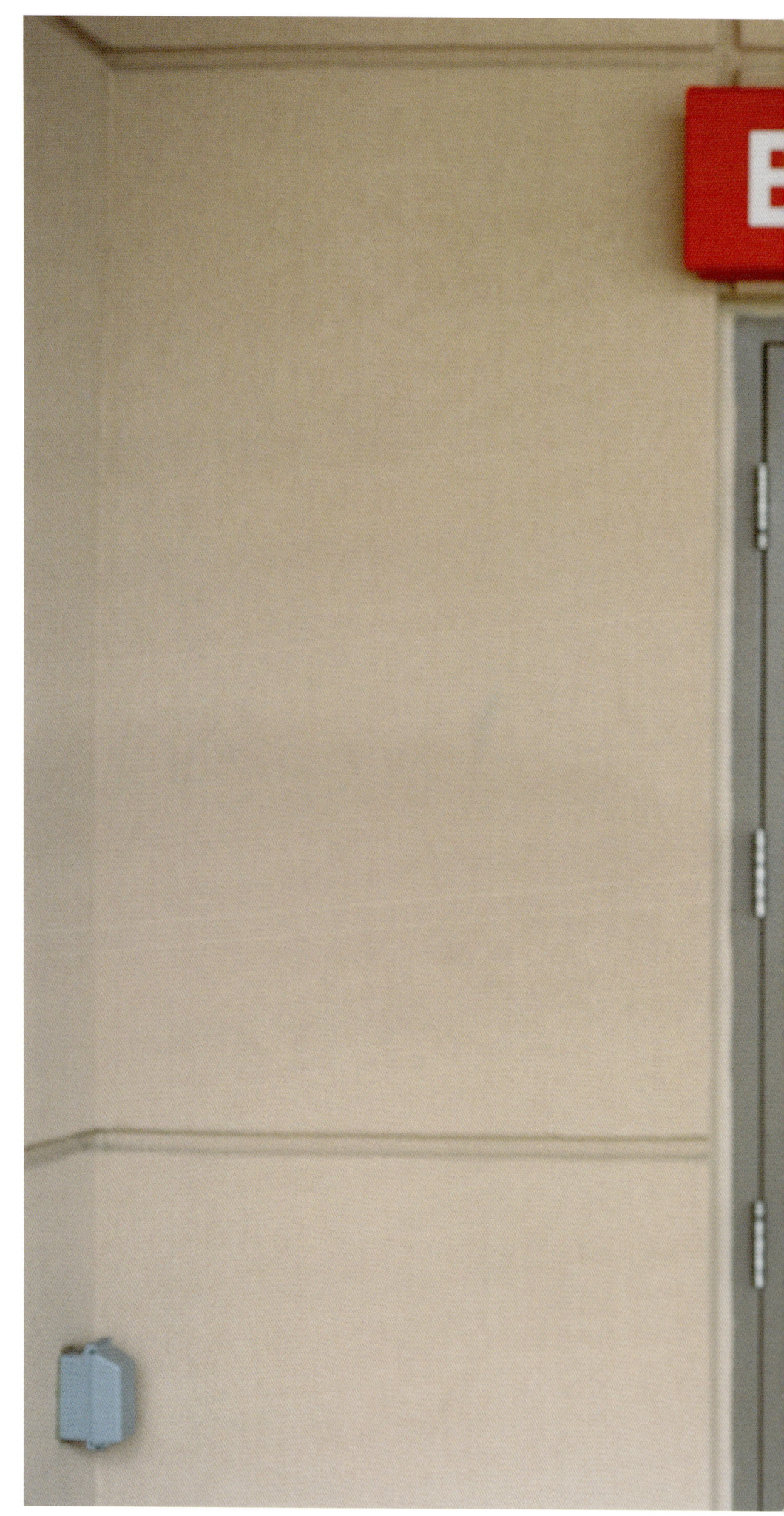

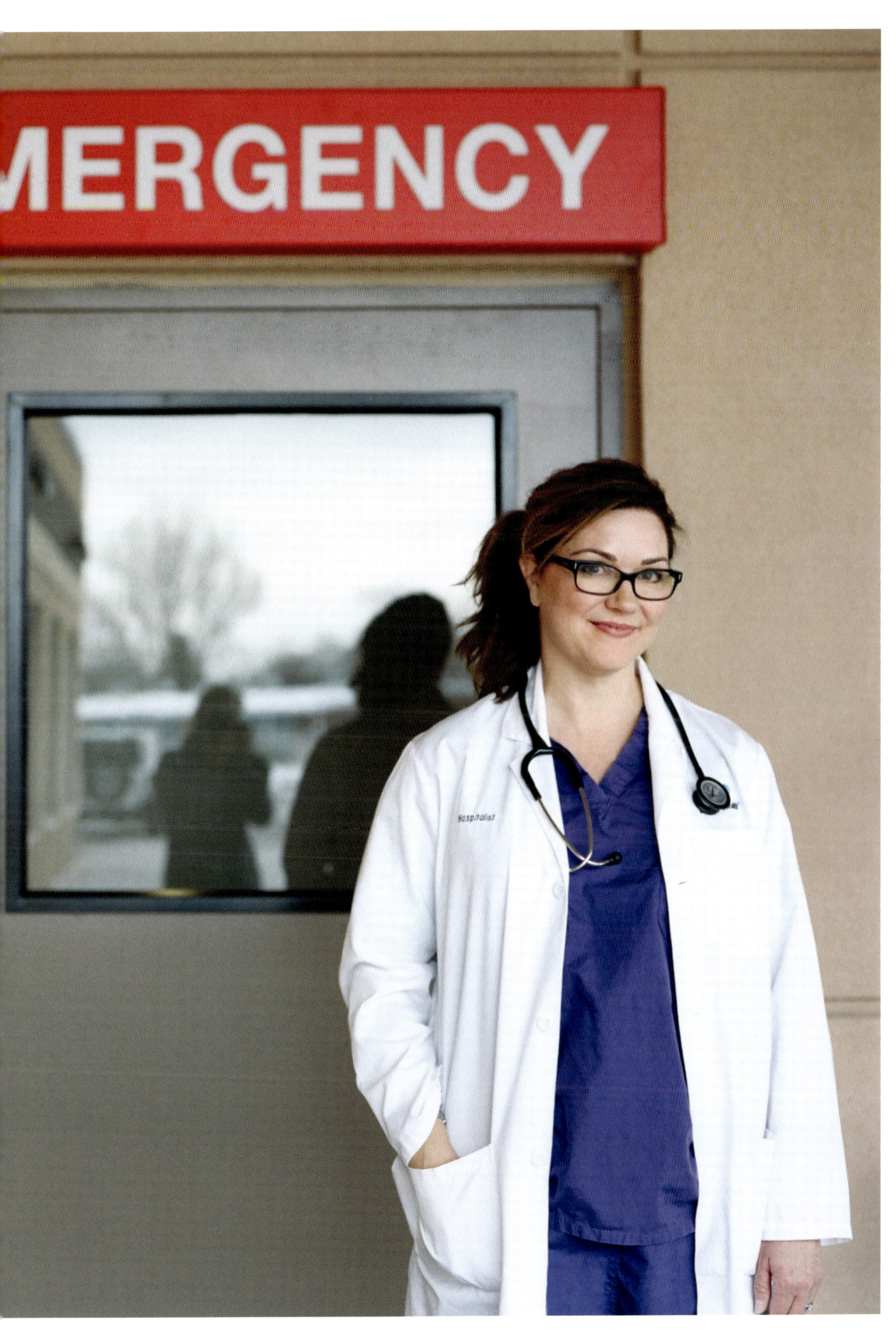

and for those in isolated areas, the pressure is even greater. Diane remembers one moment vividly: bursting into tears just because the phone rang. It was a breaking point—something had to change.

After over a decade of deep dedication to her community, Diane began a new chapter. She returned to Meeteetse after meeting her now-husband and soon applied for a position at a hospital fifty miles away in Worland (population 4,785). She also opened a clinic in Meeteetse, but once again recognized the early signs of burnout. This time, she made a different choice. Instead of pushing through, she advocated for support. Today, West Park Hospital in nearby Cody staffs the Meeteetse clinic one day a week, ensuring continuity of care without compromising her well-being.

Diane's current path in emergency medicine has offered a revitalizing structure. With a clear beginning, middle, and end to each of her patient interactions—and regular time off—she's found space to thrive again. She relishes the fast-paced nature of the ER and the problem-solving it demands, while finally having boundaries that allow her to recharge. "When I was in Saratoga, I was always on call. I couldn't relax. Now, I get to be present—in work and in life."

She's also turned inward. In 2006, a transformative Reiki session opened her to the world of energetic healing. Today, she's a Reiki Master and integrates the practice into her daily routine—another way she's learned to care for herself while caring for others.

"When you're thirty and starting your career, it's easy to lose sight of balance. Now, I have both a fulfilling career and a life I love. Achieving that took years of trial and error. But I've landed in the perfect place—a blend of both worlds, with a job I adore and a home I cherish."

The medical industry has transformed significantly since Diane began practicing. Still, one truth remains: Health is wealth. And health, as Diane knows, is about more than just the body—it's emotional, mental, and spiritual well-being. "A healthy community is a happy community," she says. "I wanted to move back to Wyoming to help make my community healthy—so it could be happy."

Dr. Diane has spent her career filling critical voids in small towns that often lack access to care—and in doing so, she's also filled the gaps within herself. Not everyone is fortunate enough to live their dream. Diane not only chased hers—she caught it. Through hard-won effort, she discovered the key to her own health, happiness, and healing.

"A healthy community is a happy community.
I wanted to move back to Wyoming to make
my community healthy—so it could be happy."

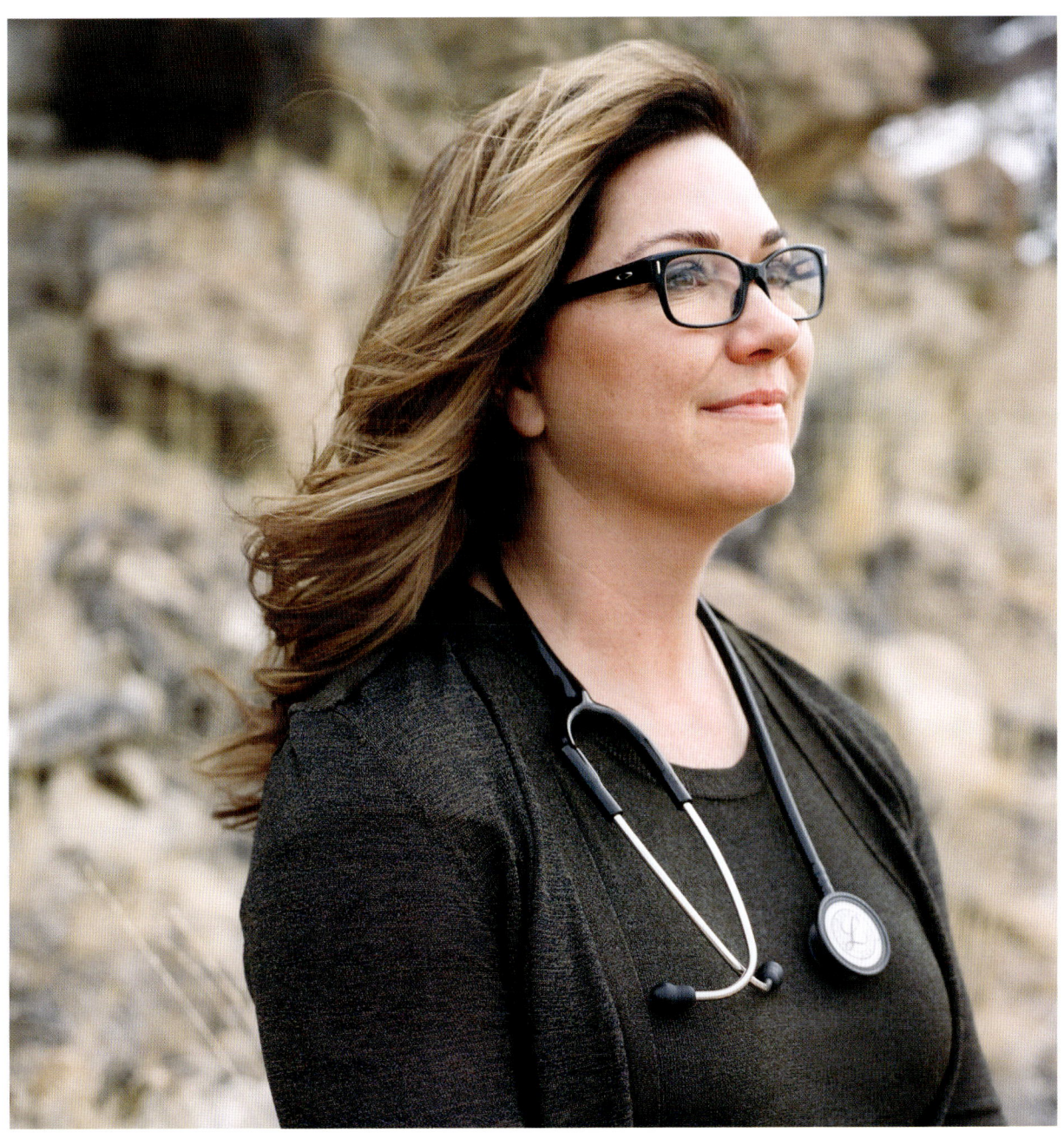

REV. DR. BERNADINE CRAFT

EPISCOPAL PRIEST, FORMER STATE SENATOR, EXECUTIVE DIRECTOR
OF THE SWEETWATER BOARD OF COOPERATIVE EDUCATIONAL SERVICES

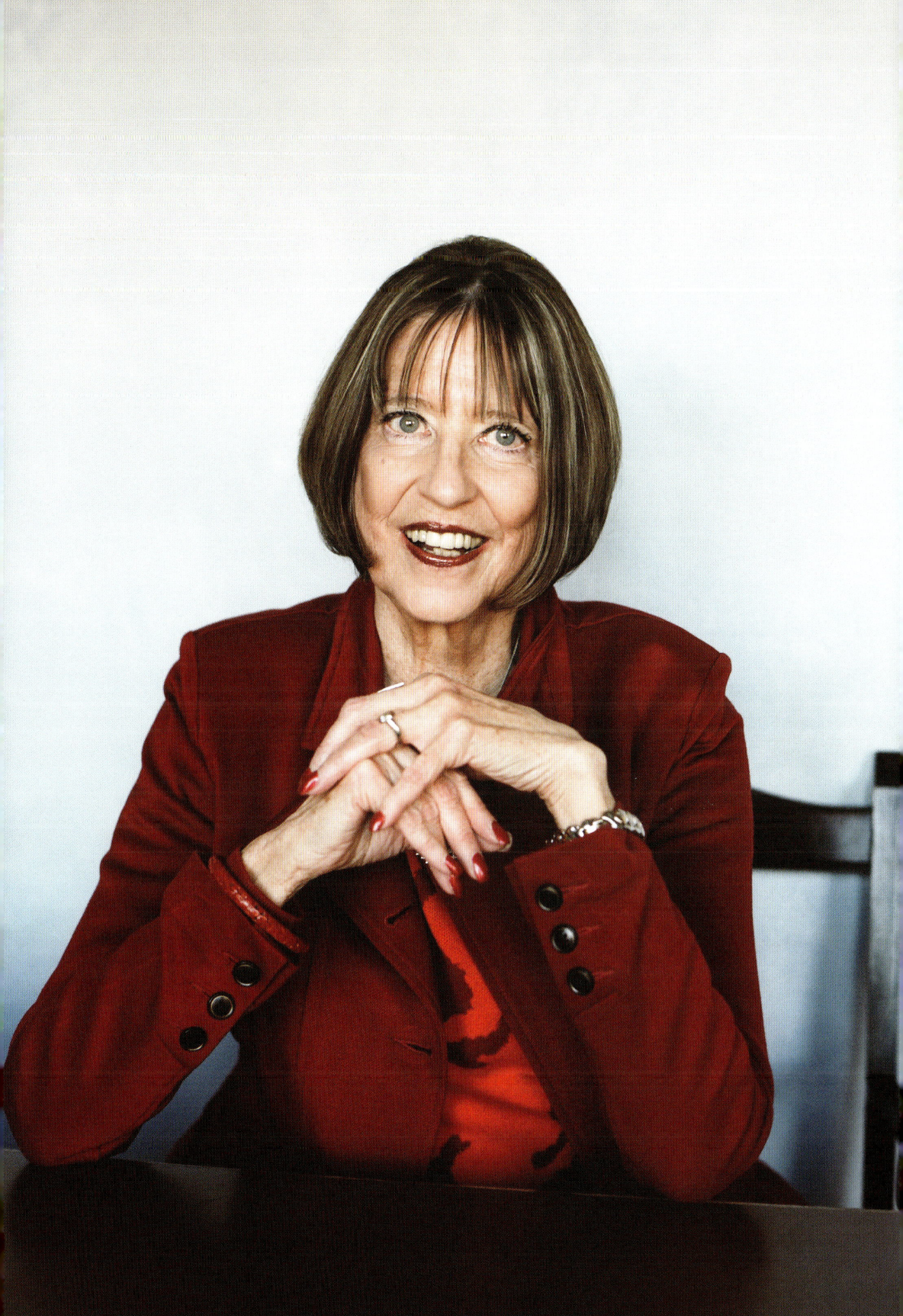

"Instead of saying, 'I can't do this because . . .'
I think what you have to say is 'I can do this;
I just have to figure out how.'"

Much like the resilient sagebrush—a hardy plant that thrives in Wyoming's high desert with little water and lots of grit—Rev. Dr. Bernadine Craft has flourished in her hometown of Rock Springs, finding strength in community and purpose in place. Bernadine lives by the philosophy "Bloom where you are planted." She has dedicated her career to serving her community and state as an Episcopal priest, former Wyoming legislator, psychotherapist, and executive director of the Sweetwater Board of Cooperative Educational Services (SBOCES).

Bernadine's journey into psychology began with a passing comment from a college theater professor who recognized her gift for empathy, listening, critical thinking, and communication. That nudge led her to a psychology class—and a lifelong calling. She earned a bachelor's degree in theater and speech communication and a master's in educational psychology from the University of Utah, followed by a PhD in professional psychology from the University of Northern Colorado. Since 1992, she has operated a private counseling practice.

Years into her career as a psychotherapist, Bernadine had another conversation that opened an unexpected door. After losing her beloved husband to cancer, Bernie found herself in a season of transition. During this time, a friend encouraged her to run for an open seat in the state legislature. Though she'd previously lobbied on behalf of counselors and chaired the Government Affairs committee for the American Counseling Association, she had never considered public office. Her deep sensitivity to others had made her question whether she could take on such a role. But after reflection, and some encouragement from her community, she ran—and won. She quickly discovered that her compassion, communication skills, and problem-solving abilities made her a natural fit for the job.

Bernadine served a decade in the Wyoming State Legislature—first in the House of Representatives, from 2007 to 2013, then in the senate, from 2013 to 2017. At one point, she was the only woman in the state senate. While she had once believed politics weren't for her, she came to describe her time in the legislature as the "golden years." Even after

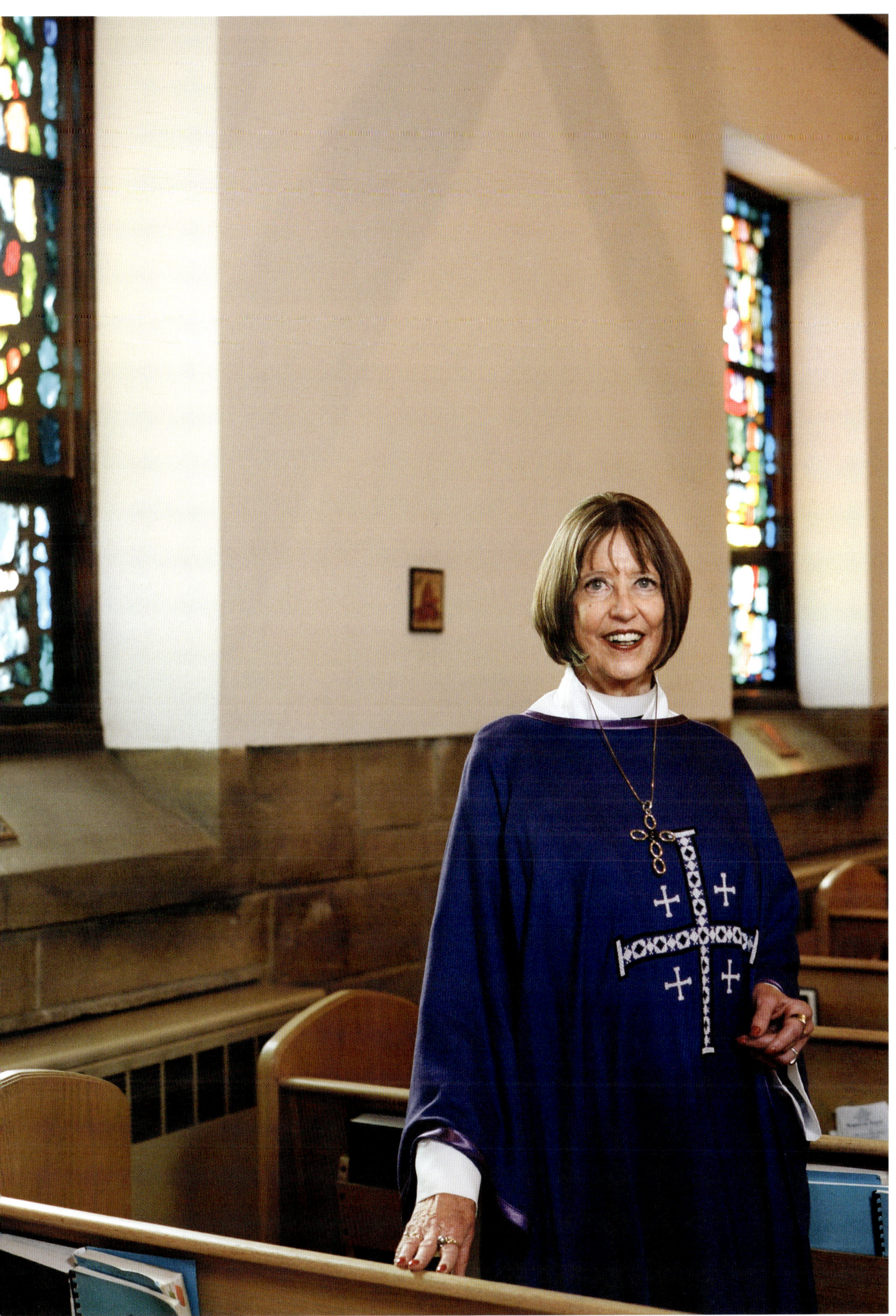

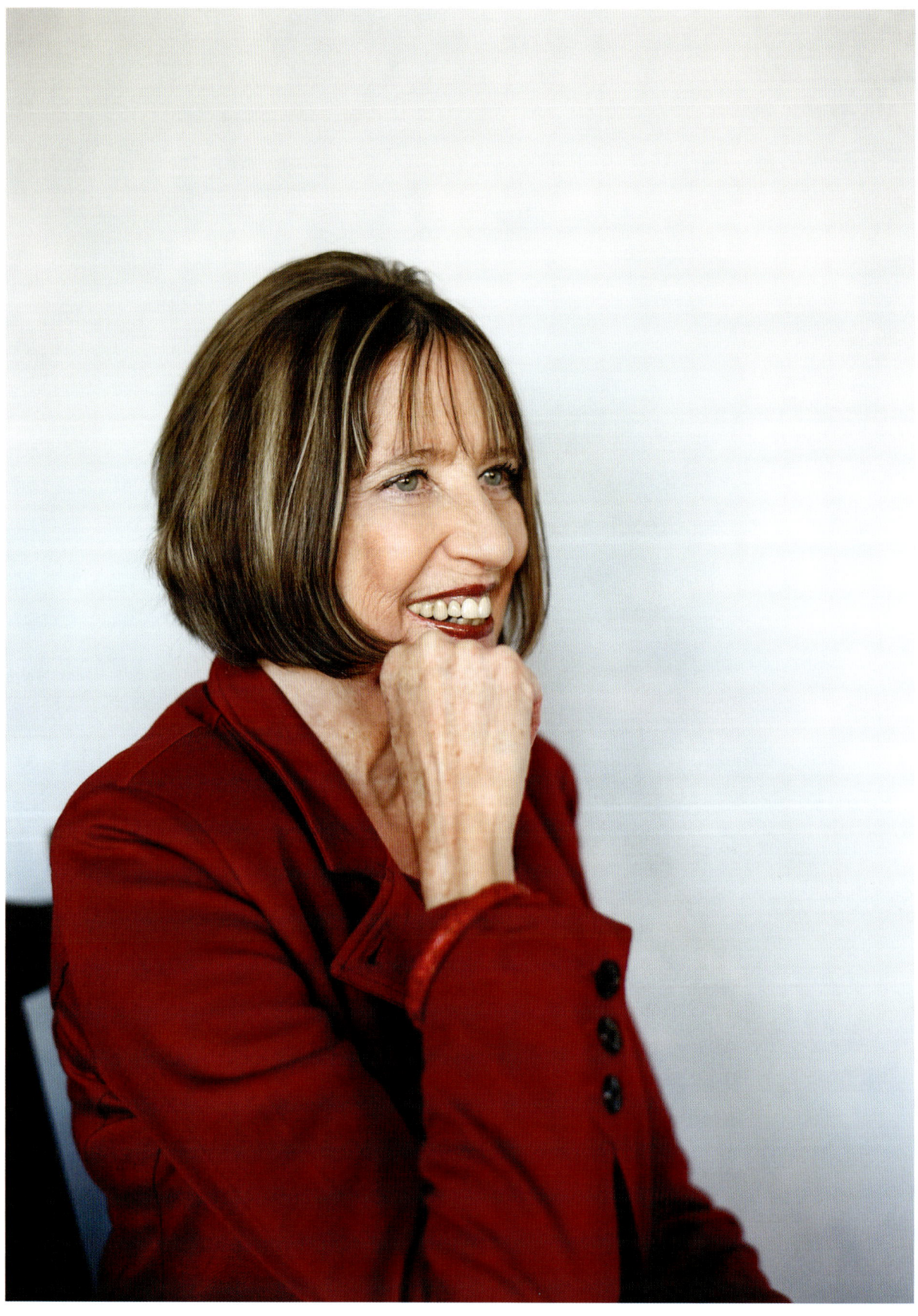

"You have to listen, and you have to be open to change, and you have to understand that the course you plotted might not be the one you end up taking."

passionate debates, legislators could leave as friends, united by a shared commitment to Wyoming—a spirit she notes has become harder to find in today's increasingly polarized climate.

Her legislative focus centered on human services. With the understanding that underfunded issues often go unheard, Bernadine worked tirelessly to be "a voice for the people who have no voice." She championed causes such as domestic violence prevention, child and family support, animal welfare, and other vital social services. For her efforts, she has been recognized by the Wyoming Education Association, Wyoming Public Employees Association, Wyoming Coalition Against Domestic Violence and Sexual Assault, AARP, and the Humane Society.

In 2014, Bernadine fulfilled a lifelong dream when she was ordained as an Episcopal priest—a milestone once impossible, as the church did not permit the ordination of women. Her ministry emphasizes inclusivity and dignity for all. As dean of Southwest Wyoming for the Episcopal Diocese, she helped create St. Christopher's Highway, a program assisting travelers in need. Her extensive community involvement includes leadership in and volunteer work with Create a Christmas, Kiwanis Club, Red Desert Humane Society, Wyoming Women's Foundation, Wyoming Humanities Council, Actor's Mission, and multiple roles within the Episcopal Church, including chairing both its Suicide Prevention Connection and the Foundation for the Diocese of Wyoming. In 2024, she received the Mayor's Arts Award for Arts Advocacy in Sweetwater County.

One of Bernadine's favorite cowboy poems reads, "When sagebrush gets in your blood, you can never really leave." In every chapter of her life, she has lived those words—working to improve, uplift, and advocate for the people and places of Wyoming.

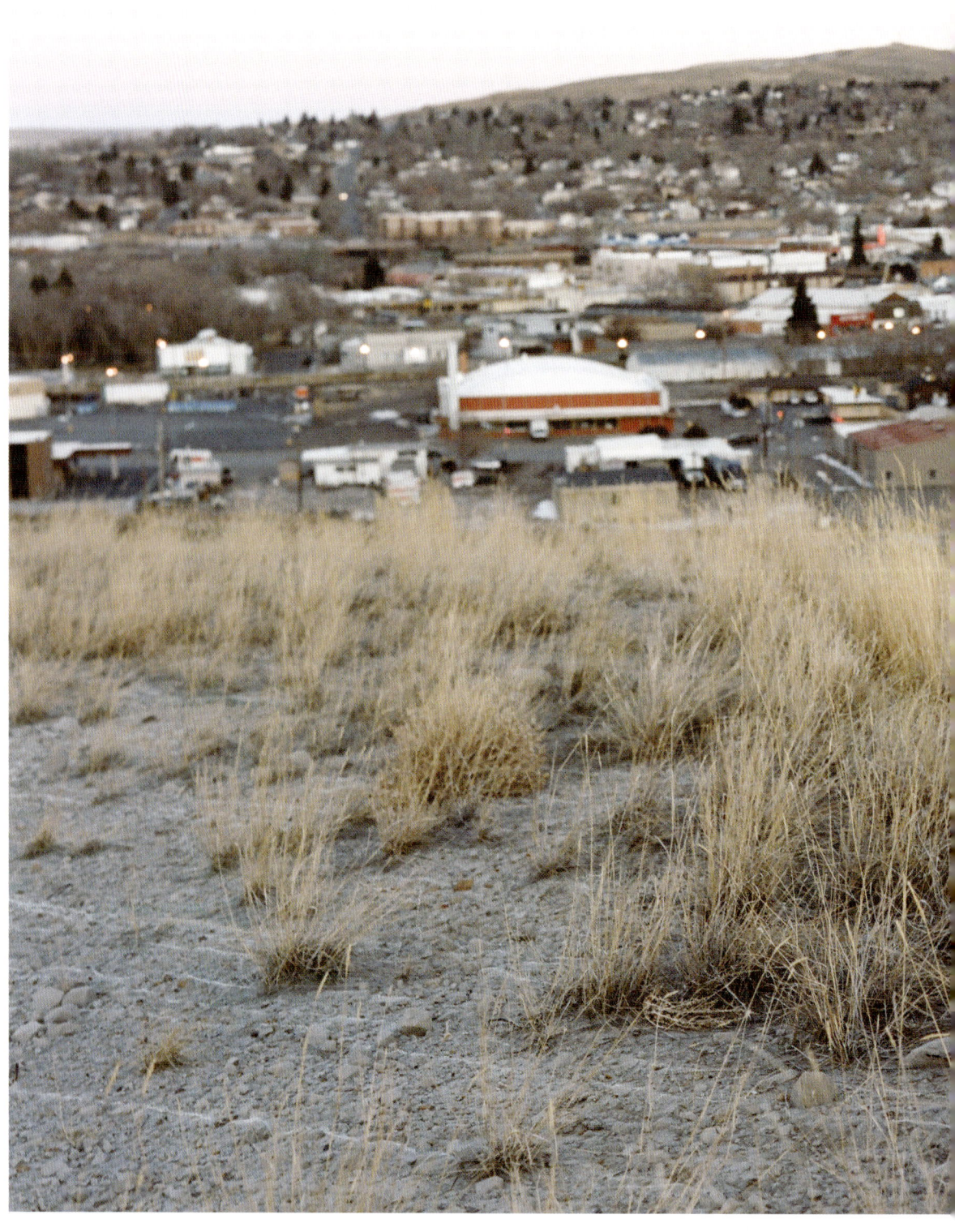

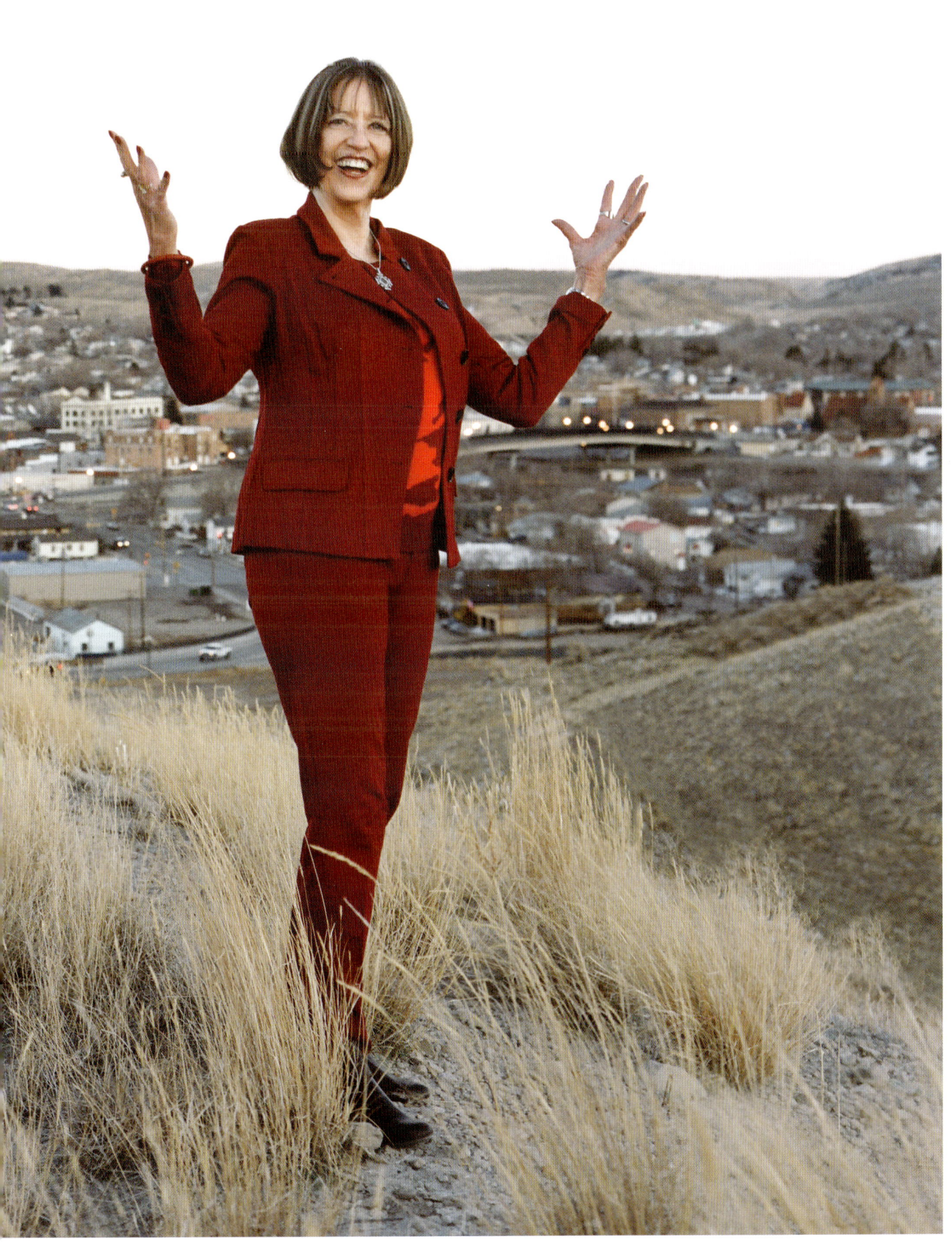

MEGAN GRASSELL

FOUNDER AND CEO OF YELLOWBERRY

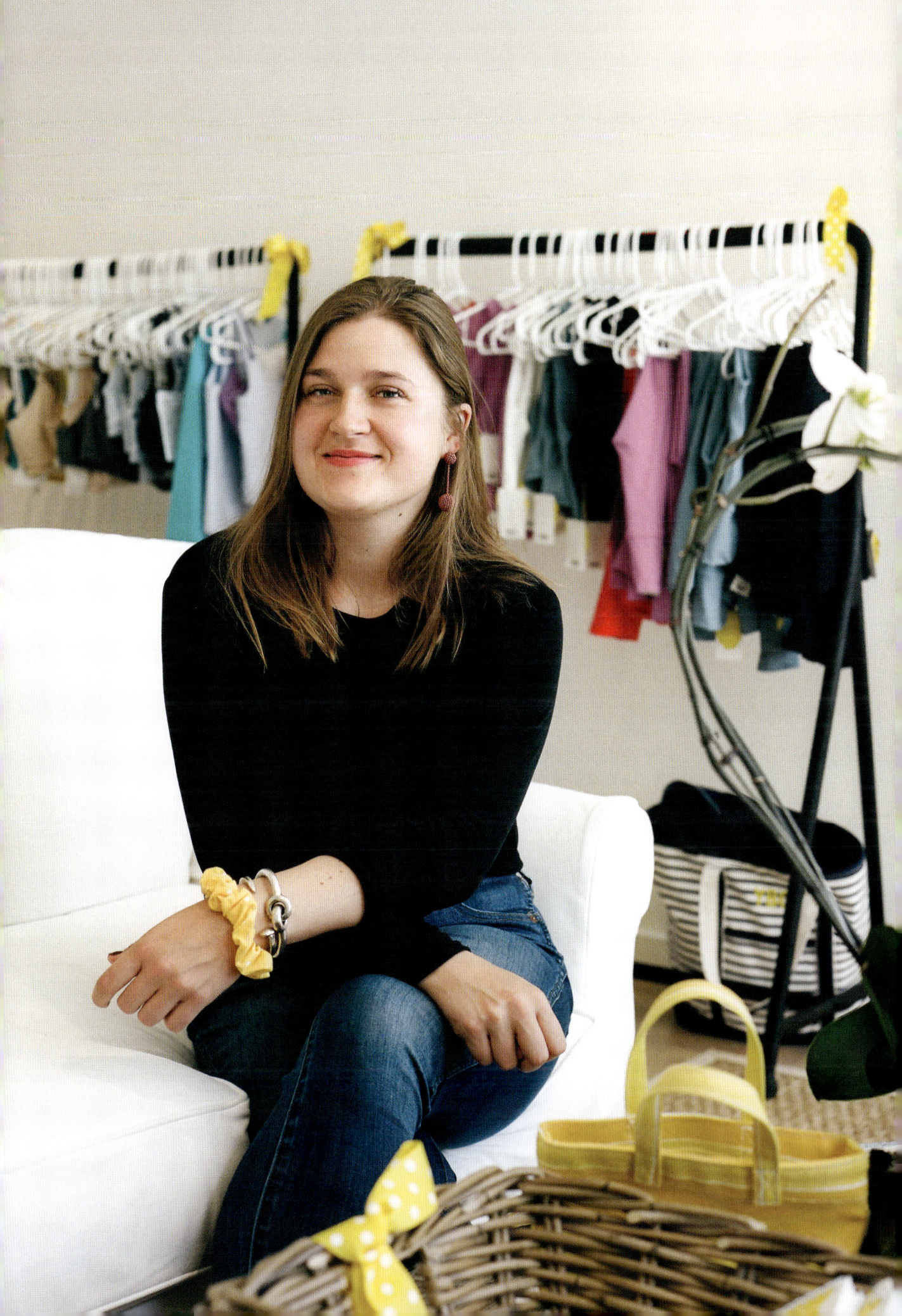

"When you grow up in a place where there are no rules, there are also no boundaries. You have all this freedom, so you're building something all the time."

Megan credits growing up in Wyoming with inspiring her adventurous journey as a business founder and CEO. Her brand Yellowberry—a bra, underwear, activewear, and loungewear company for girls aged eight to fourteen—has the manifesto "If you can dream it, you can do it."

These developing years for girls can be challenging. As the founder and CEO of Yellowberry, Megan takes a unique approach to confidence building. For her, it starts with the foundational garments for one's wardrobe. Megan grew up in the ranch town of Pinedale and later spent time in Jackson as a competitive ski racer. She describes her experience growing up in a small town as integral to her success in business.

She founded Yellowberry when she was just seventeen years old, after discovering that the only options for her younger sister's first bra were a leopard-print push-up or a sports bra. Determined to create a non-sexualized, stylish first bra option for girls, Megan launched a Kickstarter and nearly doubled her financing goals to officially launch her company and make the first product. Fun colors and comfortable fabrics are the foundation for every design. Features on *Good Morning America* and *The Today Show* rocketed her visibility. She recruited her mom to help her pack boxes and fill orders so she could study for a calculus test and complete high school while building her company. Just a few years after she launched, Yellowberry reached a huge milestone of one million bras sold.

Now in her twenties, Megan continues to revolutionize the bra industry for girls across the country. Yellowberry has partnered with American Eagle and Target. She's been named to *Time* magazine's 25 Most Influential Teens, Yahoo's 24 Millennials to Watch, and *Forbes*'s 30 Under 30 lists. She continues to be a leader for young women and girls, encouraging them to embrace their ambitions, unique strengths, and talents.

To Megan, her mission has always been bigger than just bras and is centered around a more significant effort to help girls grow up at their own pace. Yellowberry fills a void for girls who are building their confidence, speaking up, and dreaming big.

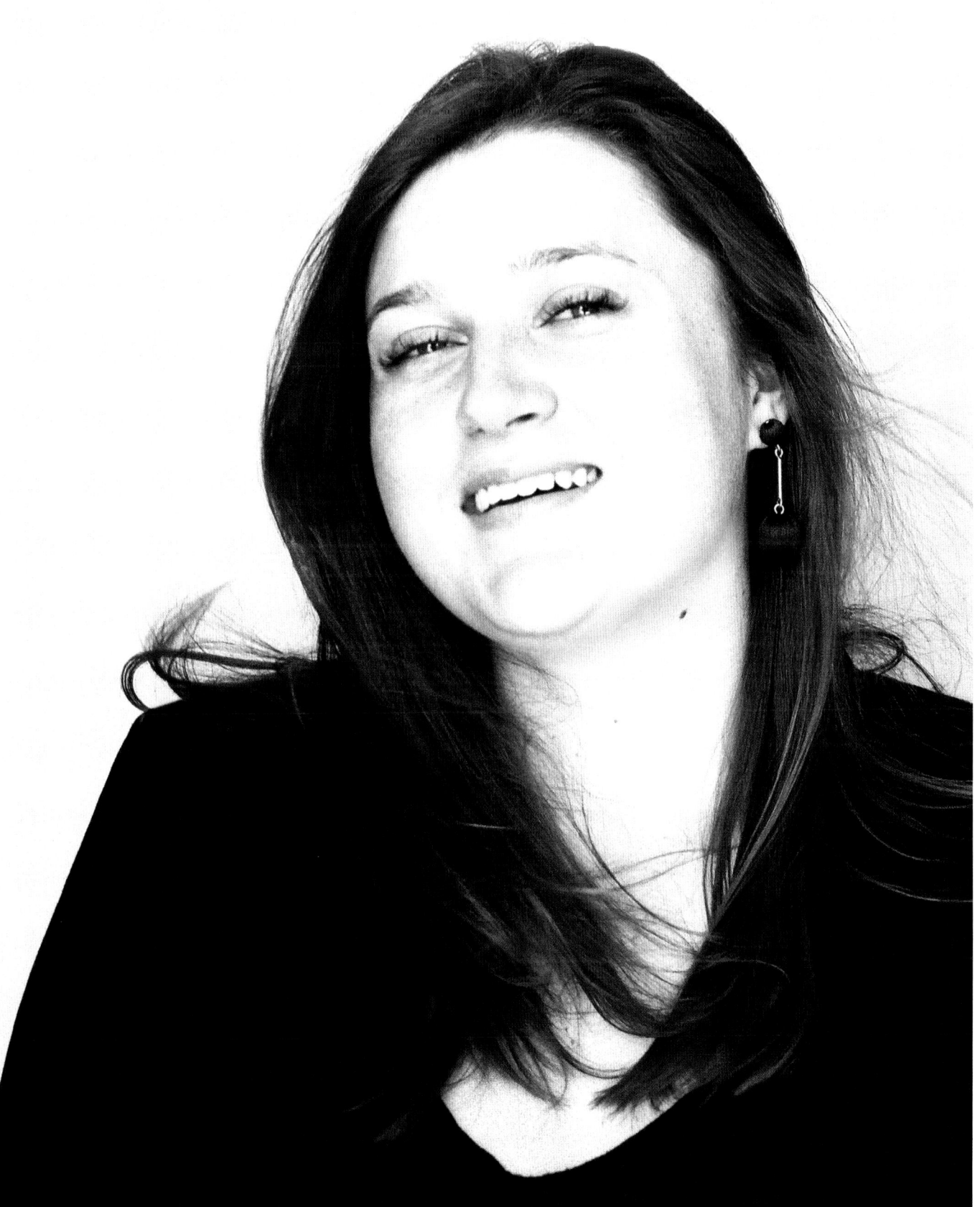

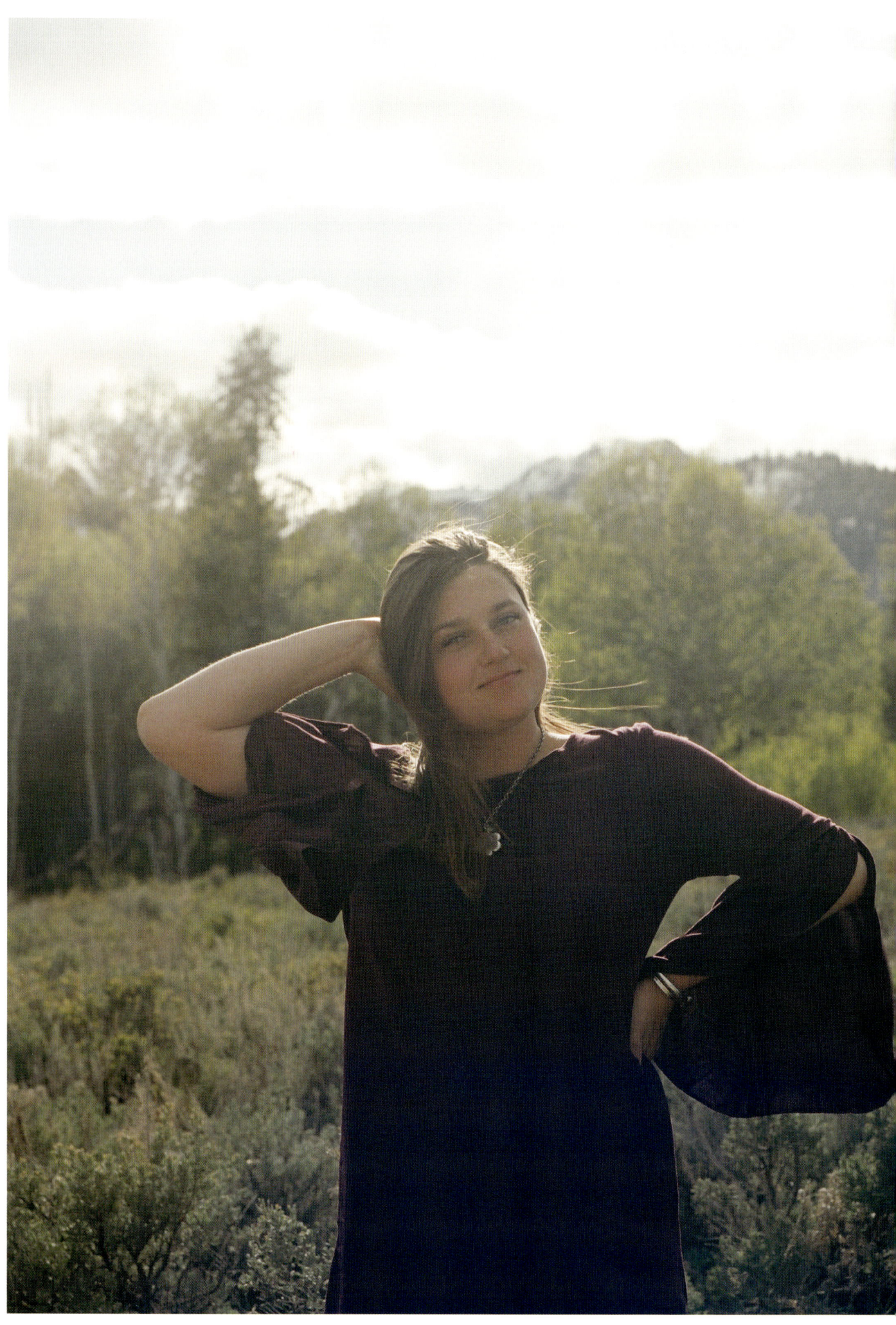

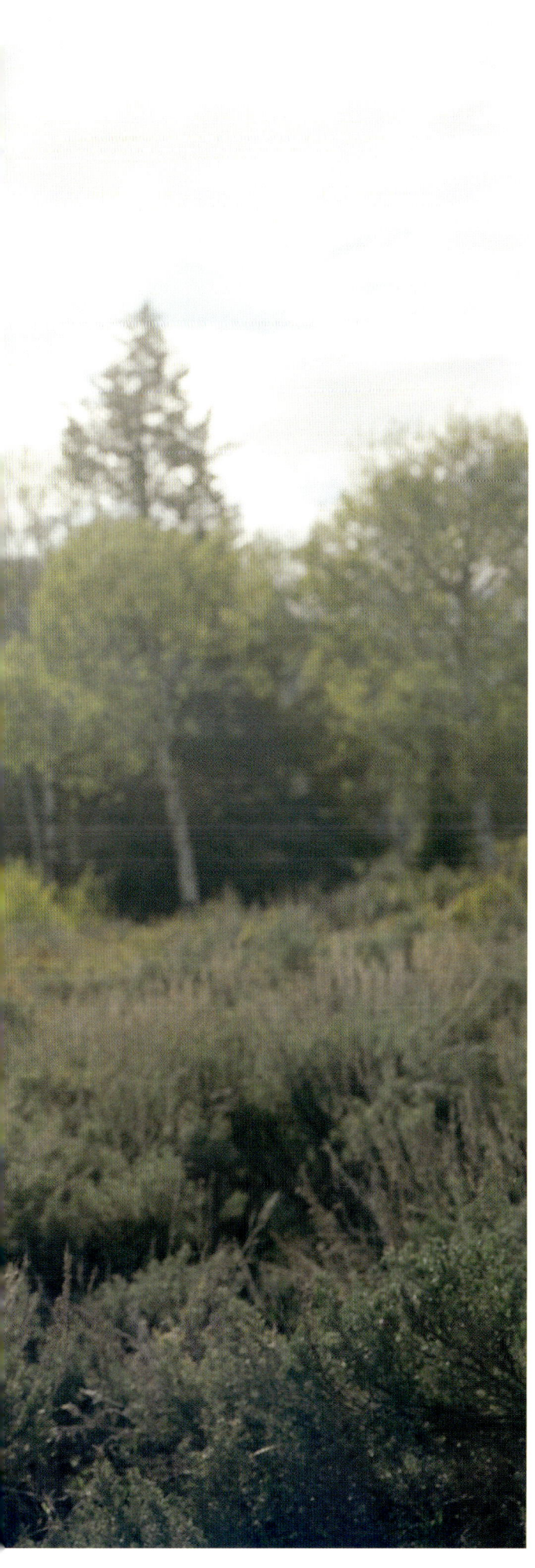

"Being smart, working really hard, being ambitious, and going after what you want is awesome, and more girls should feel comfortable doing those types of things."

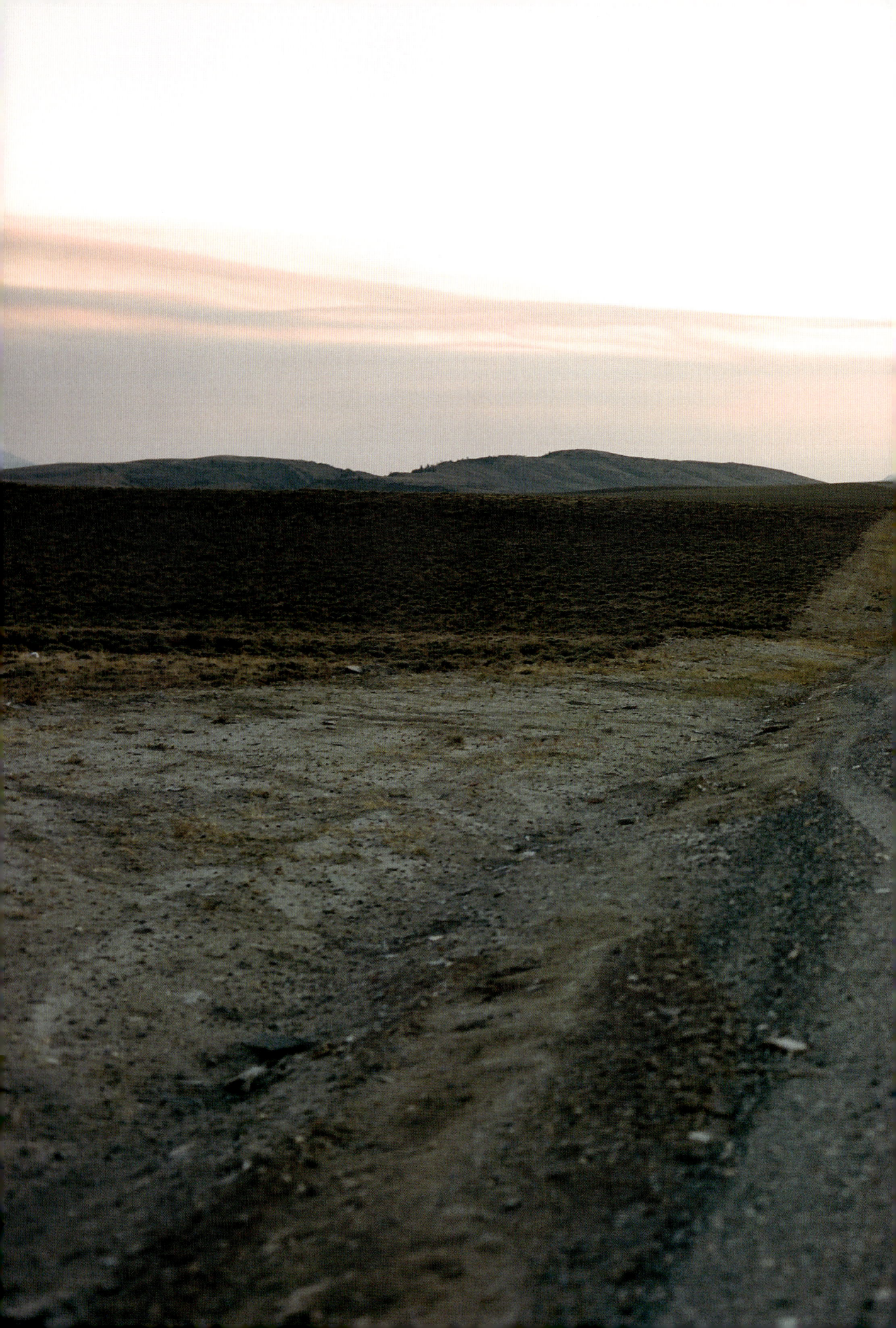

CHAPTER III

Power

Power is the space of the matriarch and community. It means holding on
to your dreams and standing strong in what you believe. You are not alone.
The collective is key to transformation. Therefore, in addition to individual
stories, this chapter explores two multi-subject stories of organizations.
Power is a spirit you continually cultivate within yourself and those
around you. By doing so, you transform the world.

MARY A. "MICKEY" THOMAN

COWGIRL, MENTOR, MATRIARCH OF THE W&M THOMAN RANCH
IN SWEETWATER COUNTY

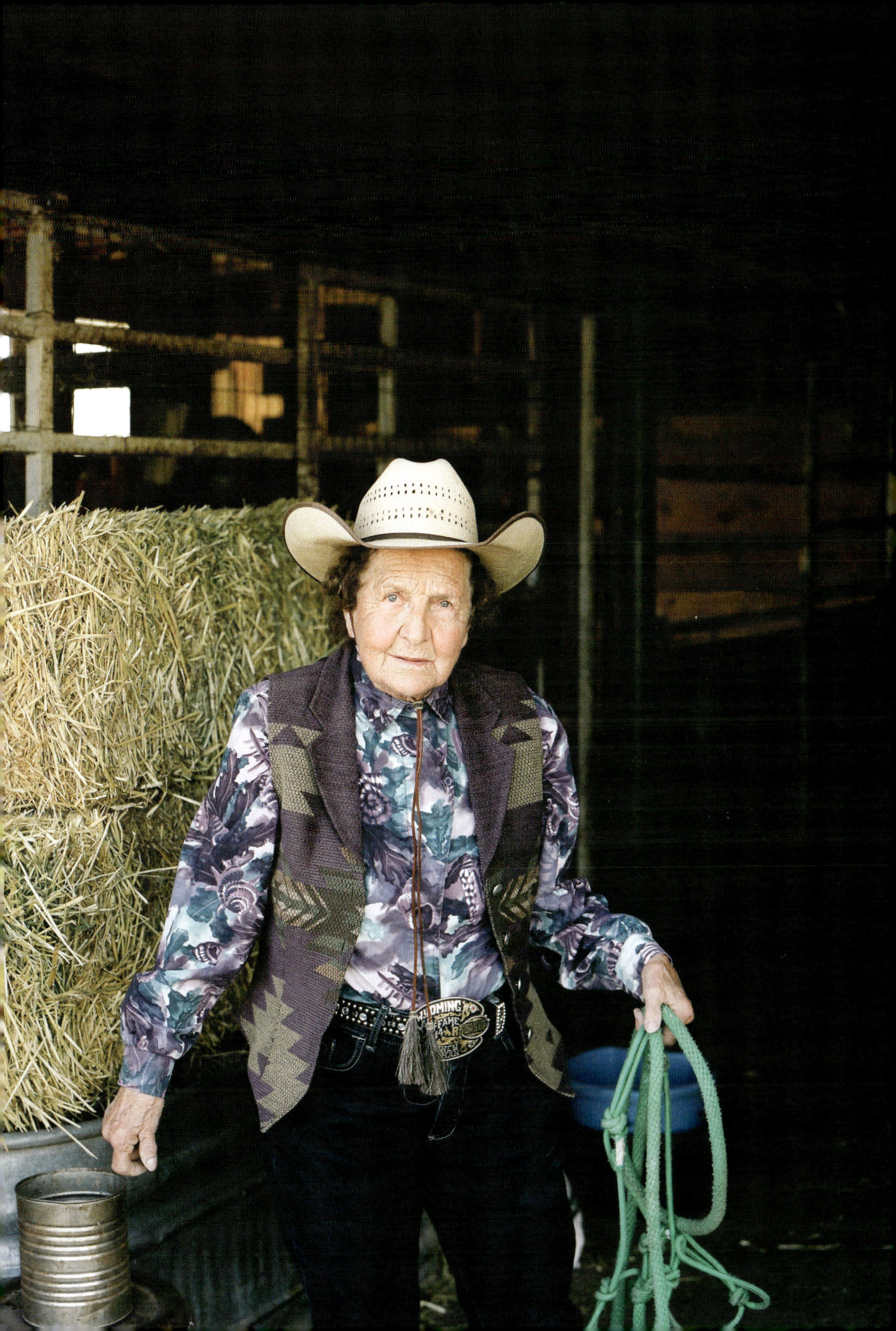

"You're kind of in control of your life to a point, but what's gotta be done, you do it."

A rodeo queen and ranch matriarch, Mickey Thoman has spent her life in the saddle, guiding both livestock and family across the rolling lands of Sweetwater County. Today, she and her three daughters run the W&M Thoman Ranch, raising fine-wool Rambouillet sheep, a uniform herd of Hereford cattle, and spirited Thoroughbred-quarter horses. Even through personal loss and the shifting challenges of the agricultural industry, Mickey has remained a steady force—determined, adaptive, and deeply connected to the land.

From the time she was able to sit on a horse, Mickey was riding. As a child, she never wanted to leave the ranch, and the rare times she had to—like when she was sent to board in town for high school—were difficult. She disliked being away from home so much that when she became a mother, she helped establish a one-room ranch school in 1957, ensuring that her children and others in neighboring ranches could stay close. The school has educated up to five students a year, both family and neighbors, since its inception nearly seventy years ago. While the ranch school doesn't currently have any pupils and it's uncertain whether it will again in the future, its legacy is profound.

Mickey lost two of her seven children in accidents and later her husband and ranching partner, Bill Thoman. When asked if she ever considered selling the ranch after his passing, she was firm: "Why would I sell it? This has been my whole life. I think that's what he would have wanted. So I'm still here, and I'm still enjoying it." Grief never leaves, she says—you just learn to accept it and work with it. For her, the best way through has always been to keep busy, to keep working.

She credits her family's ability to stay relevant in agriculture to persistence and practicality. Ranching is significant to Wyoming's economy, adding nearly $2.5 billion in revenue, and a lifestyle vital to many communities. But ranching isn't just Mickey's occupation, it's what keeps her spirit alive. For Mickey, the heart of ranching is more than hard work—it's about communication. She shares an innate connection with her animals to build trust and work in sync together. "You have to learn your animals. You learn their language." For Mickey, there is nothing more peaceful than being on the land with them. Whether it's herding sheep or working with horses, she believes every animal

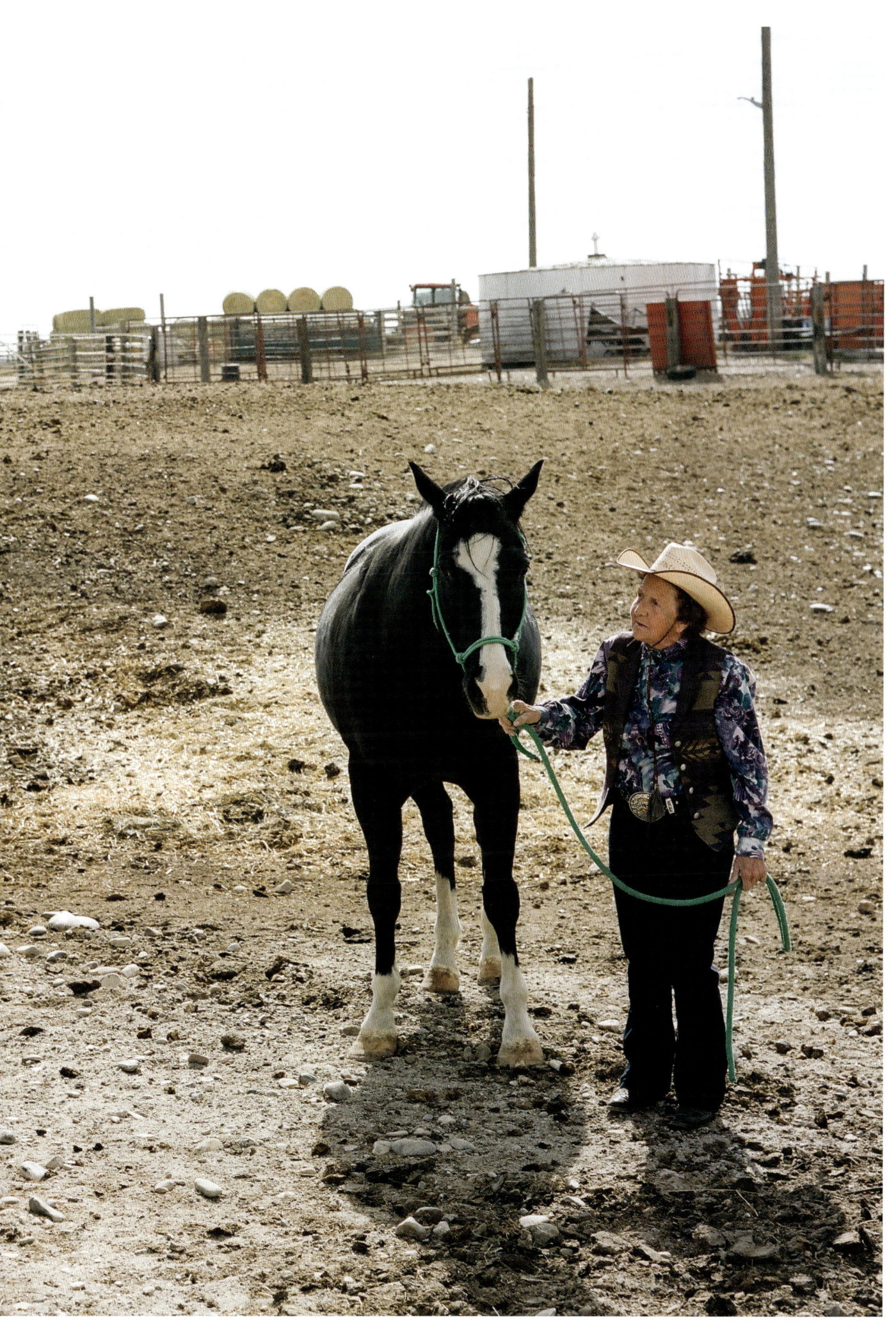

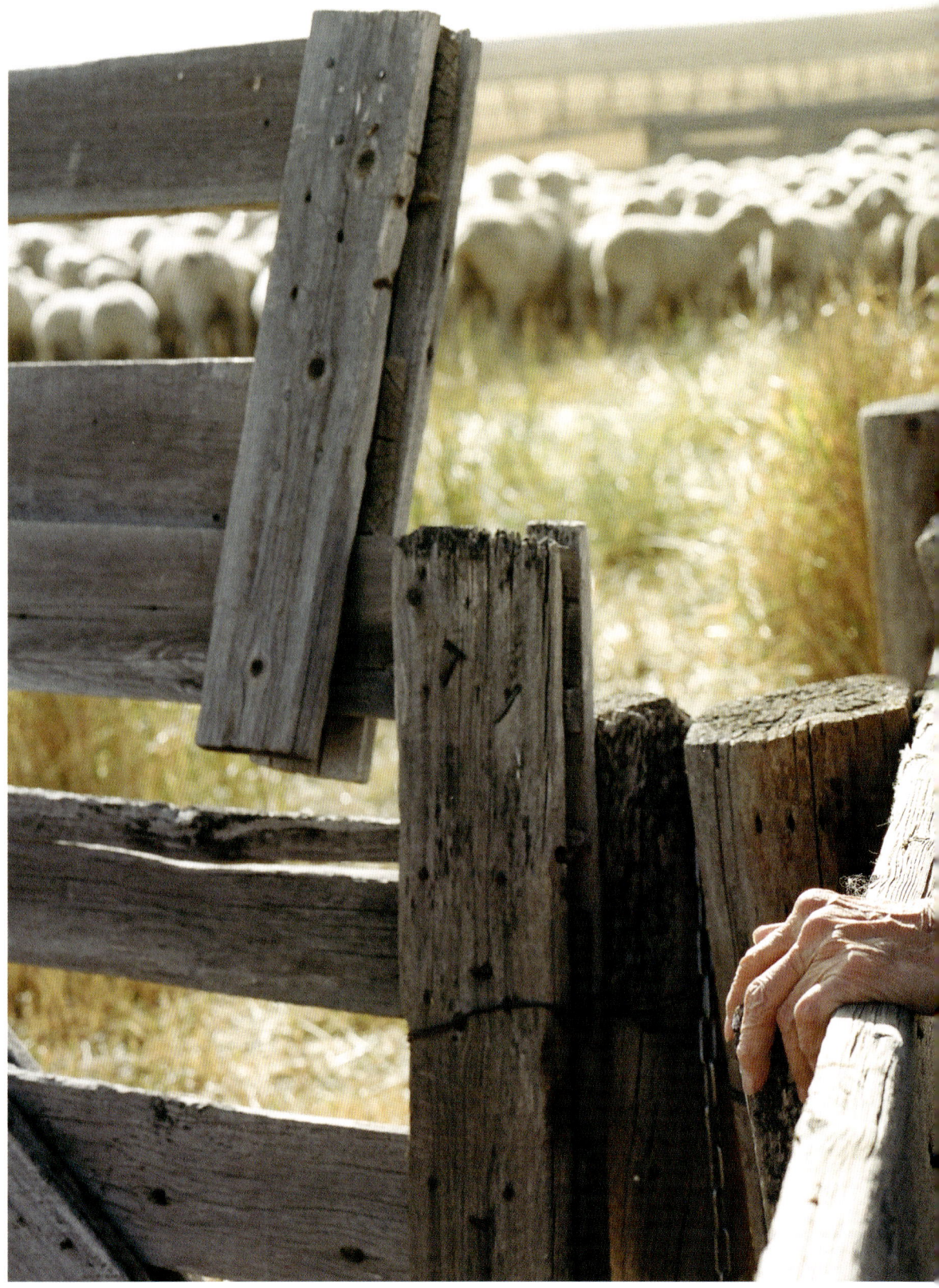

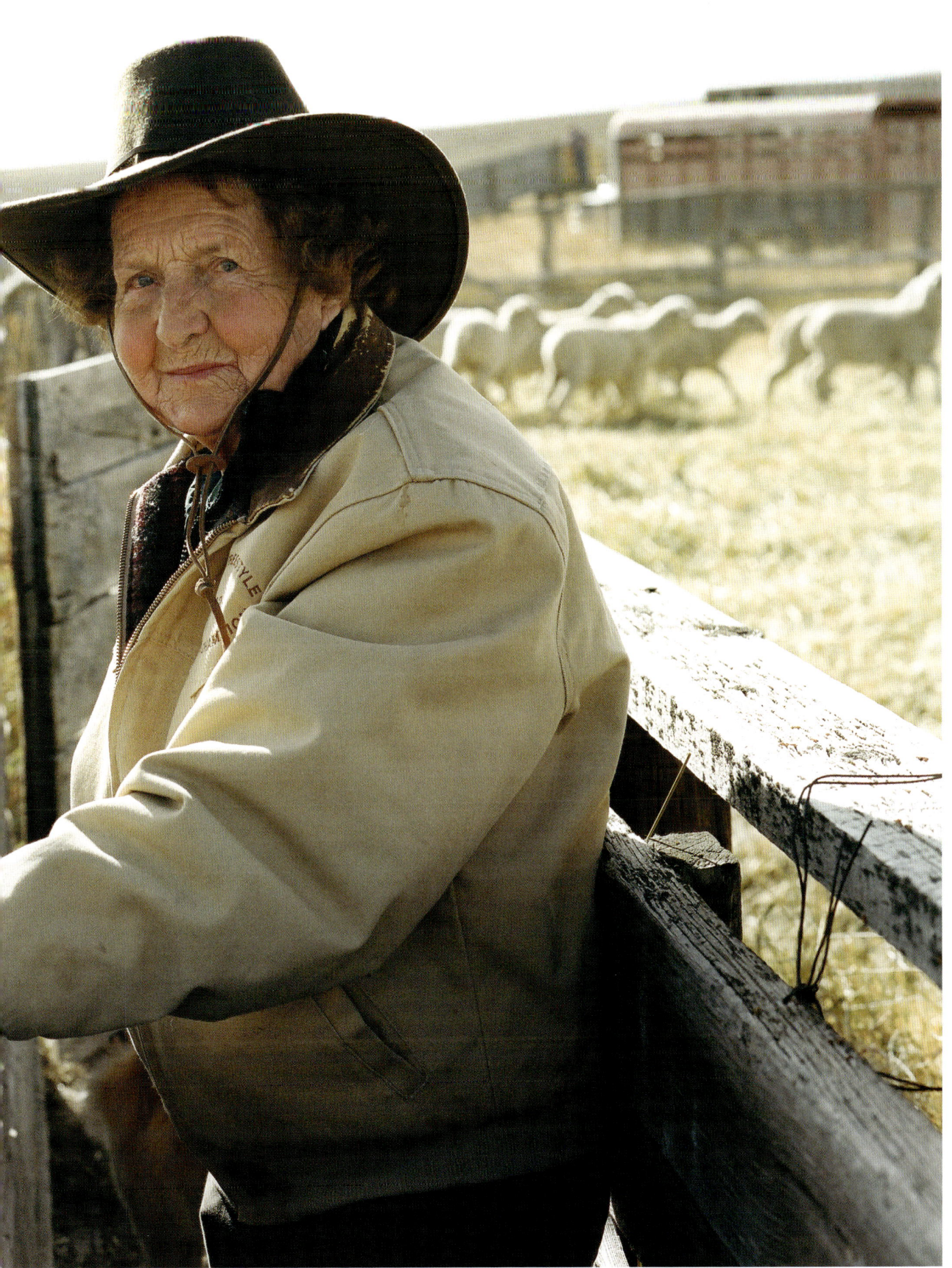

has a personality and a way of speaking, and
that trust is built in quiet moments.

It's a philosophy she applies to ranching, family,
and her deep-rooted connection to Wyoming's
Western traditions. She is one of the thirty-
three founding members of the Green River
Valley Cowbelles—a cattlewomen's association; served on the Wyoming Stock Growers
Association Board of Directors; and has been a
4-H key leader for over sixty-three years, earning multiple dedicated leader awards. In 2018,
she was inducted into the Wyoming Cowboy
Hall of Fame.

There is no place she'd rather be than out on the
land, working alongside her daughters, watch-
ing the hills turn green in the spring. "I don't
think about being a boss," she says. "I just think
about working together with my family. I just
enjoy that they're still here." To Mickey, peace
isn't something you chase—it's something you
find in a life well-lived, in work done well, and
in the simple joy of being present.

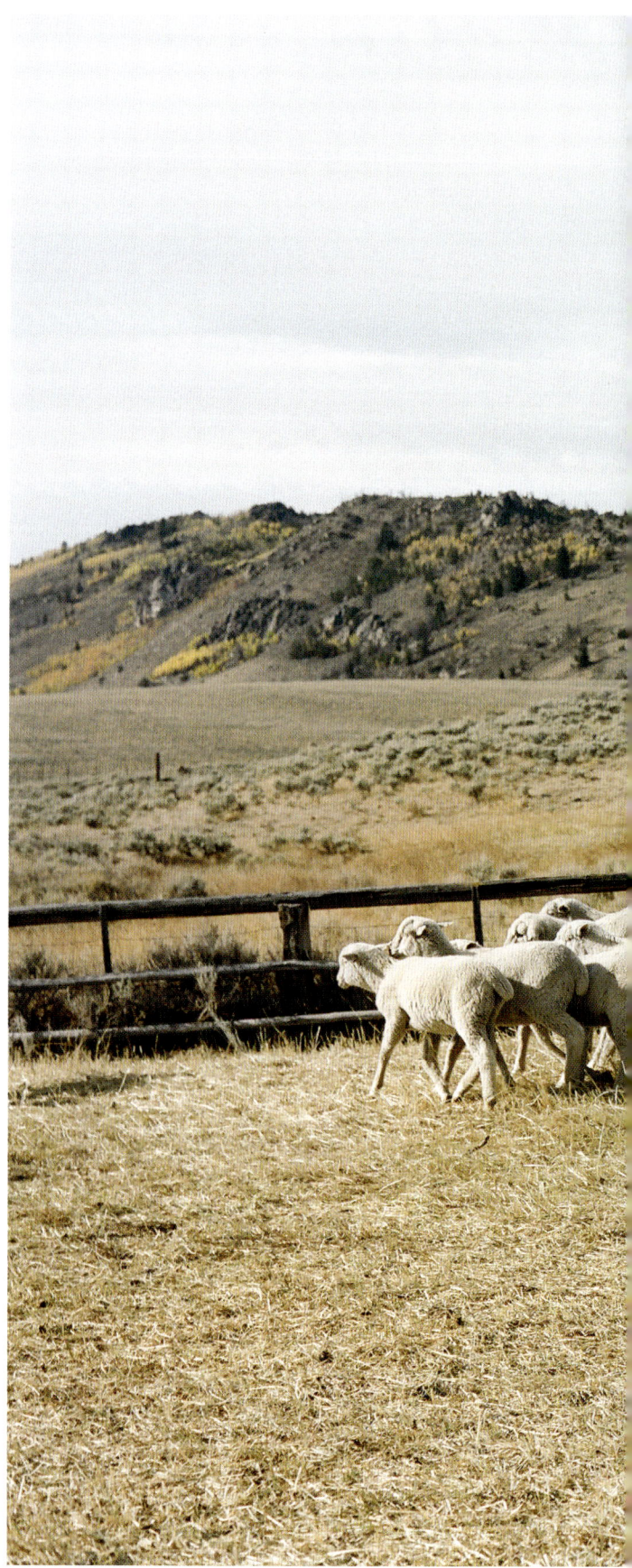

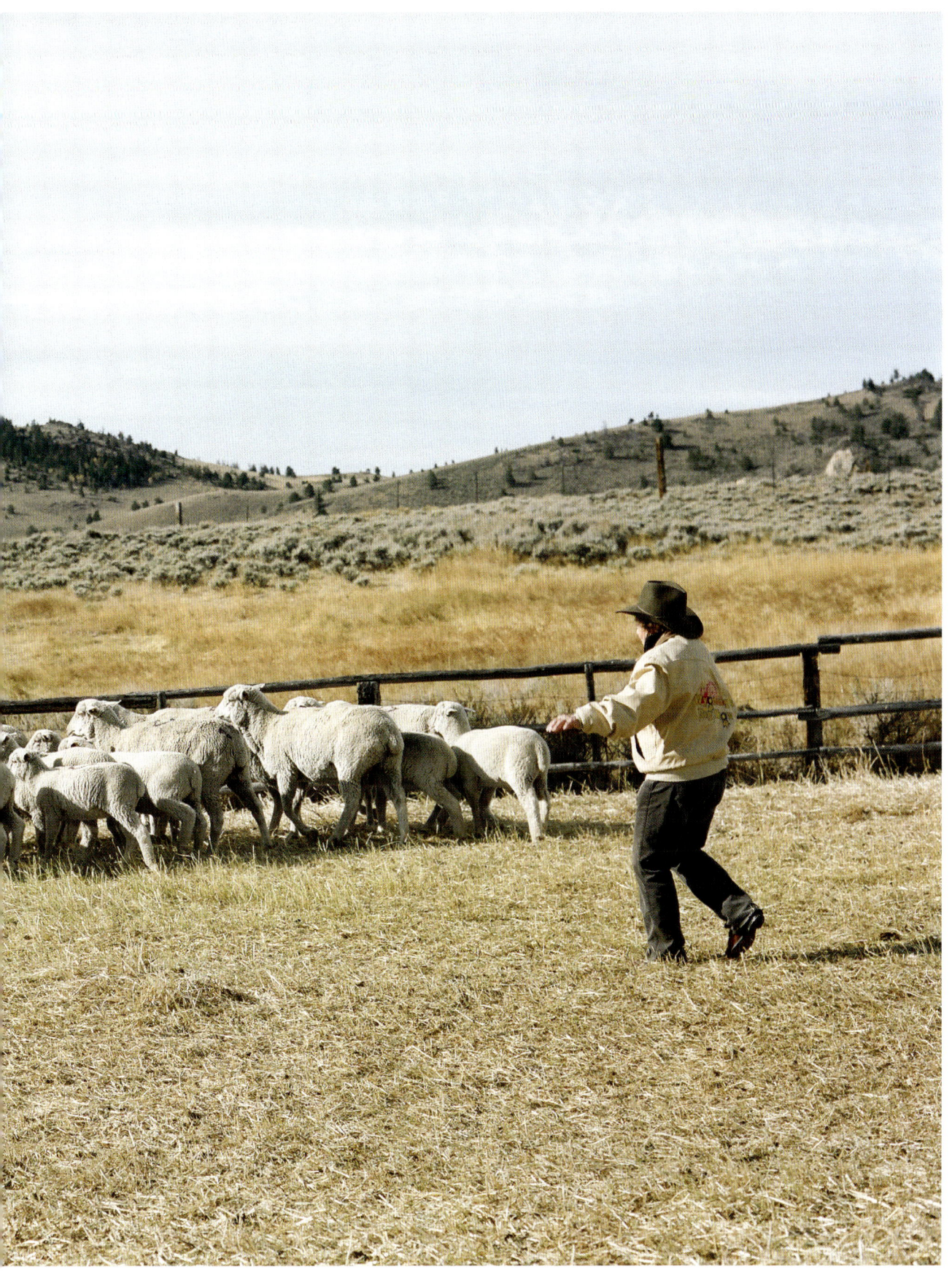

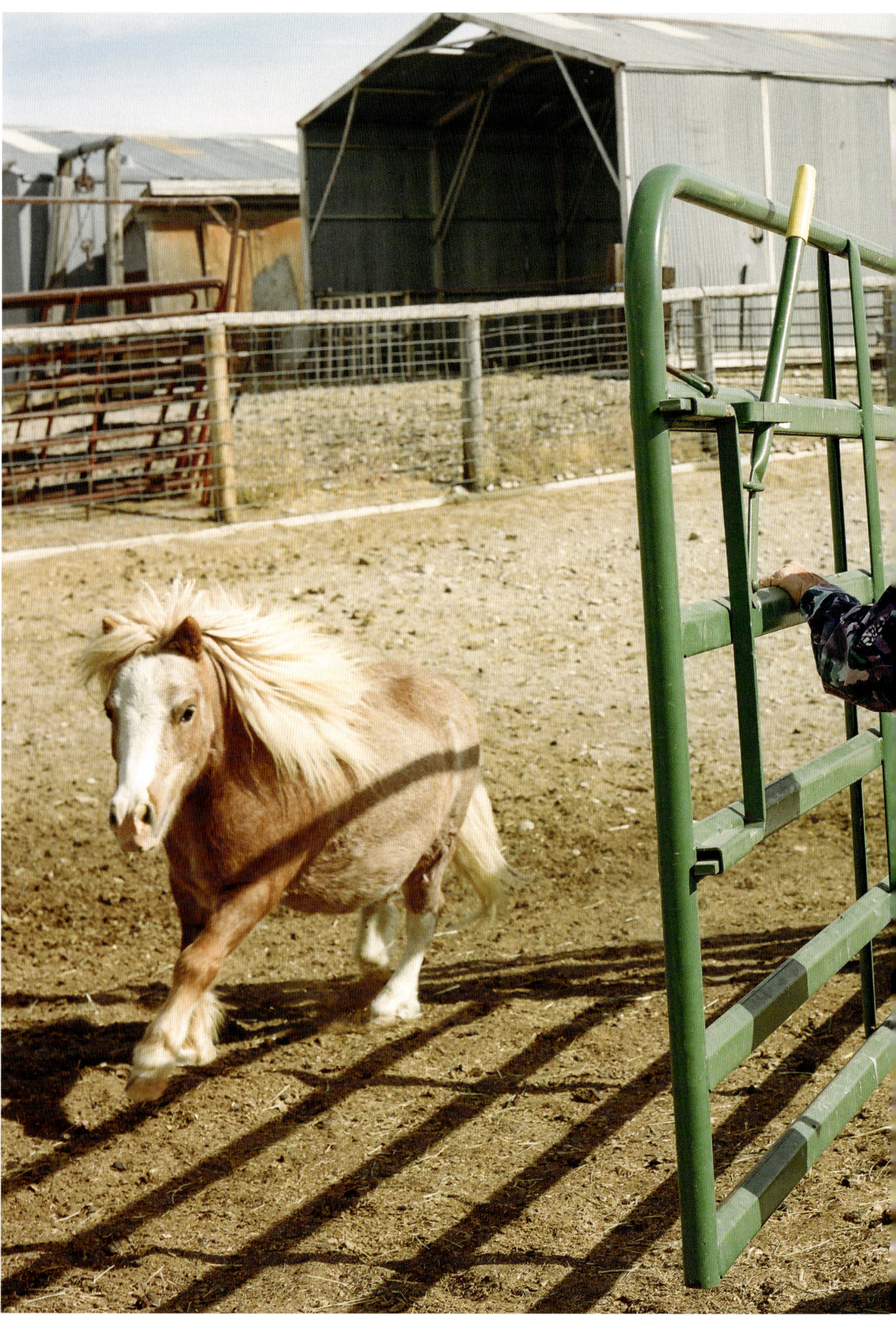

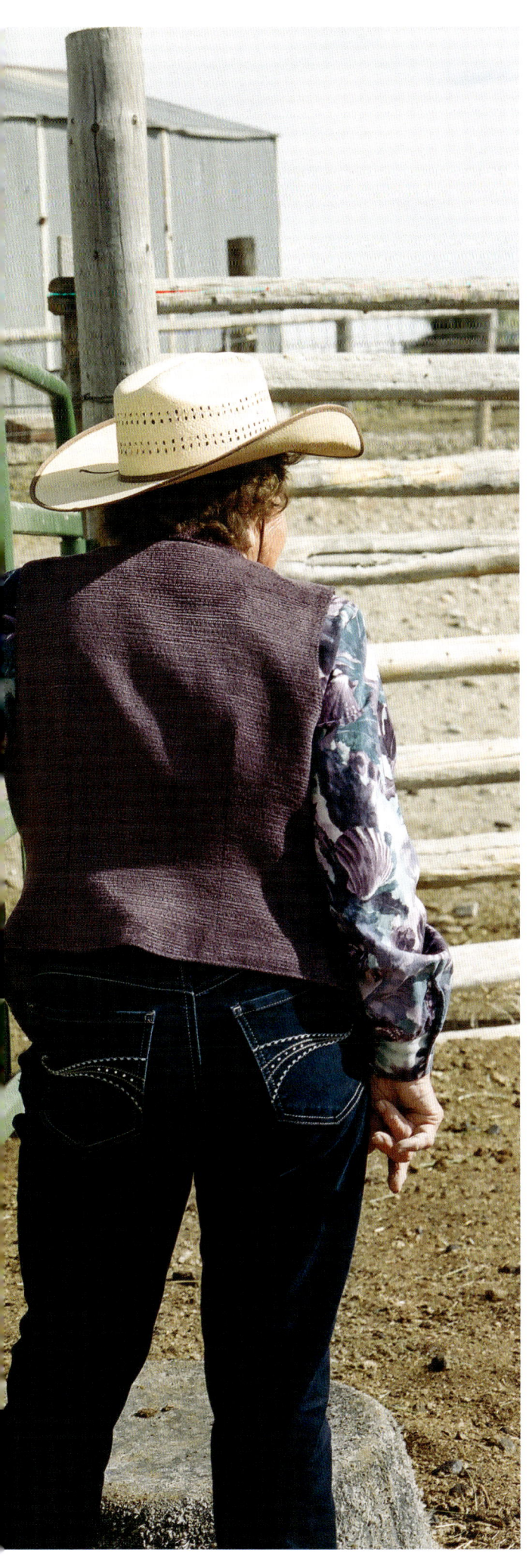

"My favorite time of year on the land is probably spring, when everything starts to turn green. And the rest of the year is my favorite time too."

CLIMB WYOMING

STATEWIDE NONPROFIT PROVIDING SKILLS AND SUPPORT FOR
LOW-INCOME SINGLE MOMS THROUGH JOB TRAINING AND PLACEMENT,
AS WELL AS MENTAL HEALTH COUNSELING

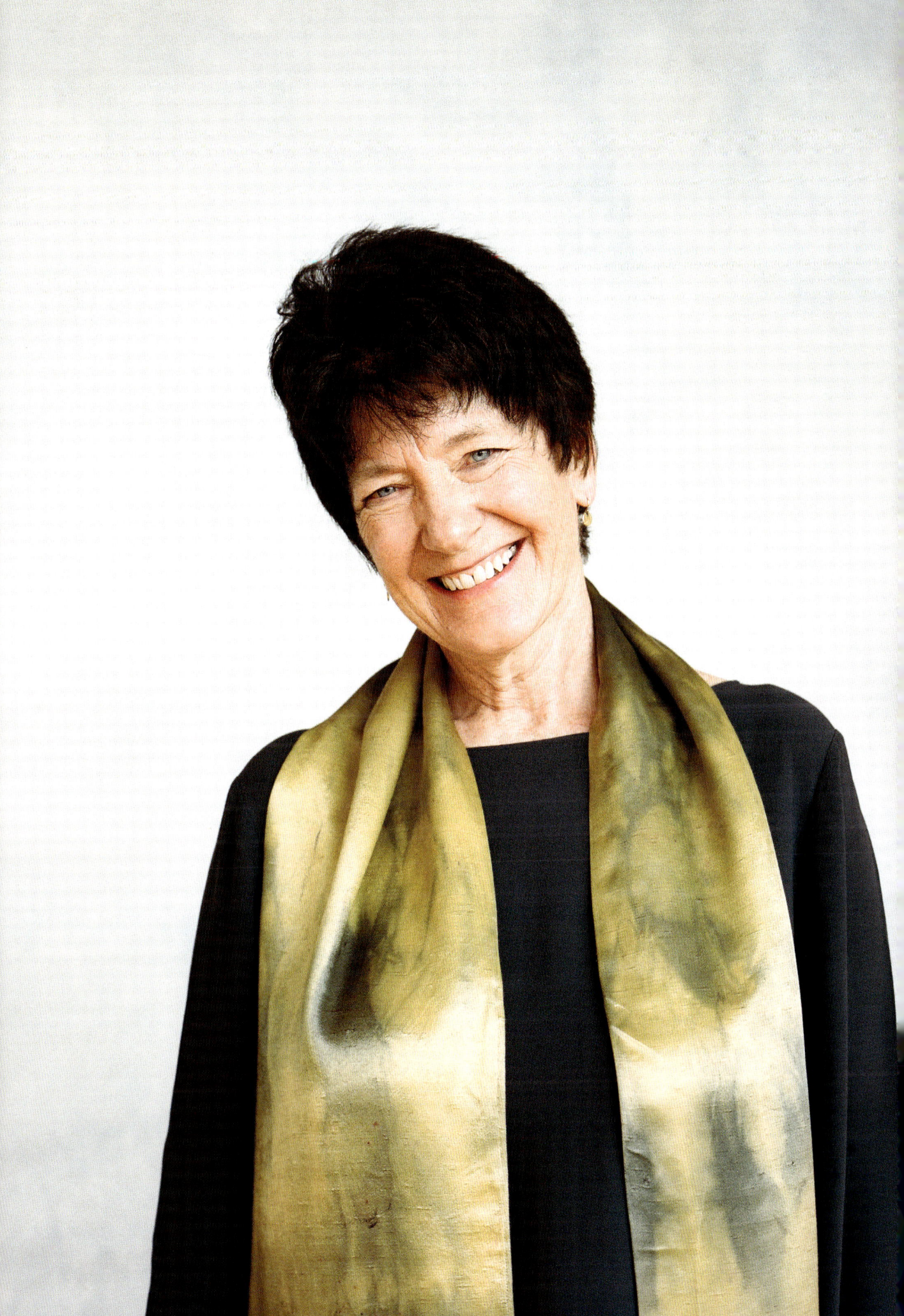

"We as women, we as individuals, can take advantage of an intense moment in time to do our work and do it well. It can change our lives."

—DR. RAY FLEMING DINNEEN, FOUNDER

Single mothers and their children experience the highest rates of poverty among families in Wyoming. Founded in 1986, Climb Wyoming has helped thousands of single moms reach self-sufficiency, with free training for careers in health care, commercial driving, office administration, and more. Climb's comprehensive program also strengthens executive functioning skills, provides mental health services, and makes connections to resources that help moms find lasting success in all areas of life. When a mom moves out of poverty, it has a ripple effect on her whole family. Her resilience and strength impact her children's lives, schools, communities, and Wyoming's economy for generations to come.

Climb's founder Dr. Ray Fleming Dinneen developed the transformative model forty years ago in partnership with her mother, Patricia Fleming, a widely sought-after psychologist and forensic expert. Their innovative approach to poverty alleviation continues to guide the organization today. Speaking about her mother's legacy, Dr. Ray recalls, "She could see the potential in everyone."

Artesia, a Climb graduate turned director in the health-care industry, speaks to her personal transformation: "To me, power can be unlimited things. It's being strong, being independent. It's being the person that you know you can be, with all that's within you." Climb's model is immersive, intense, and demands the full attention of participants and staff. Programming takes place over three months with groups of up to ten moms at a time. Climb's relationship-based approach revolves around the knowledge that the learning won't happen until a mom has structure and feels safe. Individual and group counseling help remove past barriers and support achievement of long-term employment success. Climb's therapeutic approach also gives moms tools to model healthy behaviors for their children.

Climb has developed one of the nation's most successful models for moving families out of poverty, serving 12,000 moms and 25,000 children over the past four decades. The result is a collective force of empowered, self-sufficient women who are confident and upwardly mobile, and who have created better lives for themselves and their children while helping Wyoming businesses and communities thrive.

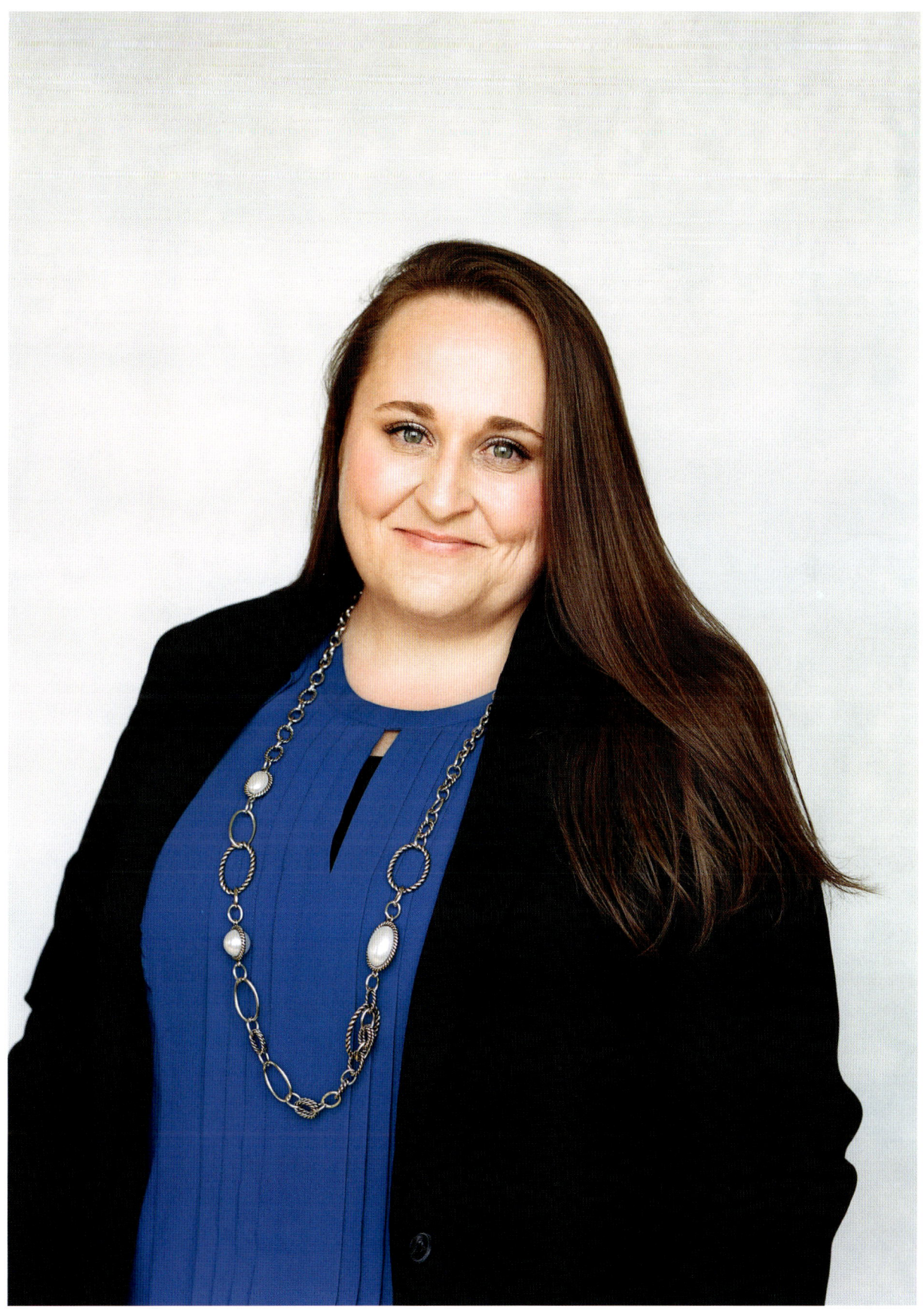

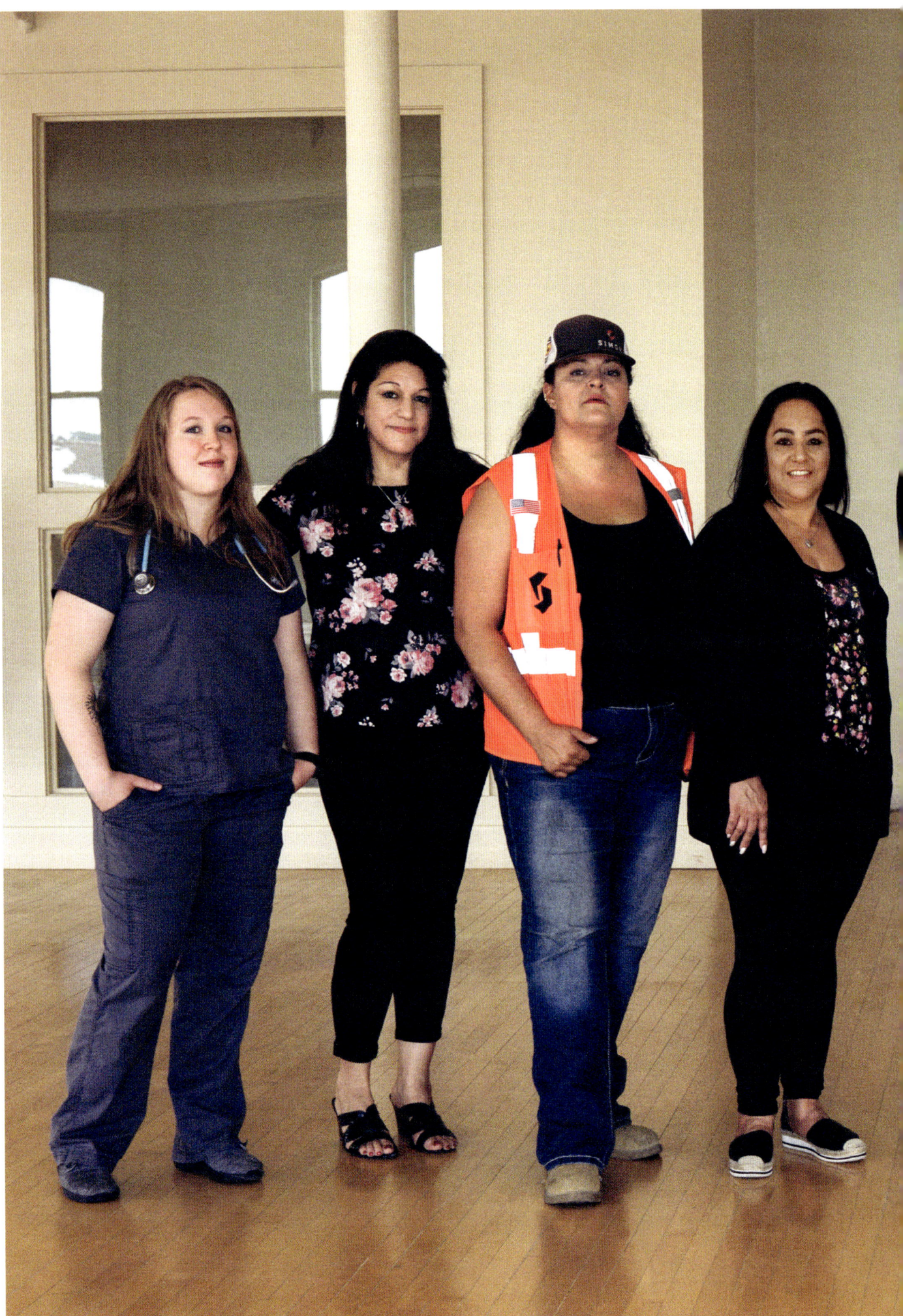

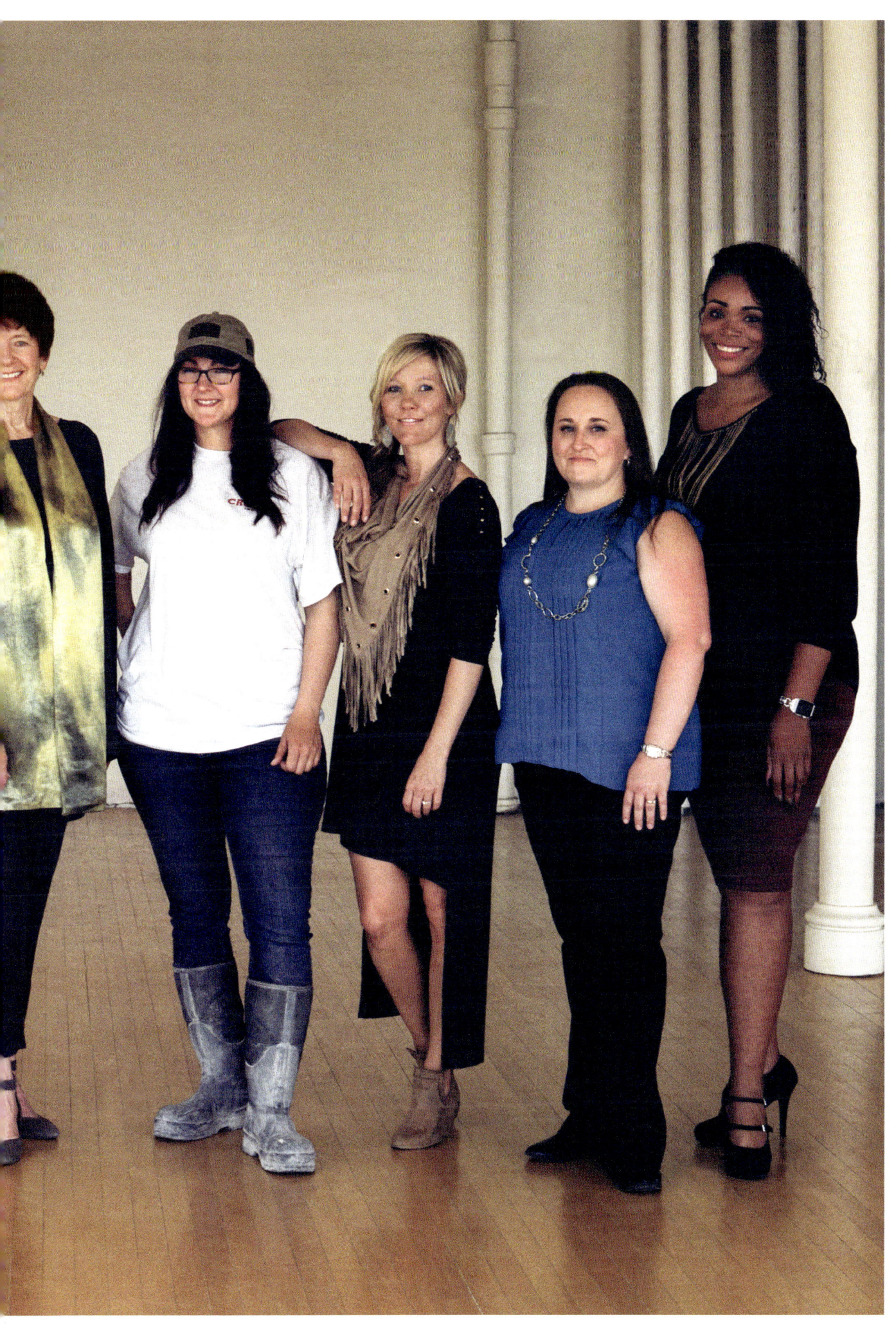

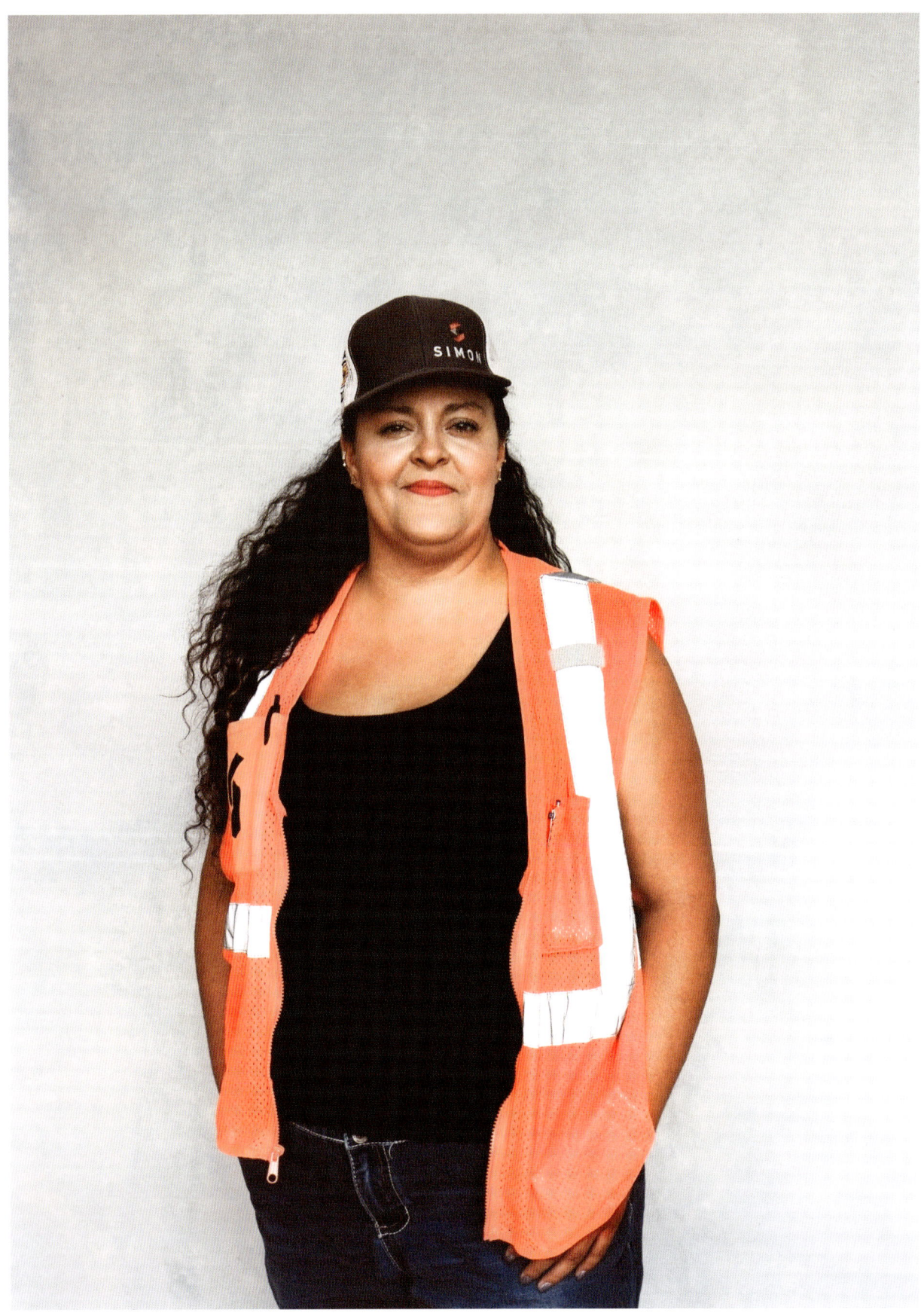

"I drive a concrete mixer. I love my job, and I'm able to buy my kids what they need and not struggle. You can do anything you put your mind to. Put the effort in; it's going to pay off."

—SARAH, CLIMB GRADUATE

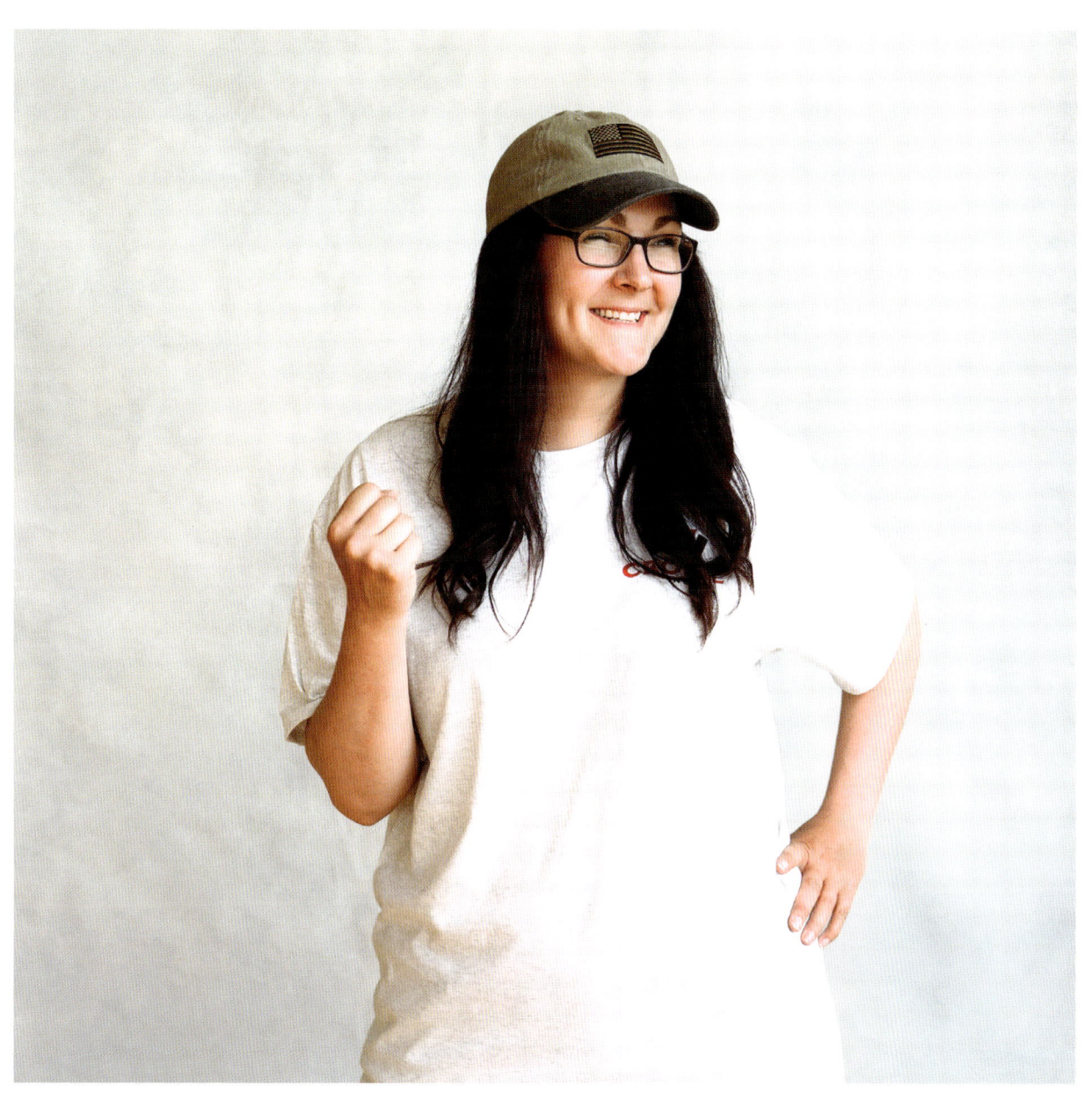

RITA E. WATSON

EXECUTIVE ASSISTANT TO THE STATE SUPERINTENDENT OF EDUCATION SINCE 1974,
COFOUNDER OF THE DR. MARTIN LUTHER KING JR. DAY MARCH IN CHEYENNE

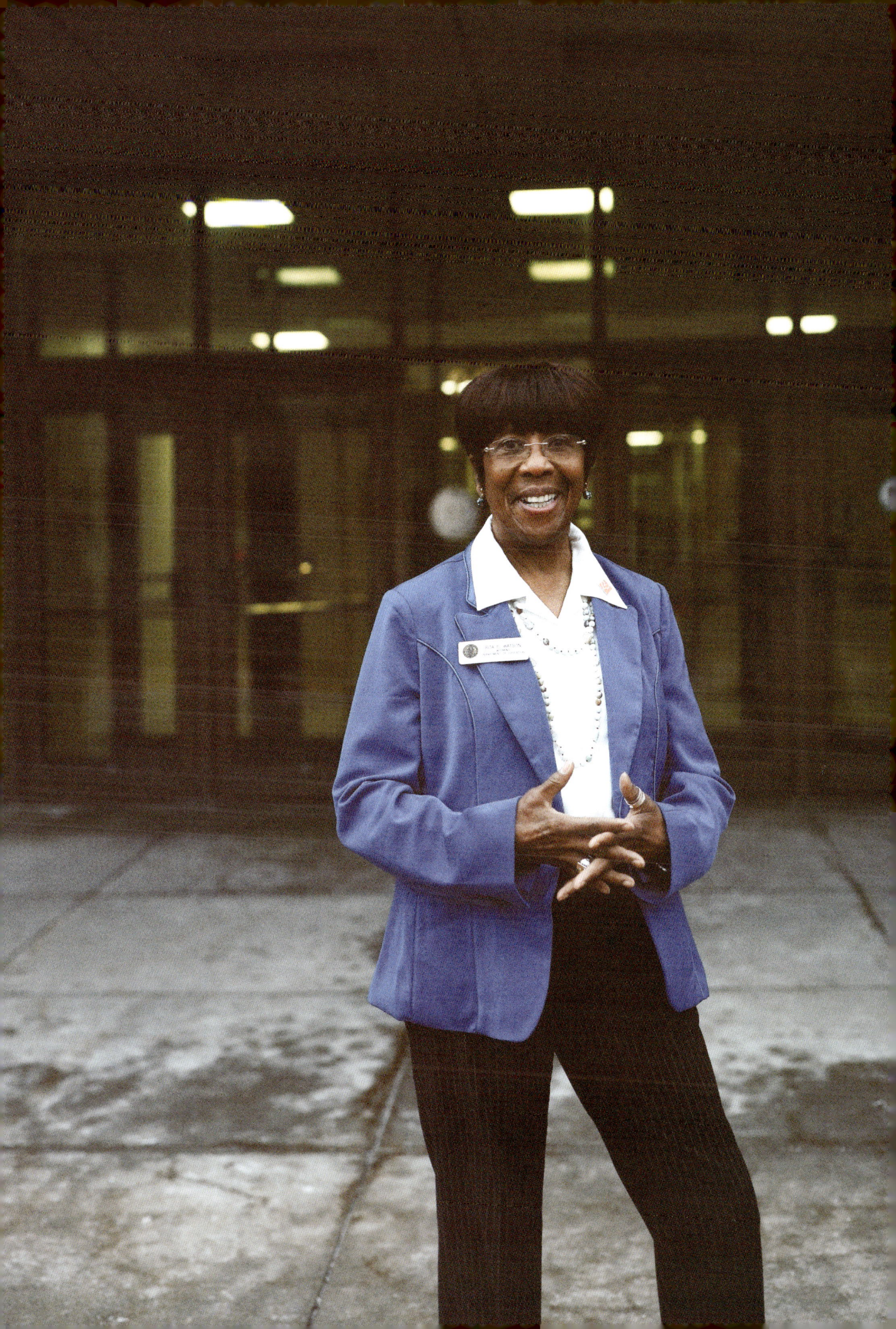

"We can make a better world. Our children need to see that there's hope and get active in the community to make life better for everybody."

"Department of Education, Rita Watson speaking. May I help you, please?"

It's a greeting countless Wyomingites have heard over the last fifty years. For half a century, Rita Watson has been the steady, welcoming voice at the Wyoming Department of Education—serving as its most enduring presence across generations of leadership and change.

Rita grew up in the Jim Crow South, in Durham, North Carolina. Life was difficult. Her mother worked as a house cleaner by day and at a tobacco factory by night. They had no indoor plumbing—an outdoor toilet served the family—and they walked up the street to collect water. Yet, her mother always made breakfast and dinner for Rita and her siblings. Their house was full of love. Later, when they moved into the city, life became a little easier.

Rita attended all-Black schools and credits her excellent education to the devoted teachers and mentors who uplifted her abilities. Outside her neighborhood, however, racism and exclusion were daily realities—dangerous ones. She learned early on to navigate a segregated world,

steering clear of certain parts of the city for her own safety.

Rita became the first Black employee at the Durham Woolworth's Five and Dime, paving the way for others to follow as civil rights slowly progressed in the United States. In 1969, her journey took an unexpected turn when her husband was transferred to F.E. Warren Air Force Base in Cheyenne. Upon arriving, Rita asked to see downtown. Her husband gestured around and said, "This is it!" Certain theirs would be a short stay, Rita took a job with the state—and ended up building a life. More than fifty years later, Cheyenne remains home and the community where Rita loves to make an impact.

Rita began her employment with the State of Wyoming in November 1969 at the Department of Health's Vital Records Services (now Wyoming Vital Statistics Services), transferring to the Department of Education in 1974. Since then, she's assisted nine Wyoming superintendents of public instruction: Dr. Robert Shrader, Lynn Simons, Diana J. Ohman, Judy Catchpole, Dr. Trent Blankenship, Dr. Jim

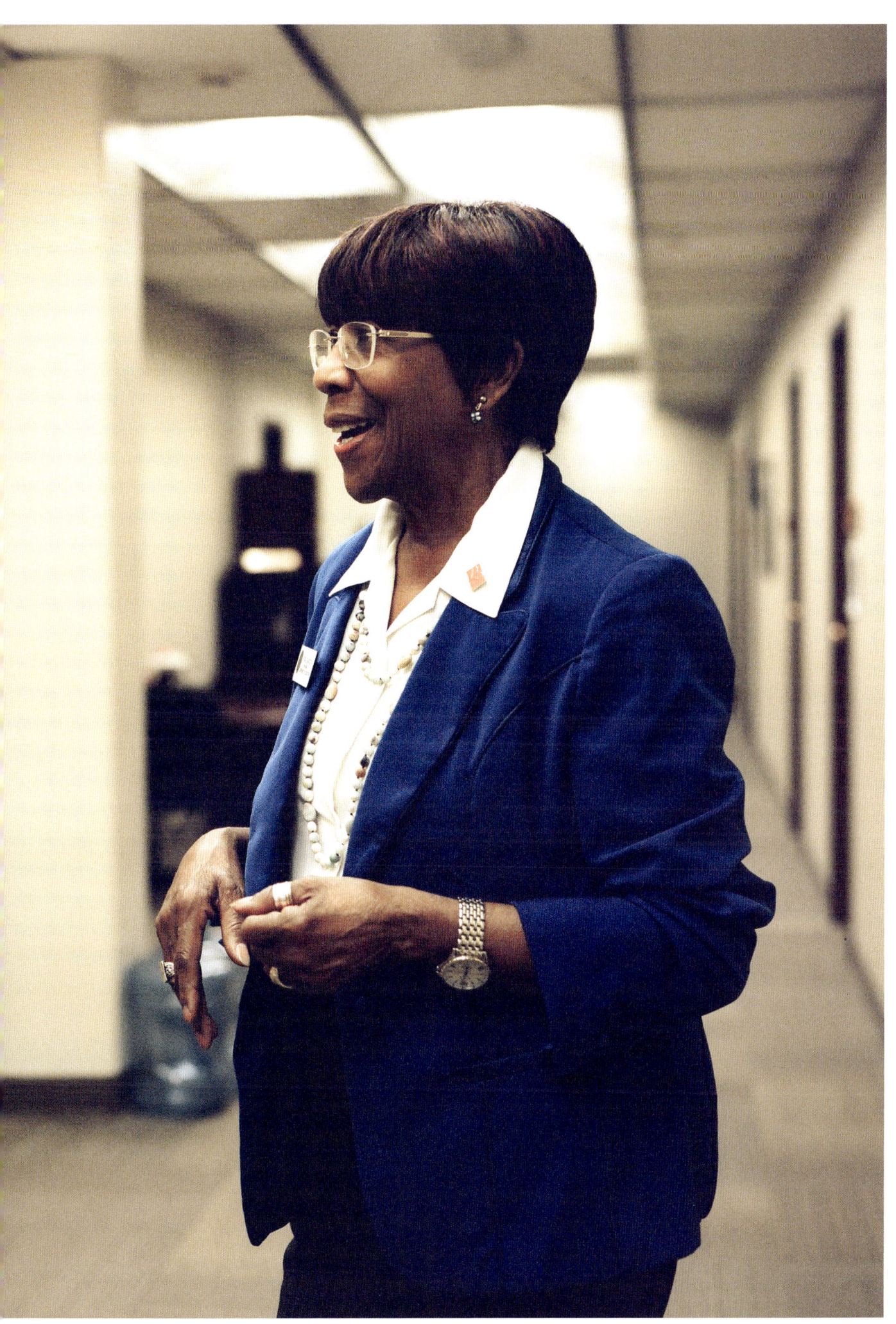

*"When you store information in your mind,
it is yours. No one can take that away from you."*

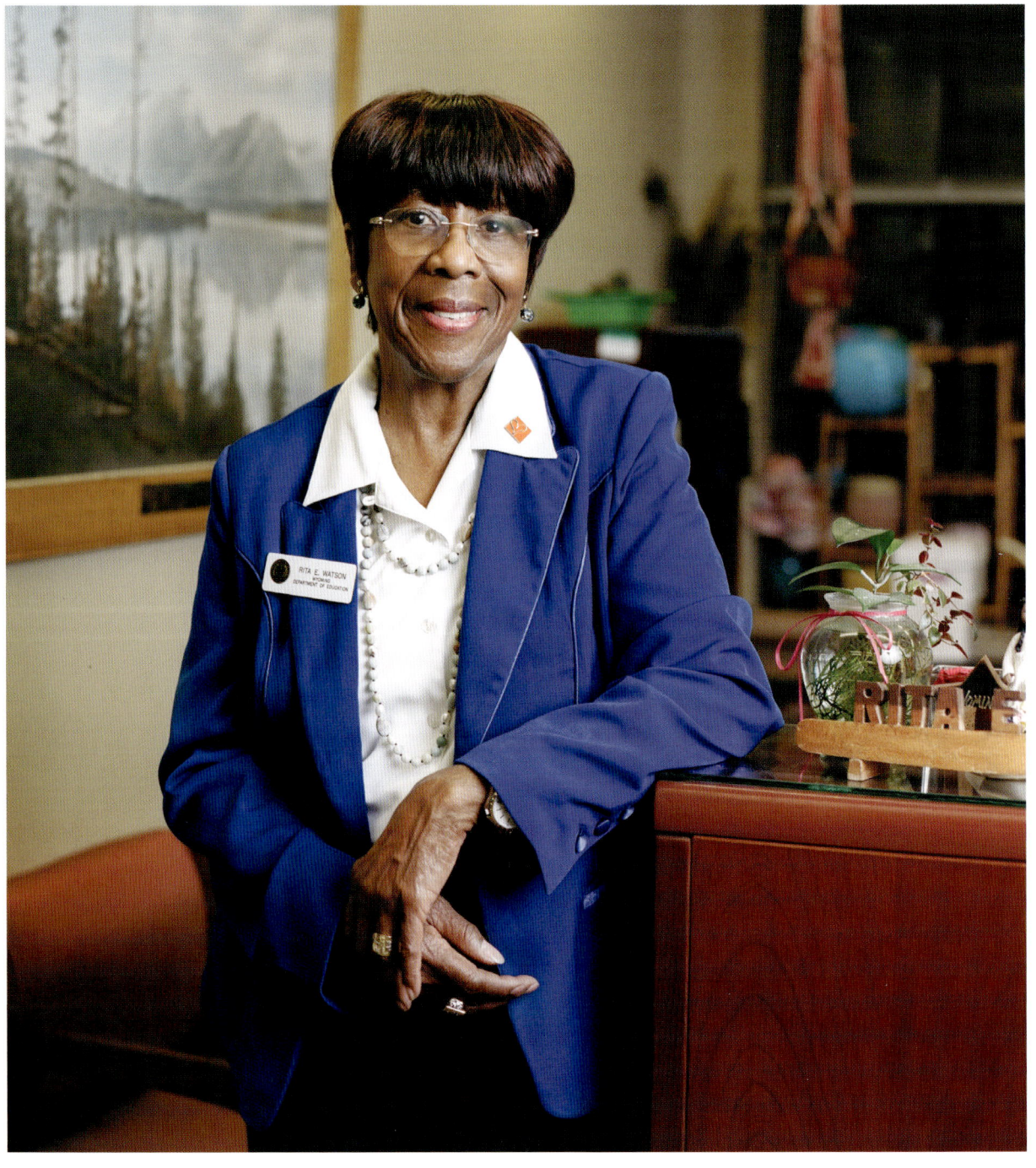

McBride, Cindy Hill, Jillian Balow, and Megan Degenfelder. She also supported two interim superintendents—Dr. Jim Rose and Richard Crandall—between 2011 and 2014. Through every administration, Rita has remained the department's beating heart.

Her commitment to education is deeply personal. The care and mentorship she received as a young student herself shaped her worldview and inspired a lifelong passion for helping others find their way. She recalls, "My teachers all through school taught us that a good education was the key to success. When you store information in your mind, it is yours. No one can take that away from you. I learned to put my best foot forward in my life." Rita loves to impart this wisdom with the next generation. That's why she's stayed. Quite simply, Rita loves her job. She loves making an impact and a difference in the lives of young people.

Outside of work, Rita is a pillar of the Cheyenne community. She's a founding member of the Love & Charity Club, best known for organizing Cheyenne's annual Dr. Martin Luther King Jr. Day March since 1982. She is active in her church, having served multiple roles throughout the years, from chairman of the trustee board to treasurer, secretary, church clerk, usher, and choir member. She is a past member of the Cheyenne City Personnel Board, Meals on Wheels of Cheyenne, and the University of Wyoming Citizen of the Century Committee. She is a member of Wyoming Chapter 6 District and School Accreditation, the Order of the Eastern Star, the Cheyenne branch of the NAACP, and the Empowerment Conference Committee.

As for retirement? Don't count on it. "I love what I do," she says. "I can't think of anything else I'd rather do . . . other than work!"

At her core, Rita is driven by a simple but powerful mission: to make a difference—in education, in her community, and in the lives of others. Exactly as she has done for more than half a century.

WYOMING LATINA YOUTH CONFERENCE

LEADERSHIP, SCIENCE, AND CREATIVITY CONFERENCE

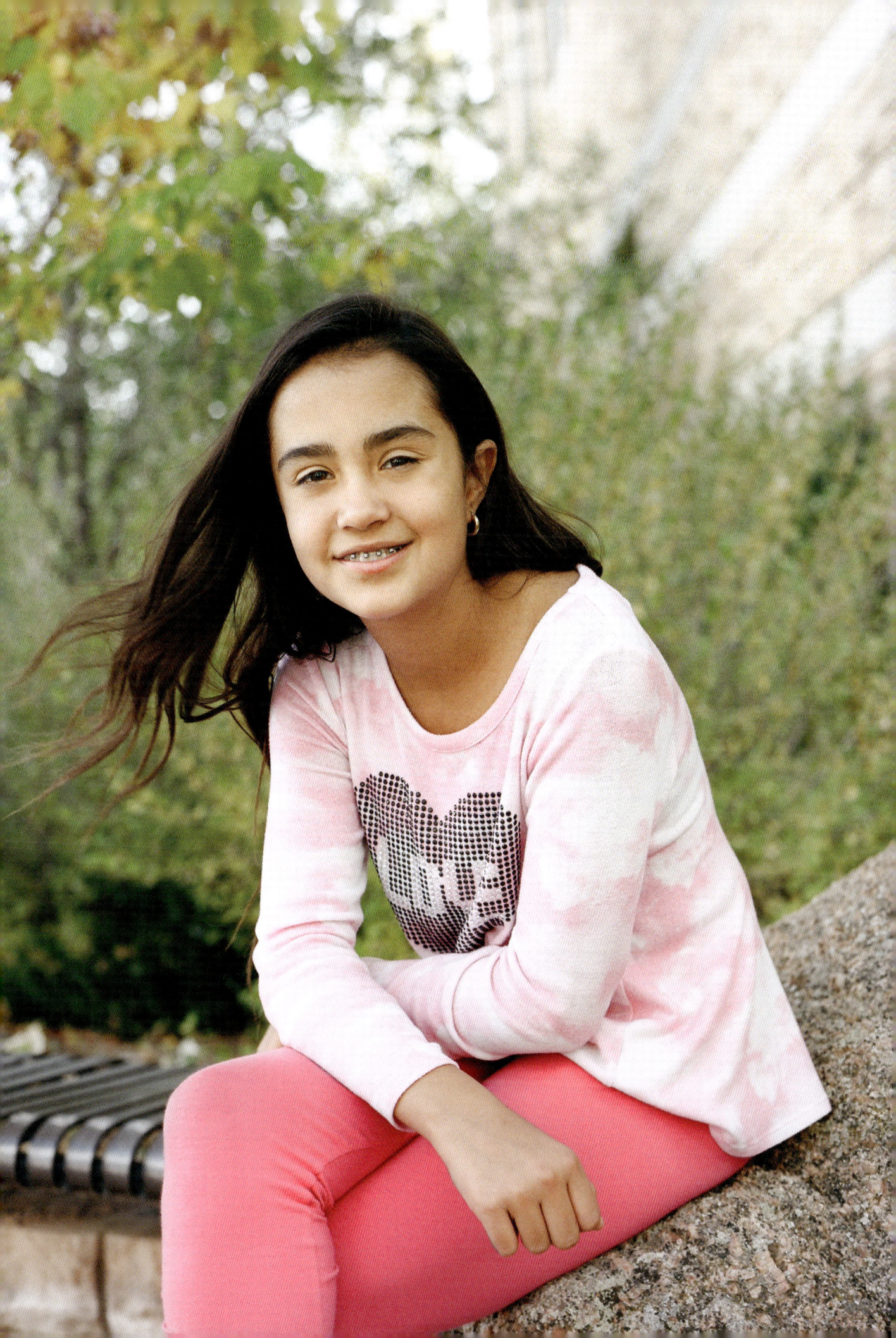

"*If you think small, you'll never get big.*"

—SKYE, WLYC PARTICIPANT

When women and girls come together, their power is amplified—and that spirit is at the heart of the Wyoming Latina Youth Conference (WLYC). The conference is a vibrant celebration of creativity, leadership, and STEAM (science, technology, engineering, the arts, and mathematics), centered around "The Power of Choice" and designed to foster "a positive mindset for growth, leadership, and academic success." WLYC aims to raise the aspirational wealth of Wyoming Latinas in grades 5 through 12.

More than 350 girls—many from isolated communities across the state—gather to connect, learn, and build community. Classrooms buzz with energy as attendees engage in hands-on workshops and hear from nationally recognized keynote speakers, all while gaining exposure to higher education. "There's no giving up; as the Nike quote goes, just do it," said Raquel about her dreams and motivation while attending the conference. The atmosphere is electric, and positivity radiates from every corner.

WLYC was founded in 2000, by Ann Esquibel Redman, a longtime community leader who

has called Wyoming home since 1950. After a distinguished career in state government—serving under Governors Herschler, Sullivan, and Freudenthal—Ann turned her focus to addressing issues disproportionately affecting minority youth, including teen pregnancy, high school dropout, and suicide. The conference she built offers a proactive, empowering alternative: encouraging Latina youth to own their ambition, cultivate self-confidence, and envision a brighter future. For her advocacy on behalf of the Hispanic community, Ann has received numerous honors, including the Lifetime Achievement Award for Women of Influence (2017), the Athena Award from the Greater Cheyenne Chamber of Commerce, and the Woman of Distinction Award from the University of Wyoming. Since 2015, Dr. Cecilia Aragon has led WLYC and continues to grow its statewide impact.

"Get that mindset—*you can't*—out of your mind. Strive for what you believe in," said Carmen, a teen adviser and past attendee. In addition to fostering confidence and leadership, WLYC places strong emphasis on overall wellness. Through workshops on building

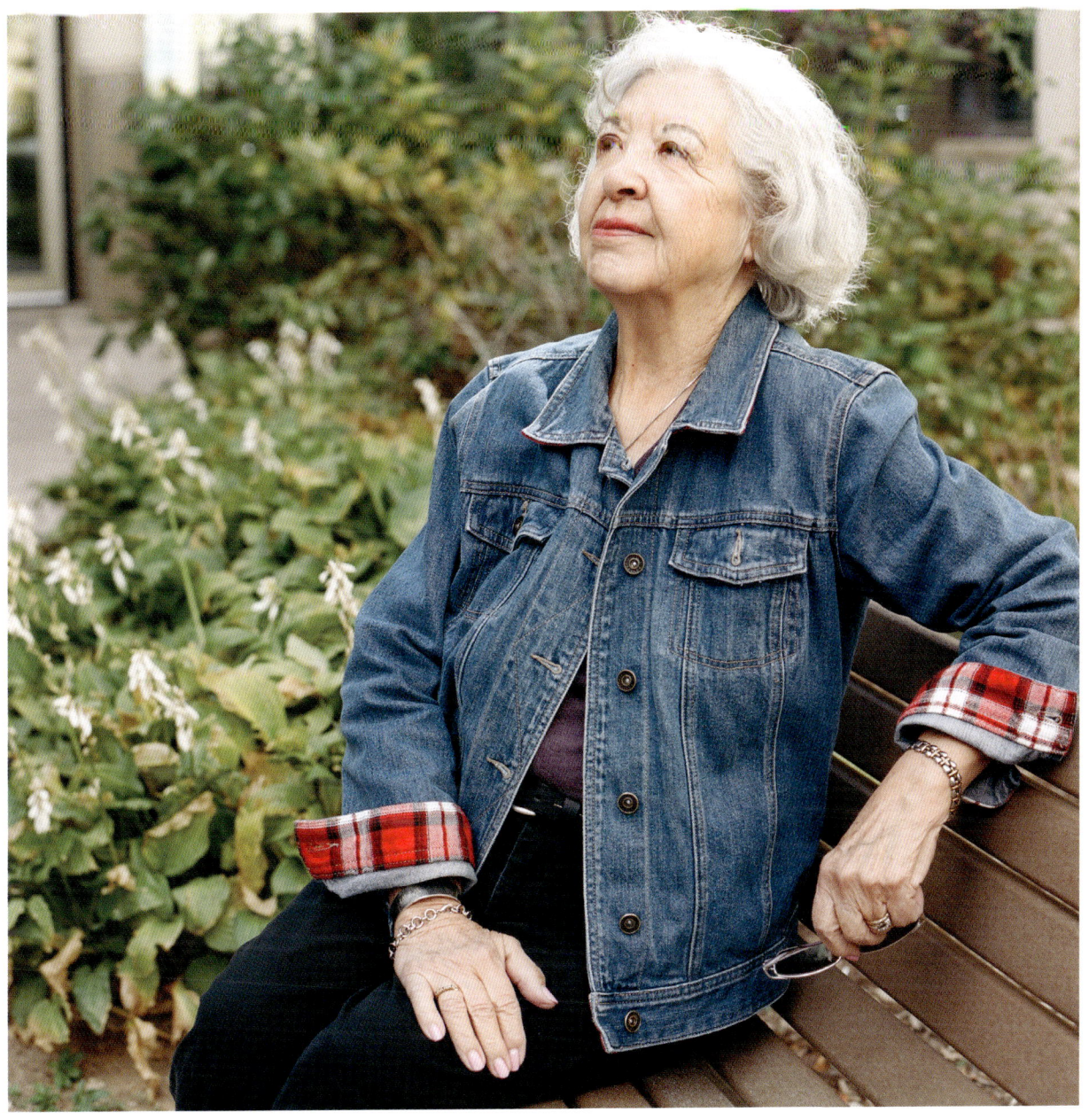

"*It's all about the power of choice.
You have the power to change your life.*"

—ANN ESQUIBEL REDMAN, FOUNDER

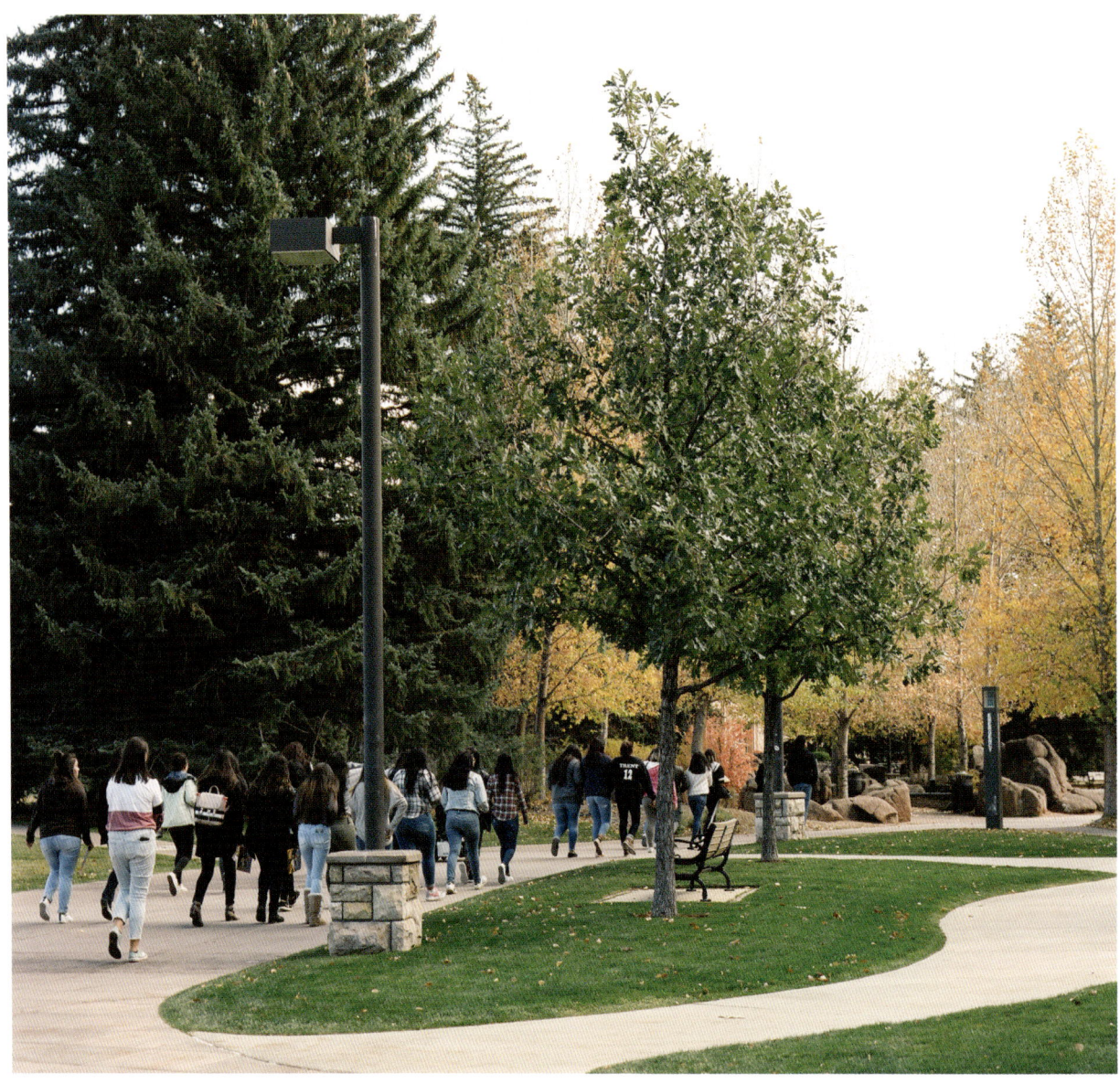

healthy relationships—including the power of setting boundaries—as well as on nutrition and mental health, the conference takes a holistic approach to empowering young women.

Expanding attendees' awareness of what can be possible for their life leaves a powerful impact. At its core, WLYC is about connection. Friendship and relationship-building are central to the experience, and many attendees return year after year—eventually coming back as speakers, advisers, and mentors once they graduate from the program.

Facing Page:
Carmen, WLYC
Participant

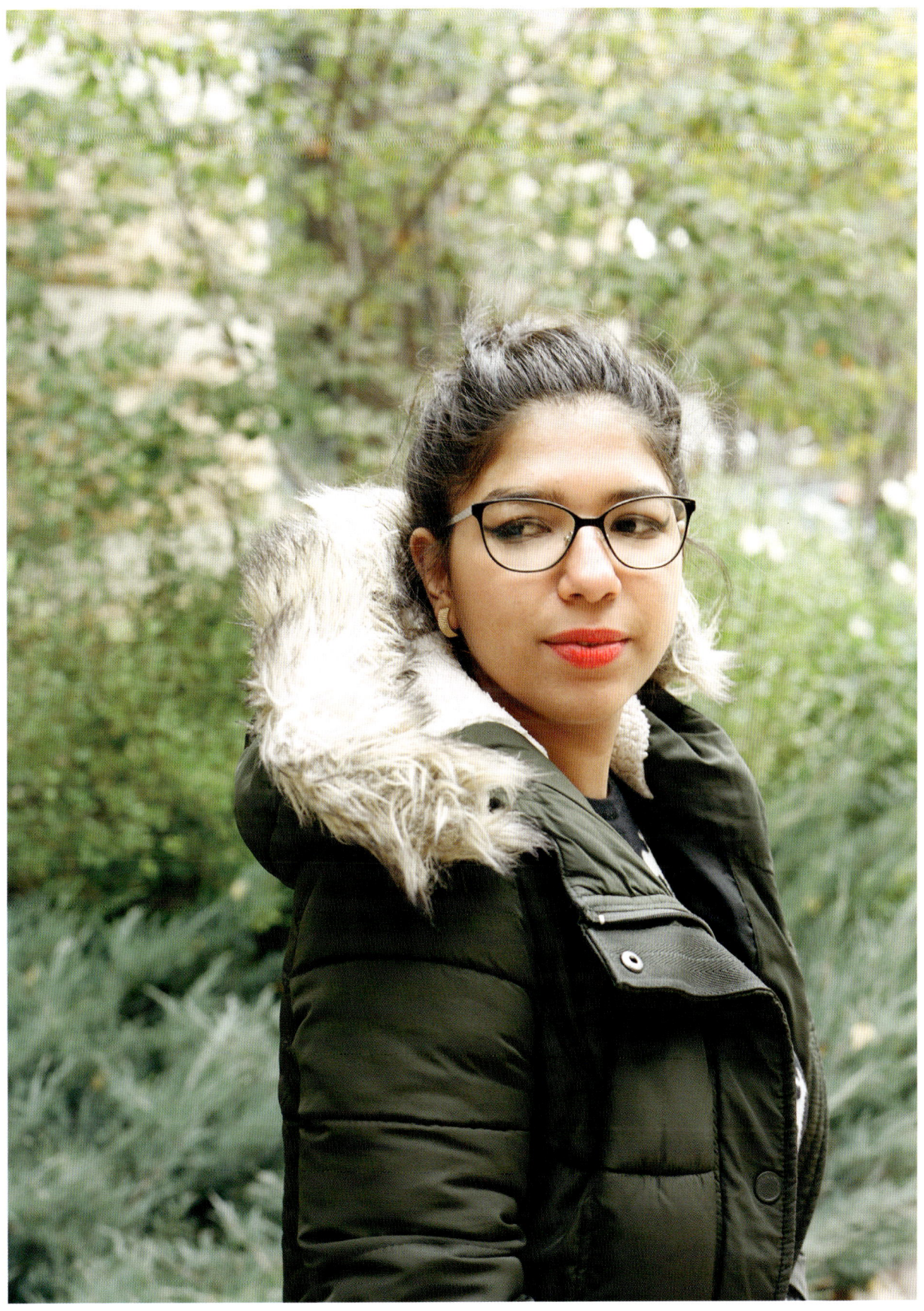

AURA SUNADA NEWLIN, PhD

ANTHROPOLOGIST, EXECUTIVE DIRECTOR
OF THE HEART MOUNTAIN WYOMING FOUNDATION

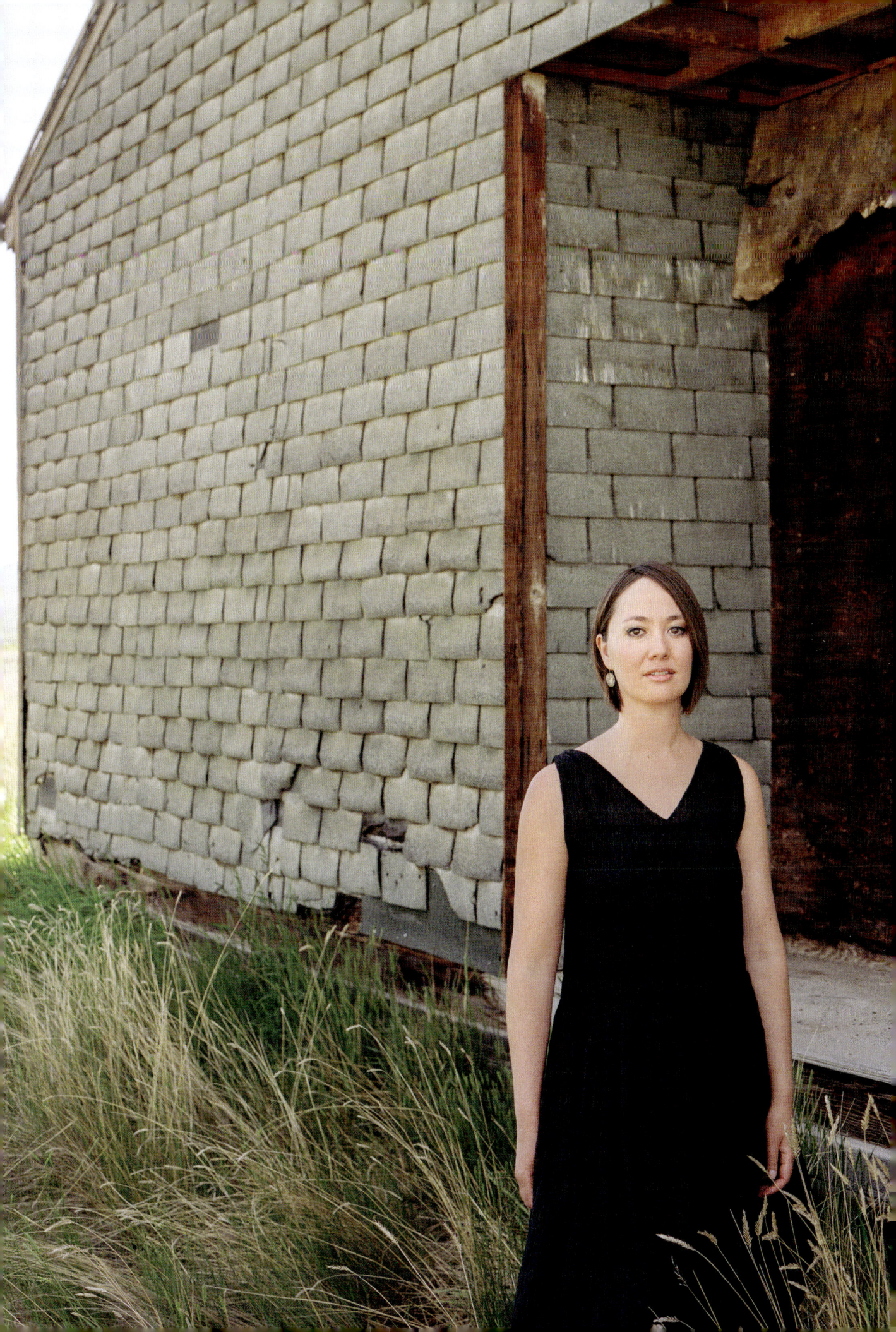

"The more that we make an effort to hear people, learn about their realities, and empathize with their situations, it is harder to fear and hate them and easier to feel compassion toward them."

Compassion. Empathy. Understanding. These aren't just values for anthropologist Aura Sunada Newlin—they're the driving forces behind her work, her worldview, and her voice.

At its core, anthropology is the study of what it means to be human—of how we make meaning, construct belief systems, and pass down the stories that shape our identities. For many, the idea of critically examining those foundations is uncomfortable. For Aura, it's exhilarating.

Her journey—one of studying human experiences and uncovering truths—has brought her back to a place rooted in both personal and national history: the Heart Mountain confinement site, where her own relatives were imprisoned during World War II, simply for being Japanese American. Today, Aura, as executive director, leads the Heart Mountain Wyoming Foundation and its world-class museum, preserving this site and sharing its legacy with the nation.

A fourth-generation Japanese Wyomingite, Aura grew up in Riverton, shaped by parents who had served in the Peace Corps and instilled in their children a global perspective. That early exposure to different cultures sparked Aura's lifelong curiosity about the human experience and led her to anthropology. "Anthropology turns everything on its head," she says. "We try to understand what it might be like to live in someone else's shoes—to see the world through their eyes."

She loves passing that perspective on to her students, encouraging them to question what's considered "normal" or "natural"—and whether those beliefs stem from truth, tradition, or simply upbringing.

Aura previously taught anthropology and sociology at Northwest College in Powell—just fifteen miles from Heart Mountain—as well as Asian American studies at the University of Wyoming. Teaching so close to the site felt serendipitous. After Pearl Harbor, up to 14,000 Japanese American citizens and immigrants were incarcerated at Heart Mountain, one of ten camps established by the War Relocation Authority.

Aura's family history is entwined with that painful chapter. Her grandmother grew up

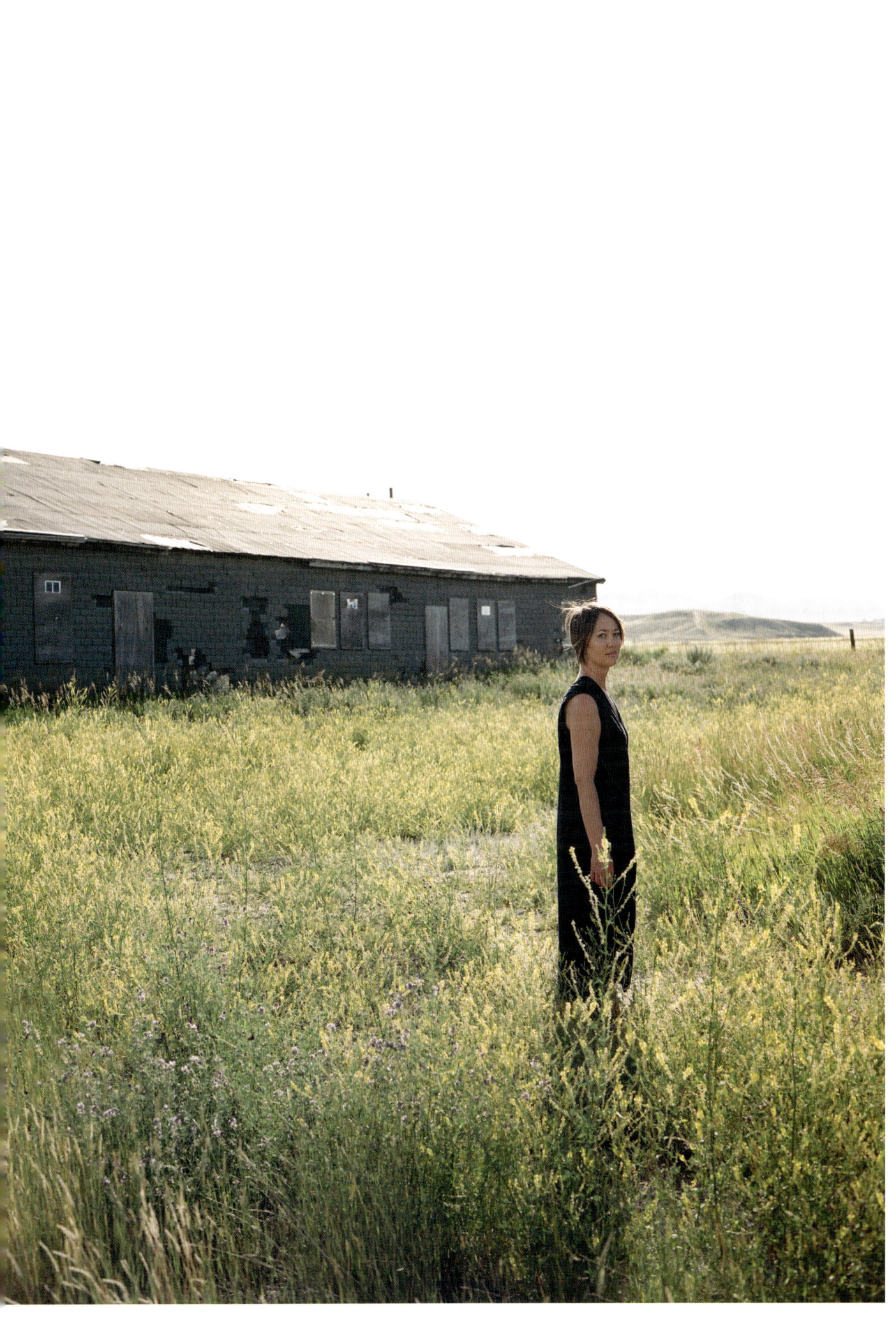

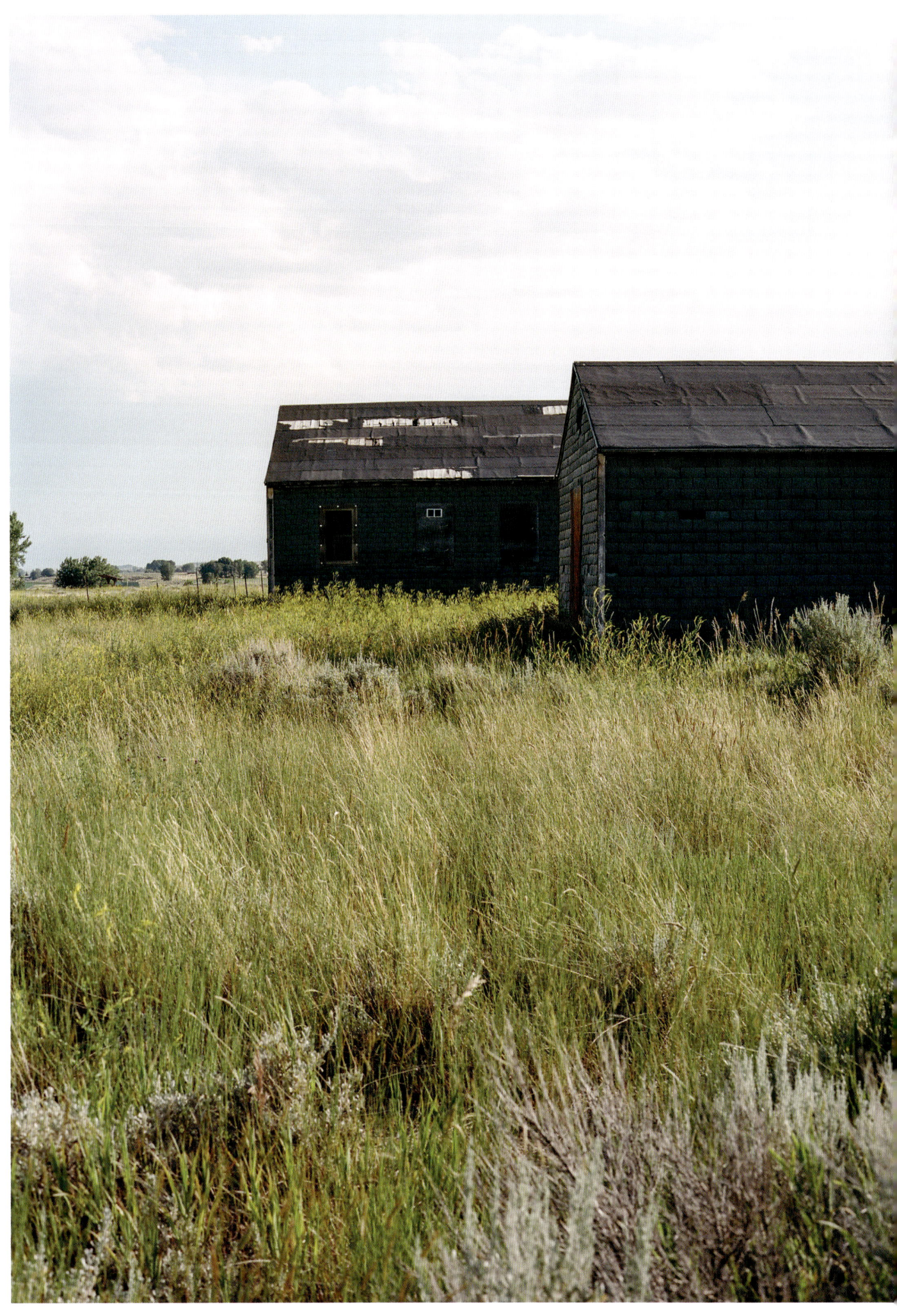

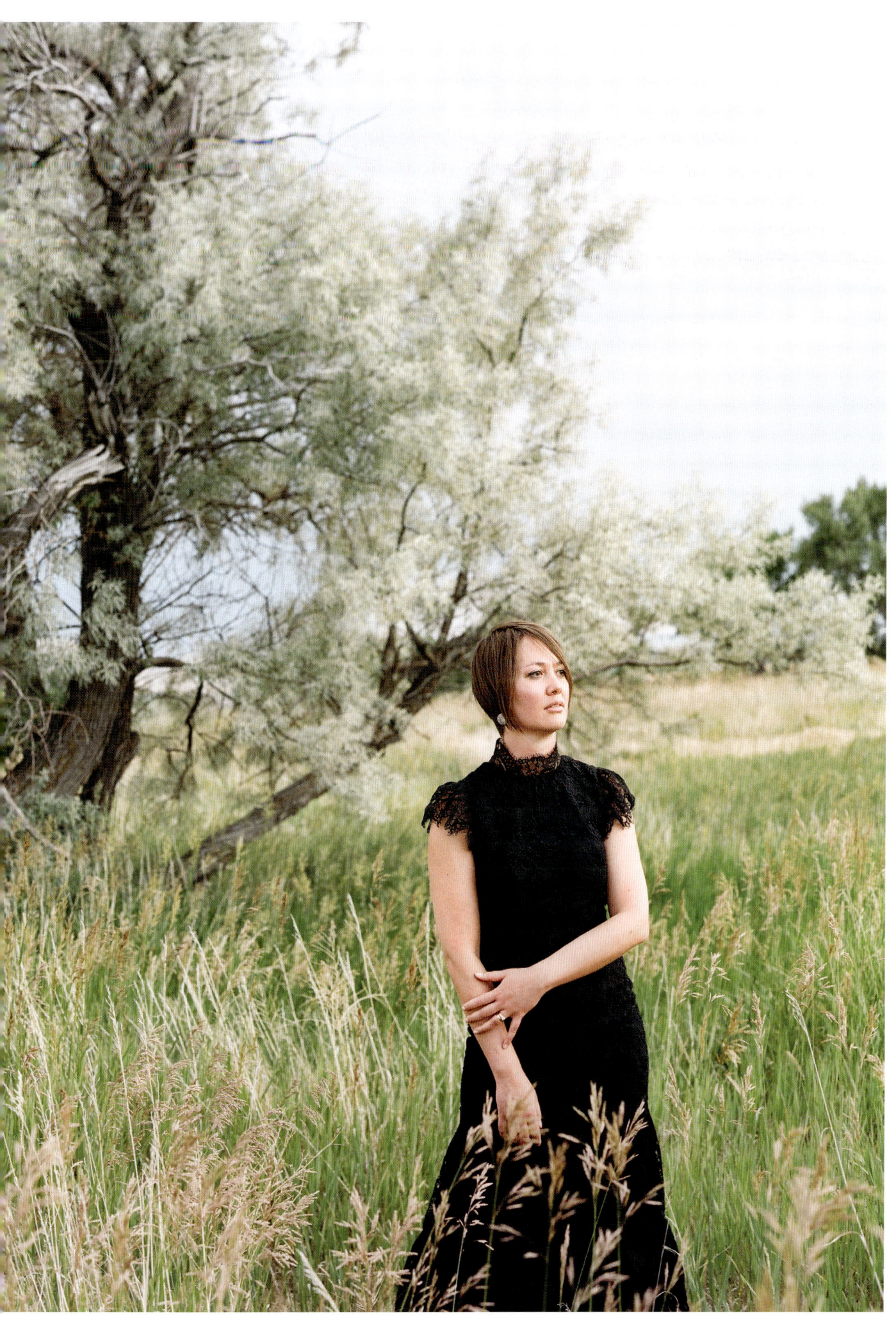

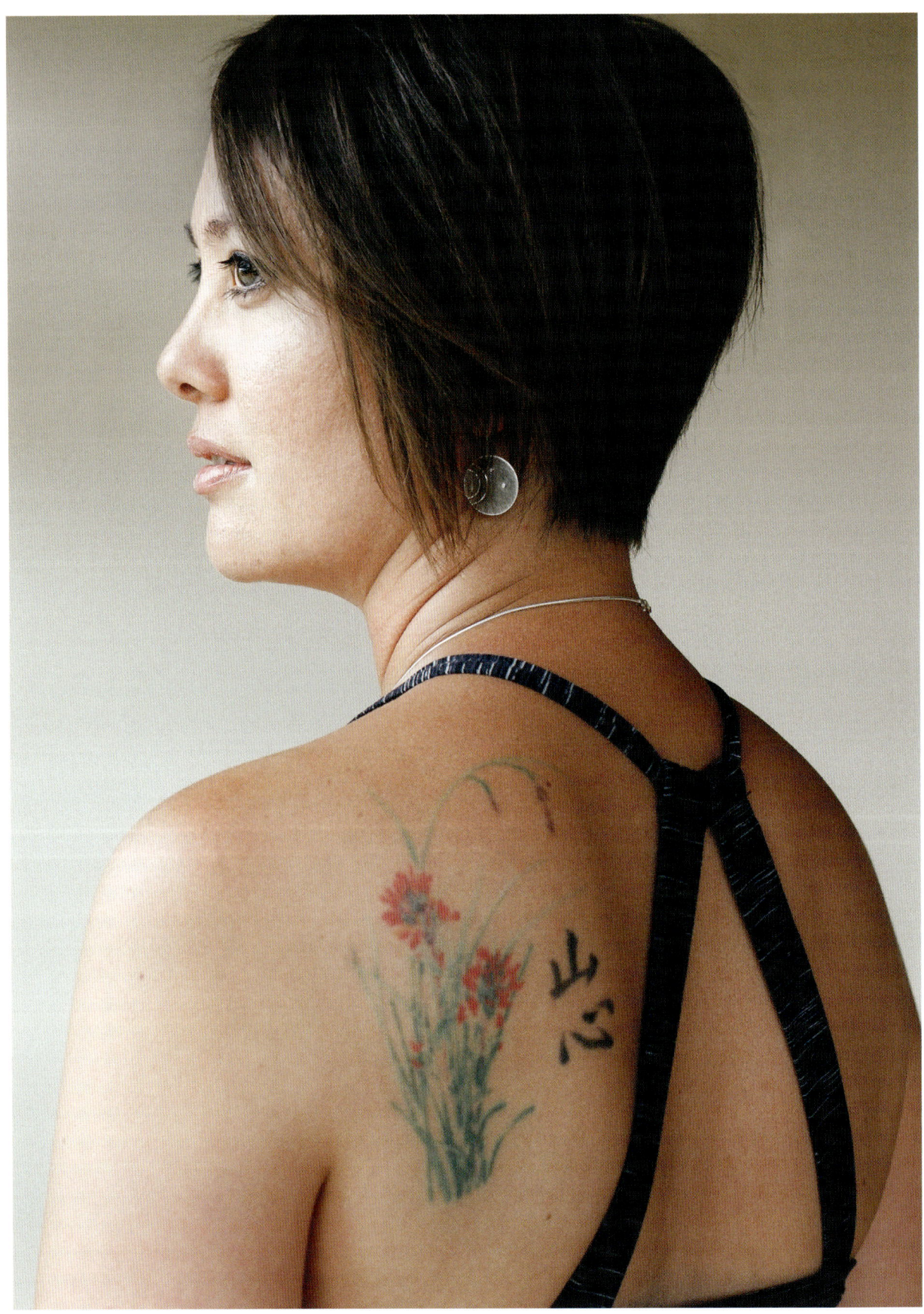

"If you are relentlessly kind and relentlessly generous, it disarms people in a way, and that brings a sense of power that is not coercive."

in southern Wyoming, where her immigrant parents made their careers as a railroader and a midwife. In the late 1930s, the family of nine moved to East Hollywood, California, and established a grocery store called the Wyoming Market. But when President Franklin D. Roosevelt signed Executive Order 9066, Aura's great-grandfather was forcibly removed and sent back to Wyoming—this time, as a prisoner. Her grandfather, then working for the Union Pacific Railroad in Green River, was fired along with other employees of Japanese descent. Though later offered his job back, he declined.

For Aura, this work is more than professional—it's ancestral. "We need to embrace the bad along with the good," she reflects. "It's part of what makes us who we are. I don't see Heart Mountain as something that belongs only to Japanese American history. It is American history. It is Wyoming history."

In her public talks across the country, Aura hopes to pass along not just the facts of history, but the passion and hope that fuel her. "I want us to be heard," she says. "Because we have an important story that needs to be told. And I like telling it."

As the world continues to change at breakneck speed, Aura encourages her audiences to think more deeply, see more broadly, and honor one another's differences—not just to remember the past, but to imagine a better future, together.

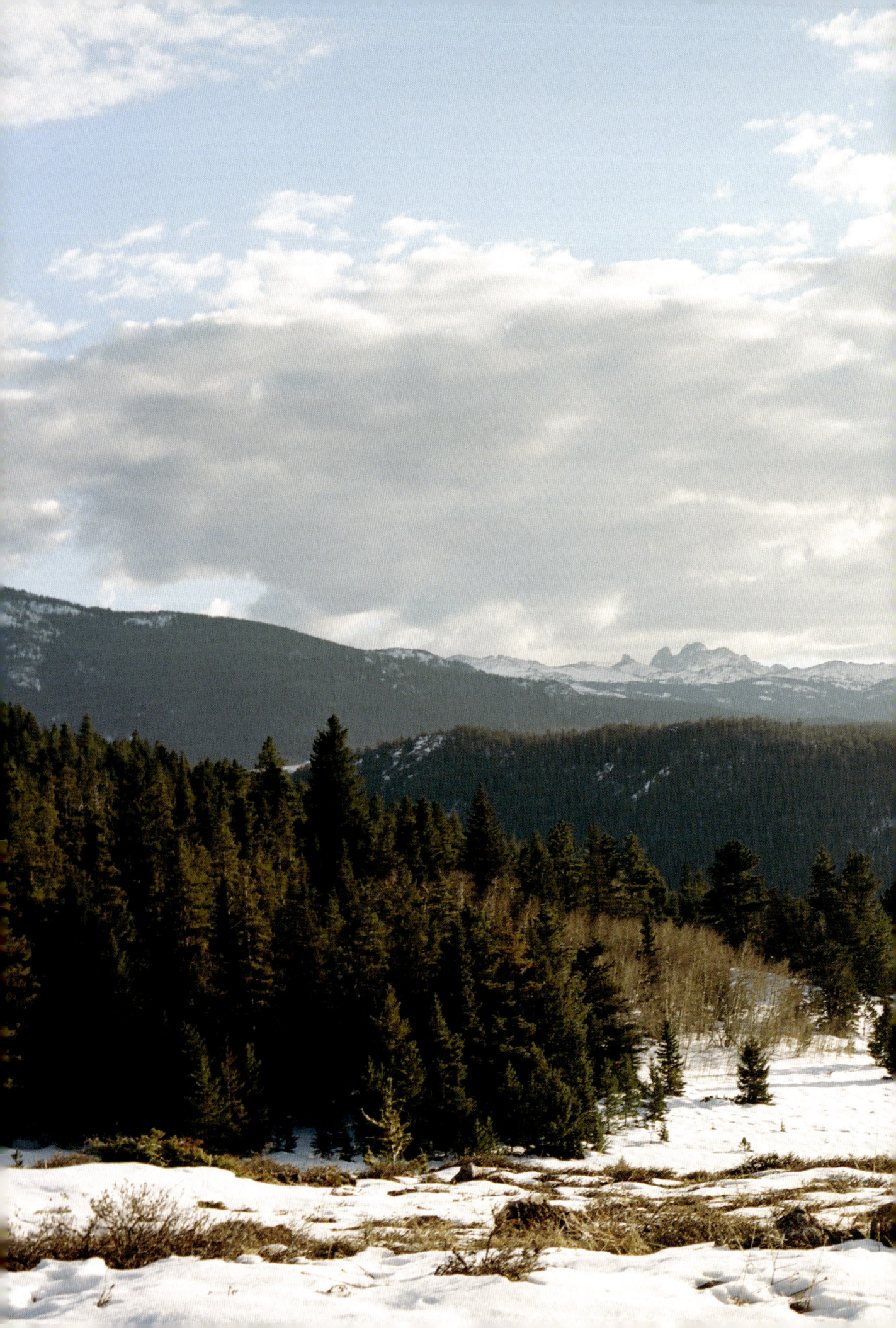

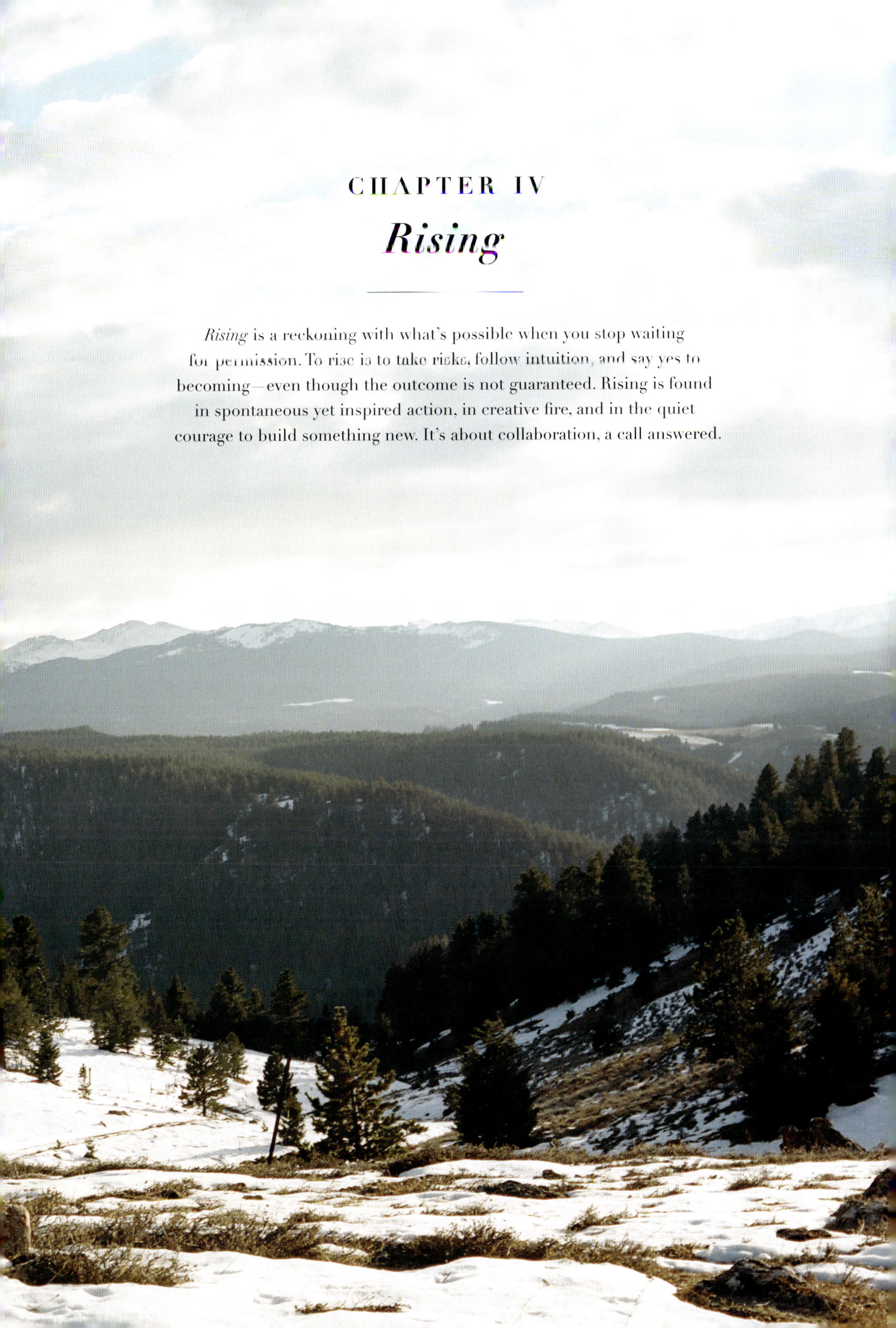

CHAPTER IV
Rising

Rising is a reckoning with what's possible when you stop waiting
for permission. To rise is to take risks, follow intuition, and say yes to
becoming—even though the outcome is not guaranteed. Rising is found
in spontaneous yet inspired action, in creative fire, and in the quiet
courage to build something new. It's about collaboration, a call answered.

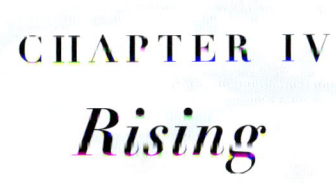

Behind the Scenes:
Into the Air with Commander Lauren Gurney

In this part of Wyoming, high winds whip across the prairie as predictably as the cycle of ocean tides. After being grounded for the morning and all afternoon, a moment of calm finally permits us to ascend. It's a biting early winter day, and our only window to fly is now. We leap from our relaxed conversation into a whirlwind of action. Commander Lauren Gurney, her copilot, and two paramedics all grab their gear, urgency igniting every movement. I clutch my camera, mentally calculating the remaining film on the roll. Adrenaline buzzes in my veins.

We bolt to the tarmac, the scent of aviation fuel sharp and exhilarating. There's limited time for staged portraits because we need to commence the test flight as soon as possible, with the current weather window. "Turn here!" I shout. The gravitas of the scene before me is so impressive, with Commander Gurney and the imposing presence of the Black Hawk helicopter behind her. The light is sharp. I capture a few stoic shots and know I've "got it" before Lauren leaps into the cockpit. Inside, the flight deck resembles a complex puzzle, a hundred buttons illuminating the metal dash. There is zero automation in this bird. My pulse quickens as Lauren meticulously sequences every command, ensuring readiness. Meanwhile, I fix a set of headphones around my ears and buckle into a shoulder-harness seat-belt system. One of the paramedics lends his muscle to tug the straps tighter.

As the engines roar to life in a thunderous symphony, I feel the vibrations resonating throughout my entire body. Even through headphones, the Black Hawk's blades oscillate with a deafening roar. This flight is not about comfort. Lauren, totally in her element, glances back to flash a thumbs-up and a confident smile. It's go time.

We hover for a moment before dancing upward, floating at first, then with velocity to break free into the endless Wyoming sky, into weightlessness, into thinner atmosphere, and beyond. F.E. Warren Air Force Base and Cheyenne's city limits are soon out of sight. Only pastel plains remain as the world below recedes.

The evening light fades to dusk and eventually dark. I watch Wyoming's only female medevac pilot and her team practice complex technical maneuvers that, during combat, save lives. I'm jostled left, right, up, and down. Thank goodness for this harness keeping me somewhat seated. Lauren's skill, ability, and tact are obvious, even to my totally novice eyes. Here's a pilot who could have chosen a much safer path in life but directed herself to one of danger to serve others. She's a woman on a mission.

I'm on the knife-edge. I visualize the enormous pressure and intensity of flying into a war zone, where life and death are the literal stakes. What drives someone to want this?

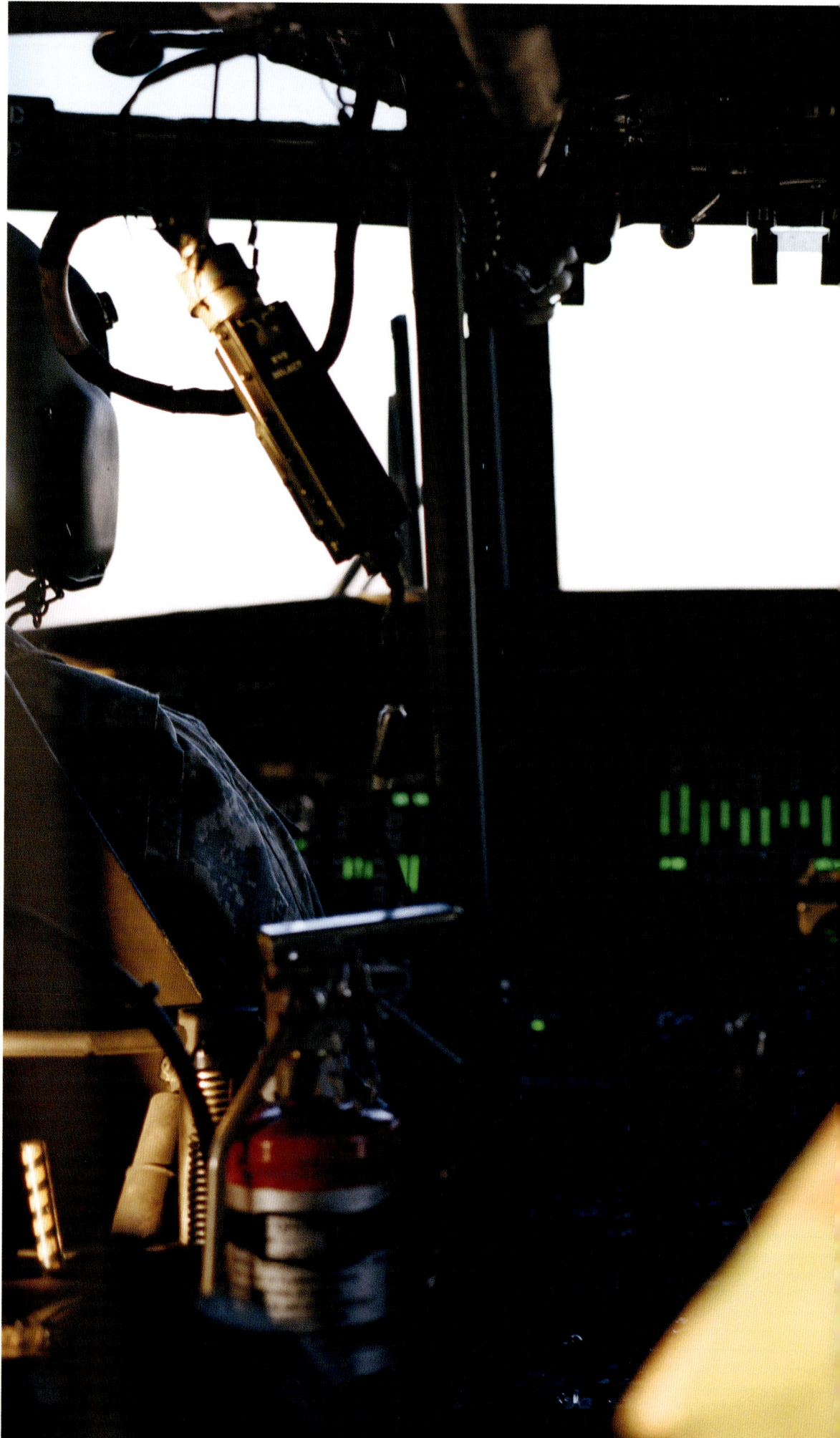

WARNING, SEAT
DO NOT ERATE UNL
DEPRESS VERTICAL RELEA
PUSH SEAT BUCKET T

COMMANDER LAUREN "LOLO" GURNEY

WYOMING'S ONLY FEMALE DUSTOFF MEDEVAC PILOT,
COMMANDER OF G CO. 2-211TH AVIATION REGIMENT

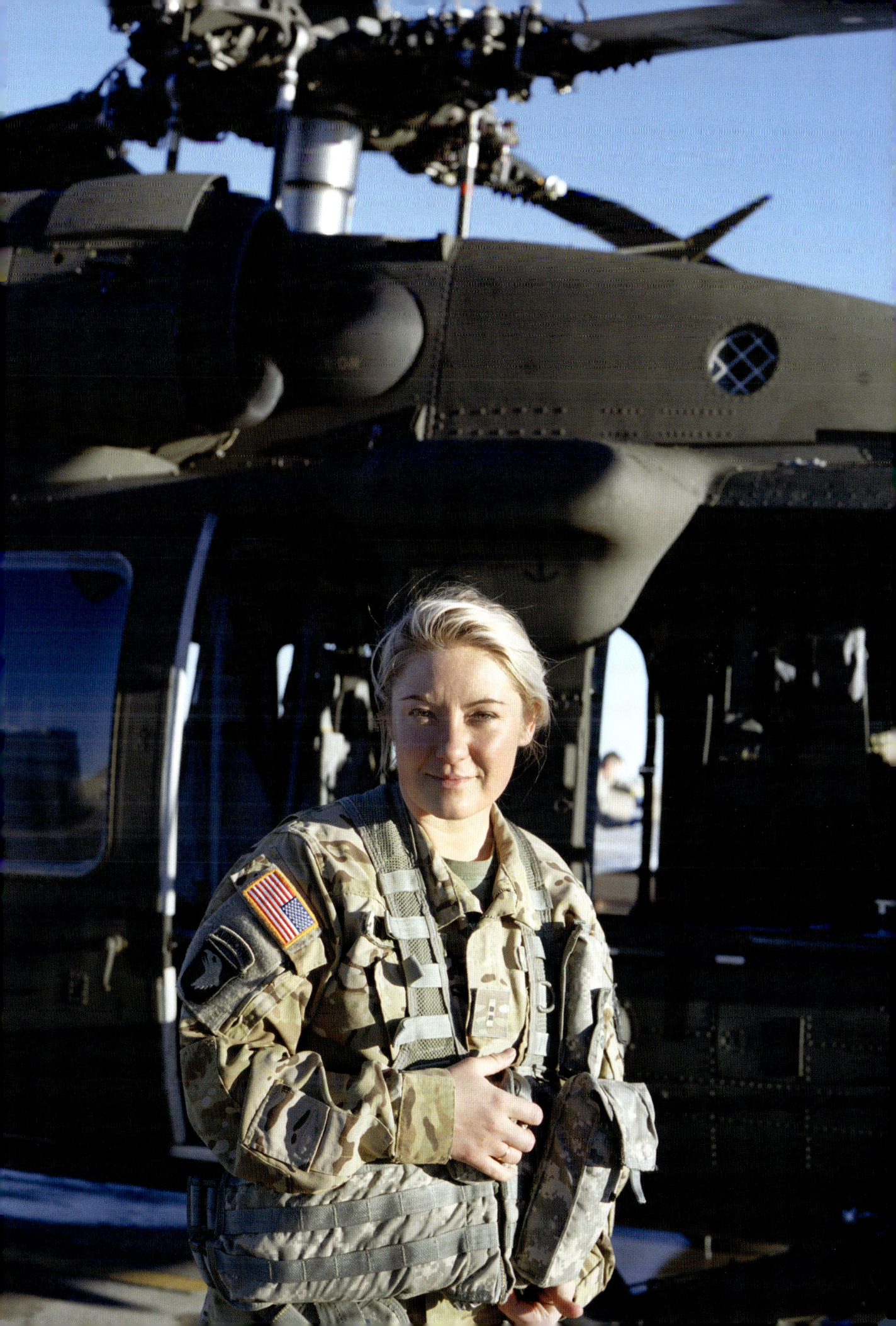

"It clicked 100 percent to be a medevac pilot and save lives. DUSTOFF stands for 'dedicated unhesitating service to our fighting forces,' and I feel that so inherently in my bones once I get into a helicopter."

Wyoming's only female army medevac pilot and the first woman to serve as a commander for the rotary wing regiment in Wyoming, Lauren Gurney is a leader whose mission in aviation is to save lives. She pilots Sikorsky UH-60 Black Hawk helicopters, but her flight journey had whimsical beginnings—first sparked by the movie *Dumbo*. As a child, she'd leap across her home with arms outstretched, determined to defy gravity.

Lauren began honing her tactical instincts early. Between the ages of nine and nineteen, she raced cars with her dad and worked as a mechanic on his pit crew. At sixteen, she was named "Mechanic of the Year" by the Sports Car Club of America. Problem-solving, understanding systems, and knowing how machines work laid the foundation for flying the complex aircraft she commands today.

Her grandfather Doc Gurney was one of her most influential mentors. A Korean War paramedic, a veterinarian, and a NASA Valkyrie project technician, he modeled a life of service, science, and boundless curiosity. Inspired by him, Lauren was captivated by space, medicine,

and a call to fly. She enlisted in the army at seventeen and studied pre-medicine in military college, initially intending to become a doctor—until she met Black Hawk pilots. Five years later, she graduated with honors from flight school.

Lauren has since served multiple overseas deployments, including combat missions in Iraq and Syria, where she was the officer in charge. She's been a pilot in command and a maintenance test pilot with the Wyoming National Guard since 2016, and a medevac pilot since 2010. For her, DUSTOFF— "dedicated unhesitating service to our fighting forces"—is more than an acronym; it's a lived mission.

Aware that warfare is destructive and not everyone comes home, Lauren is proactive with her mental health. During a particularly intense deployment, she reached out to a mindfulness coach via social media and began working with her over satellite phone. Since then, she has continued cultivating mindset tools and practices, leading from a deeper, more grounded place. That inner work has paid off. As the

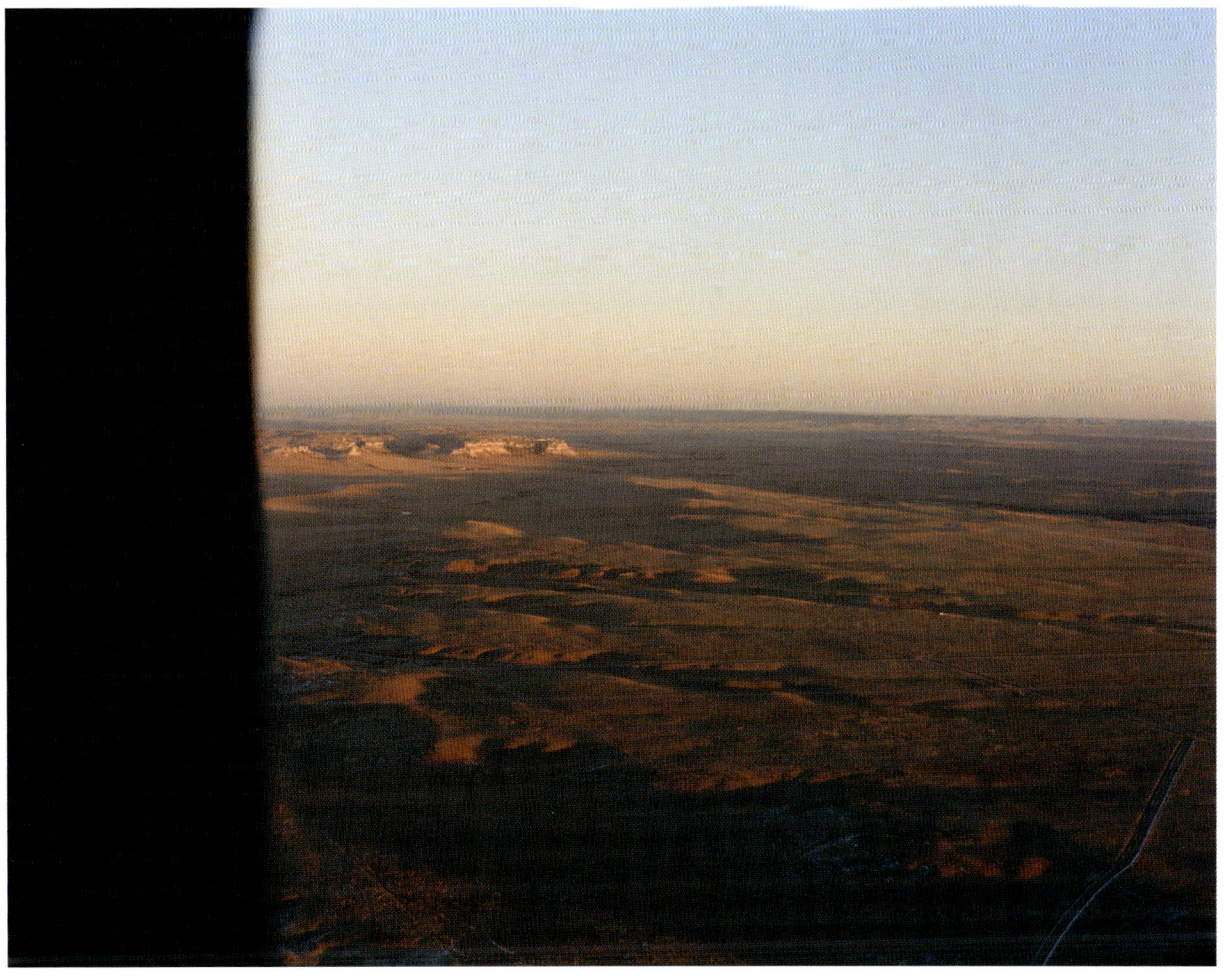

first woman in Wyoming to command G Co. 2-211th Aviation Regiment at F.E. Warren Air Force Base in Cheyenne, she has led the Army Aviation Support Facility to the number-one operational rate in the country.

When she's not piloting an aircraft or guiding her team, Lauren expresses her creative joy as a self-taught baker and chocolatier. She's owned multiple baking businesses over the years—including Jackson Cake Co. and CoCopelli Chocolatier in New Mexico—and has baked in every country she's been deployed. For Lauren, baking is an outlet: a way to build community through love and connection.

Flying, she says, is never a solo mission. Trust and teamwork are the heart of DUSTOFF. Lauren and her team place their lives in each other's hands every time they lift off. It's in those relationships—grounded in purpose, precision, and care—where Commander Gurney truly soars.

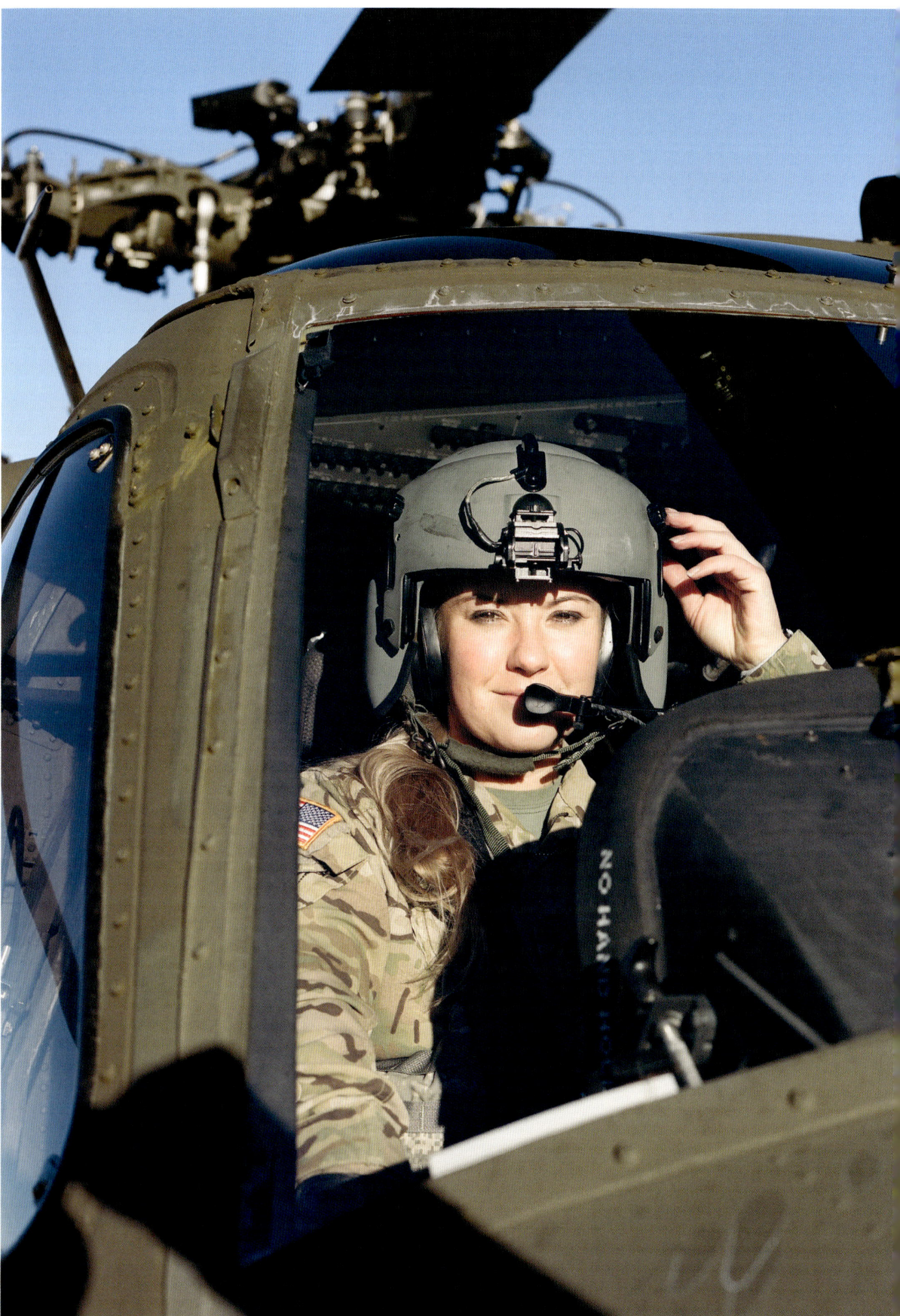

"You are so powerful. One of the mantras I say to myself is, 'Great big dreams, tiny little steps.' And whatever those tiny steps are—whether it's the college application, the military application, the volunteer group that builds houses and you want to be an engineer—trust every single dream that you have, and chase them with abandon."

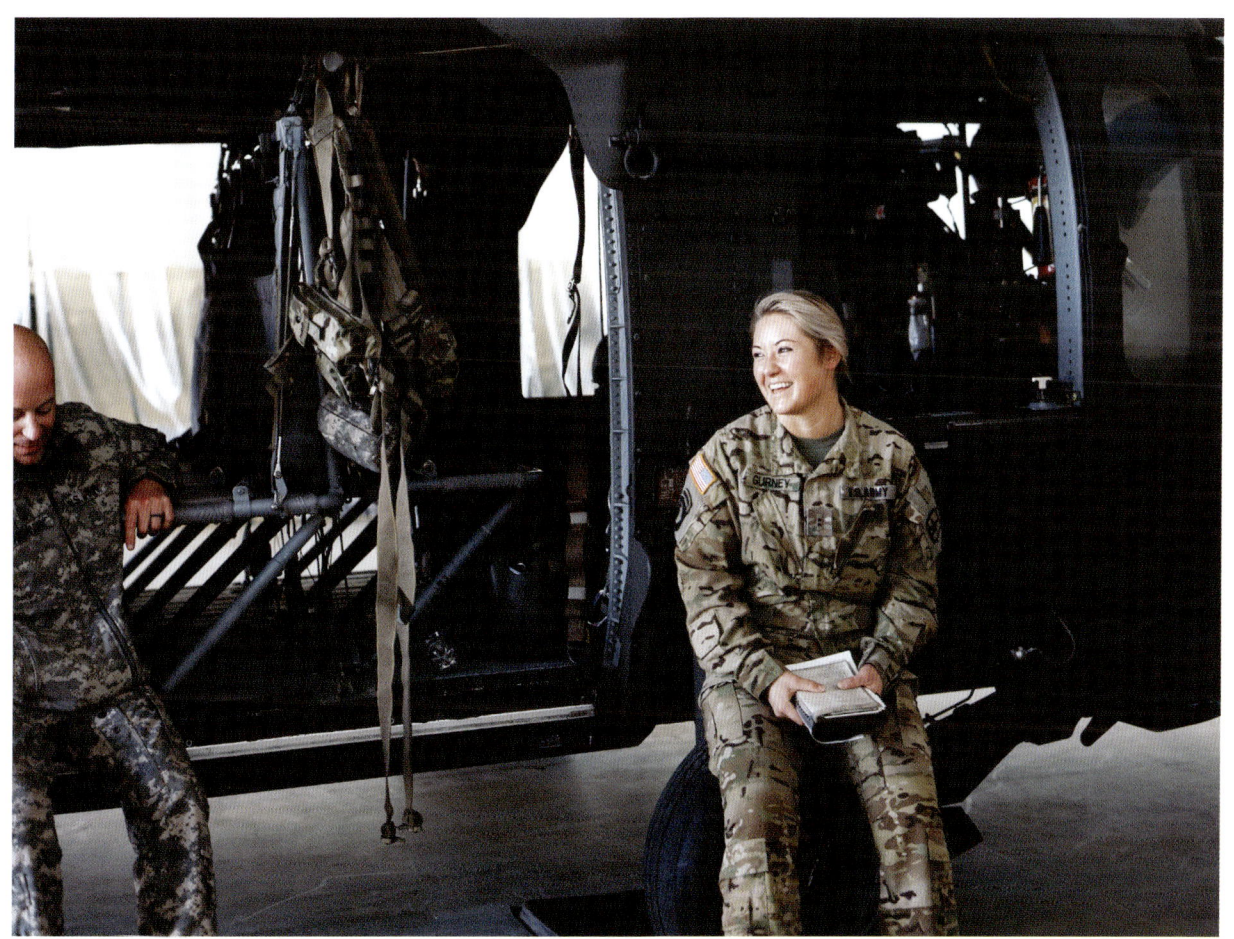

ROSIE BERGER

COMMUNITY LEADER, FORMER LEGISLATOR

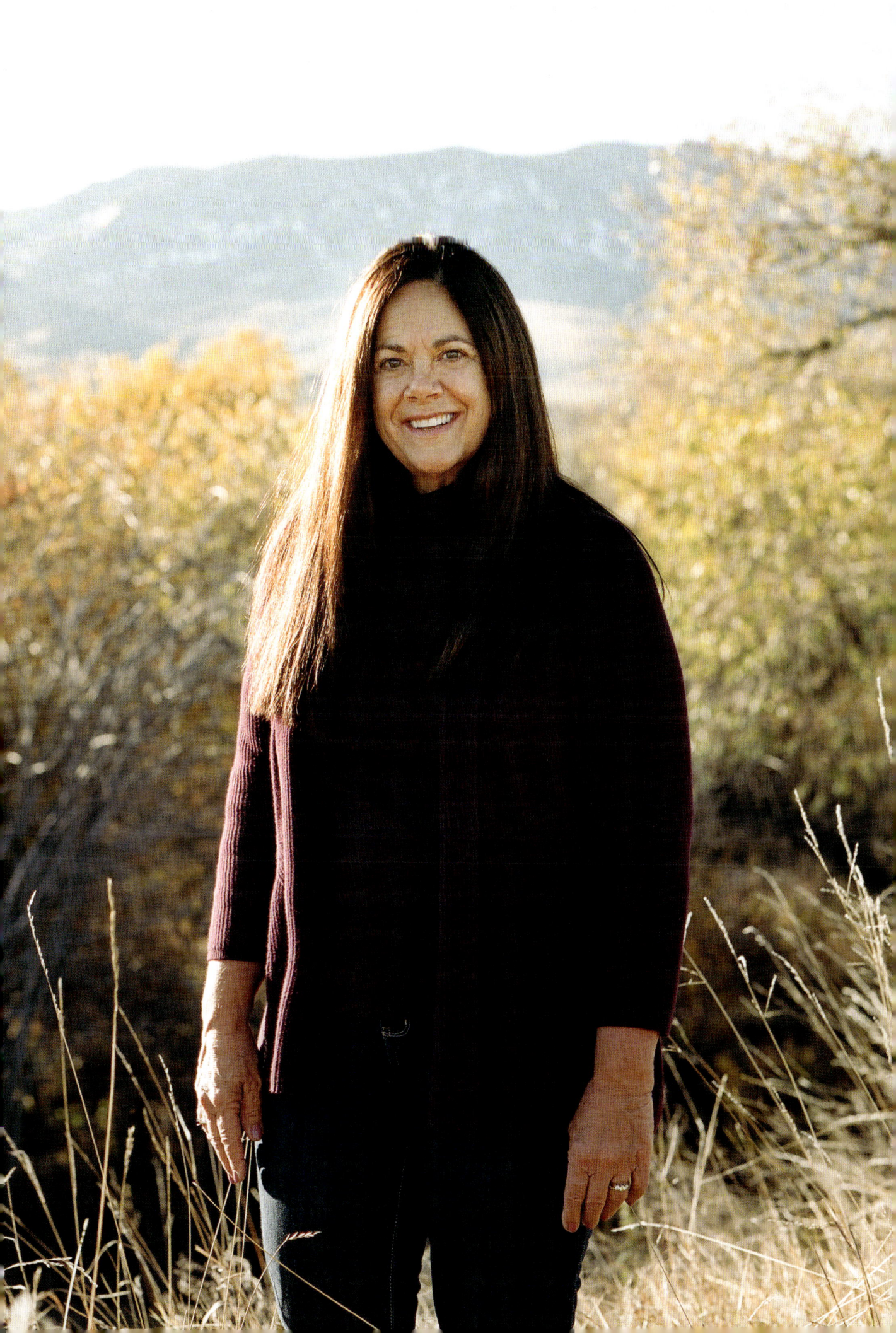

"Every time I've taken a risk, I've learned something from it, I've bettered myself, and I've become a better human being. What I've learned from failure is that it teaches me how to get to the next step. At the end of the day, win or lose in any of these opportunities, you will be a better person. So—jump in!"

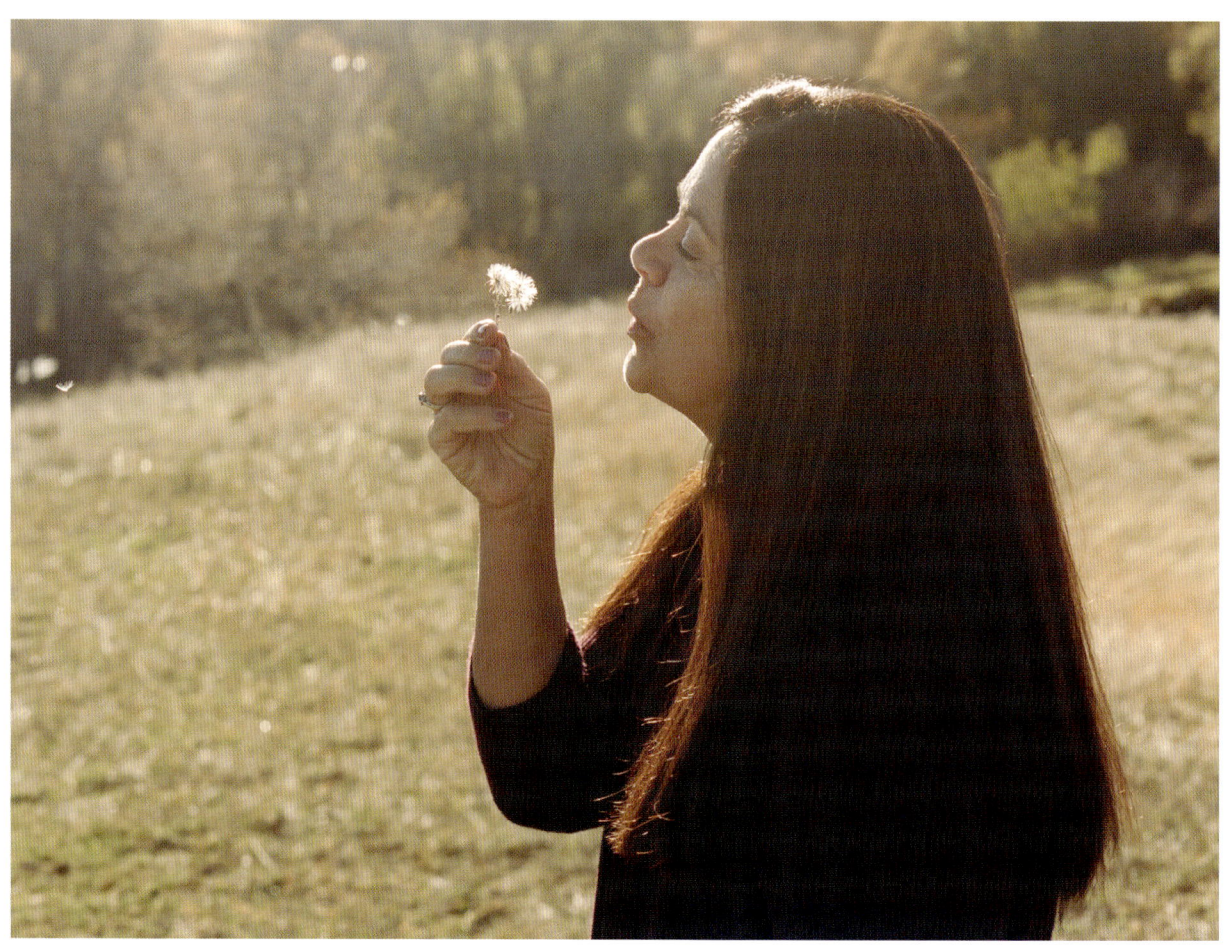

Raised on a dairy farm in Daleyville, Wisconsin, Rosie set bold intentions by age thirteen: She would get a good education, learn French, and travel the world. A natural risk-taker, she studied art history at the University of Wisconsin and worked in Switzerland before returning to the States and embarking on a road trip west. It was there she fell in love with the Rocky Mountains and ultimately made her home in Sheridan, Wyoming, where she has lived since 1978.

The eldest of seven children, Rosie stepped into leadership early. "When you live in a family that doesn't have very much, to know that what you have is a lot. That appreciation has never left me," she says. A deep love for neighborhood, family, and community are among Rosie Berger's most defining values.

For eighteen years, Rosie co-owned and managed Brittain World Travel, on Sheridan's Main Street—a role that cemented her confidence as a community leader. Her passion for civic life grew from there. She served as president of the Sheridan County Chamber of Commerce and on numerous boards—including the Sheridan Arts Council, WYO Theater, the Wyoming State Parks and Cultural Resources Commission, and the Sheridan Dog and Cat Shelter, among others—and worked with the Wyoming Film Commission.

Rosie's leadership is rooted in collaboration, civility, and the pursuit of consensus. During her fourteen years and seven terms in the Wyoming House of Representatives, she worked with four governors and contributed to nearly every aspect of state government. Her legislative legacy includes work on judicial reform, landowner rights, economic development, health care, and the prevention of animal cruelty. She served as chair of the House Appropriations Committee, speaker pro tempore, and majority leader. Nationally, she held leadership positions with the Council of State Governments West and the National Conference of State Legislatures.

Rosie lost her campaign for an eighth term—a seat that would have made her the second-ever female Speaker of the House in Wyoming. But to her, risk and failure are inseparable from growth.

Spontaneity, hard work, and a willingness to say yes to new opportunities have guided Rosie throughout her life. She continues to lead and mentor across the state, serving as a facilitator for Leadership Wyoming, where she is also a proud 2002 alum. Her civic engagement includes service on the Wyoming Judicial Nominating Commission, the Brinton Museum National Advisory Council, the ENDOW Initiative, Climb Wyoming, the Wyoming Women's Foundation, and other statewide organizations that align with her mission to uplift and serve.

At Rosie's core, it is love that fuels everything she does. For her enduring impact across Wyoming's communities, nonprofits, and future leaders, she was awarded the Governor's Woman of Distinction Award in 2023.

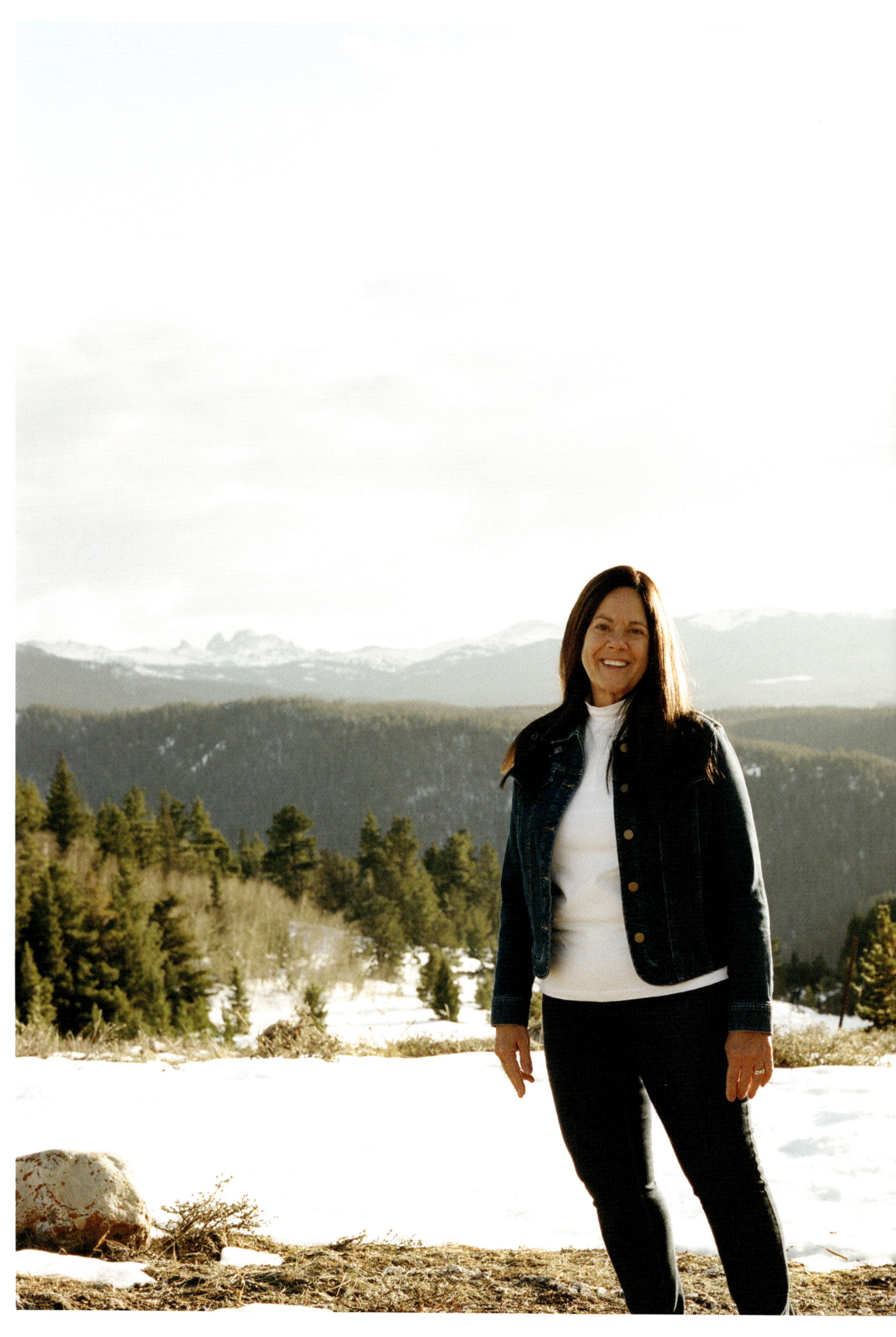

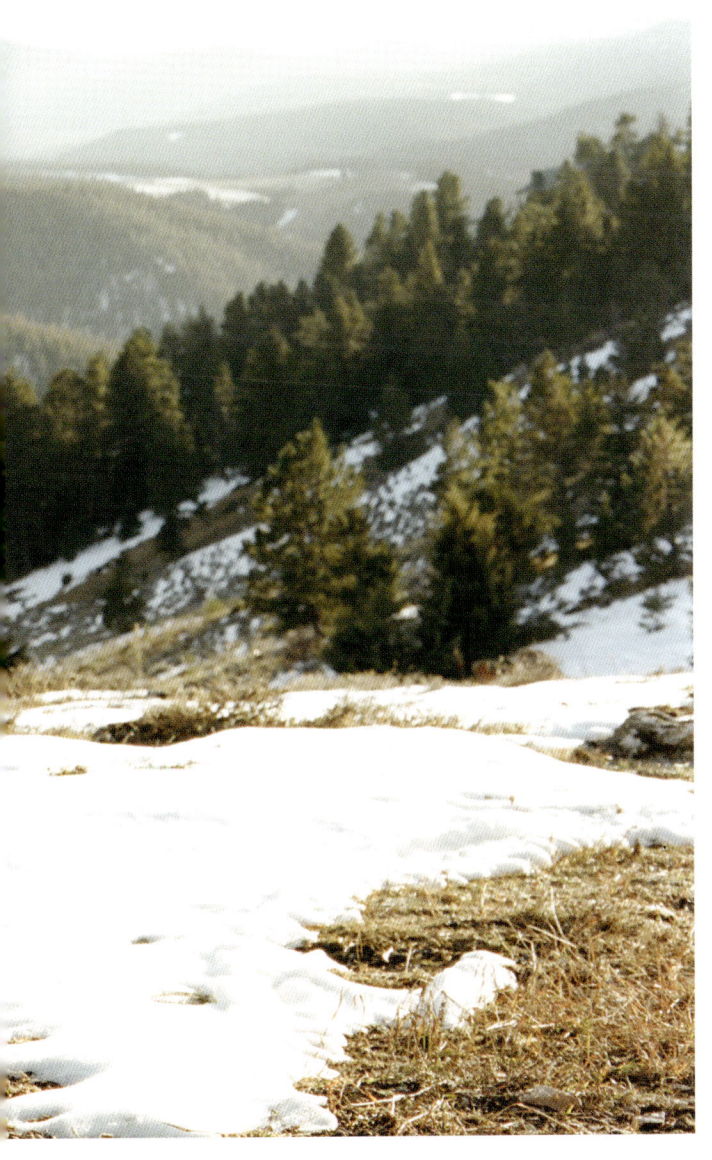

"*Spontaneity
is such a spirit.*"

ELIZABETH
FERNANDEZ

FOUNDER, ARTISTIC DIRECTOR, AND CHOREOGRAPHER OF
ROCKY MOUNTAIN SCHOOL OF THE ARTS AND ROCKY MOUNTAIN DANCE THEATRE

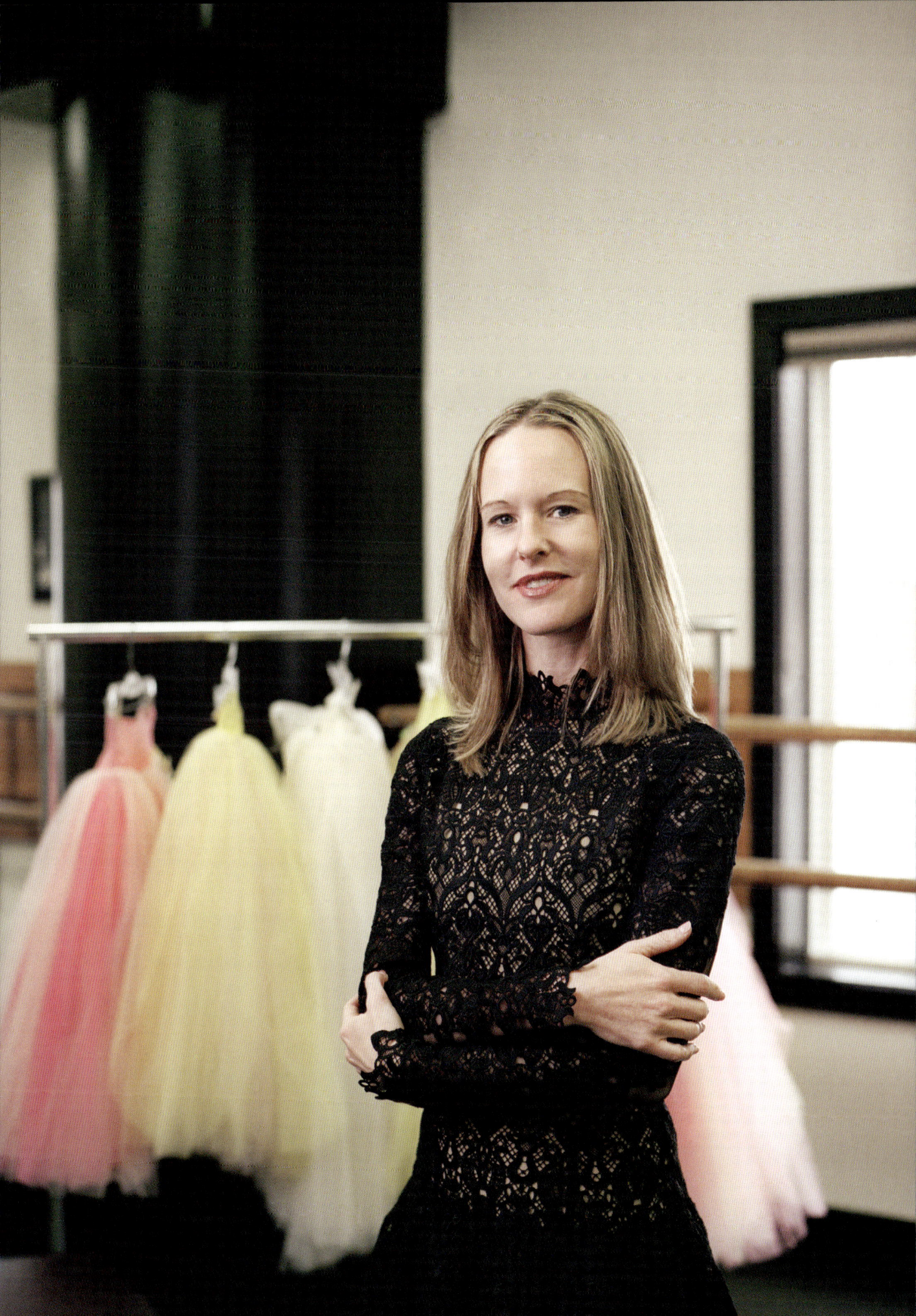

"The arts are an avenue of reflection, creativity, discussion, and perspective. Through the arts we are able to more easily bridge gaps that sometimes, with words, can be too divisive. Reflection and perspective are the most powerful tools to open the door to understanding and new thought processes."

Liz Fernandez has an insatiable passion for movement. As the executive and artistic director of the Rocky Mountain School of the Arts and the Rocky Mountain Dance Theatre (RMSA/RMDT) in Cody, she is relentlessly committed to her mission: creating space for reflection, connection, and perspective through the performing arts. It's what dance gifted her—and what she's devoted her life to sharing with students and audiences alike.

Liz took her first formal dance class at eight years old—considered late for ballet, a highly technical discipline. Her mother enrolled her in dance to help her overcome her shyness. It worked. Movement became her voice, her outlet, and her way of communicating with the world. "Movement is a type of communication. That's the type of communication that I'm most comfortable with, and I'm able to express what I want to say through movement." By sixth grade, Liz had already made up her mind: Dance was her calling, and she would one day open her own studio.

After high school, Liz auditioned for several collegiate dance programs, only to be turned away for not having a strong enough technical foundation. The ballet director at the University of Northern Colorado shared similar concerns—but saw potential and offered her a place in the program. Determined to catch up, Liz threw herself into her training. She took private lessons in addition to her college coursework and studied at a nearby studio to build the skills others had developed over years. Her hard work, musicality, and determination paid off. Liz graduated with honors, earning degrees in dance teaching/movement analysis and dance kinesiology.

True to her sixth-grade promise, Liz returned home to Cody after college and opened her own school. In 1997, she and her mother, Cynthia Kaelberer (a piano teacher), launched Rocky Mountain School of the Arts. They began with just nineteen students in a small upstairs building in downtown Cody, with one dance studio and one piano room. It wasn't

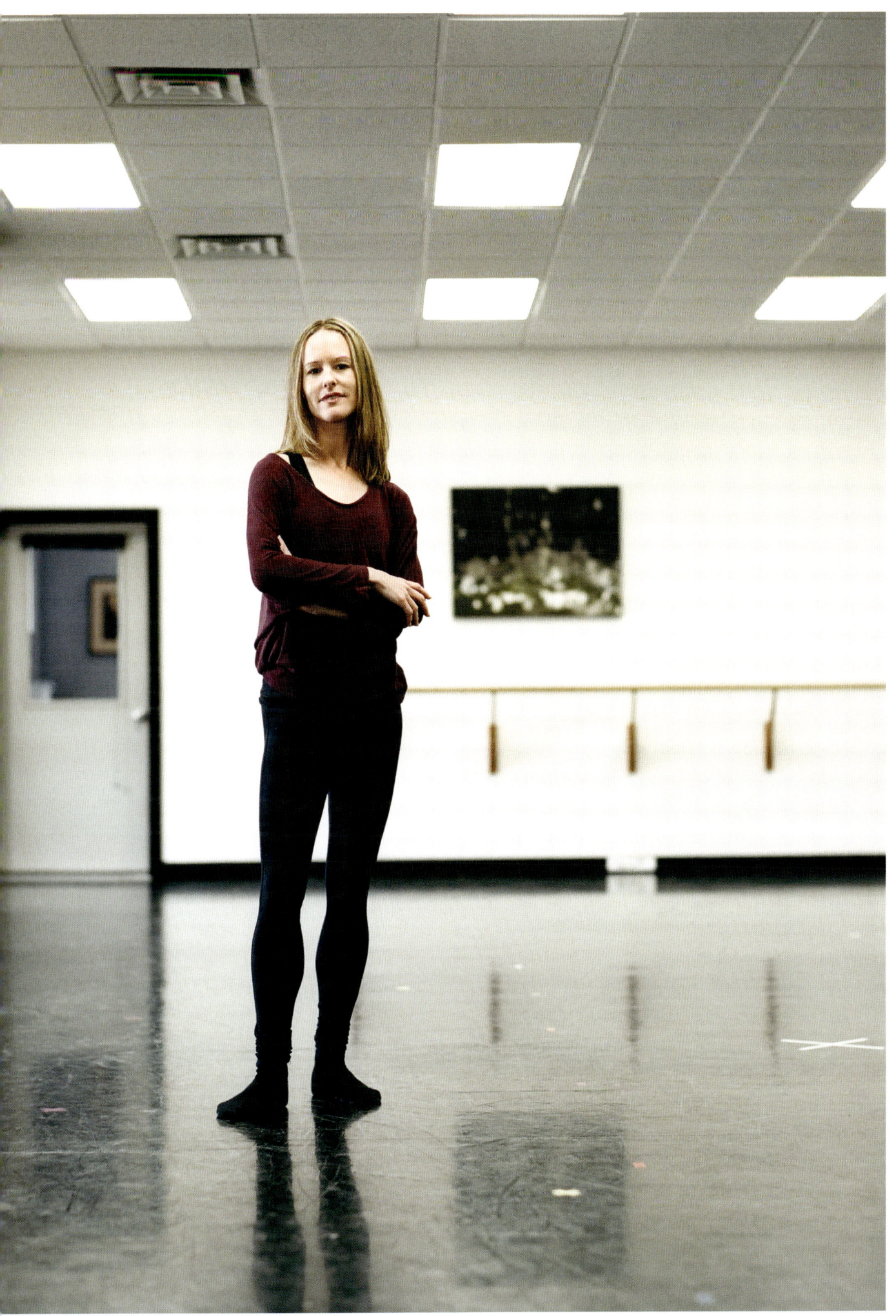

long before they outgrew the space. Since 2004, they have expanded into a dedicated facility, complete with three studios, a specialized stretching area, observation windows, a music room, and a dance store. For over twenty-five years, 3,000 students and counting (including myself!) have been a part of RMSA/RMDT.

But Liz's ambitions didn't end at teaching. Soon after founding the school at age twenty-two, she realized something was missing: creative fulfillment. Choreography became her outlet—a way to evolve artistically, reinventing and challenging herself. Whether composing contemporary ballads or theatrical productions, each piece she creates carries its own heartbeat and identity. Choreography, for Liz, is where discipline and soul collide.

To support her growing vision, Liz founded the nonprofit Rocky Mountain Dance Theatre. Through it, she produces large-scale annual performances such as *The Nutcracker* and her original musical, *The Wild West Spectacular*, based on Buffalo Bill's legendary *Wild West* show. Under Liz's direction, both RMSA and RMDT train students of all ages across ballet, pointe, tap, jazz, hip-hop, and contemporary dance, as well as musical theater. Her approach emphasizes both technical precision and expressive artistry. She holds her students—and herself—to a high standard of discipline and commitment.

Liz's work goes far beyond teaching steps. Through the performing arts, she empowers young dancers and actors to build self-discipline, confidence, individuality, and artistic voice. She promotes dance and theater not only as art forms, but as vital forces for introspection, growth, and community in Wyoming.

A lifelong learner, Liz is certified at the highest level through the Russian American Foundation's Bolshoi Ballet Academy. Her dedication sets the tone for her students, who rise to meet her passion with their own. Like Liz, they discover their potential, sharpen their focus, and find a second home in the studio—a place where movement speaks volumes.

"*I think in the beginning what drew me to ballet was the discipline, the exactness, and the preciseness of what ballet is. Why I felt compelled to pursue dance as a career—it was the only place that felt like home. Even to this day, I feel most comfortable in a dance studio.*"

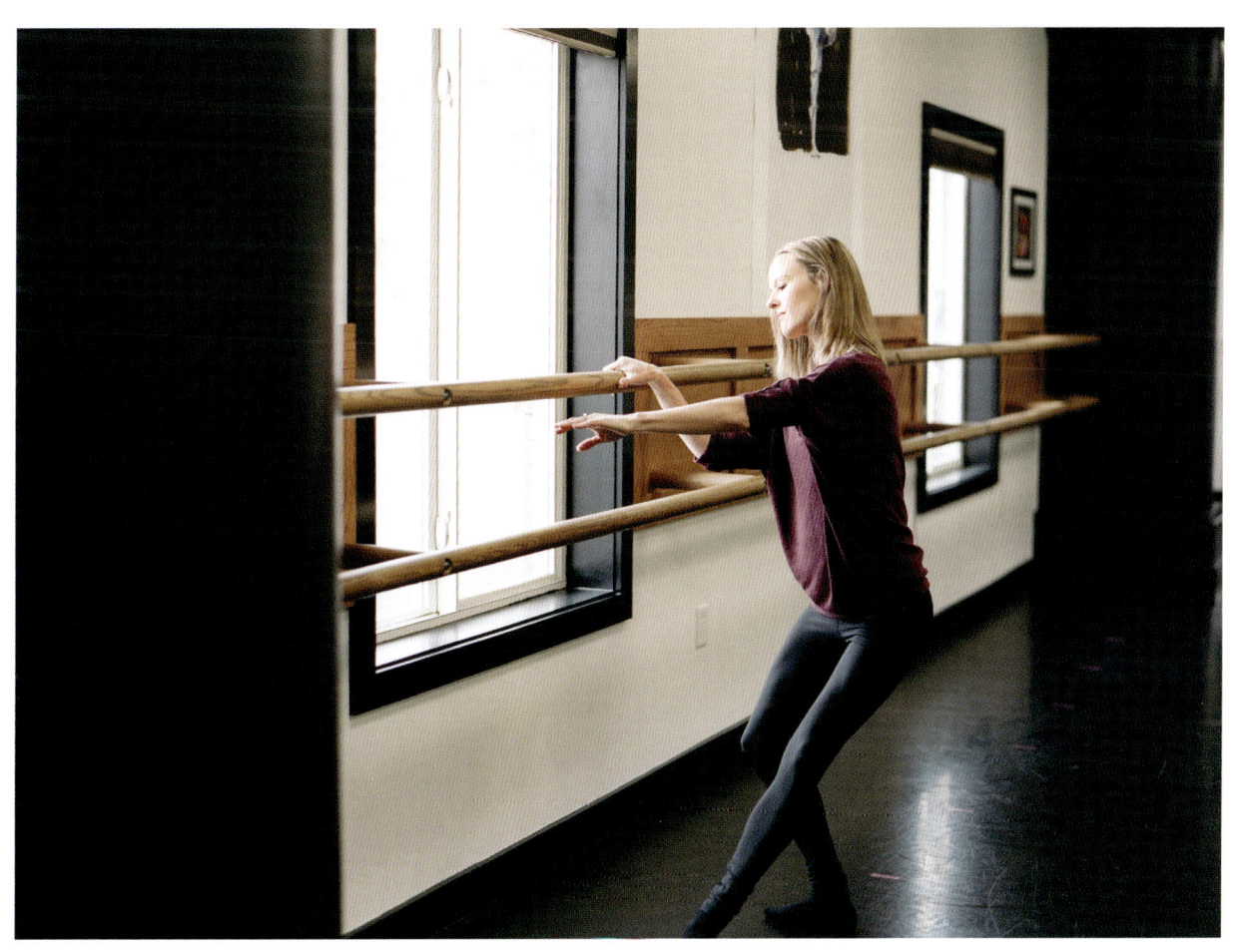

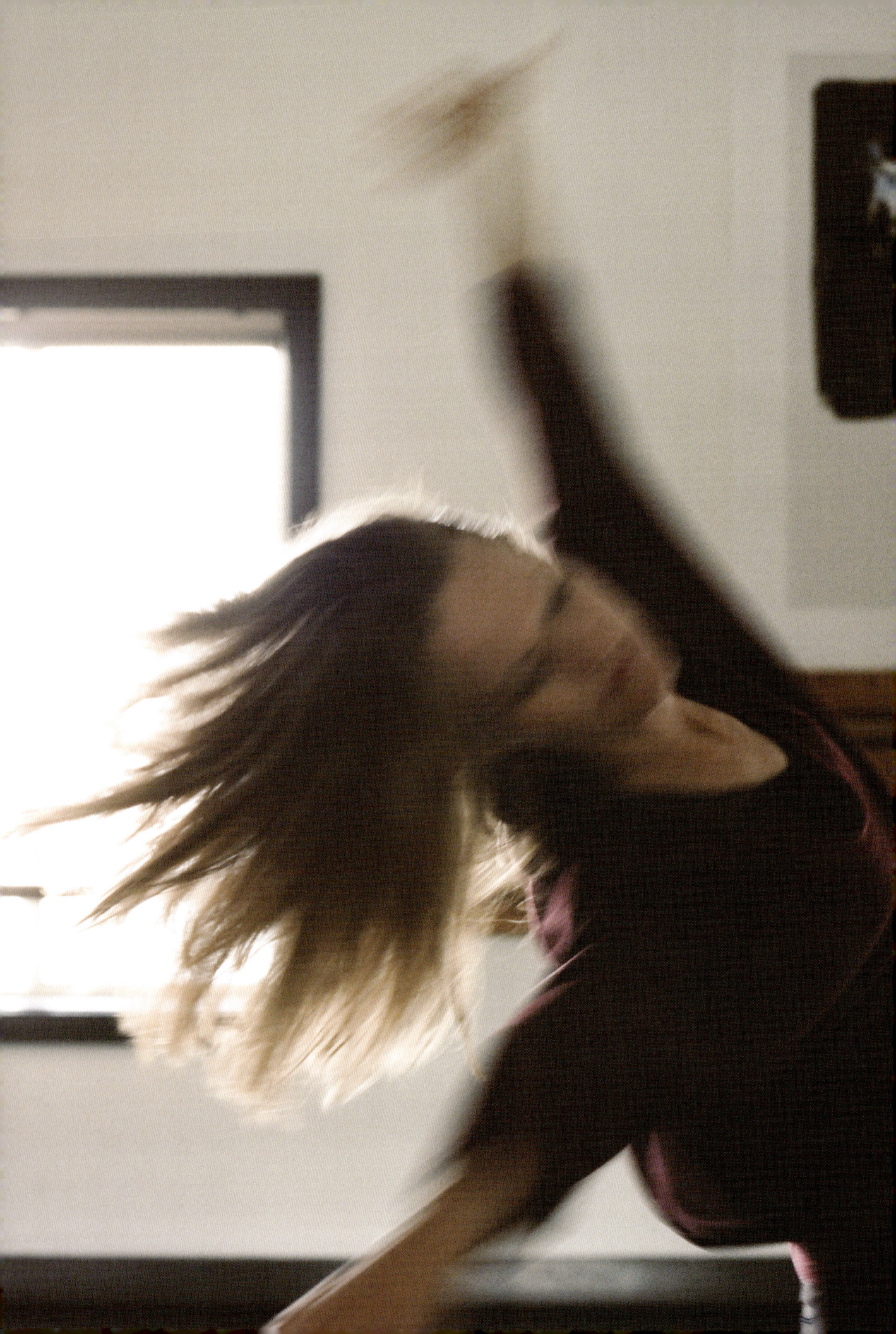

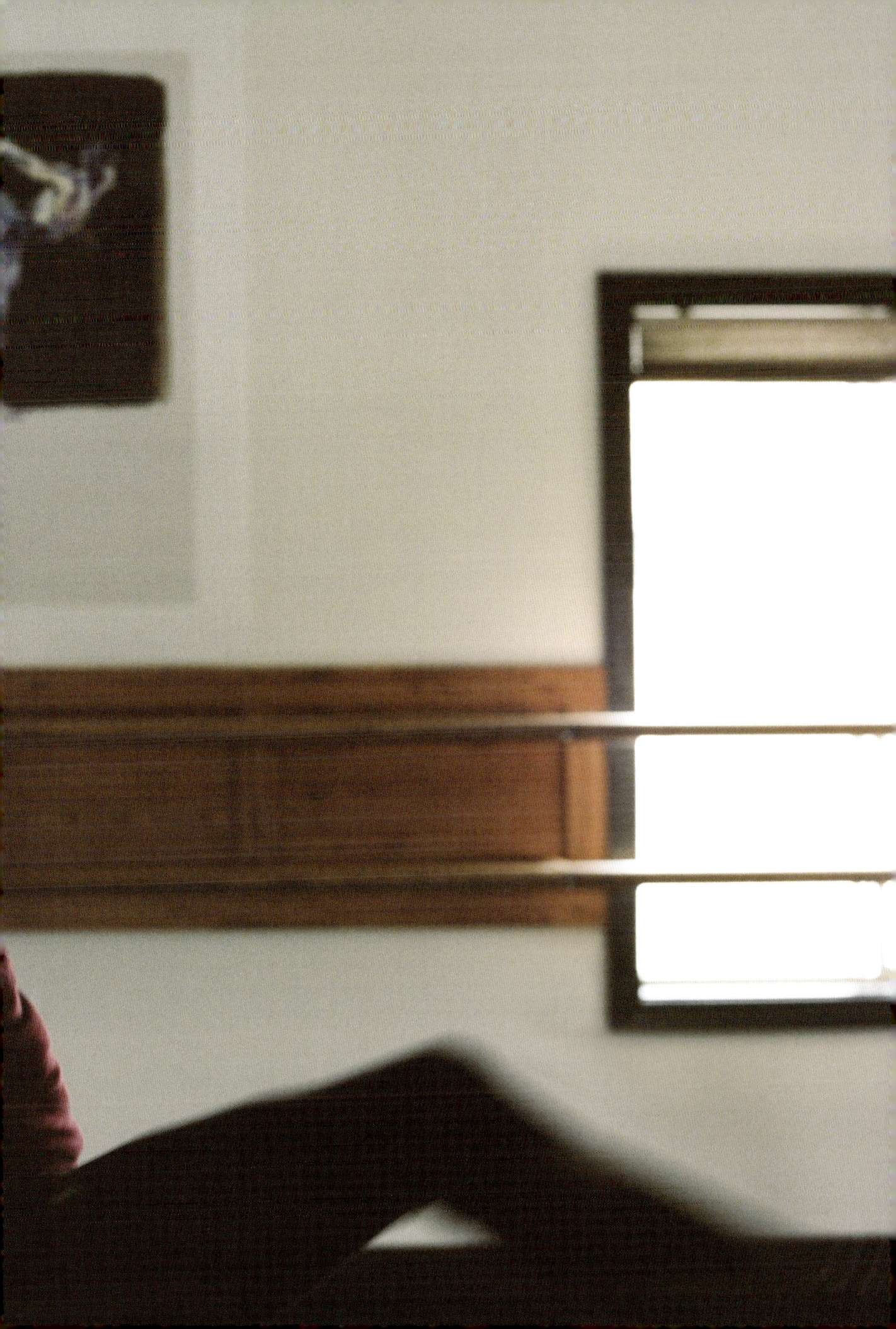

JILL
WINGER

HOMESTEADER, INFLUENCER, PODCASTER, RESTAURATEUR, BEST-SELLING AUTHOR

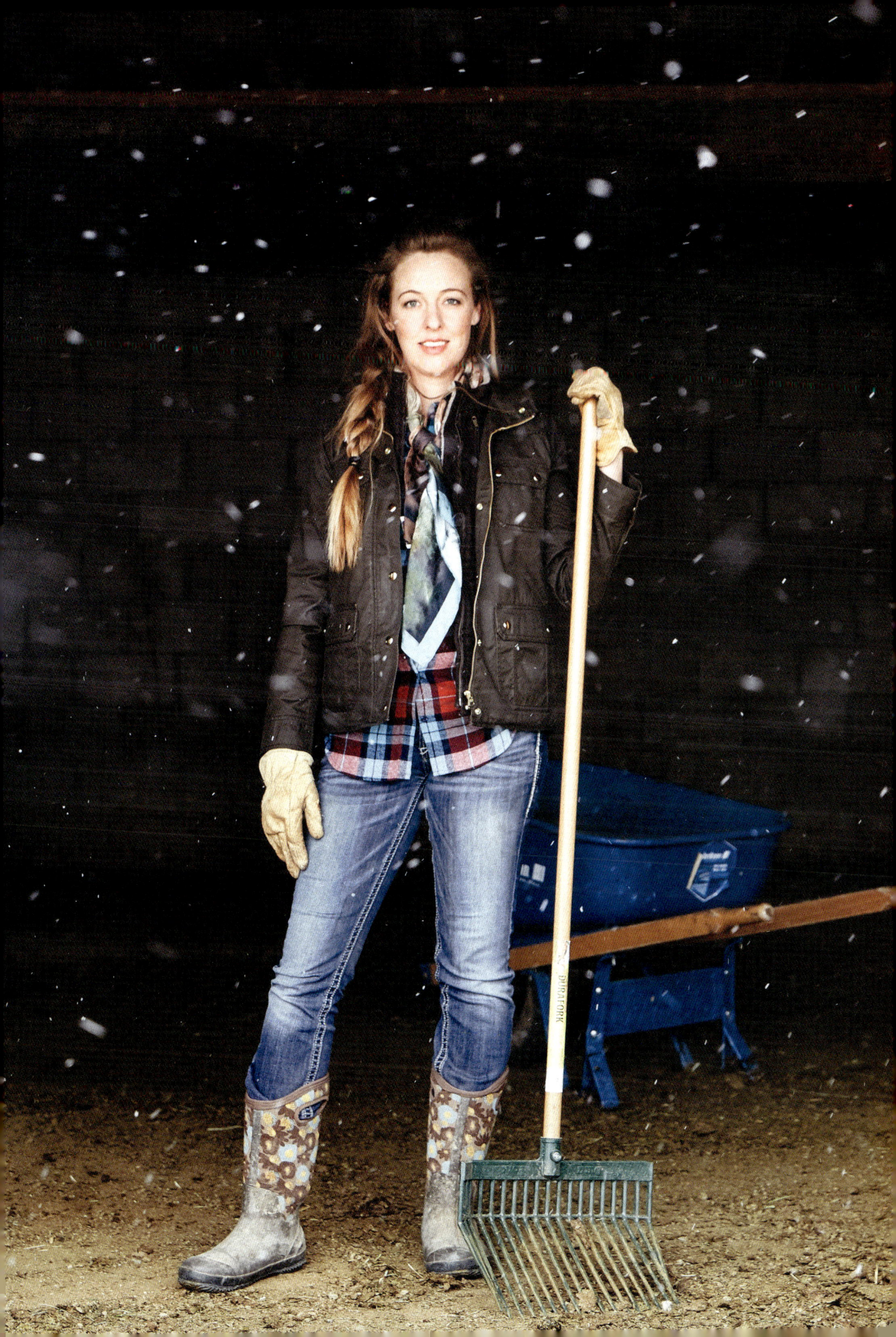

"Look at what lights you up and follow that spark. I believe that every single person has something special that they're meant to develop and share. For me, it's homesteading, and I love entrepreneurship as well. Find out what that is for you, and chase it like crazy."

Rain, snow, wind, or shine—Jill Winger and her family live off the land as much as possible. As the founder of the Prairie Homestead, one of the foremost homesteading brands in the country, Jill has helped tens of thousands of people reconnect with a slower, more intentional way of life. Since 2010, through her podcast, books, and courses, she's inspired a global audience to grow their own food and embrace the fulfillment of an analog lifestyle.

"Why do we have to live like everyone else?"

That single question sparked a radical shift in direction for newlyweds Jill and Christian, her husband. Their unconventional path began with the purchase of a rundown, sixty-seven-acre property forty miles from the nearest town of Chugwater (population <200). Driven by a surge of inspiration, they started a compost pile, bought a few chickens, and began restoring the land—learning as they went. Jill recalls how the transformation wasn't just physical; it ignited something seismic within her. The connection, joy, and purpose she found through homesteading became a flame she never wanted to extinguish.

Jill launched the *Prairie Homestead* blog in 2010 to share her journey with other like-minded souls. Since then, she's grown her brand into a powerful platform for intentional living, attracting a worldwide following. Her debut cookbook, the *Prairie Homestead Cookbook*, became a best seller, earned an Amazon Editor's Pick designation, and won Best Cookbook in the 30th Annual Reading the West Book Awards. Her second book, *Old-Fashioned On Purpose*, was also an instant best seller. In it, Jill invites readers to question what we've lost in our race toward convenience and digitalization.

Living off the land, for Jill, holds the keys to awakening through simplicity and hands-on labor. But she didn't grow up farming or cooking from scratch. For many years, microwaved burritos were her specialty. Her rise as a homesteader, entrepreneur, and teacher has been forged through trial and error, determination, and a genuine hunger to learn and share.

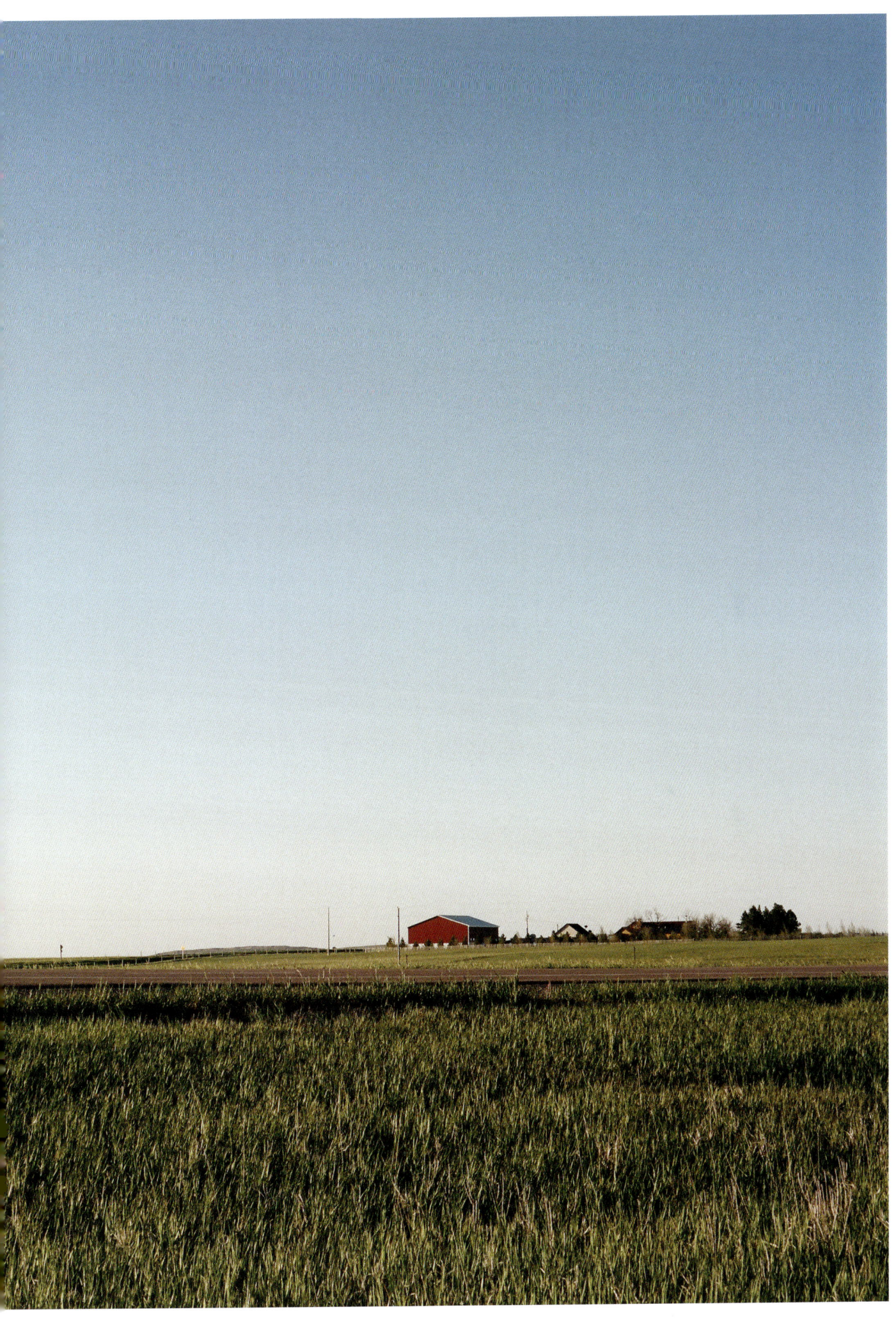

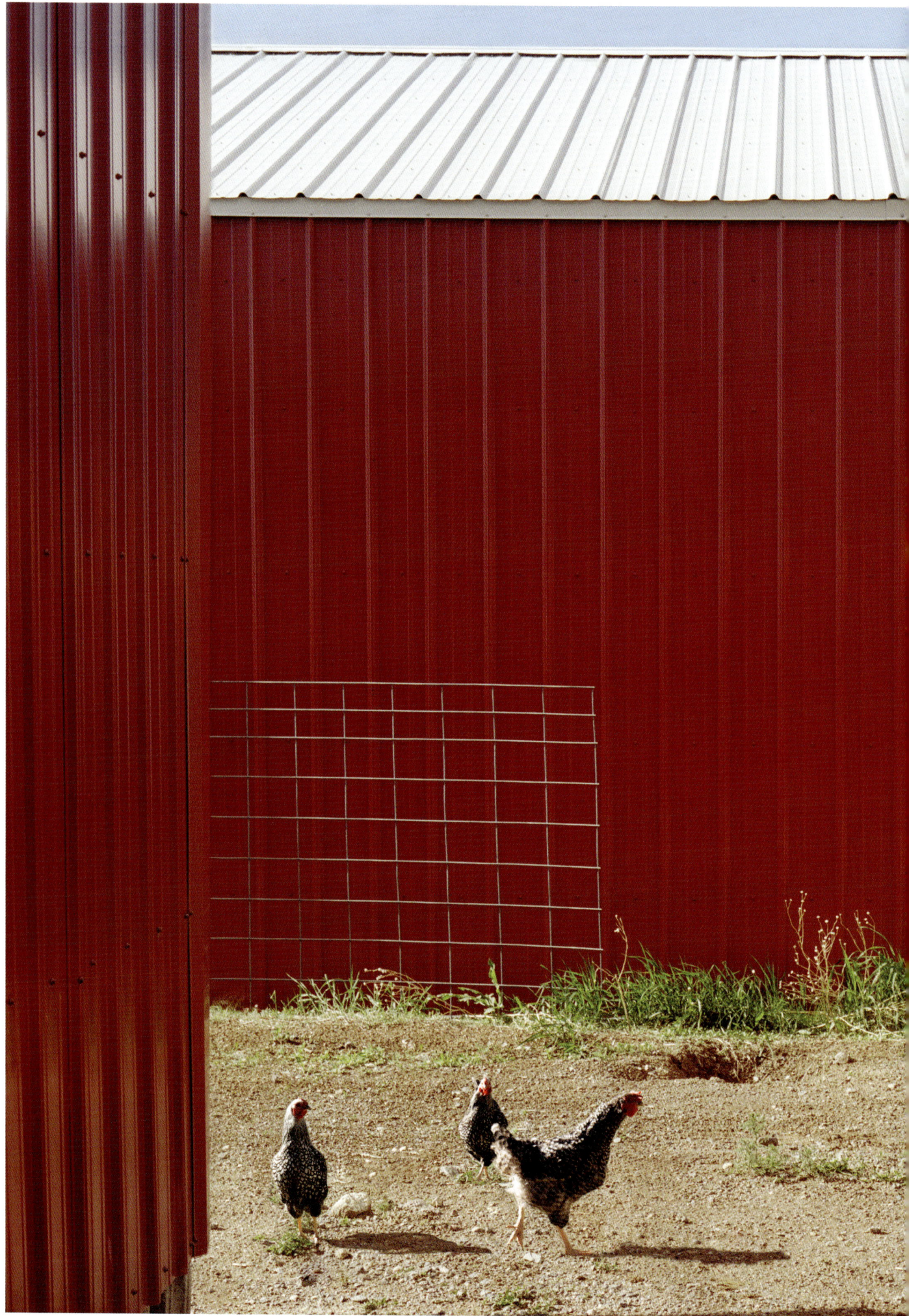

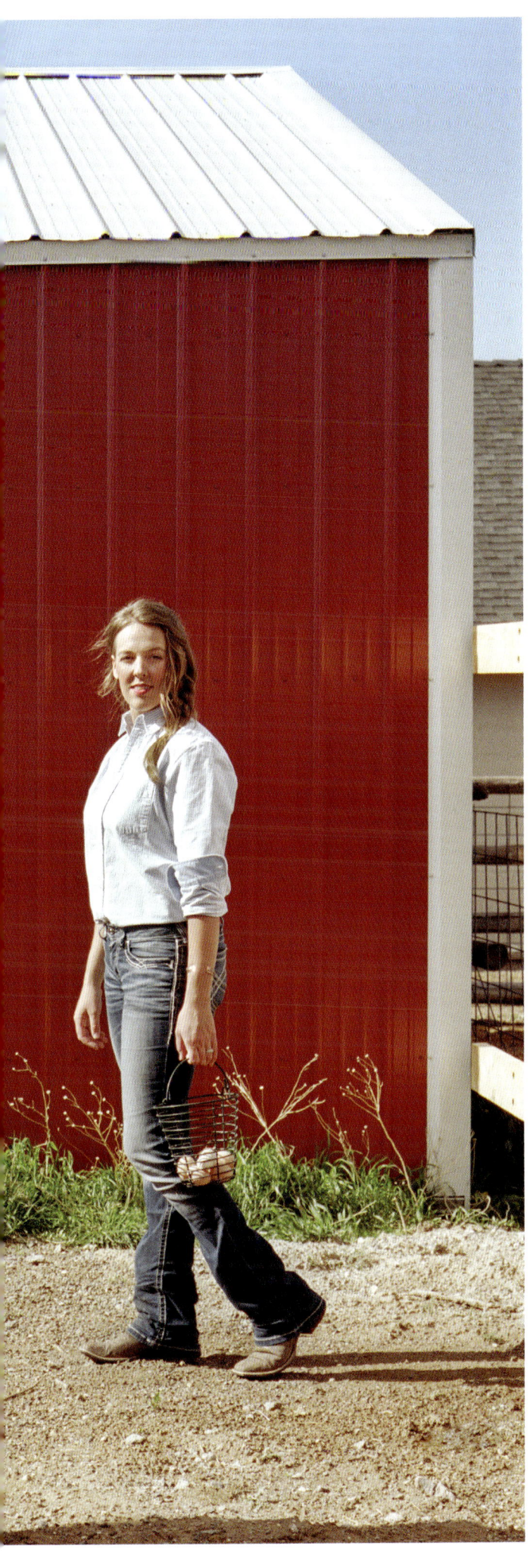

Jill shares weekly insights on her top-ranking podcast, *Old-Fashioned on Purpose*, which has surpassed nine million downloads. She and her family also raise grass-fed beef through their Genuine Beef Company, shipping nationwide from their Wyoming ranch. But Jill's impact extends well beyond her homestead and online community.

Her latest venture brings her philosophy full circle: the restoration of the Chugwater Soda Fountain, Wyoming's oldest operating soda fountain. There, in downtown Chugwater, she builds community in person, serving farm-to-table meals that highlight local beef and seasonal, whole ingredients. It's a living example of her mission in action—preserving the past while nurturing the present.

Jill is committed to helping others incorporate rural arts and self-sufficiency into their lives—regardless of location—and to reclaiming the physical and mental benefits that come from living more simply. Her work has been featured in *Cowgirl* magazine, *Woman's Day*, *HuffPost*, *The Wall Street Journal*, *People* magazine, and on Wyoming PBS.

As Jill continues to expand her influence and teachings, one constant keeps her grounded: the drive to ask deeper questions.

"What have we left behind in our race for progress?"

Her quest to answer that question helps her navigate the complexities of the modern world—and share her discoveries with anyone seeking deeper connection, purpose, and a sense of aliveness.

"When we look at things like canning or gardening or keeping animals, it's better for our health; science is starting to back this up. That's why I'm such a fan of encouraging folks, even if you live in an apartment in New York City, to weave these rural arts and skills into your life. Not because you're trying to be trendy, but because it's going to bring you a lot of benefits and peace in the process."

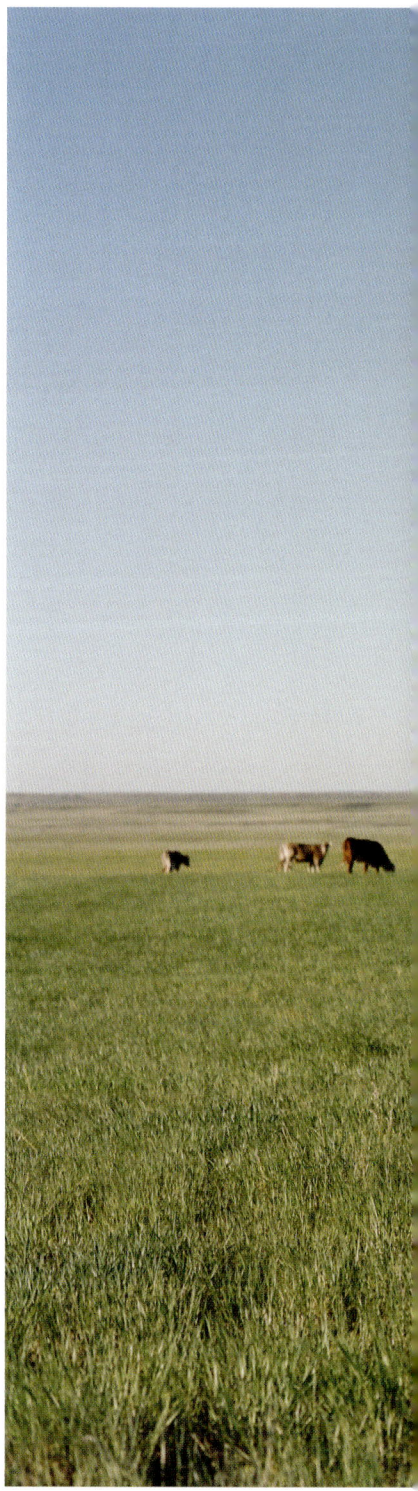

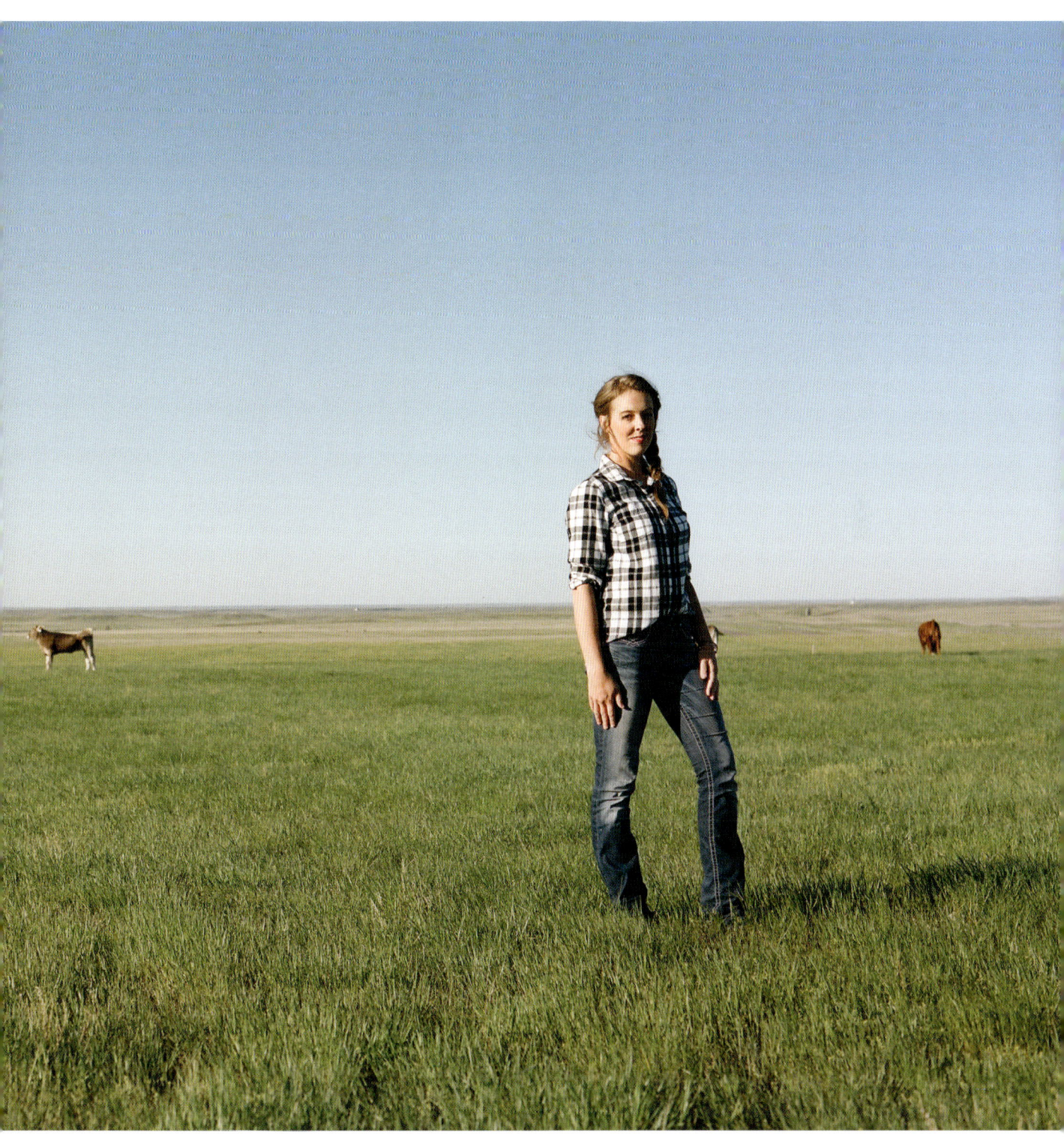

HILLARY WALRATH

WILDLIFE BIOLOGIST, CONSERVATIONIST, RESTORATION PROGRAM MANAGER
FOR TROUT UNLIMITED, FOUNDER OF THE SEEDSKADEE WOMEN'S FLY FISHING FLOAT

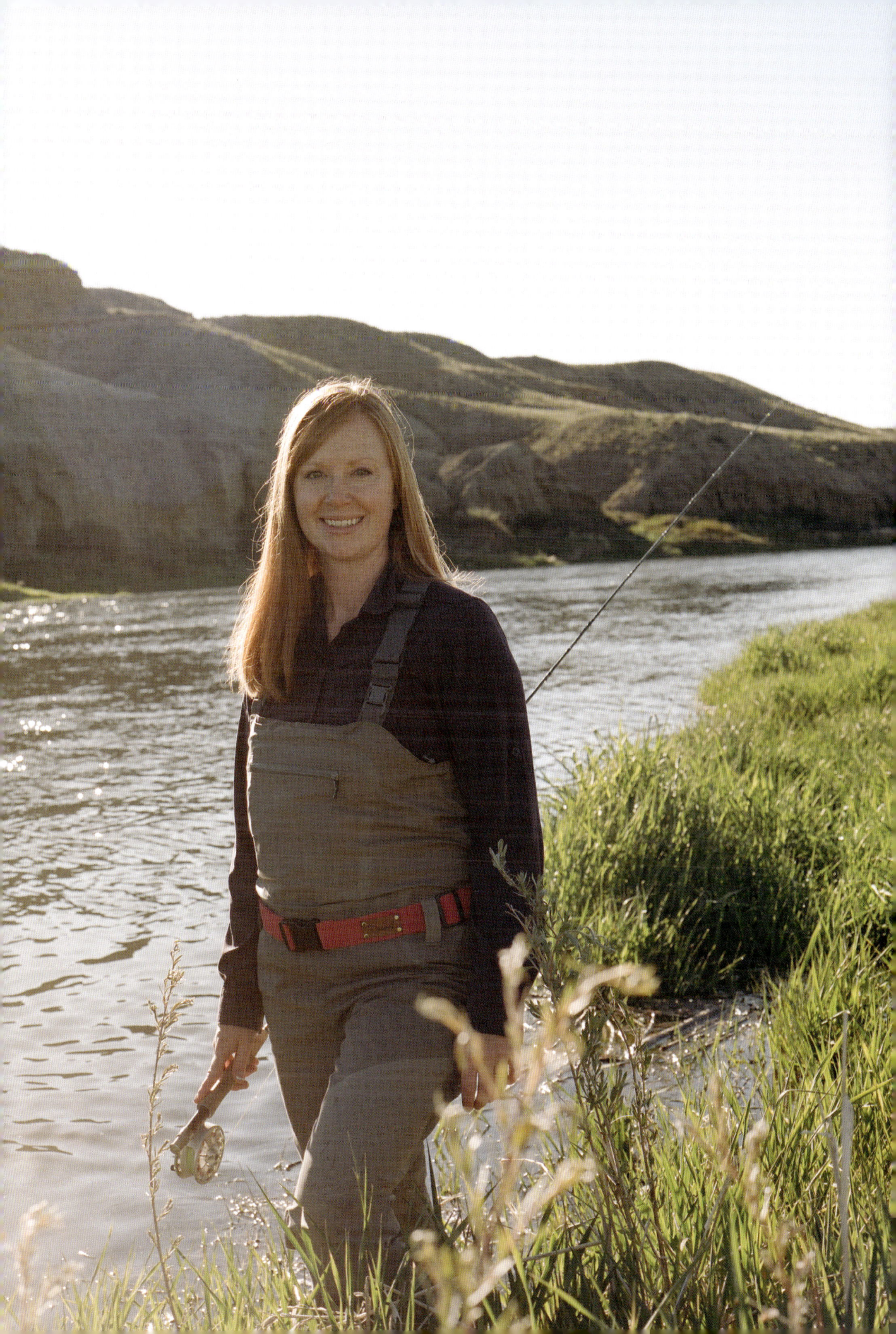

"The river connects with my soul and who I am. Having the opportunity to give back to rivers and these beautiful places is the best opportunity and what I love most about the work that I do."

Water is life. In the West, where water is scarce, it becomes even more precious. For wildlife biologist Hillary Walrath, water is more than a resource—it's home. Rivers are her happy place. Her life and career revolve around protecting them.

Hillary grew up on a remote ranger station in northern Idaho, where the Lochsa River flowed through her backyard. Her childhood was spent exploring the untouched habitat outside their family cabin, which instilled a deep sense of independence, joy, and connection to the natural world. From an early age, she knew she wanted to become a biologist, drawn to the animals and ecosystems that gave her so much fulfillment. Though she initially imagined a future as a marine biologist, her path narrowed to wildlife and aquatic biology. She went on to earn a master's degree in rangeland ecology and watershed management from the University of Wyoming.

A summer job as a fisheries technician solidified Hillary's focus. She describes fish as powerful indicator species—vital for understanding the health of an entire ecosystem and the megafauna that depend on it. Now, as a restoration program manager for Trout Unlimited, her mission is to find creative, intelligent solutions that benefit both wildlife and landowners. With growing populations come increasing pressures on natural resources. Hillary works closely with landowners to secure funding and implement updates that both support their operations and enhance wildlife habitats.

One standout example is the watershed-wide Henry's Fork Fish Passage Project, which began in 2018 as a single diversion improvement. It has since grown to include more than fifteen improved diversions and over fifty miles of reconnected river. The project brings together six ranch operations, Trout Unlimited, and local partners to upgrade irrigation systems—making them more efficient for landowners and passable for fish. These win-win solutions build trust, momentum, and lasting collaboration between communities and conservationists.

An avid fly-fisherwoman and conservationist, Hillary is passionate about helping others connect with Wyoming's wild places. She founded the Seedskadee Women's Fly Fishing

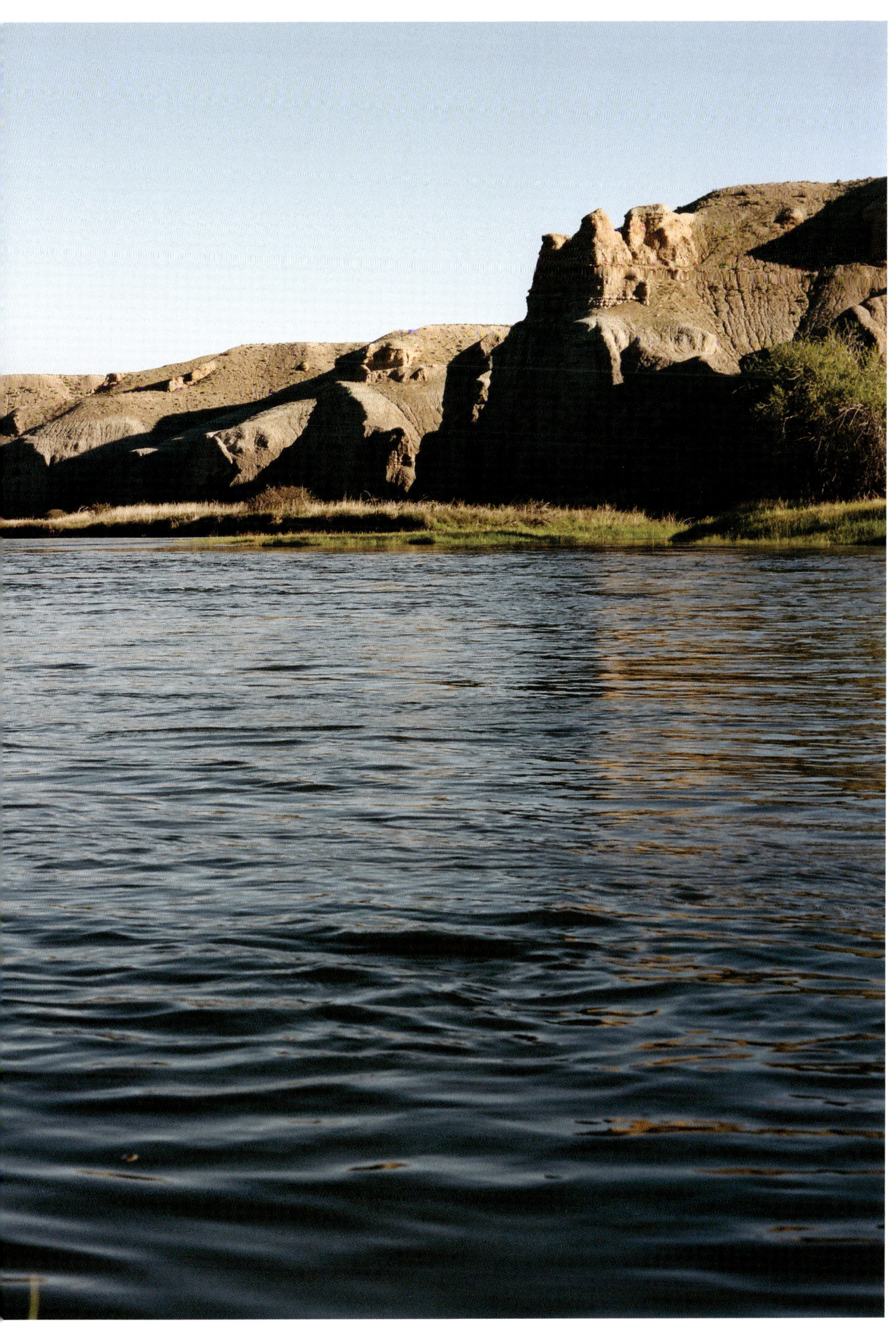

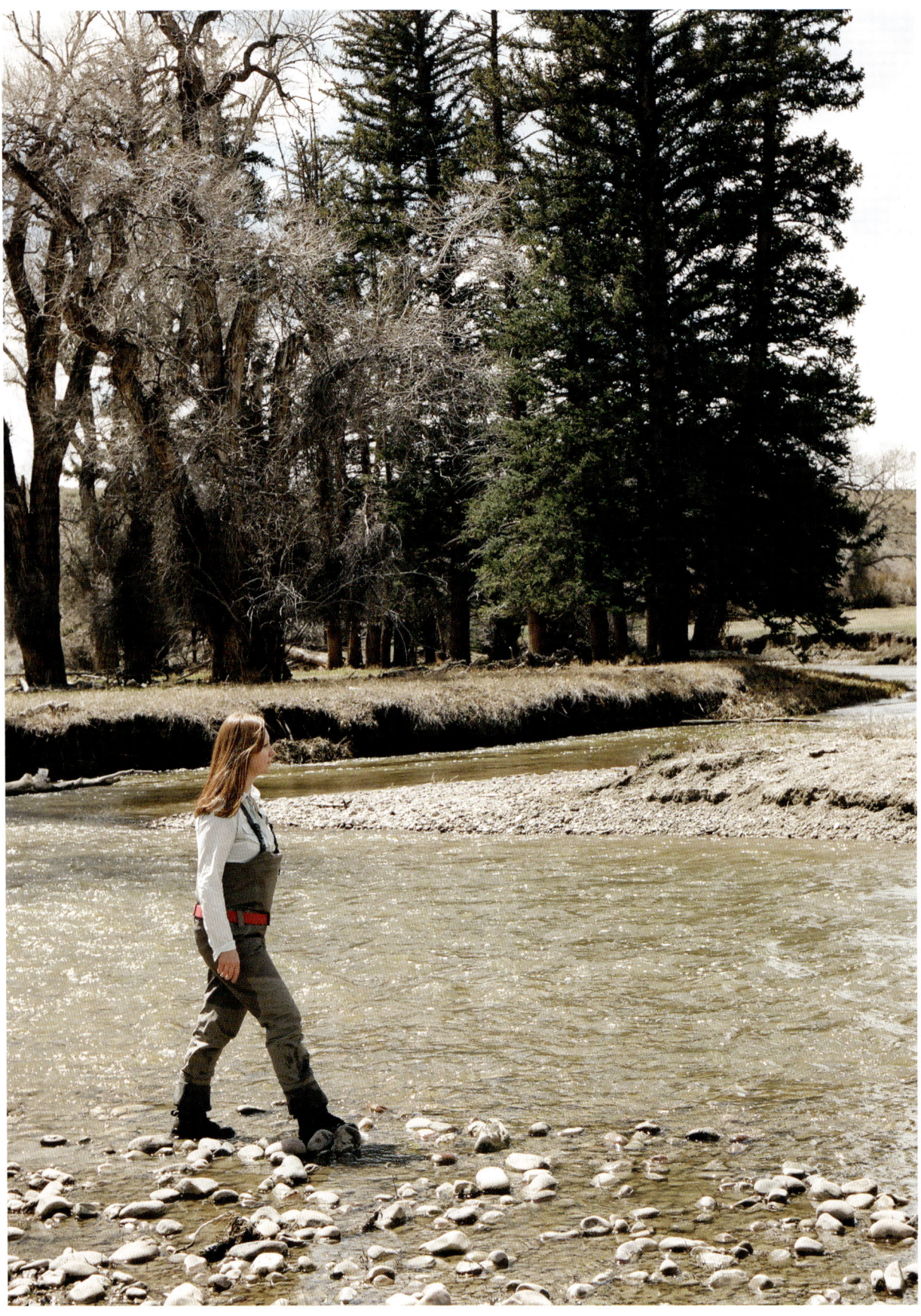

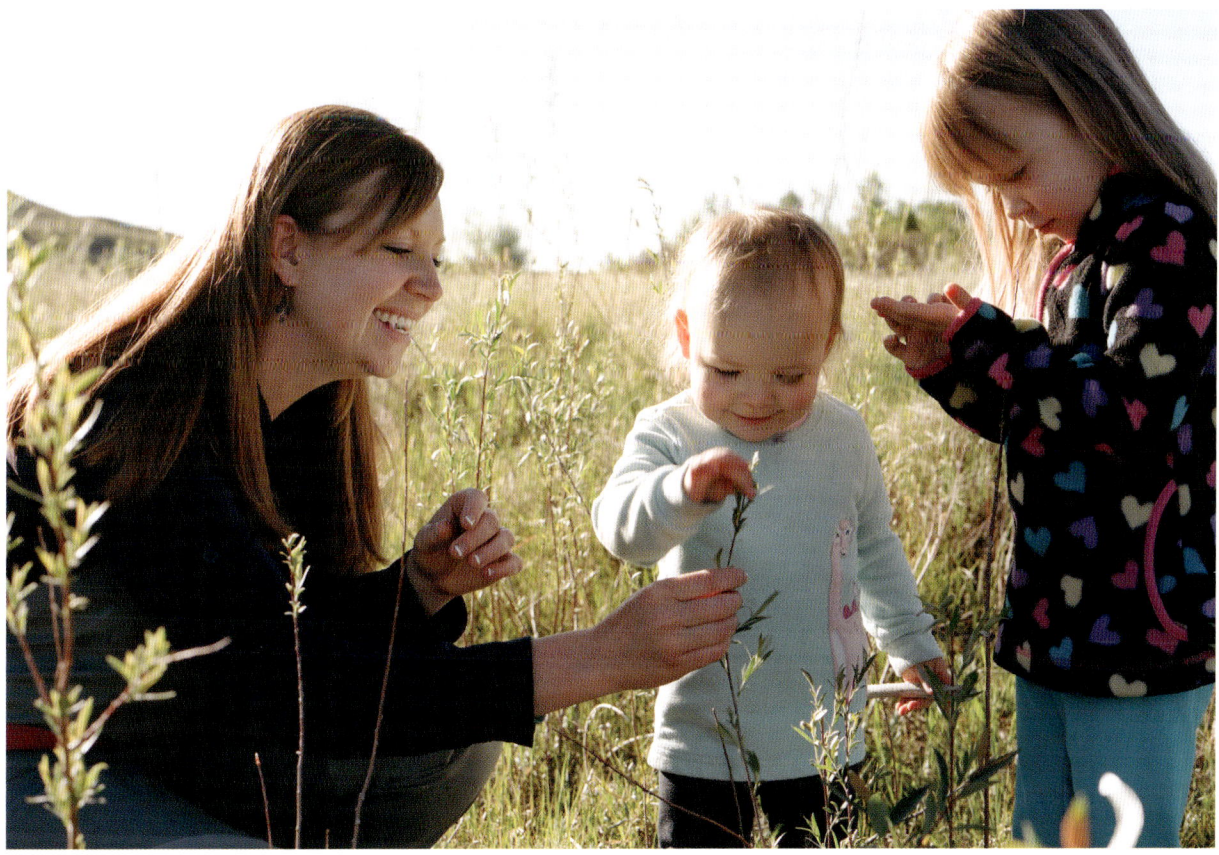

Float, an annual event on the Green River in the Seedskadee National Wildlife Refuge. Designed to empower women to get on the water and learn to fish, the float is about more than sport—it's about confidence, connection, and conservation. As a mother of two daughters, Hillary was struck by how often she was the only woman on the river. She created the float to help women feel confident getting outside with their families—building awareness and appreciation for this rare and thriving ecosystem.

The Seedskadee National Wildlife Refuge, one of seven in Wyoming, is a ribbon of life through the high desert sagebrush steppe. It supports more than 300 animal species, from moose and sage grouse to trumpeter swans and cutthroat trout. The Green River Corridor is a vital migration route for birds, big game, and small mammals alike.

Caring for the river is deeply fulfilling to Hillary. It's a way to give back to a resource that has given her so much. Her devotion not only protects these ecosystems but ensures their future. Federal public lands comprise 48 percent of Wyoming. Hillary intimately knows that when these lands are used, enjoyed, and loved by the people, they are more likely to be preserved—rather than sold or privatized.

It's this intersection of conservation and public connection where Hillary thrives—cultivating a deeper love, appreciation, and commitment to protecting Wyoming's wild, life-giving waters.

"People need these wild places to disconnect. We live in a very fast-paced world, and technology is great, but it doesn't solve all of our problems. It's so important to make people aware of these wild places, so they want to keep them around for future generations."

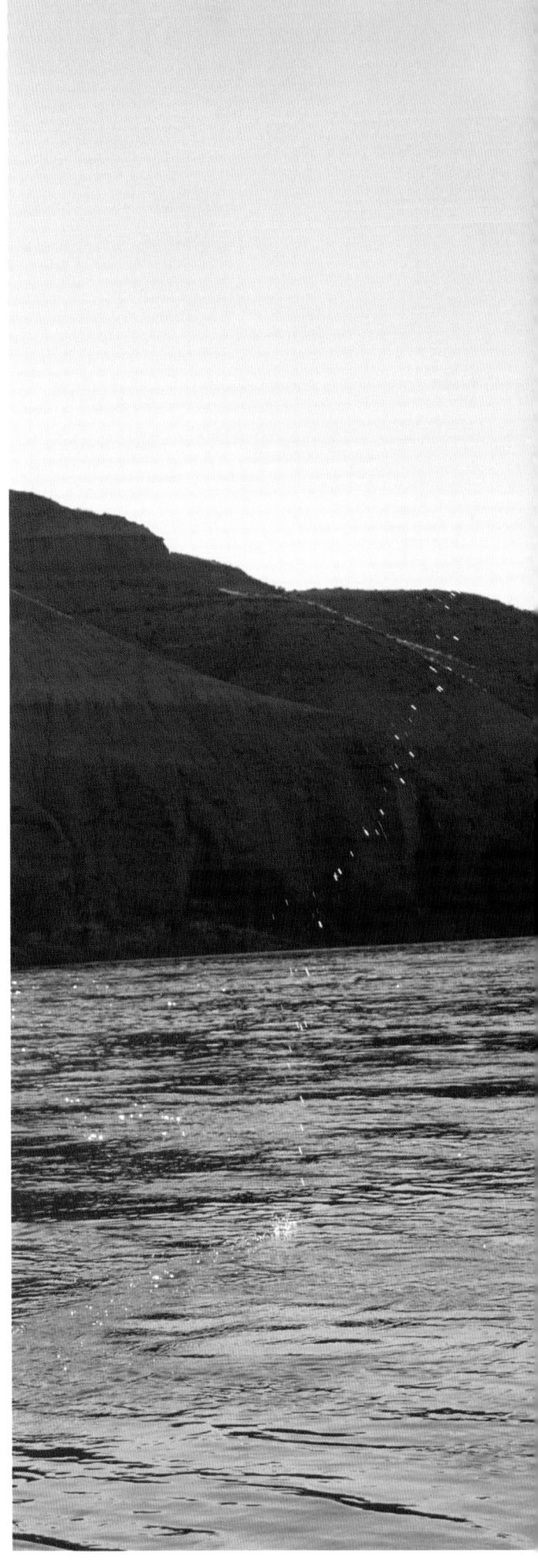

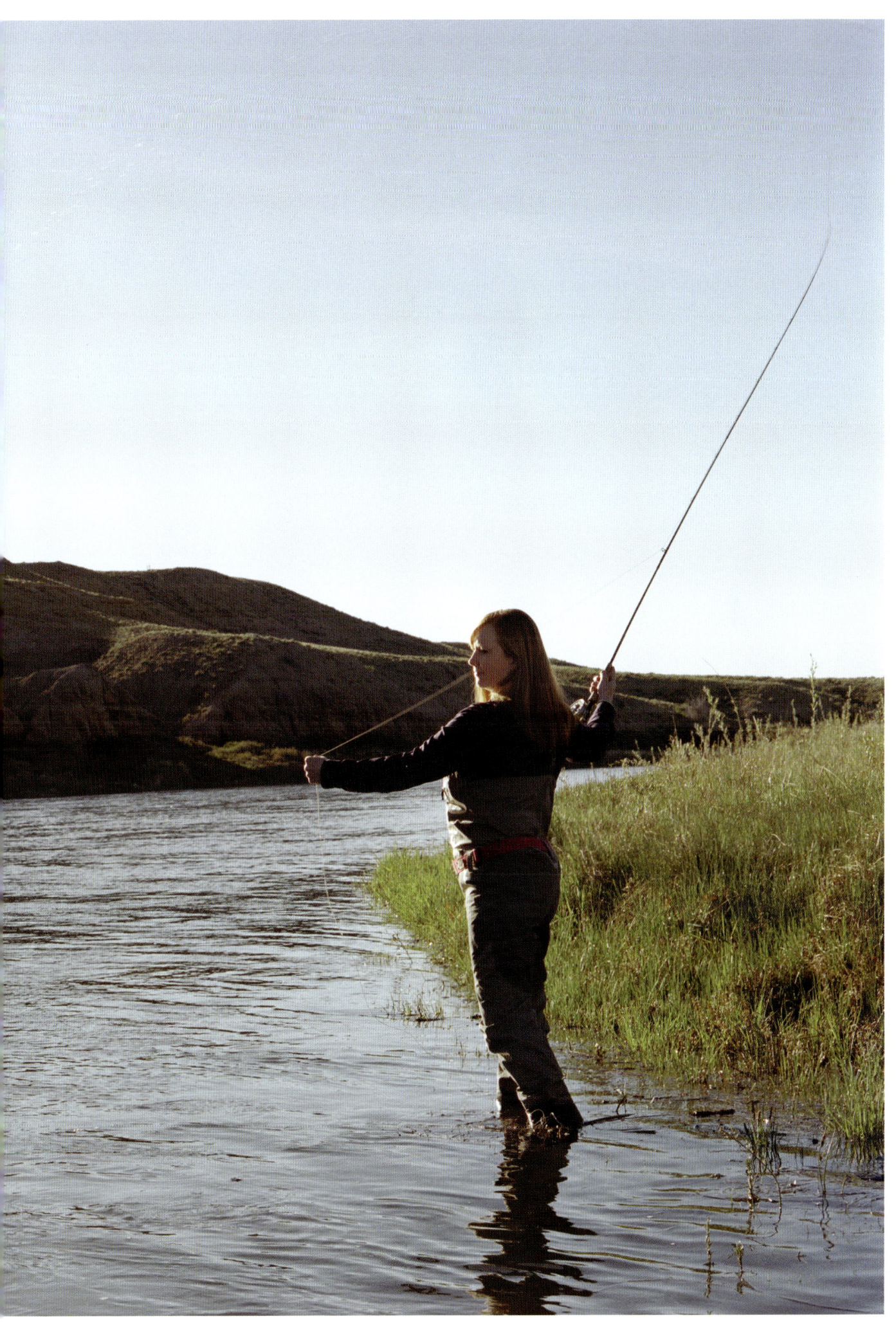

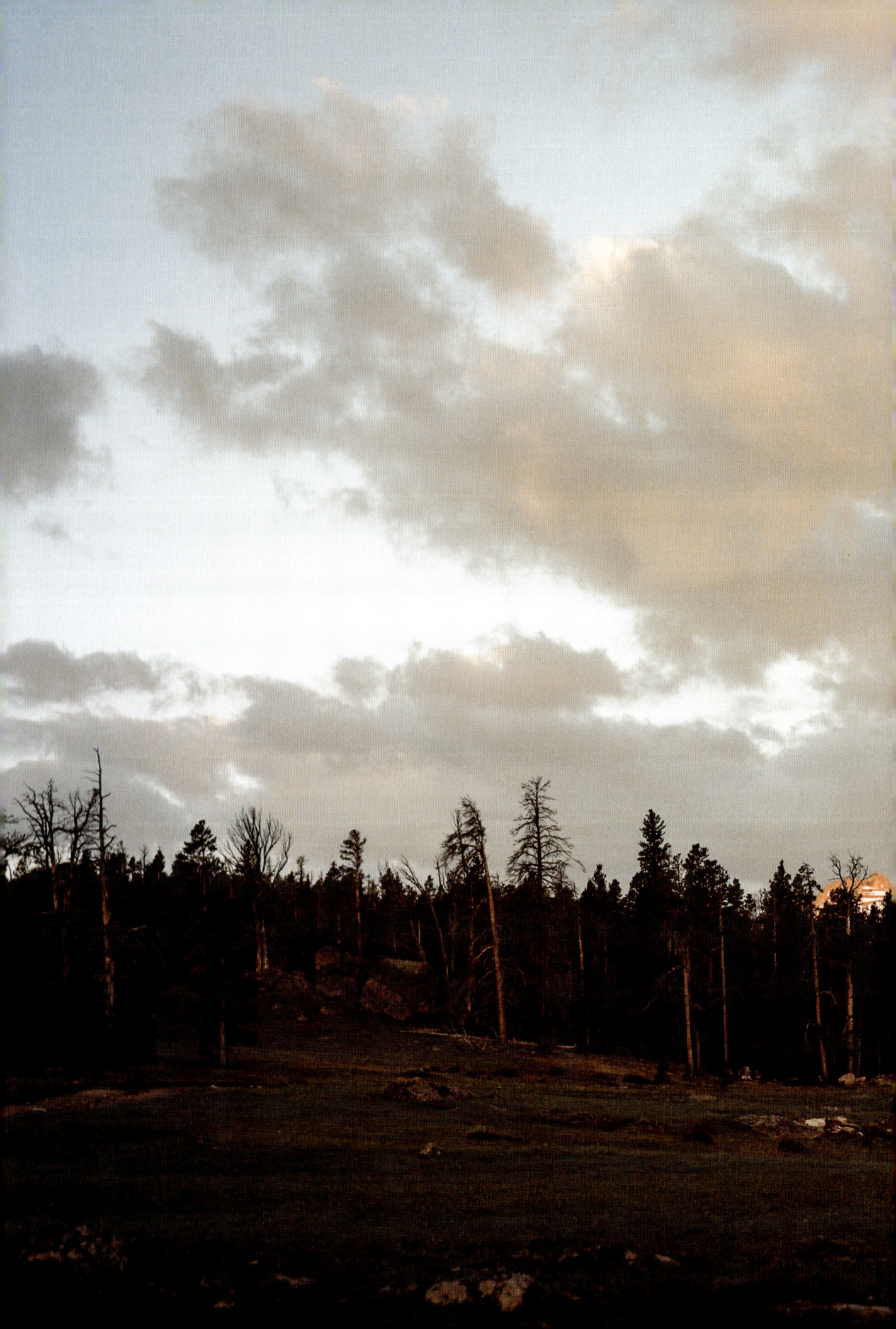

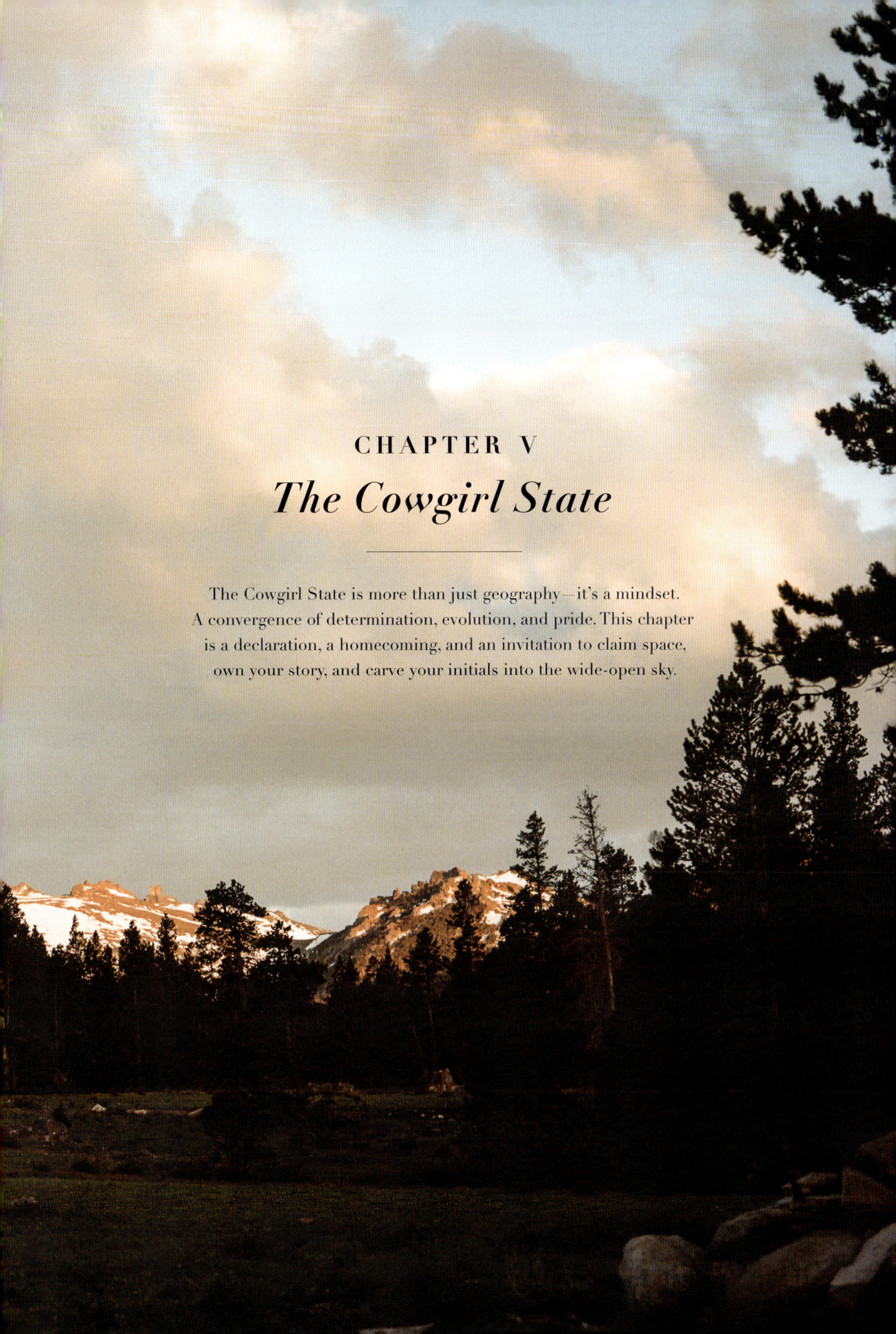

CHAPTER V
The Cowgirl State

The Cowgirl State is more than just geography—it's a mindset.
A convergence of determination, evolution, and pride. This chapter
is a declaration, a homecoming, and an invitation to claim space,
own your story, and carve your initials into the wide-open sky.

Behind the Scenes:
Up with the Sun and Jessie Allen Gottwald

I awake at 4:30 a.m. in a rustic, one-bedroom cabin built decades ago. It's mid-June and pitch black, and I am a little over three months pregnant with my first child. It is difficult to start the day so early, but this is our only window for production. The Diamond 4 Ranch will welcome its first guests of the season next week, and my exhibit deadline looms just four months away in October. Heavy winter snowfall delayed our access to the ranch until now. The chance to capture sunrise images is brief, so the day begins before light.

The previous afternoon, I drove with Jessie Allen Gottwald—owner of the Diamond 4 Ranch, a wilderness guest ranch that sits high in the Wind River mountains—for over an hour, through tribal land, from Fort Washakie on the Wind River Reservation. Zigzagging up the grassy green mountainside on a narrow dirt road, we navigated bumps, mud, and lingering snowbanks. After ascending the rough terrain, we arrived at a wide clearing surrounded by forest at 9,200 feet. Aside from the man-made cabins and horse corrals of the Diamond 4 Ranch, it's endless, expansive terrain. The "Winds" are a rugged range that boast hundreds of alpine lakes, abundant wildlife, and the largest active glaciers in the lower forty-eight states. This has been Jessie's off-the-grid home every summer and fall of her life.

In the cold, early dark, I pull on a wool top and down jacket, load my Contax with a fresh roll of 120 mm Kodak Portra 400 film, and prep several more. A glimmer of light skims across the grassy meadow. The vast Wyoming sky begins to stir. I step outside and take a breath. Even in June, the air bites at this elevation. I follow a narrow dirt path through the field to Jessie's cabin. She's bundled and ready. We head for the corrals.

As dawn stretches across the landscape, Jessie saddles three of her favorite horses: her gelding LeDoux and two packhorses, Misty and Ike. She and LeDoux go way back—he was her rodeo queen horse growing up, and he's still her go-to rope horse for brandings. Misty and Ike were born on the ranch and now spend their lives traveling deep into the backcountry. There's an easy, familiar rhythm between them. Jessie is an expert handler.

We climb the hillside as the sun crests the mountains. Jessie, her loyal pup Scout, and the trio of horses are bathed in sharp, golden light. She guides them past lichen-covered boulders, weaving through blooming wildflowers—shooting stars, mountain bluebells, and cinquefoil. Scout waits patiently, alert for a command. Stonecrop and bitterroot, both freshly bloomed, dot the terrain. The air is calm, the world still. Beyond Jessie, Scout, LeDoux, Misty, and Ike, there's only wilderness—rugged, remote, and real.

My tiredness from the early wake-up and long journey to the ranch dissolves, alchemized into something grounding and quietly electric. I understand now why Jessie can't live without this place. I take the final frames of our session as a full moon sets, making way for daylight's embrace.

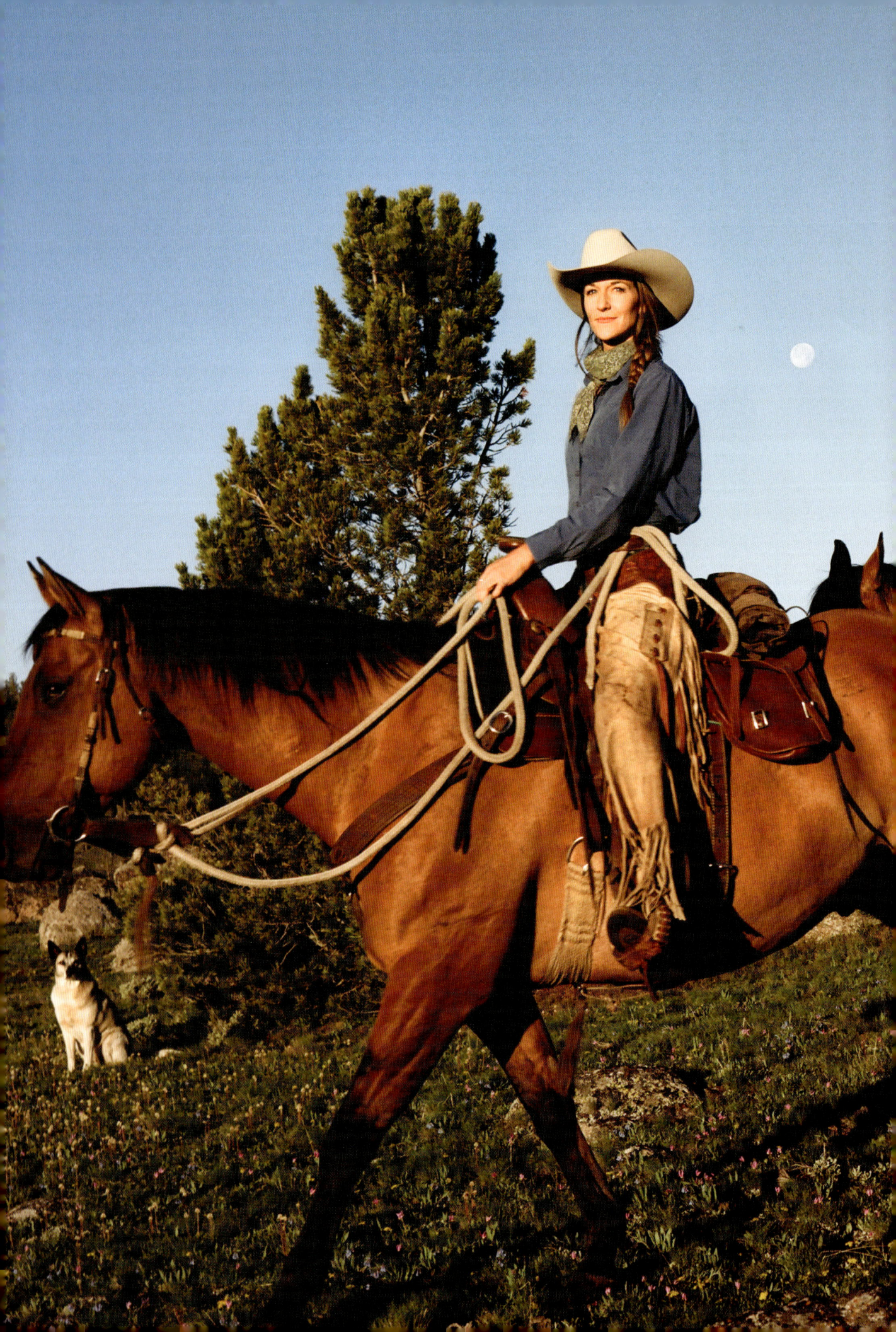

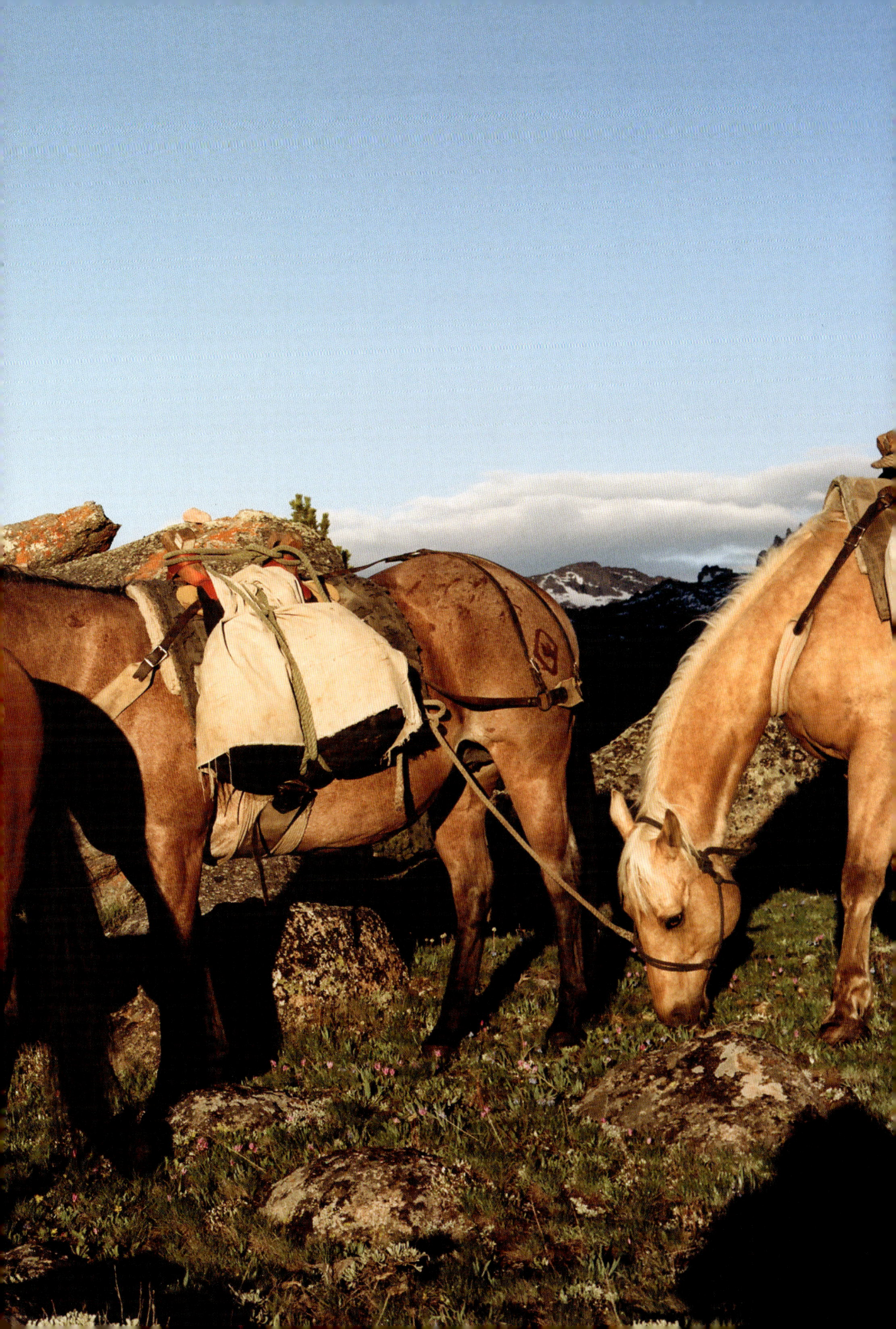

JESSIE ALLEN GOTTWALD

DIRECTOR AND OWNER OF ALLEN'S DIAMOND 4 RANCH, YOGA INSTRUCTOR, HUNTING GUIDE, NATIONAL OUTDOOR LEADERSHIP SCHOOL INSTRUCTOR, FORMER MISS WYOMING

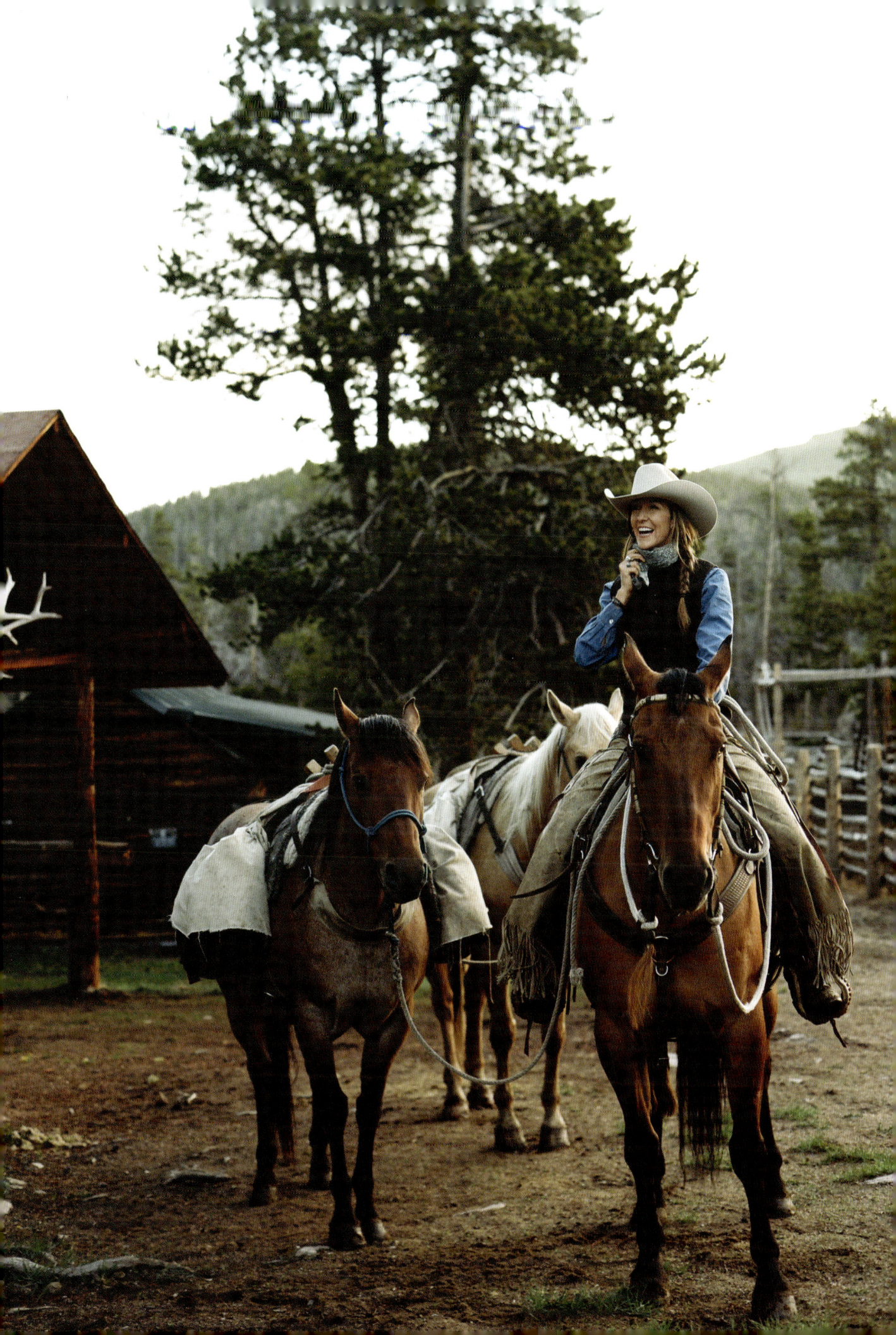

"I really appreciate that being in the mountains, your focus is fully present . . . It's where I feel most connected and alive."

A hundred horses scatter. Hand-built, rustic cabins blend into the forest at the meadow's edge. Ahead, the commanding skyline of the Wind River mountains rises, jagged and immense. The entire scene feels otherworldly. Here at the Diamond 4 Ranch, owner Jessie Allen Gottwald is building something rare: connection and community in wild, untouched terrain.

Jessie's parents built the ranch in the 1970s, and it's been a licensed outfitter since 1973. Jessie has carried that legacy forward with strength and vision. At just thirteen, Jessie led her first solo trip—guiding a group of older male fly-fishermen. Initially skeptical of her youth and skill, they quickly shed their doubts after a successful catch.

Jessie's Wyoming roots run deep. Her ancestor Senator John Fosher cast the tiebreaking vote in 1871 to retain Wyoming's groundbreaking suffrage legislation. A sixth-generation Wyoming woman, Jessie honors her family's legacy of service with a community-oriented mindset. While studying at the University of Wyoming, she served as an FFA state officer,

performed on the university dance team, and spent a semester in Washington, DC, as an intern for Wyoming's congresswoman. These experiences shaped her leadership path and inspired her to compete for—and win—the title of Miss Wyoming in 2014, which took her to the Miss America stage the following year.

As a guide, teacher, and facilitator, Jessie leads guests into tens of thousands of acres of wilderness accessible from the ranch. She offers weeklong women's yoga retreats, as well as horseback riding, fly-fishing, and hiking trips for individuals, families, and groups. In the fall, she guides archery and rifle hunters in pursuit of elk, deer, moose, and antelope. As the only female hunting guide on the ranch—and the one with the highest harvest rate—Jessie continues to challenge expectations.

In the offseason, she guides students through backcountry expeditions with the National Outdoor Leadership School (NOLS). An adventurer at heart, she lives with deep curiosity and an explorer's mindset. She completed her yoga teacher training in Thailand, worked as a handler in Alaska's grueling Yukon Quest

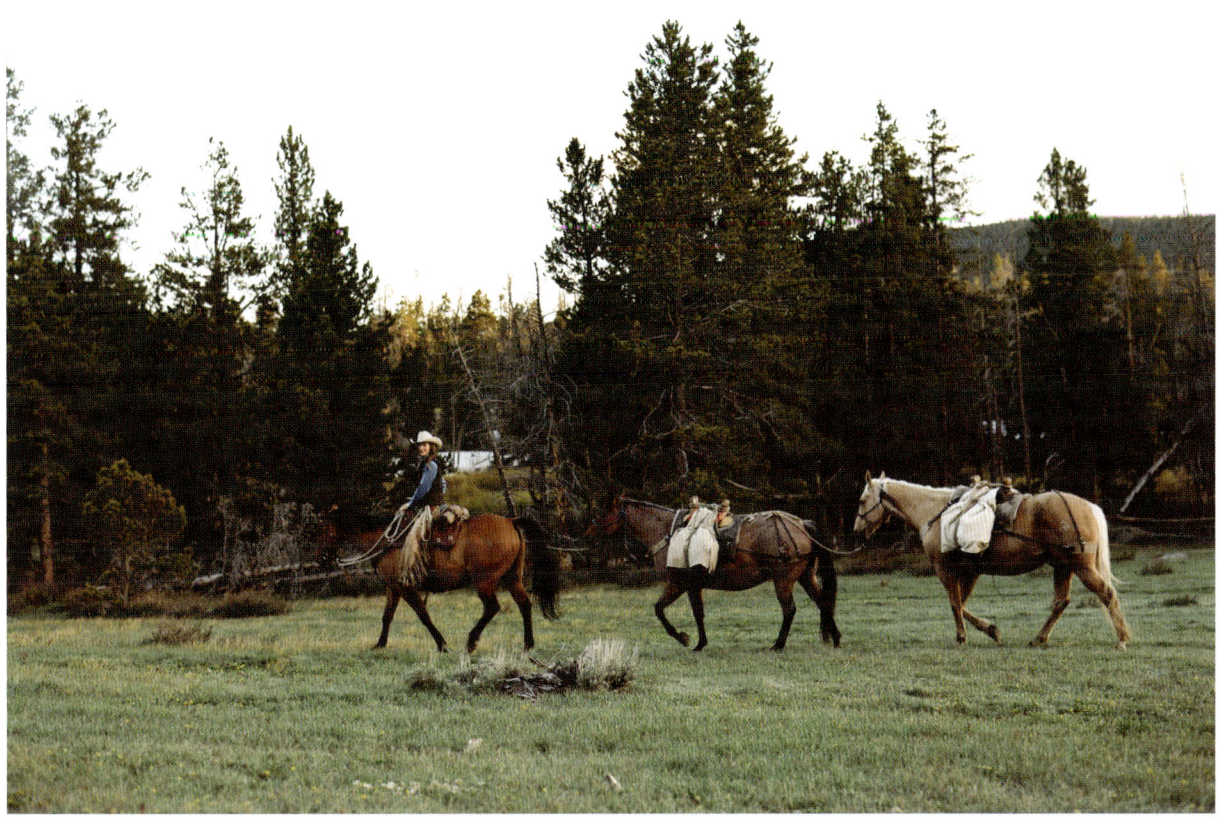

thousand-mile dogsled race, and spent four months traveling solo through New Zealand—working at dairy farms, horse-trekking operations, and sheep stations.

Surrounded by terrain so untouched, it's impossible not to feel small in the best way. As Jessie puts it, "I really appreciate that being in the mountains, your focus is fully present. You are in the here and now. And yes, your mind can wander when you're riding alone for hours, but it always comes back to the present. It's where I feel most connected and alive."

Jessie channels that awe into transformational experiences in the mountains. As an outdoor facilitator, she helps her clients bridge divides, find common ground, and foster a broader sense of human connection. In a world that often feels increasingly artificial and consumer-driven, Jessie knows access to untouched nature is essential—for staying open, grounded, and inspired.

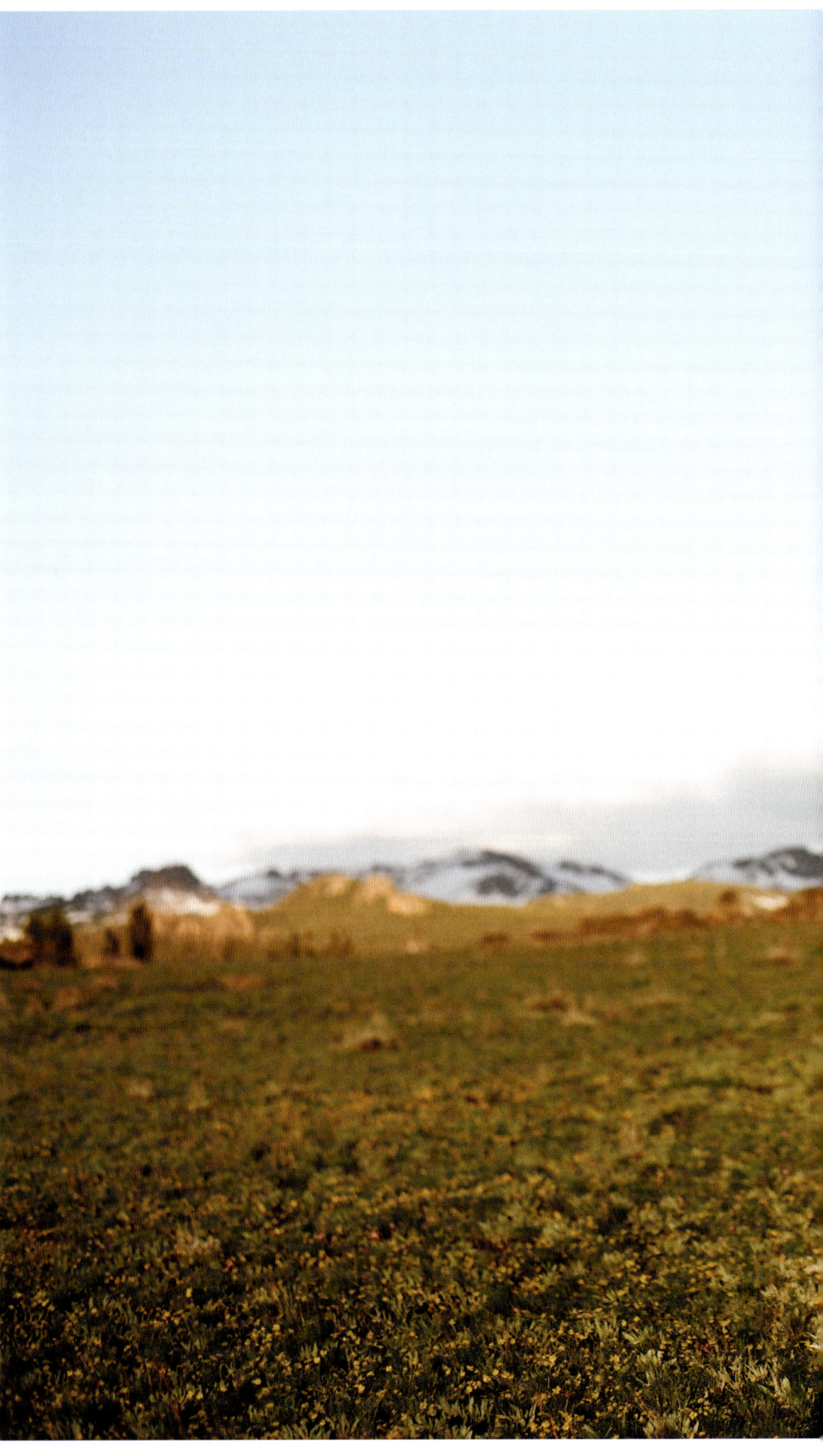

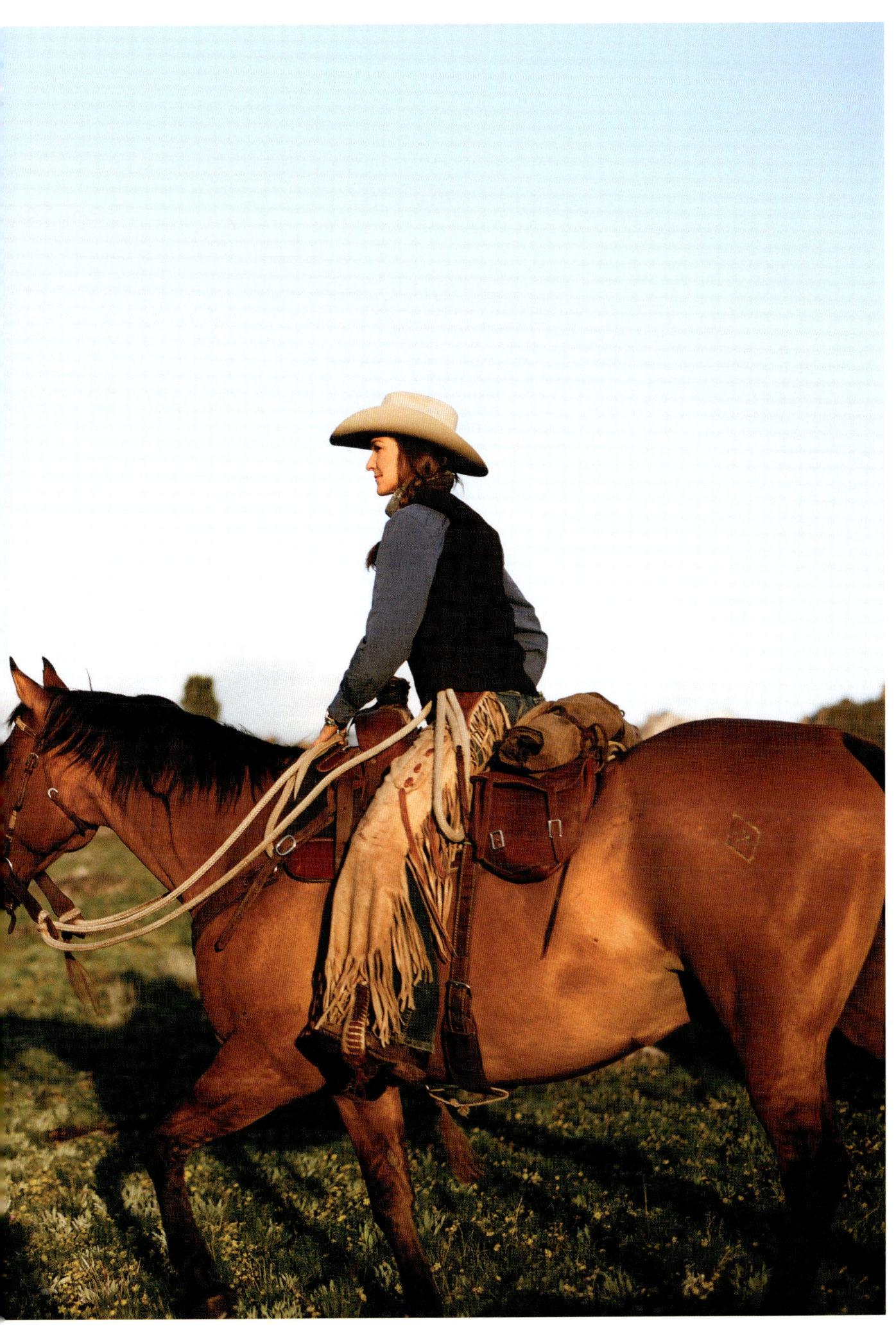

"*There is so much opportunity in being an anomaly. It's a powerful tool to not only break stereotypes and shift people's perspectives but to connect with people in a variety of ways. My goal is to diversify myself as much as possible because that allows the opportunity to bridge gaps, find common ground, and build a broader connection with people.*"

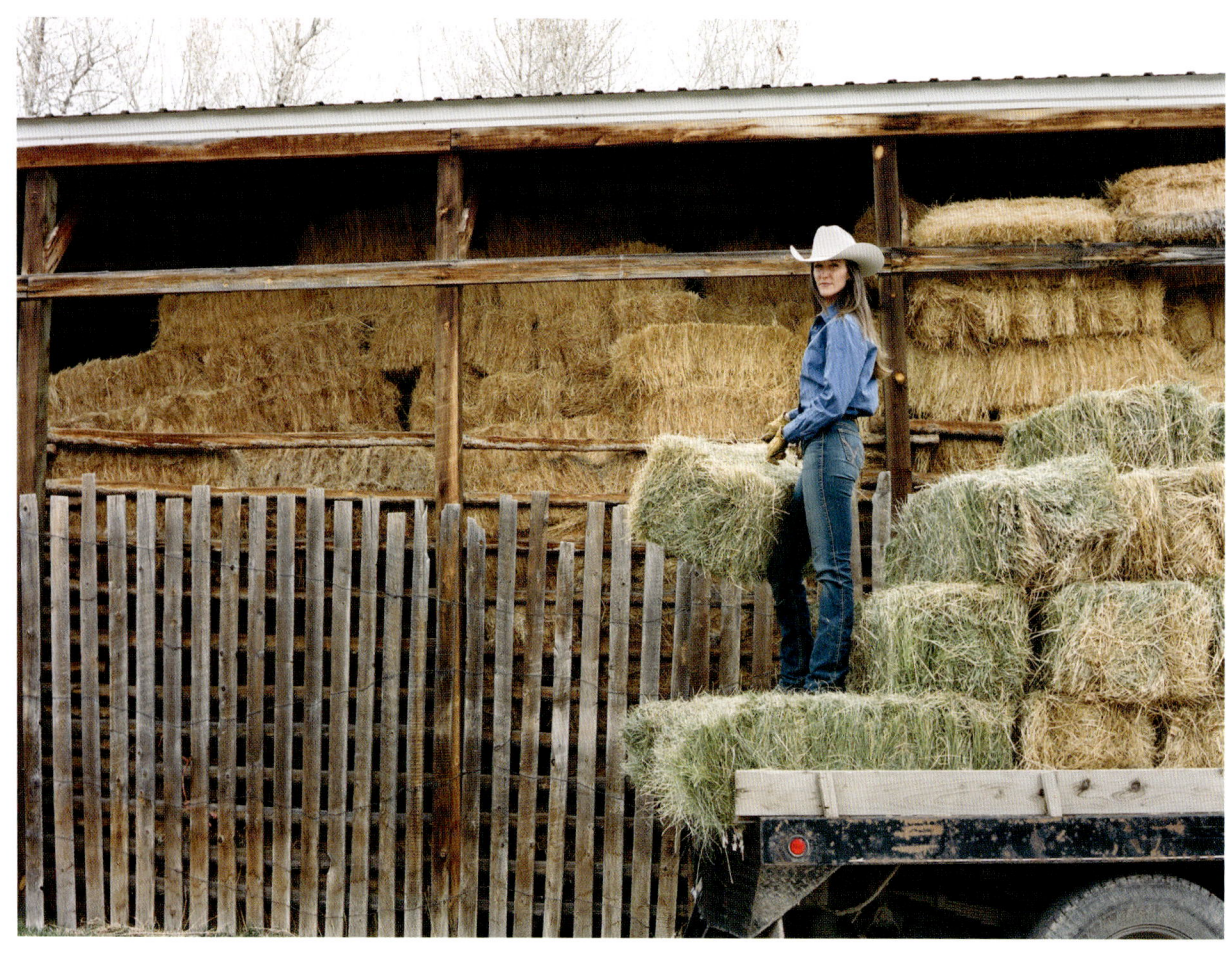

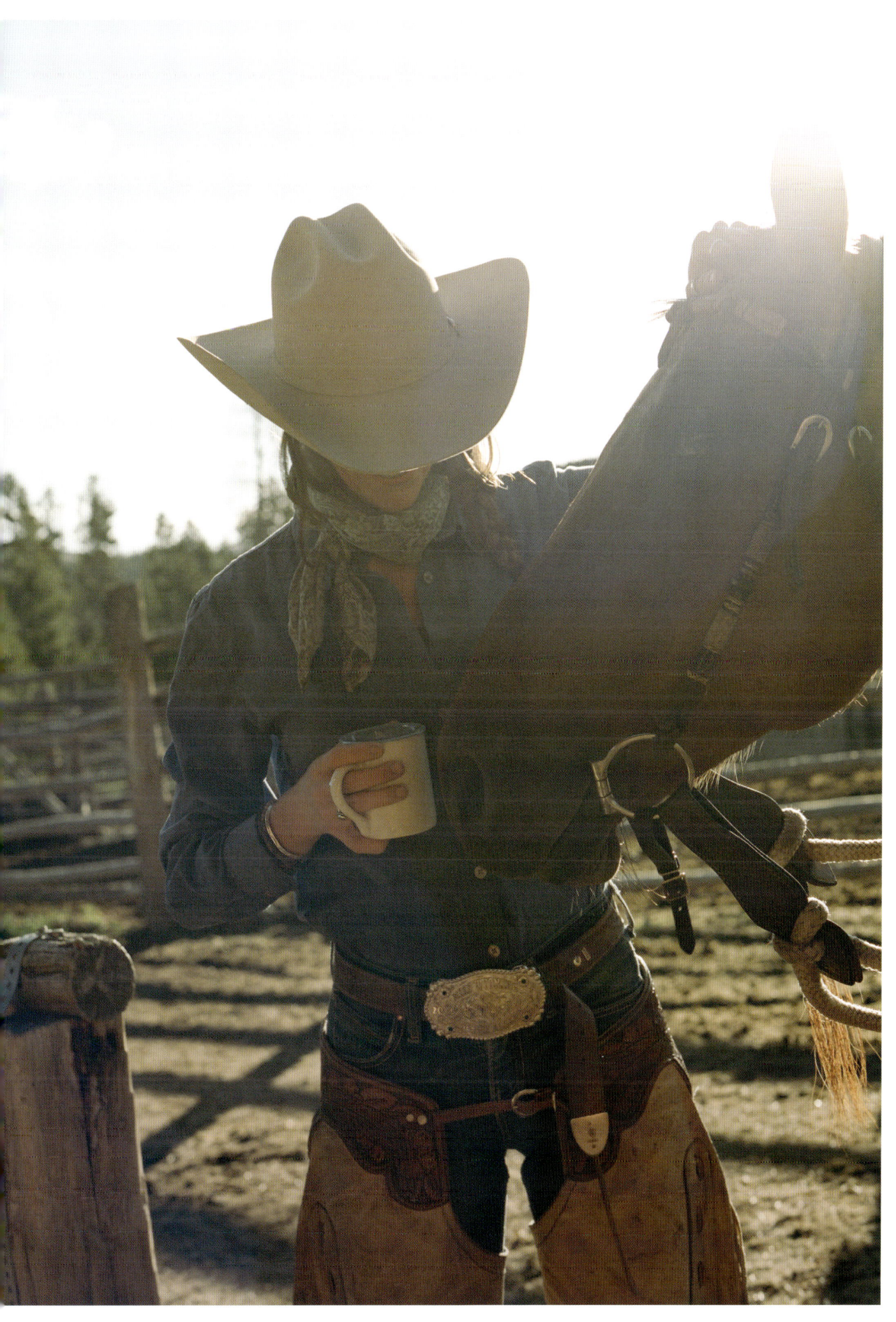

ANN
SIMPSON

COMMUNITY AND MENTAL HEALTH ADVOCATE,
CHAMPION FOR THE ARTS

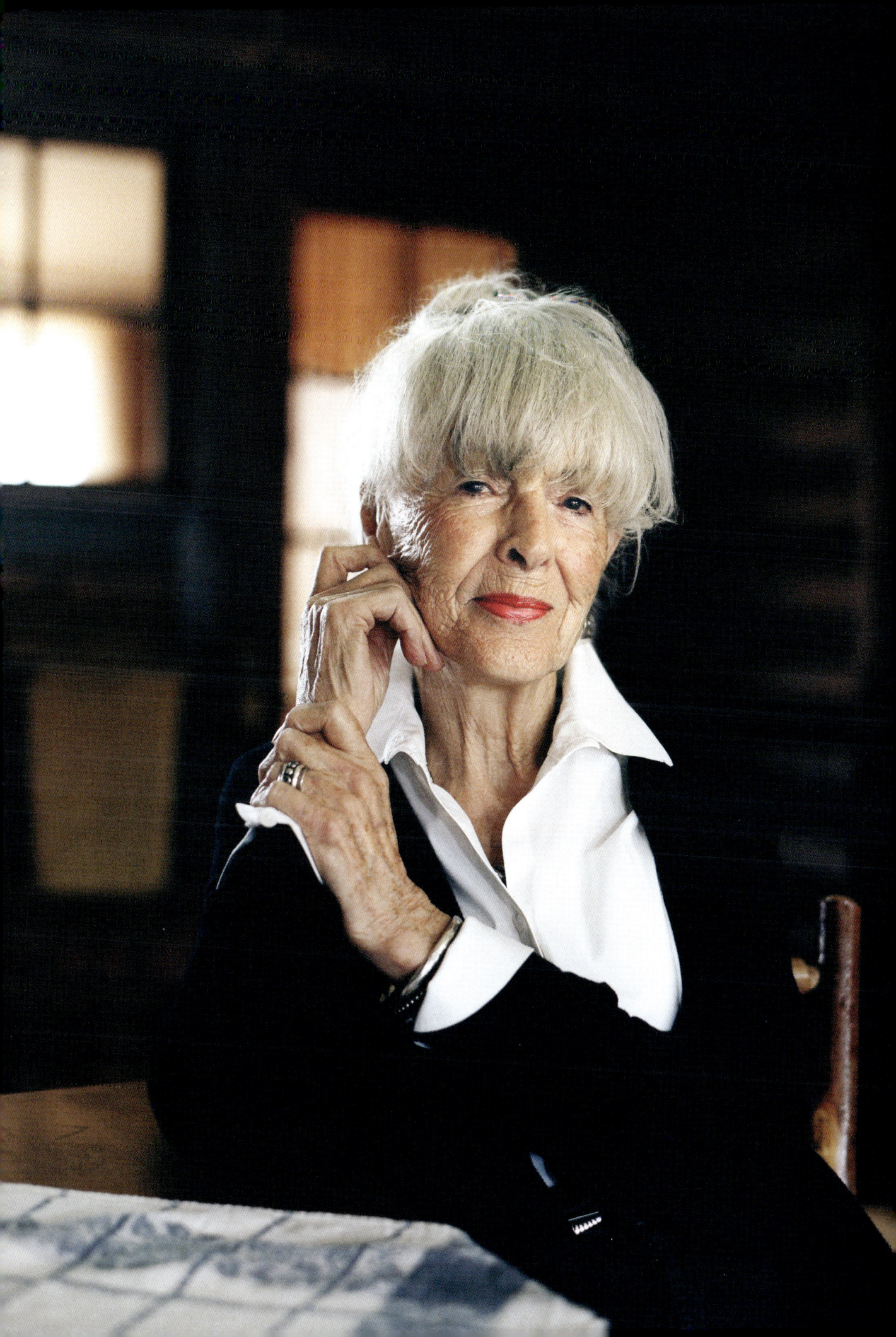

> *"Life is to make the most of what you have done and let go of regret. I think the goal is to gain wisdom about ourselves and life. We are constantly evolving with the goal to become a richer person."*

Ann Simpson's expansive spirit took root on a small farm in Greybull. As a child, she never imagined leaving her small town—or even envisioned what life had in store for her. As she recalls, "It just evolved." A self-described hyperactive, headstrong child, Ann spent her days in the garden or tending to the family's chickens and horses alongside her father. That sense of routine and closeness shifted abruptly when her father died suddenly of a brain tumor during her junior year of high school.

Following the tragedy, Ann's mother moved her and her sister to Laramie, where their brother was attending the University of Wyoming. To support the family, her mother took a job as a house mother (presently called a dorm RA), and this new chapter opened Ann's eyes to a larger world. Though the transition was difficult, it launched her on a path of personal growth—one marked by resilience, curiosity, and expanding horizons.

It was in Laramie that Ann met her future husband, Alan Simpson (who, sadly, passed away in 2025). Their love story spanned seventy years and gave Ann the opportunity to travel, engage with diverse communities, and develop the broad, gracious presence for which she's best known. Her self-worth and confidence have always served as her compass, guiding her to "do what's right." The people and cultures she encountered—both at home and abroad—inspired many of her lifelong initiatives.

From her early years in politics alongside her father-in-law, Milward Simpson, to decades of public life with her husband in the Wyoming State Legislature and the U.S. Senate, Ann learned a fundamental truth: When you extend yourself to others with sincerity, they respond in kind. This simple but profound realization has shaped her service ever since.

Early in their marriage, an army posting in Germany for the future statesman sparked one of Ann's earliest initiatives: launching the first American Field Service (AFS) study-abroad program in Cody, which opened doors for Wyoming youth to travel internationally while also bringing students from around the globe to experience life in the American West.

As a mental health advocate, Ann was deeply involved with the Congressional Wives Mental

Facing Page: Ann Simpson with her daughter, gallerist Sue Simpson Gallagher.

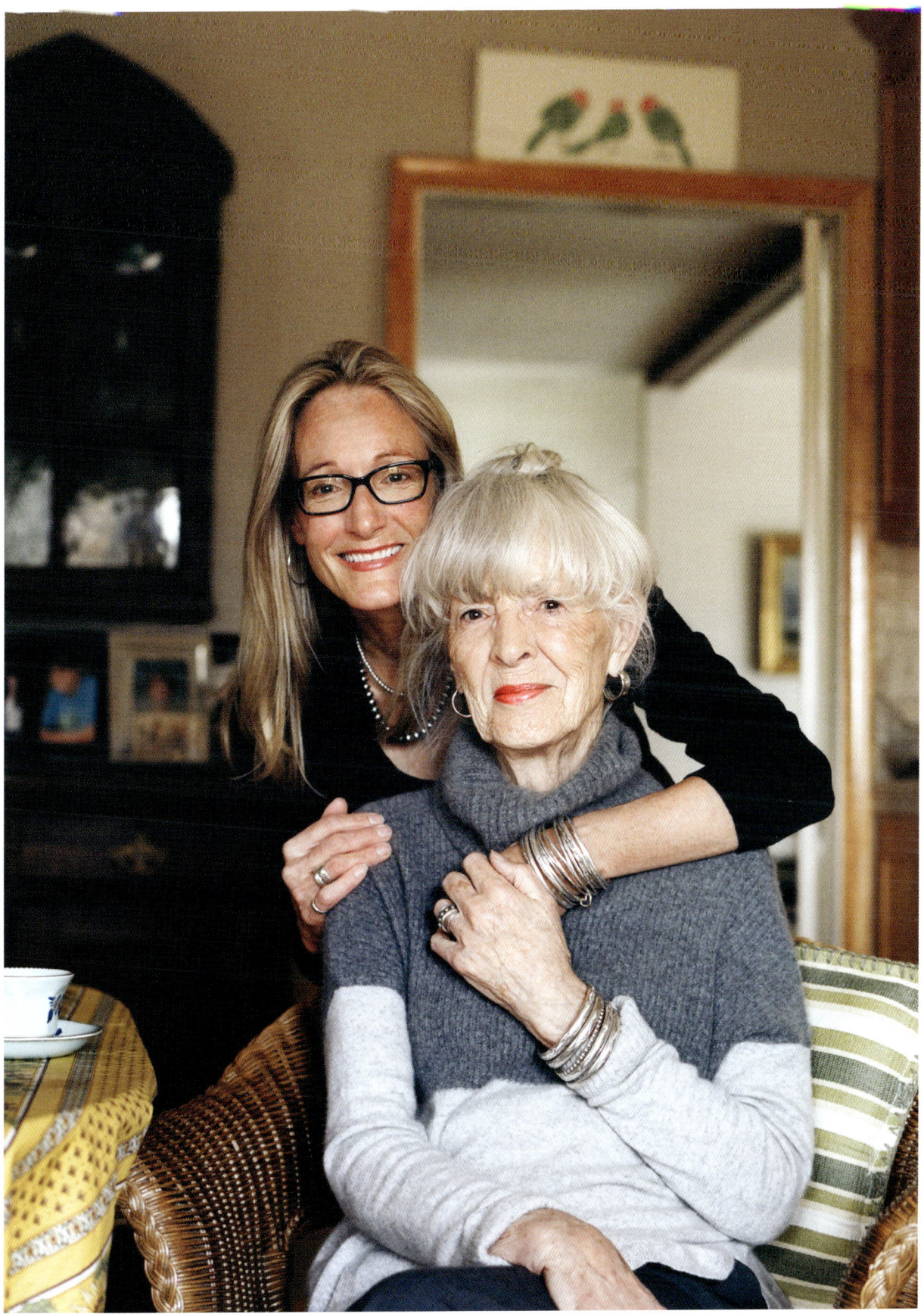

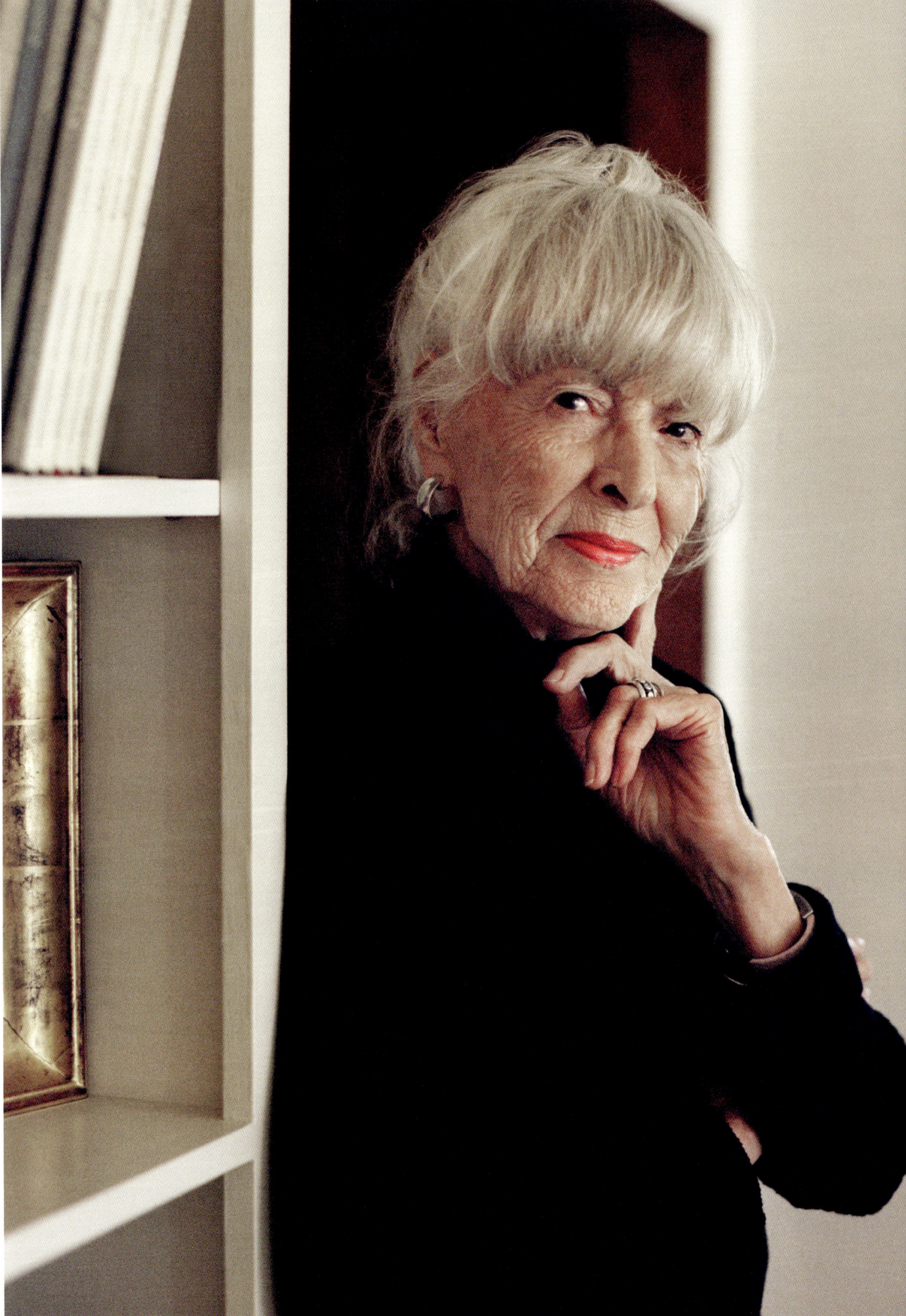

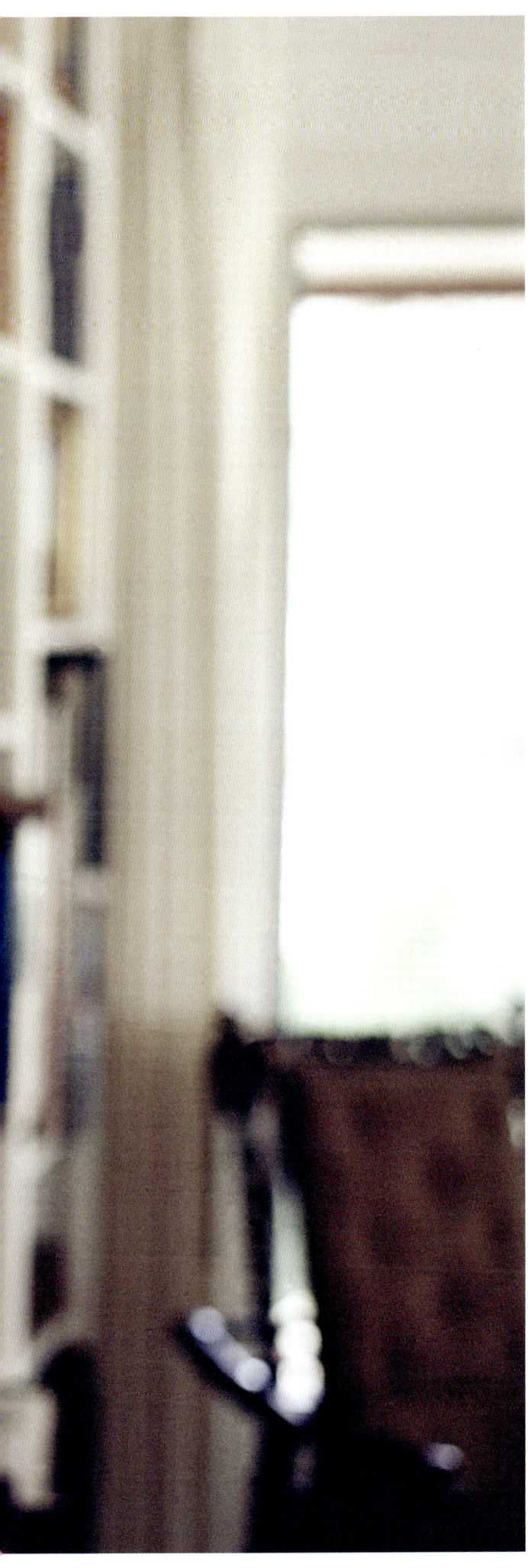

Health Group, working alongside Tipper Gore and Nancy Domenici of New Mexico to shine a national spotlight on mental illness. She also supported children with dyslexia through her work with the Lab School of Washington. Ann embraced the challenge of her demanding schedule in Washington, DC—which included advocacy work, political commitments, and a full-time career as a realtor—reflecting on what felt like eighteen-hour workdays. That season of life showed her she could handle just about anything and underscored her boundless capacity for service.

A champion of the arts, Ann helped establish the University of Wyoming's most successful outreach initiative: the Ann Simpson Artmobile. Named in her honor, the Artmobile has traveled across Wyoming's 97,914 square miles for more than three decades. Showcasing works from the University of Wyoming Art Museum's collection, the mobile program brings not only art but also hands-on creative experiences to communities that might otherwise have limited access. Regular visits are made to K–12 schools, libraries, visitor centers, senior centers, and other community spaces across the state.

From humble beginnings on a Wyoming farm to a lifetime of service, advocacy, and outreach, Ann Simpson has quietly and powerfully shaped her world. Through the opportunities she seized and the wisdom she shared, she has not only impacted her community, state, and country but carved a lasting legacy of personal and public transformation.

Ann has, without question, left her mark.

"I think the feeling of self-worth is very important for all of us. That's what holds us back, when you don't have self-worth."

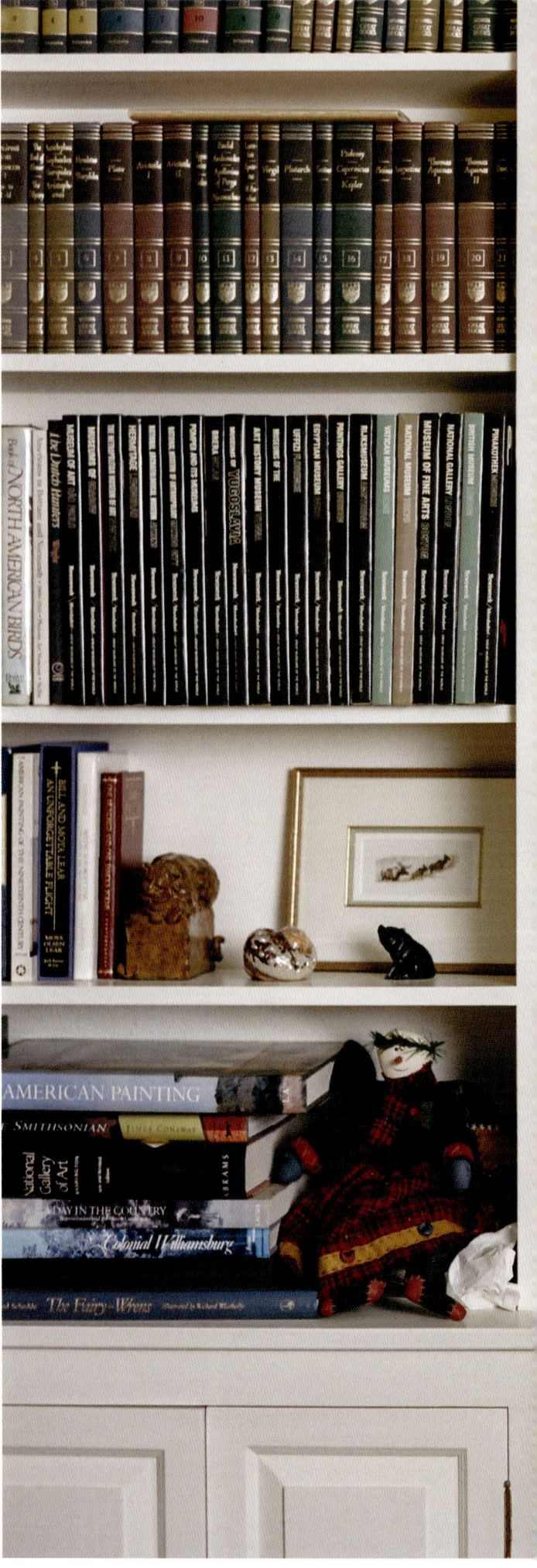

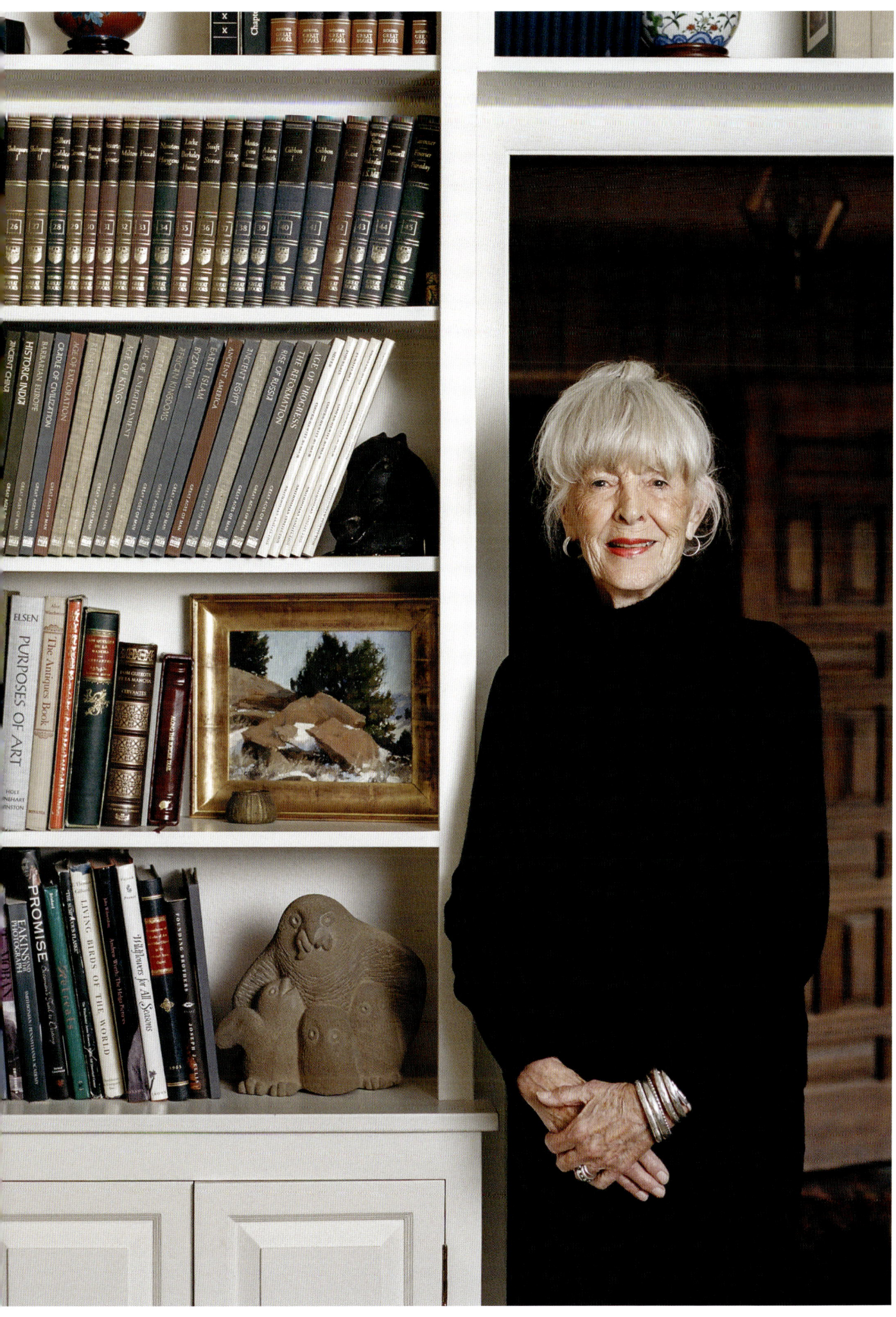

MARNIE PETERSON

SCIENTIST, INVENTOR, ENTREPRENEUR

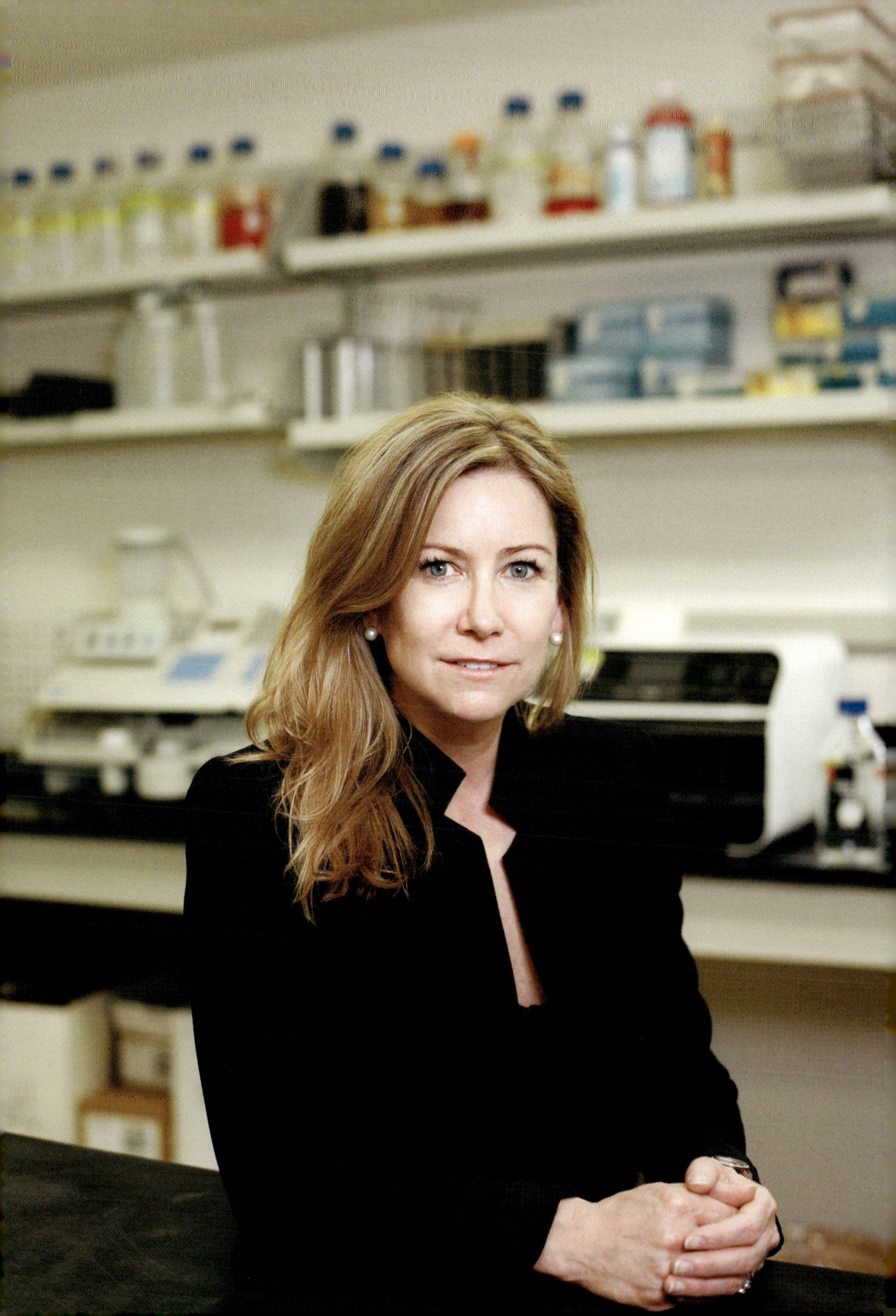

"I just love science. It's the undercurrent of all that we are and all that we do. And I love having young people come in, learn, and watch their lives and career paths progress and their impact grow."

When Marnie Peterson was growing up on a rural farm in Iowa, her daily life was centered around science and nature. She witnessed the cycle of life and death through caring for farm animals, and learned about biology and chemistry through hands-on agricultural experiences—crop cycles, soil health, and the rhythms of the land. Her father helped her grow bacteria on petri dishes for local science fairs, while her mother, an X-ray technician, introduced her to the human body and healthcare systems. These early exposures, combined with her natural acumen in STEM classes, laid a strong foundation for Marnie to thrive in a field historically dominated by men.

She began her professional journey in pharmacology, working for seven years as a hospital pharmacist at a teaching facility. A life-changing opportunity to study health care in Thailand sparked her deep interest in infectious diseases and global health. That passion took root and grew during her time in the United Kingdom, where she worked under Dr. Laura Piddock, a leading expert in antibiotic resistance. Upon returning to the United States, Marnie joined the University

of Minnesota, where she led a major research lab, earned several patents, and mentored the next generation of scientists.

For twenty-five-plus years, Marnie's been an innovator in the discovery and development of new therapeutics, as well as an expert in infectious diseases. After becoming a mother, Marnie and her husband sought a new pace of life and relocated to Wyoming in 2014. There, she continued to push an innovative and ethical approach to scientific research: what she calls "farm to bench."

Marnie and her team conducted research using live animal tissue, specifically pig tissue sourced from a local hog farmer. This tissue—a by-product of pigs being butchered for food that would otherwise have been discarded—was repurposed for drug development and testing. Because pig and human tissue are highly similar, this method reduces the need for live animal studies while improving the accuracy and efficacy of clinical trials. It also promotes sustainability by helping local farmers make full use of their livestock.

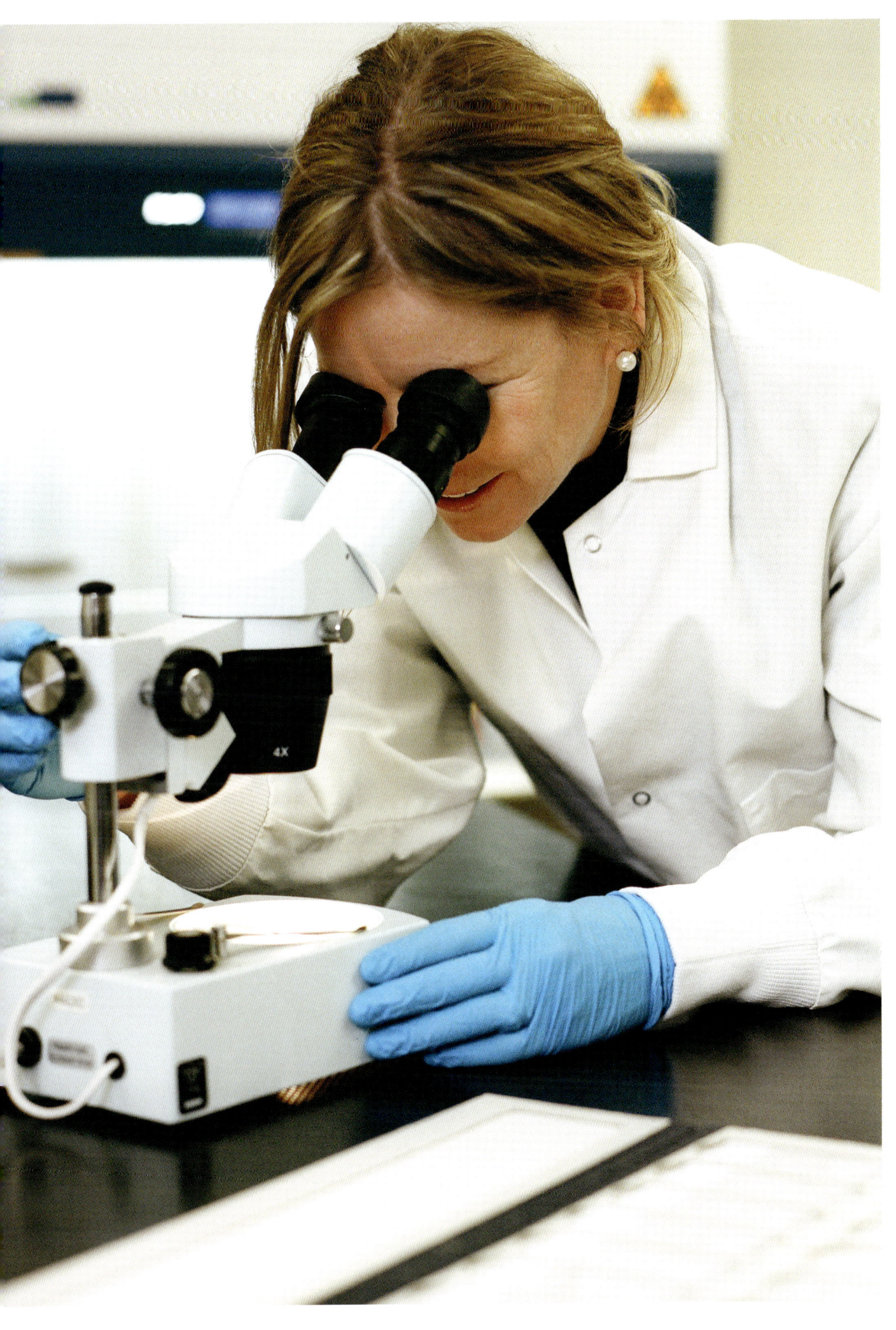

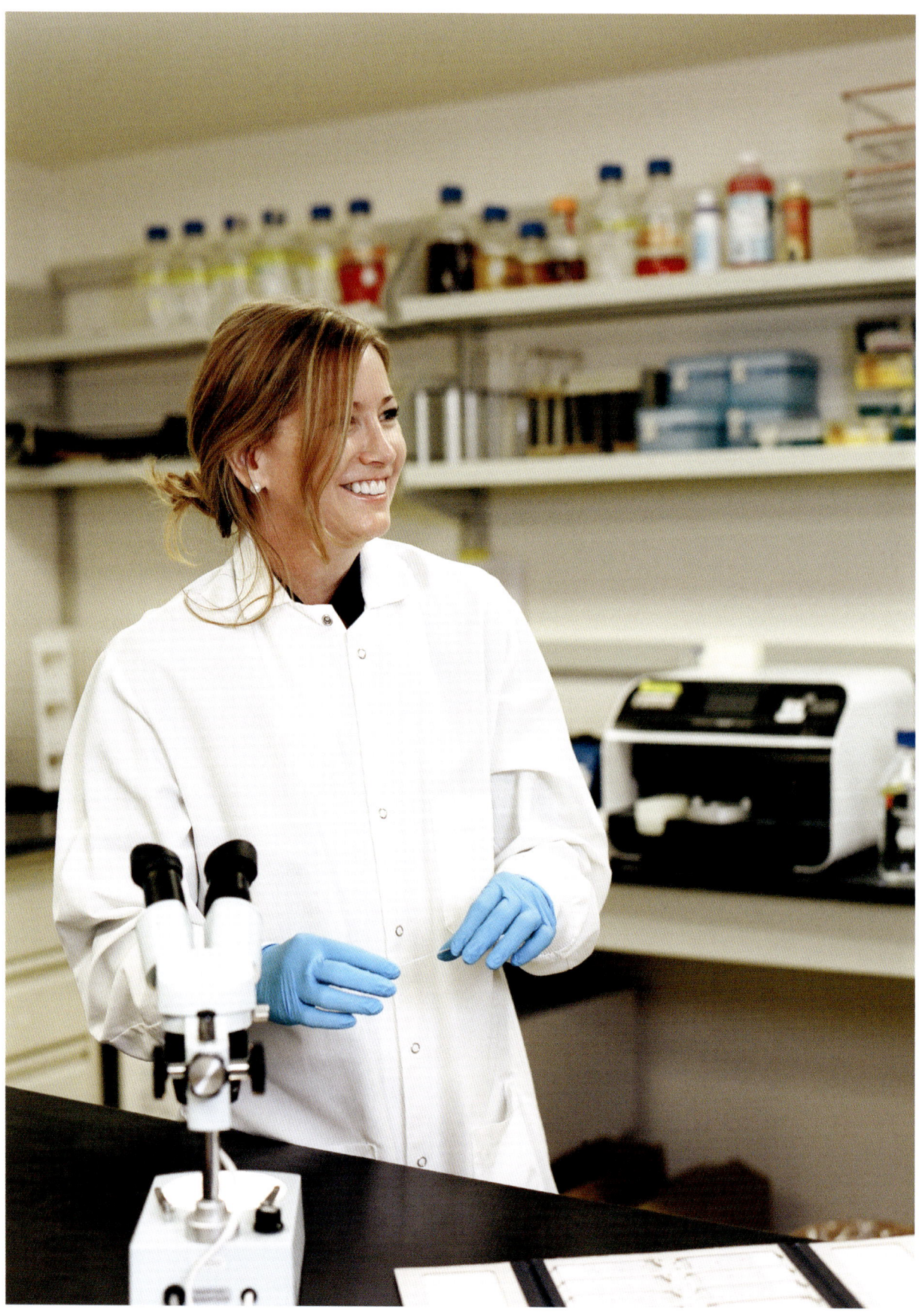

"When people ask me when I became interested in science, it's almost as if I can't remember, it goes back so far. Growing up on the farm and seeing animals born and unfortunately die of illness and disease, you get really connected to the life cycle. The underpinning of it all is biology, chemistry, and all things science."

Marnie has been developing and refining this method for over two decades, becoming a leader in this niche but increasingly essential area of biomedical science. In the spring of 2025, the FDA announced their commitment to phasing out animal testing and exploring new approach methodologies (NAMs), like live animal tissue alternatives. As Marnie puts it, "It's important how and the way we do science"—a belief that guides her commitment to conscientious, responsible research. The world is catching up.

In 2016, she founded and became CEO of Extherid Biosciences, focusing on new approaches to preclinical research, including live animal alternatives that accelerate and predict clinical outcomes. In June 2020, she merged her company with Dr. Samantha Westgate in the United Kingdom. As chief scientific officer (CSO) and U.S. managing director of Perfectus Biomed, Marnie led a boutique research firm that provided custom scientific services to pharmaceutical, medical device, and biotech companies. Her team helped clients develop new technologies, strengthen their intellectual property, and deliver innovative health solutions to market. Marnie and Dr. Westgate sold the company in October 2022, but Marnie remains active in the research world as a consultant and CSO for hire. Her unique approach to technology development led to research collaborations with the FDA, academics, and global companies in the pharmaceutical, medical device, and cosmetics industries.

Marnie is especially inspired by the next generation. Sharing her love for science is of the utmost importance to her. She routinely mentors up-and-coming scientists at the University of Wyoming and around the globe.

SARA
WOOD

REGENERATIVE FARMER, HERITAGE GRAIN GROWER,
COMMERCIAL FLOUR MILL OPERATOR

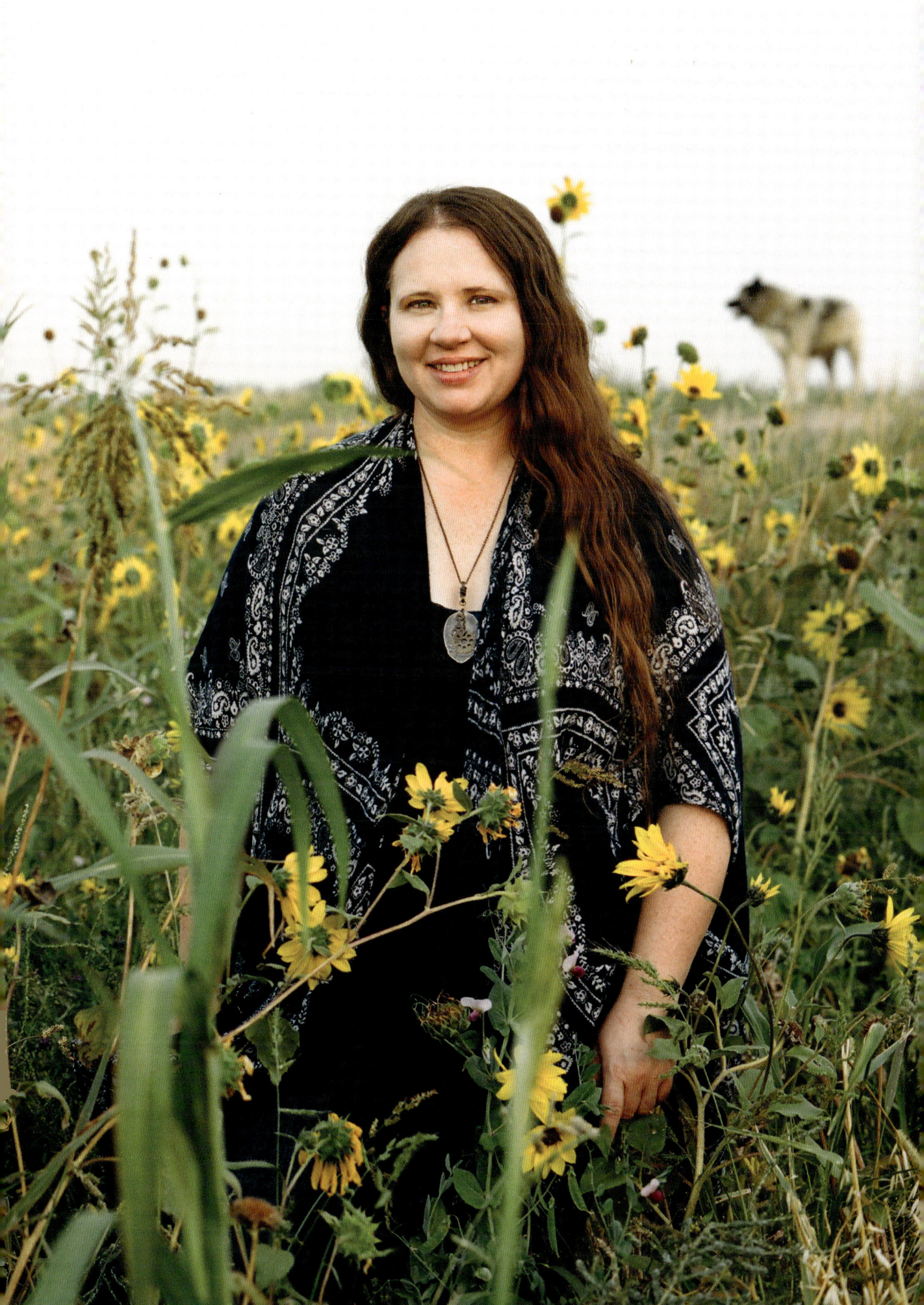

"A big part of my mission is connecting people to their food, how what they have on their plate is grown, and creating a larger connection to the farming community and to agriculture."

Driving down a country lane outside of Powell, you'll find a field unlike the rest. There isn't one crop neatly planted in rows, but seven, all wildly intermixed and ranging in height from ground cover to upwards of five-foot stands. It's seemingly unkempt, but there's a method to what looks a little like madness. If you listen carefully, you'll hear a cacophony of sounds—bumblebees, leaf-cutter bees, wasps, and other pollinators. The aptly named "salad field" is the center of fourth-generation farmer and fifth-generation Wyomingite Sara Wood's regenerative farming and heirloom grain operation.

Sara gets a lot of attention for her salad field, but she never expected to take over the family farm—let alone become a full-time farmer. Her family arrived in the Bighorn Basin in the early 1900s and has worked the same land since 1946. Farming demands a particular kind of grit: passion, resilience, a deep love for the land, and a willingness to face uncertainty head-on. Weather, market prices, and the rising cost of supplies are all beyond a farmer's control. For many, after years of hard work and little reward, selling to developers makes sense.

But Sara wanted a different future. If their farm was going to last another one hundred years, something had to change.

In 2017, a question sparked her transformation: *Why are so many people gluten-intolerant?* That curiosity led her to heirloom and heritage grains—ancient, pre-hybridized varieties of wheat, oats, barley, and rye. She uncovered how much biodiversity had been lost in modern agriculture and decided to act on that discovery. Leaving her corporate job, she convinced her father and uncle to completely transform their traditional farm, which grew conventional crops like sugar beets, corn, and beans, into a regenerative agricultural operation. In came regenerative practices: cover crops, companion plants, rotational grazing, and no-till soil management.

Their goal wasn't just sustainability—it was self-sufficiency. By moving away from chemical fertilizers and pesticides, they nurtured the health of their soil and crops naturally. But the boldest—and riskiest—move was abandoning the traditional commodity market in favor of a direct-to-consumer model.

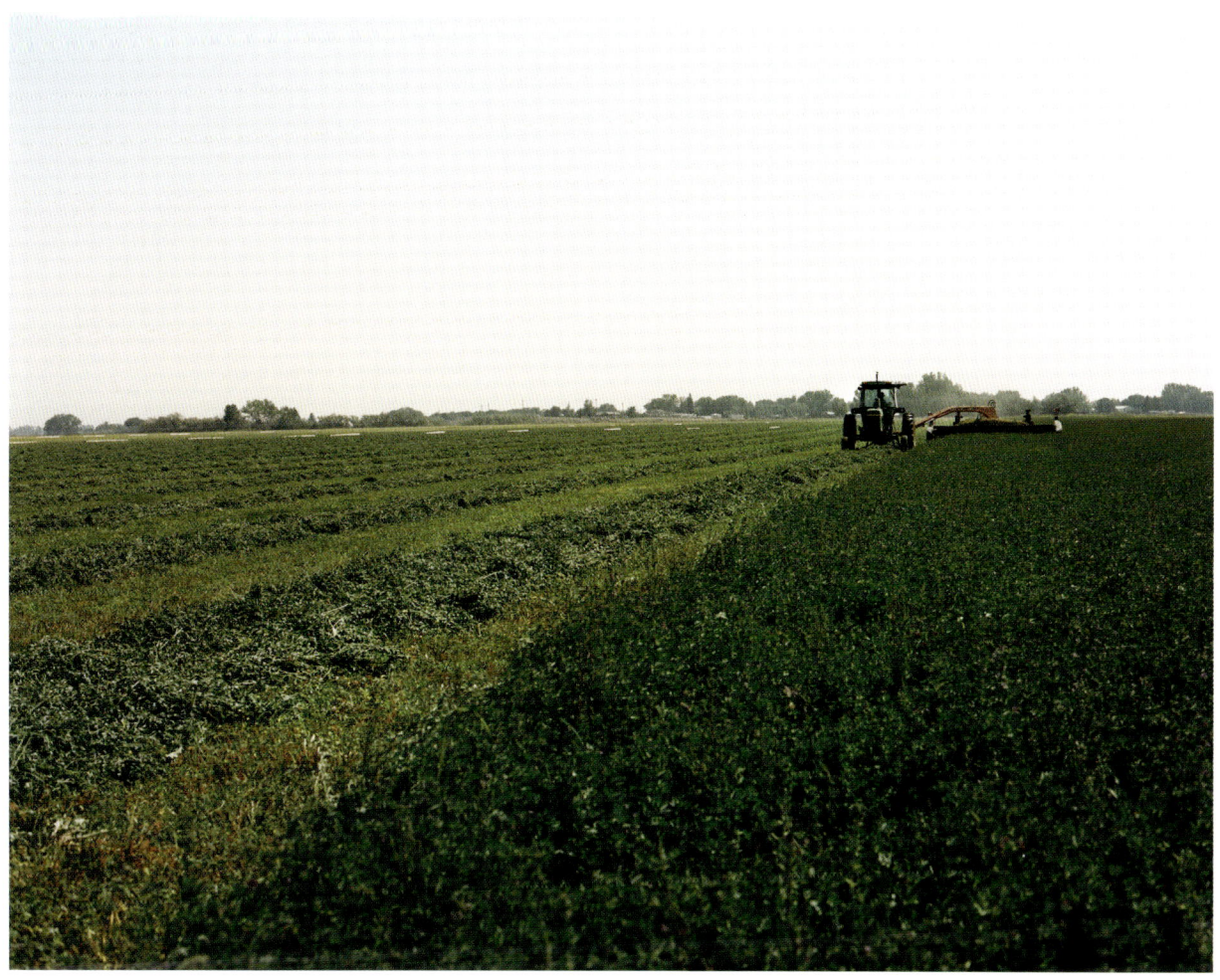

As the owner and founder of Wyoming Heritage Grains, Sara believes good food should be nutrient-dense, sustainably grown, and locally rooted. Connecting people to where their food comes from—and how it's grown—is at the heart of her mission. One of her unexpected joys has been learning to mill her own flour, producing White Sonora pancake mix, Red Fife wheat berries, and a variety of freshly milled flours and grain products. From seed to table, none of her yield leaves the state before being shipped to consumers.

Though she's often seen as an outsider for doing things differently, there's nothing new about regenerative agriculture. The salad field serves as an excellent conversation starter. Curious farmers stop to ask questions—and that's exactly what Sara hopes for. Beyond growing food, she's on a mission to build community within agriculture and empower other farmers to rethink what's possible.

Sara's work is rooted in this principle: that thoughtful stewardship, collaboration, and innovation can nourish not just the land but the people who depend on it.

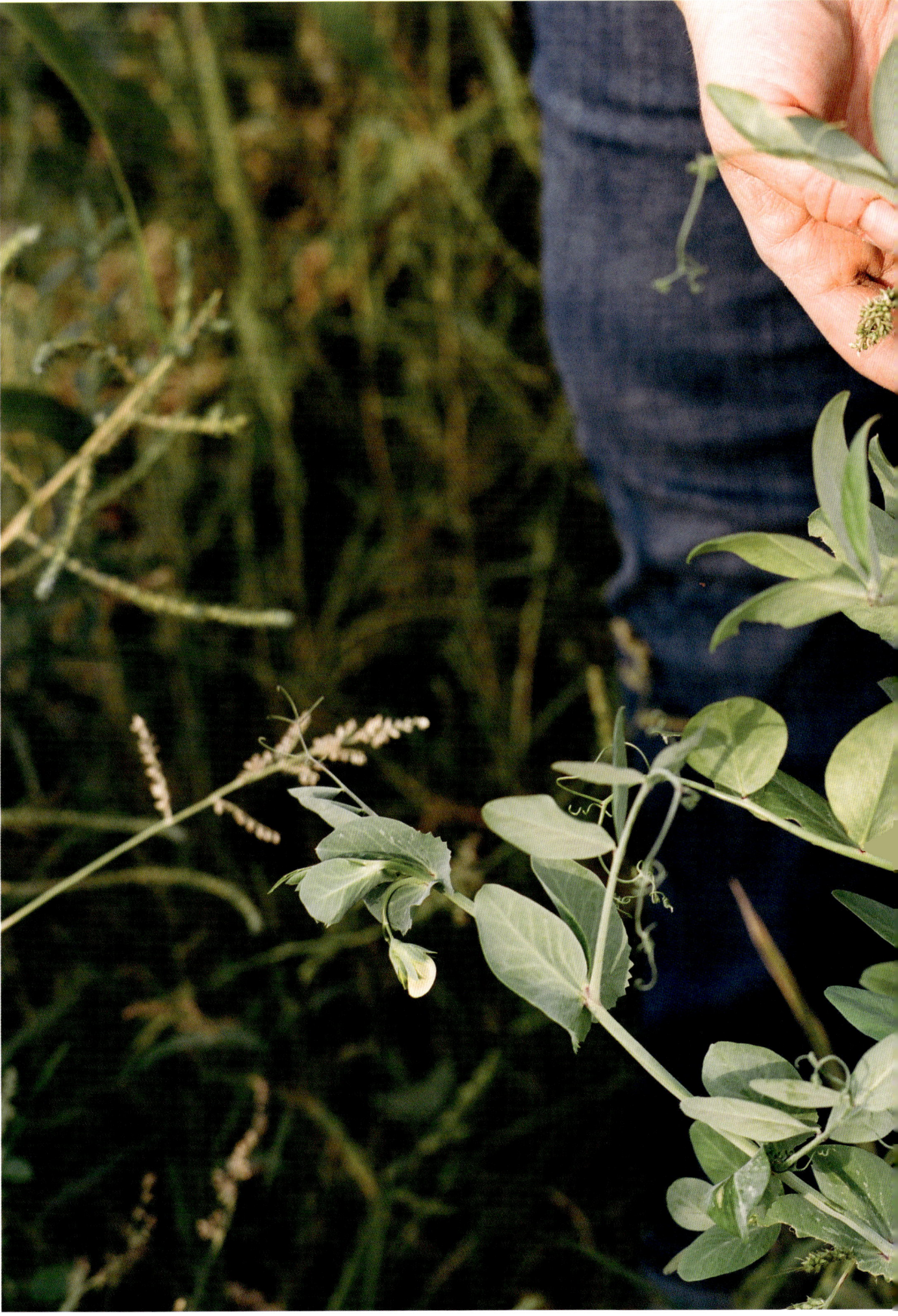

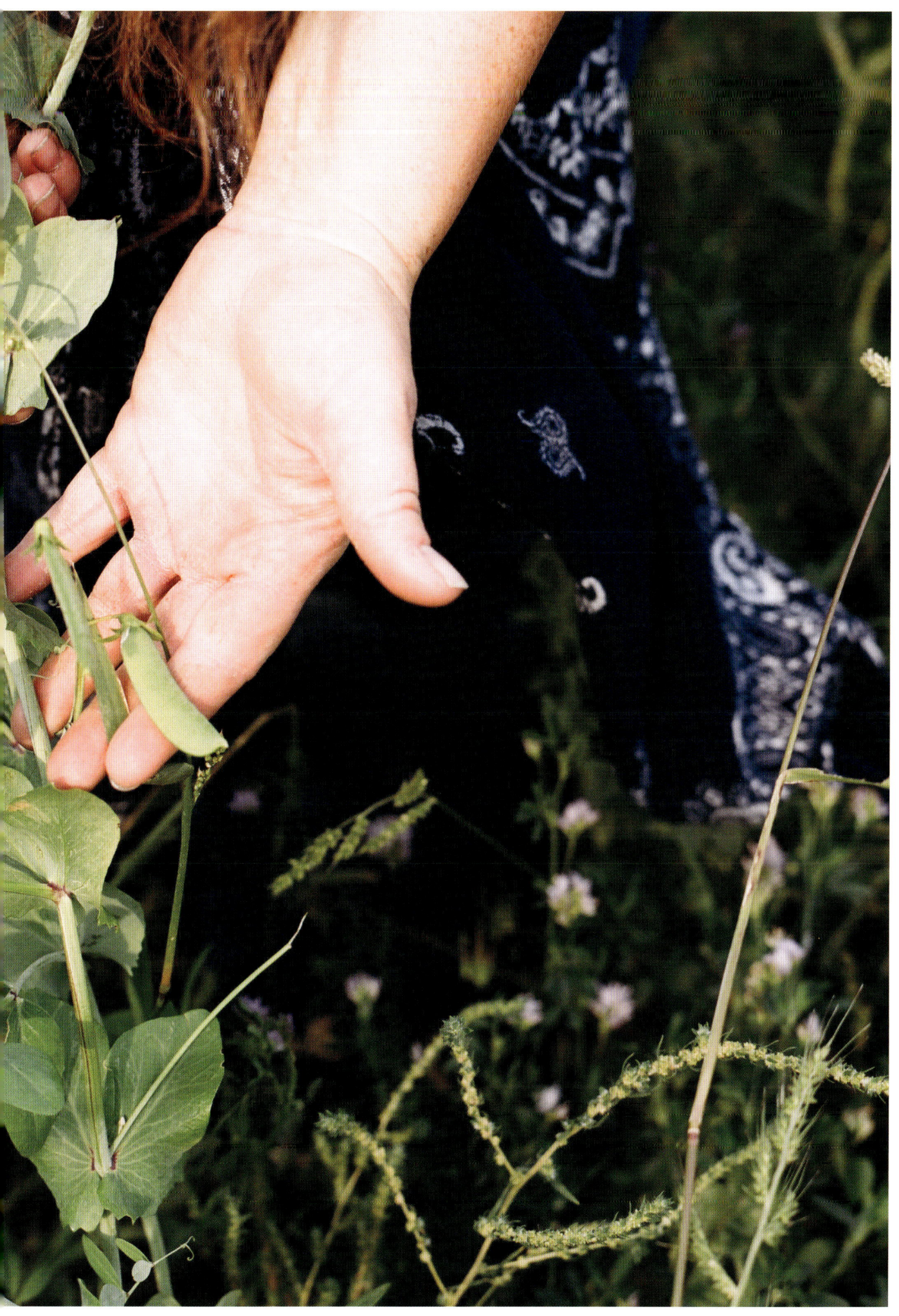

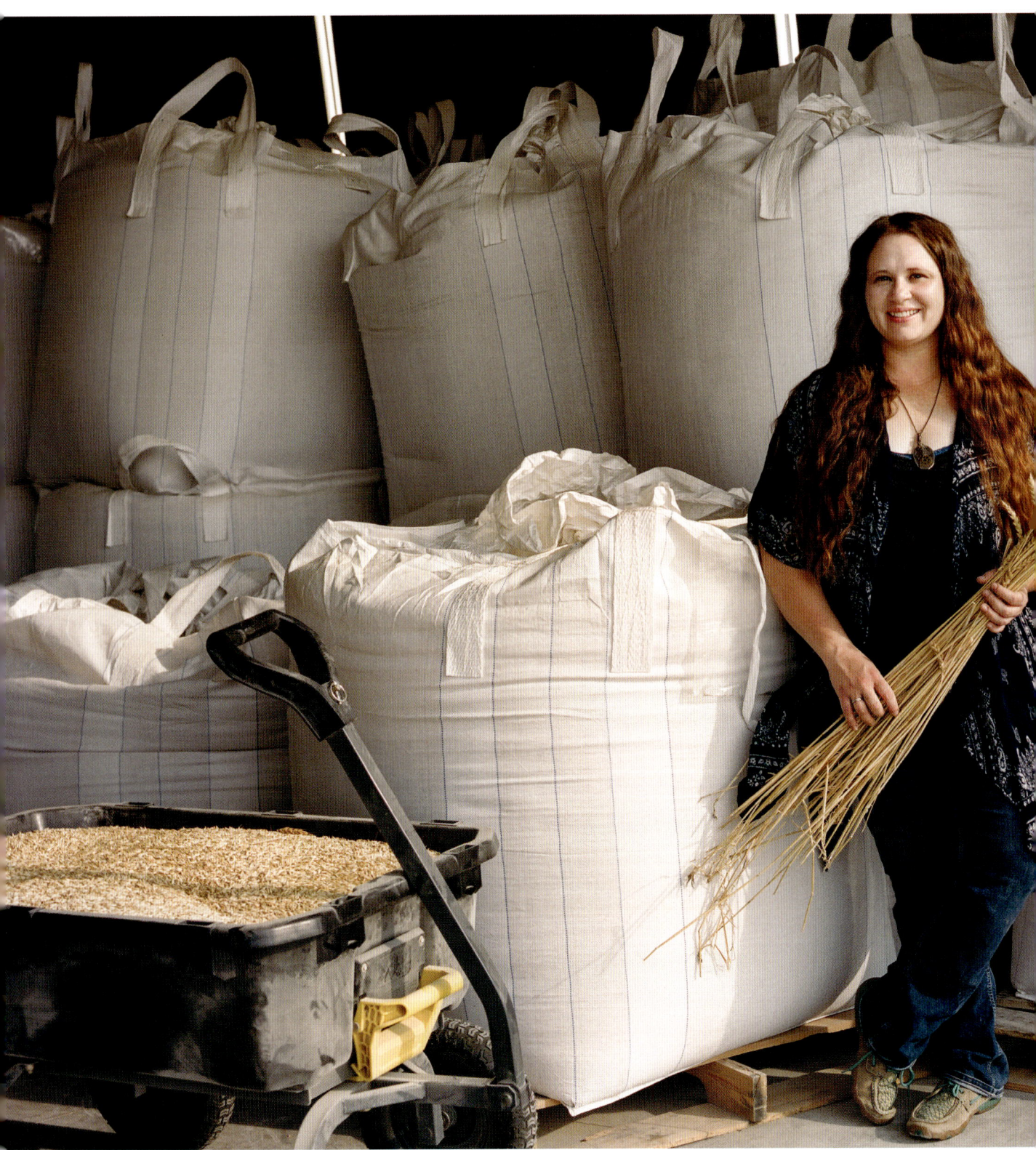

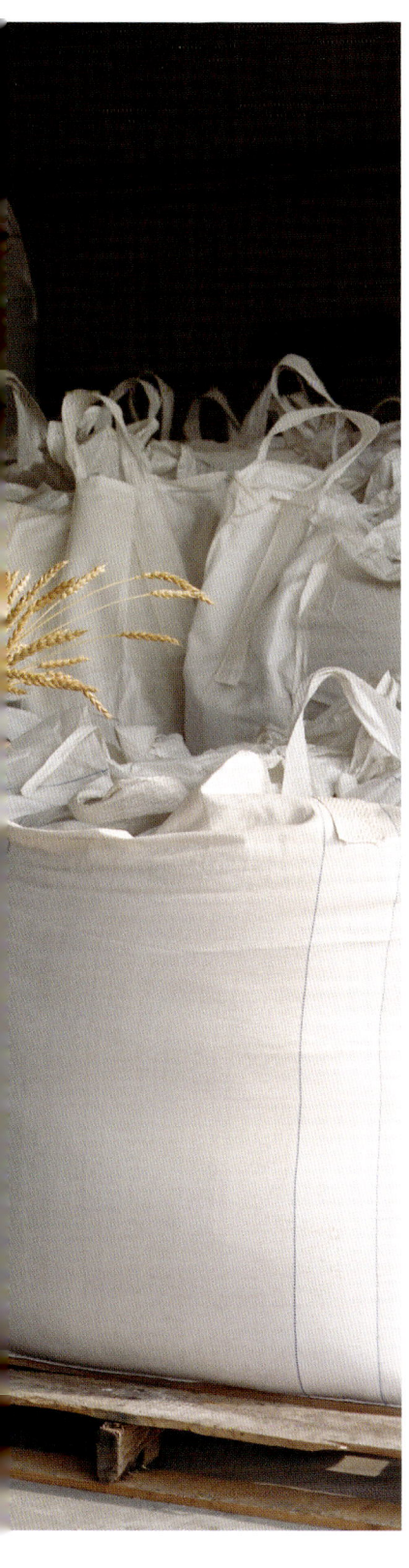

"Farming is an ecosystem. You can create your garden, lawn, home, or whatever you have as an ecosystem. Everyone has a role to play to foster diverse plant species and beneficial insects, but if we don't all work together, our ecosystems will continue to deteriorate, as well as our health."

JASMINE PICKNER BELL, "GOOD ROAD WOMAN"

TWO-TIME WORLD-CHAMPION HOOP DANCER, EDUCATOR

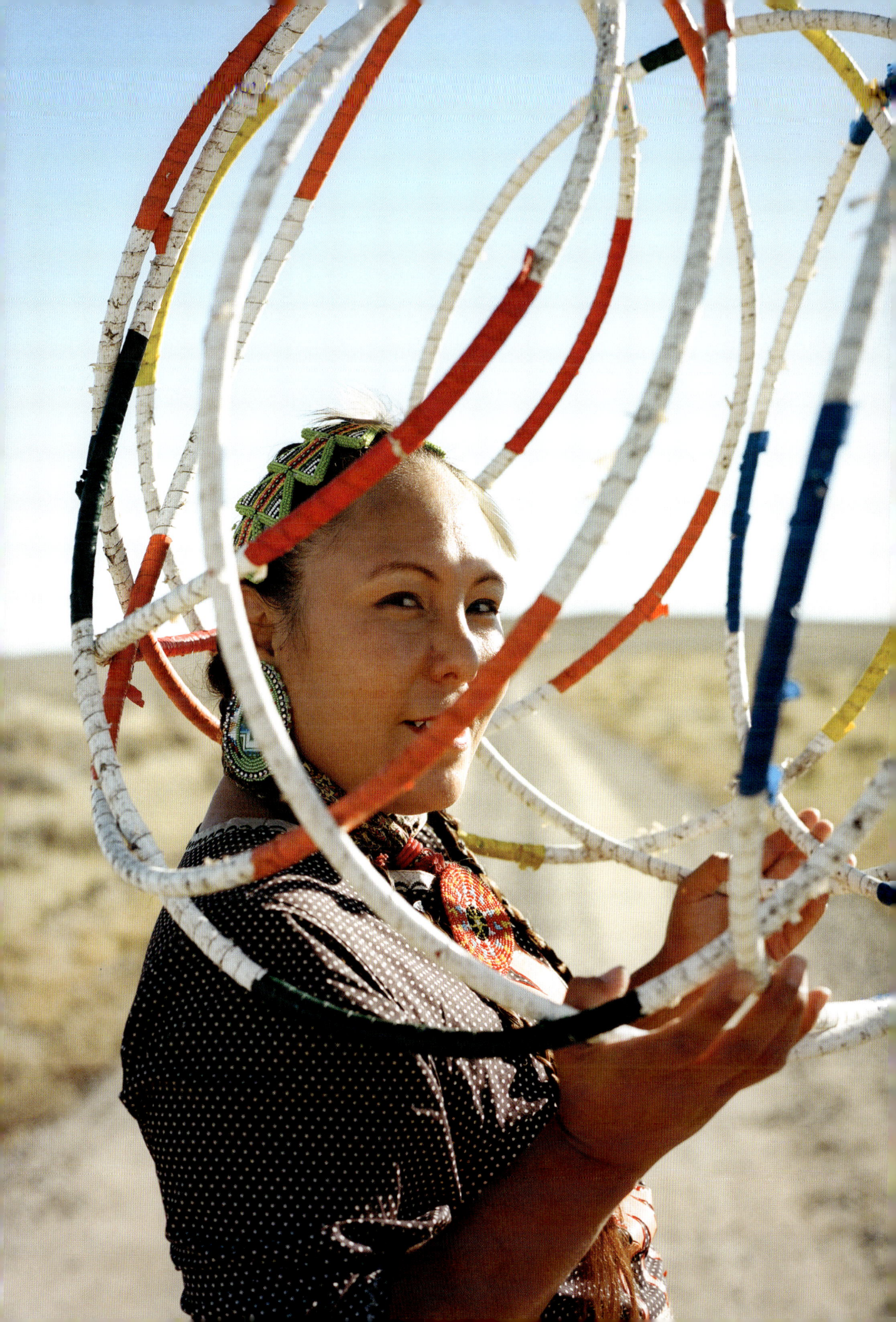

"The hoop dance has taught me that you keep moving forward no matter what. Sometimes a hoop might fall and a design may fall apart. But you pick up those hoops, you keep going, and you keep dancing. No matter what, as hard as life gets, you're going to be able to jump through that hoop."

Jasmine Pickner Bell, also known by her Dakota name Cunku Was'te Win', meaning "Good Road Woman," shares the sacred tradition of hoop dance with the world. A two-time world-champion hoop dancer, Jasmine is a member of the Crow Creek Sioux Tribe (Hunkpati Oyate). She carries a legacy of healing, storytelling, and cultural preservation—one hoop at a time.

She began training under her father, renowned hoop dancer Dallas Chief Eagle. Traditionally, the hoop dance was a male-only discipline, but Dallas recognized in his daughter a powerful blend of strength, spirit, and outspokenness—a force capable of restoring balance between masculine and feminine energy within the sacred circle.

Jasmine fully stepped into this calling following the tragic death of her brother, also a gifted hoop dancer. In his honor, she danced in his place at the World Championship Hoop Dance Contest—and won. Jasmine became the first woman to hold the title and the first to compete wearing a dress rather than traditional male attire. She returned the following year to defend her title and won again, further solidifying her role as a trailblazer and cultural torchbearer.

Often described as "the renewal of the collective human spirit," the hoop dance is a sacred act of healing, prayer, and unity. Though Jasmine spins constantly throughout her performances, she never feels dizzy. "You're aligned with a higher purpose," she says. As she passes each hoop around her body, she shares, "Your prayers are being connected and lifted up. You're not only telling a story through the designs of the hoop dance, but you're also praying and healing the people who are in need at that time."

Each of Jasmine's designs holds personal or spiritual meaning. Some come to her in dreams or on long drives. Others are family heirlooms, passed from generation to generation. Each dance begins with one hoop—representing the self—and expands to include as many hoops as

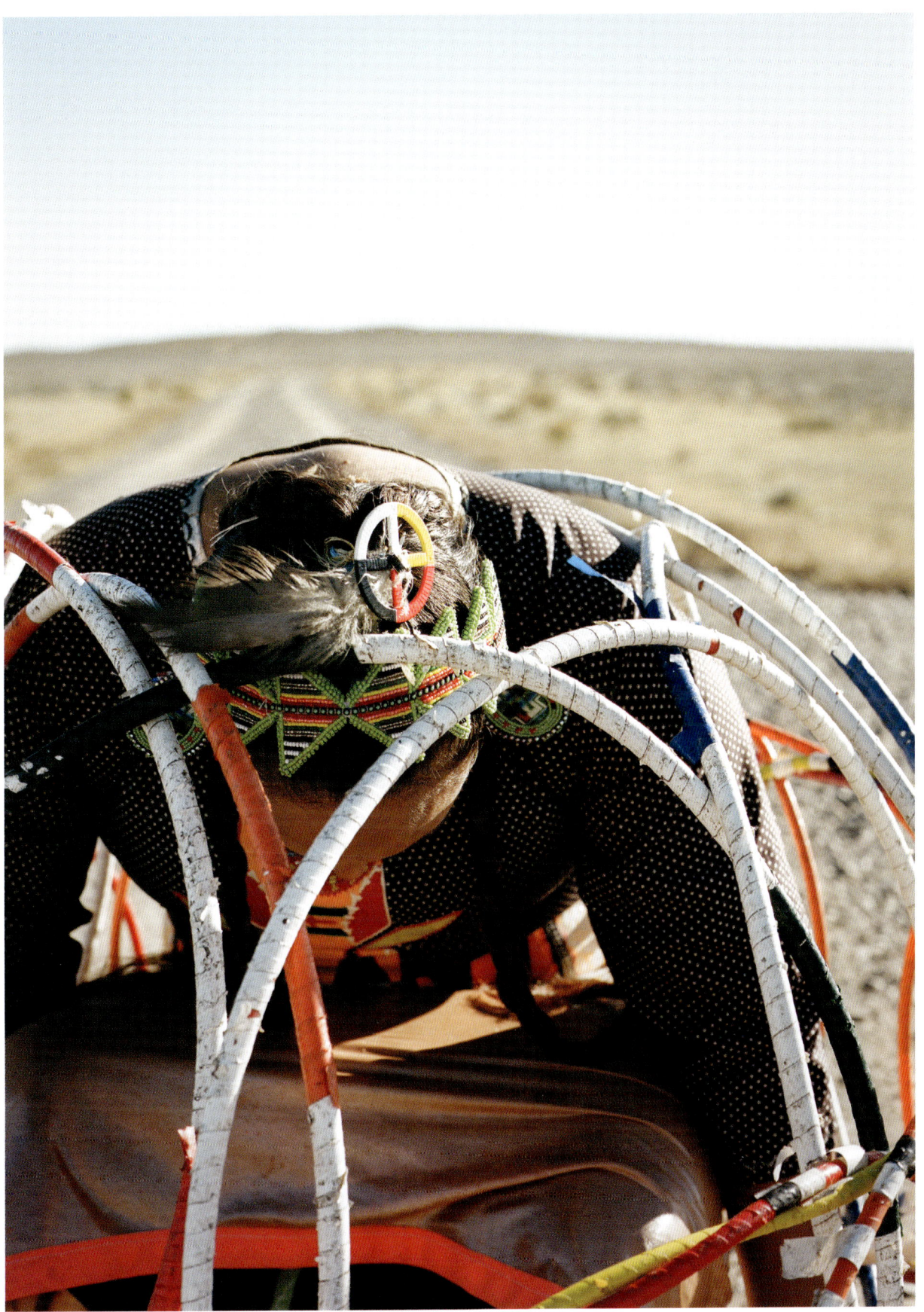

the message requires. Jasmine has danced with up to forty-eight hoops at once.

The sweat lodge shape pictured on the previous page is exclusive to Jasmine's family, created by her father as a tribute to the ceremonial roots of the dance. One of Jasmine's original designs, the flower symbolizes humanity coming together as one.

Education is central to Jasmine's mission. She teaches children, helps preserve Indigenous traditions, and invites her audience to experience the dance with her. After her performances, she often brings audience members onstage to share in the joy and meaning of the hoops. As Jasmine says, "When you get done hoop dancing with me, you're going to feel better. You're going to go home and have a story to tell. You're going to be able to share that story with your friends and family. And that's what it's about for me and why I include the audience. Let's connect together and really have that opportunity to share our hoops and leave here with a smile on our face."

For Jasmine, the hoop dance is more than performance—it's a way of life. She lives with her family on the Wind River Reservation, where her husband, Luke Bell, drums for her performances alongside the North Bear singers. Together, they bring tradition to life, lifting hearts and connecting spirits through the sacred rhythm of the hoop.

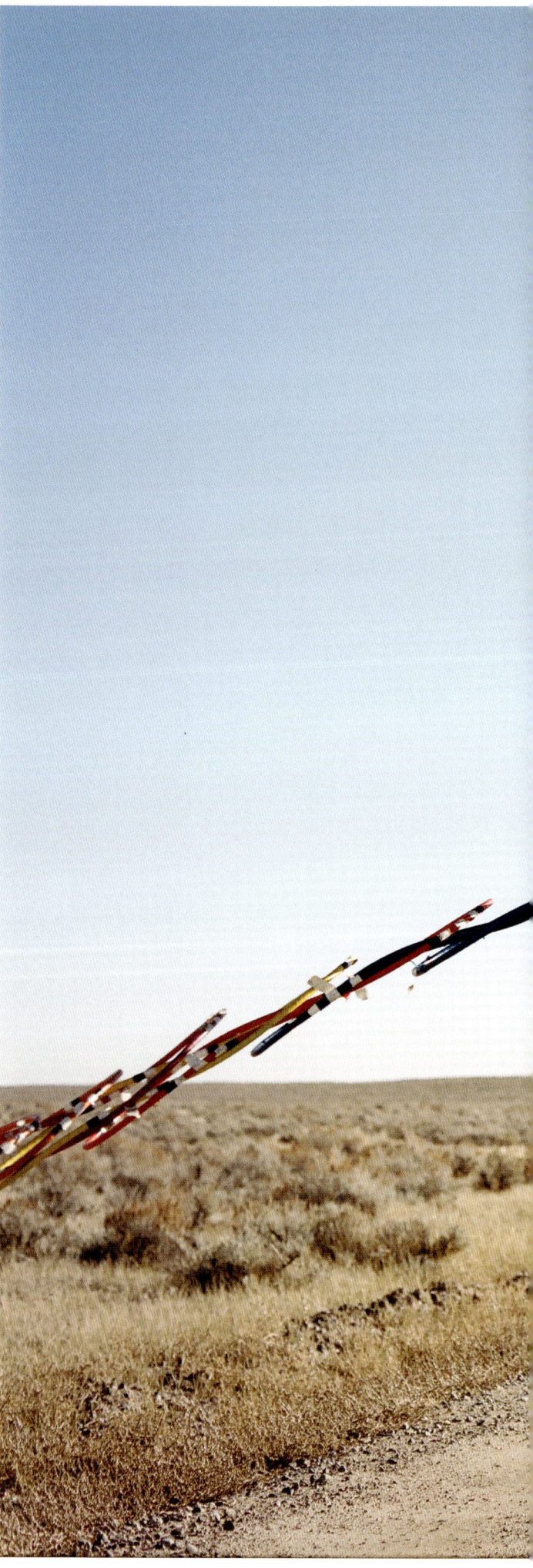

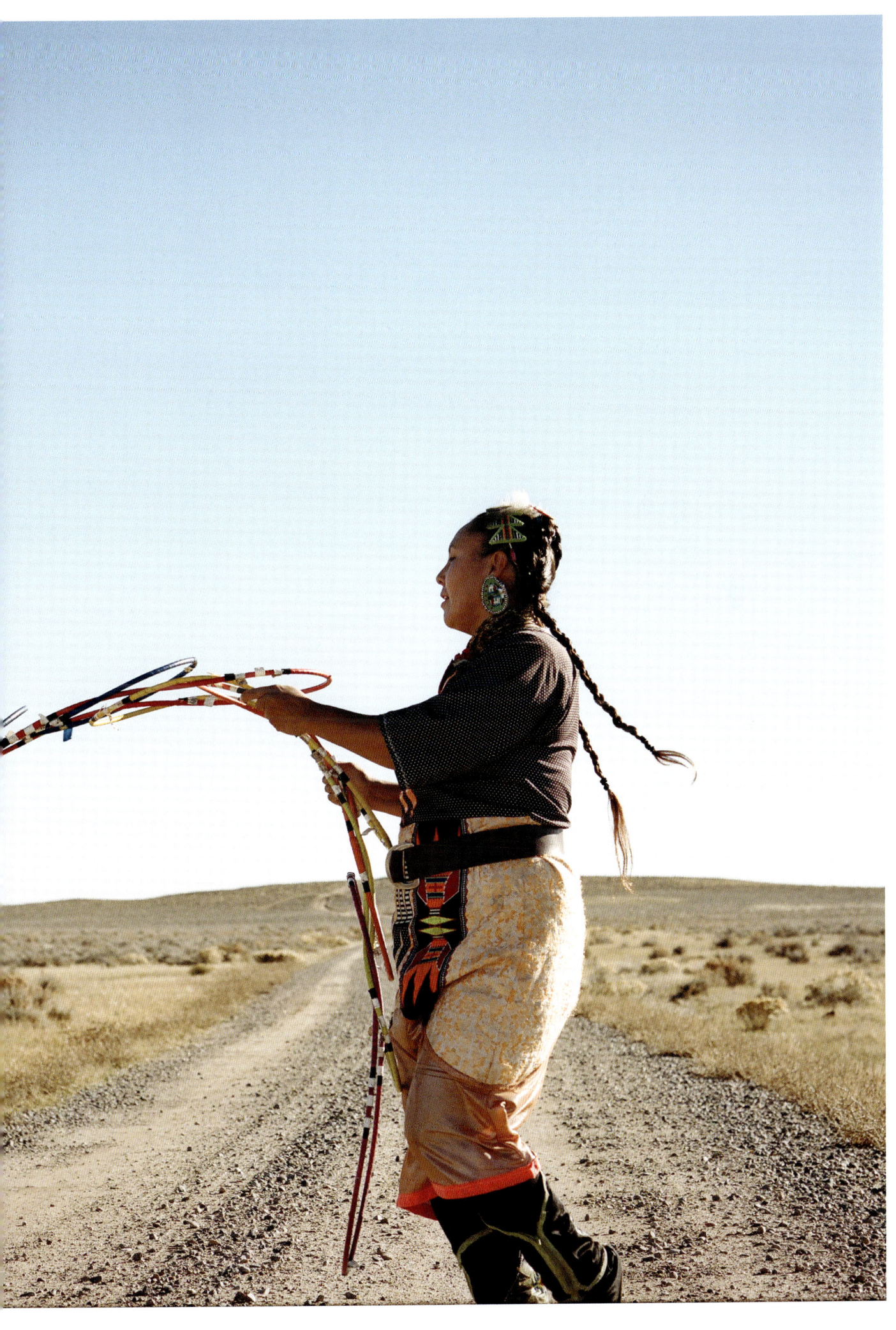

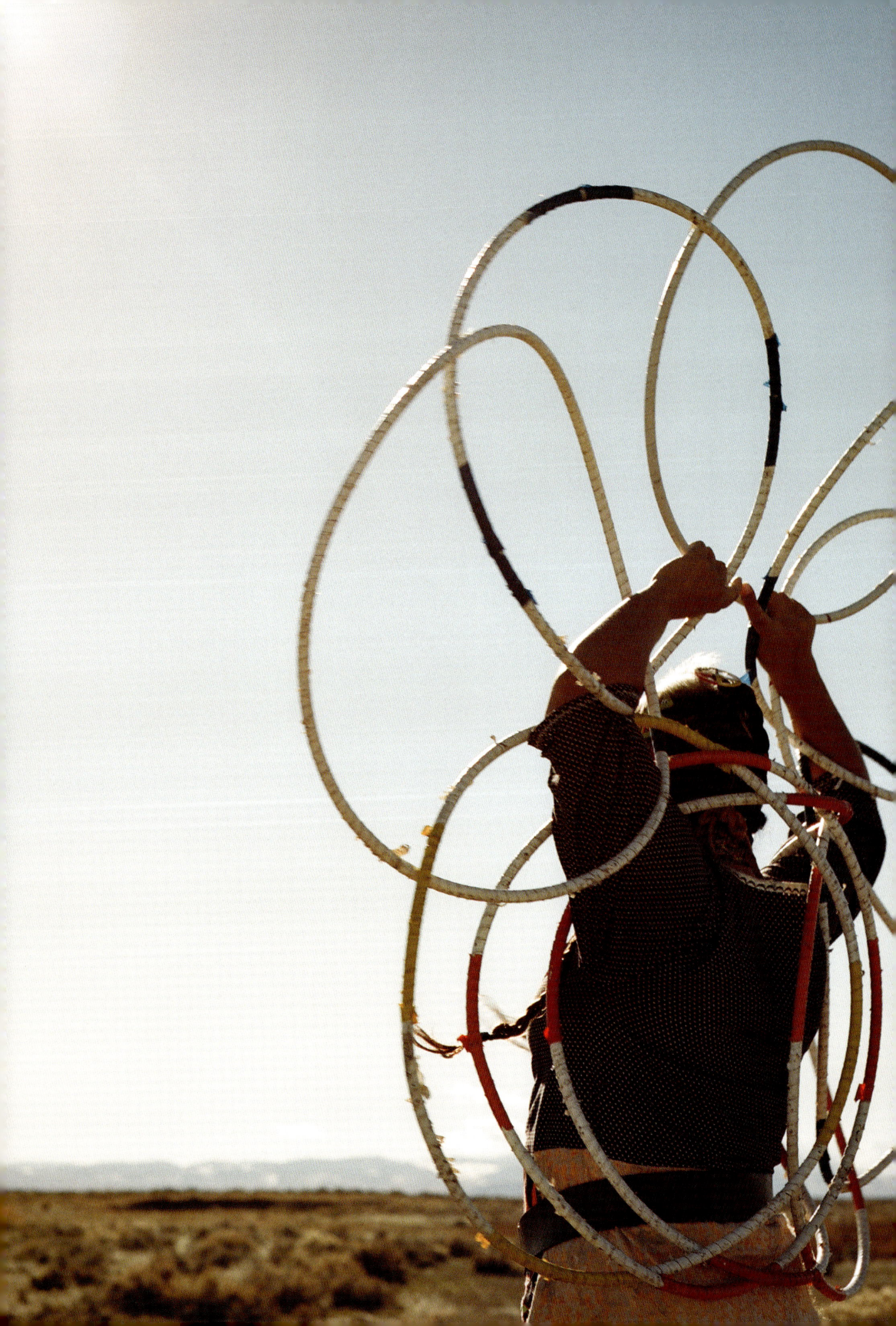

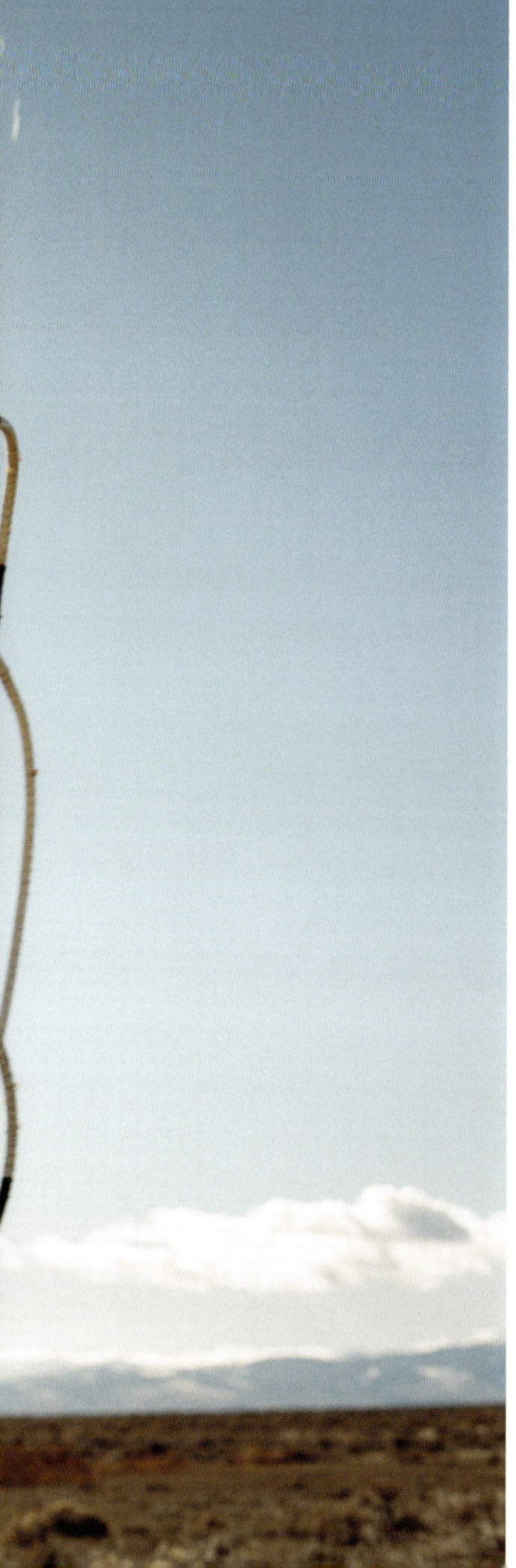

"When I look at my hoops, it's like going through life. Creating these designs represents stories that I've been through but also the relationships that I've connected as I went along. That's where the story of the hoop dance for myself comes from."

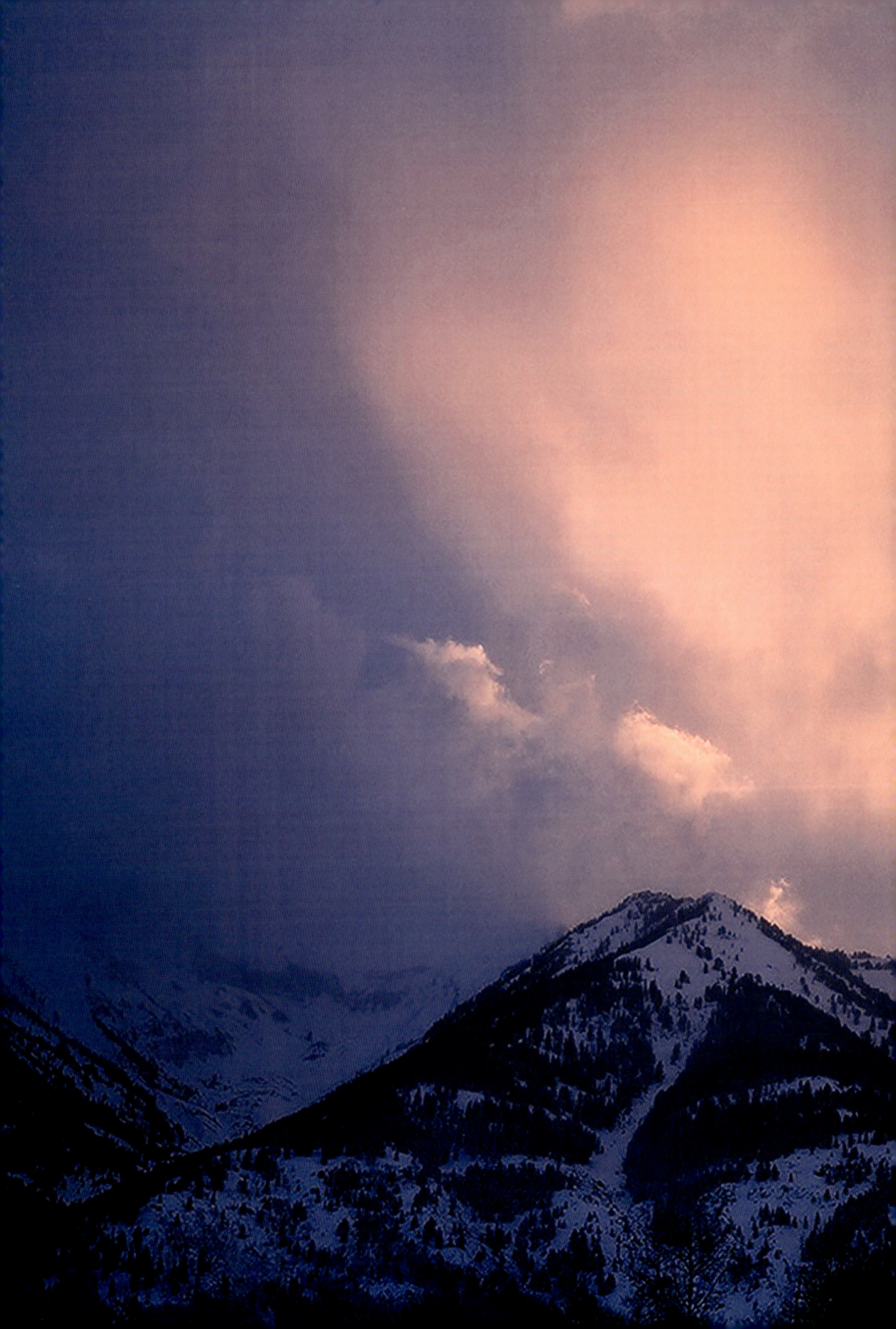

The Creative Process

———

Some of my favorite words of wisdom come from my photography mentor, J. L. "Woody" Wooden, and are simple: "Be receptive." He's a master at capturing lightning—literally! His intuition allows him to sense the precise moment to press the shutter, preserving that nanosecond of electricity. That same skill—of being open, aware, and attuned—is just as essential in life as it is in art.

You may think creativity is something reserved only for artists, but in reality, it's the foundation for how you move through the world. Creativity isn't just the production of art—it's in the way you solve problems, navigate challenges, and shape your daily life. It's in how you think, how you speak to yourself, and how you approach each day. It's the way you build, adapt, and persist.

Creativity is also an act of devotion. The act of constructing demands your receptivity and your discomfort. You make yourself open to new ideas, unexpected opportunities, and even uncomfortable truths. For much of the time, you may be tempted to return to safer, more familiar waters, yet persistence and dedication are paramount to discovery. The only way out is through.

When you exist in a receptive state more often than not, you cultivate space and your creative power. Trading distractions and unhelpful patterns for behaviors, networks, friendships, mentors, and community that feed your soul and energize your spirit ultimately allows you to be your most potent self. Building this project invited me into that dynamic energy over and over again.

While I did have specific visions and goals, like building the exhibit and producing a certain number of stories for the project, I didn't have a predetermined path to get there. Perseverance, passion, and a lot of sensitivity to the present moment coalesced to create the stories, podcast, exhibit, and this book. Every effort led me to the next step.

Film

As a young girl, I loved to make photo albums after a trip or an adventure. I'd carefully lay out the images on the page and write down snippets of who, where, and what happened. But I never formally picked up a camera until much later in life. For many years, classical dance and performance were my creative outlets. My curiosity toward people and their stories led me to graduate with a degree in history, yet I craved a more creative path as my profession. My mom suggested I explore the commercial photography program at Northwest College (NWC) in Powell, my hometown. Two weeks before classes started, I called then-department head Craig Satterlee, who enthusiastically signed me up for the introductory photography classes. While I had zero knowledge of ISOs or apertures, I jumped in feetfirst. From 2008 to 2010, I set myself on a completely new track.

On the walls of one of our classroom studios were posters from the great Rodney Smith, an iconic commercial photographer (now, sadly, no longer with us, but very much alive at the time), who only shot medium-format film and created the most whimsical, poignant images. His style was captivating, playful, and stunningly beautiful. I was completely enamored of his work and became his summer intern immediately after I graduated NWC—an opportunity that kicked off my New York City journey.

While the program at NWC was largely digital, we spent a semester shooting and developing 35 mm black-and-white film as well as large-format 4x5". The printmaking lab was no longer in commission, but my teacher and mentor Anthony Polvere guided me through the process of printing in the darkroom, ensuring I was exposed to that technique before working for Rodney, one of my photographic heroes.

While shooting film has made a comeback in certain niche industries, the photo world today is overwhelmingly digital, and this is true for most of my commercial work too. But when it came to this project, shooting medium-format film was an intentional choice for several reasons.

First, it provided a break from my digitally captured commercial assignments—where everything is more produced and retouched. The women in these pages are strong, powerful, and real. Their portraits should be too. Film, with all its imperfections and unpredictability, felt like the right fit. And frankly, it was more fun. I spent less time editing in front of a screen and more time immersed in the actual process.

Then there's the mystery of it. The magic. With digital, I can check my shot immediately. With film, I can't. There's no instant gratification, no quick reassurance that I *got it*. Capturing an image on film required extra receptivity. Through keen observation and anticipation, I'd strive to document the most impactful intersection of energy, presence, and authenticity. Each frame must be intentional and thoughtful. Film isn't cheap; every click of the shutter matters. It forced me to slow down, to be fully present.

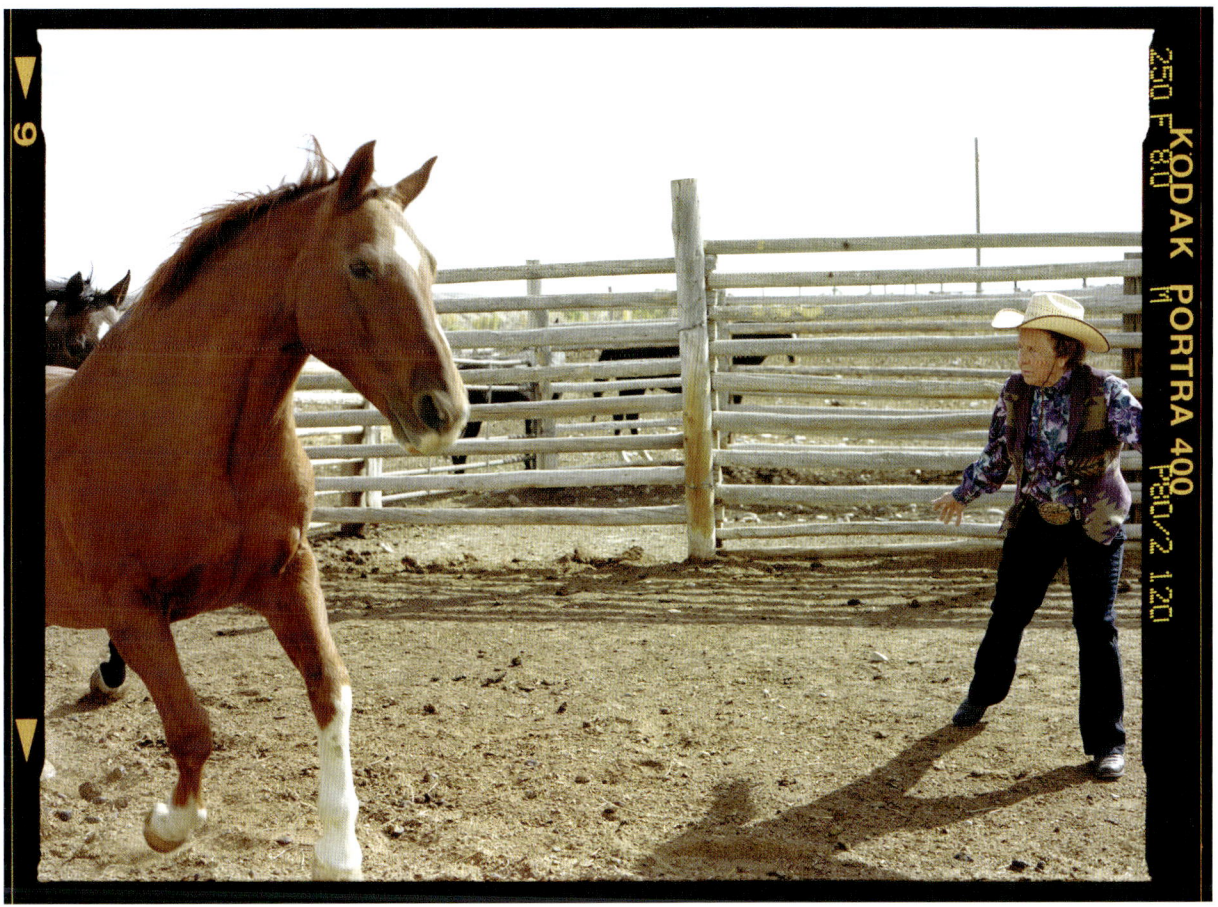

And then there's the physicality of it—the grain, the texture. That tangible, almost tactile quality that mirrors Wyoming's rugged landscapes and the strength of the women who call this place home.

Finally, I knew I wanted these images to be *big*. The kind of prints that demand space. Shooting medium-format gave me the depth and resolution to make that happen. I could drum scan the negatives at 100 MB, pulling every detail into massive, high-quality prints.

This project was shot on a Contax 645 camera using primarily Kodak Portra 400 film. Though it is primarily full-color, there are a few black-and-white images scattered throughout, and those were captured on Ilford Delta 3200 film. The film was developed and digitally scanned by Steve Block of Photo Impact Imaging, in Hollywood, California.

While I took the portraits of all the women and landscapes for this book on film, the behind-the-scenes production images in the field, as well as images of the exhibits, were captured digitally. For behind-the-scenes production shots, when it was typically just me and the women in their environment, I used a tripod and self-timer mode to capture the moment.

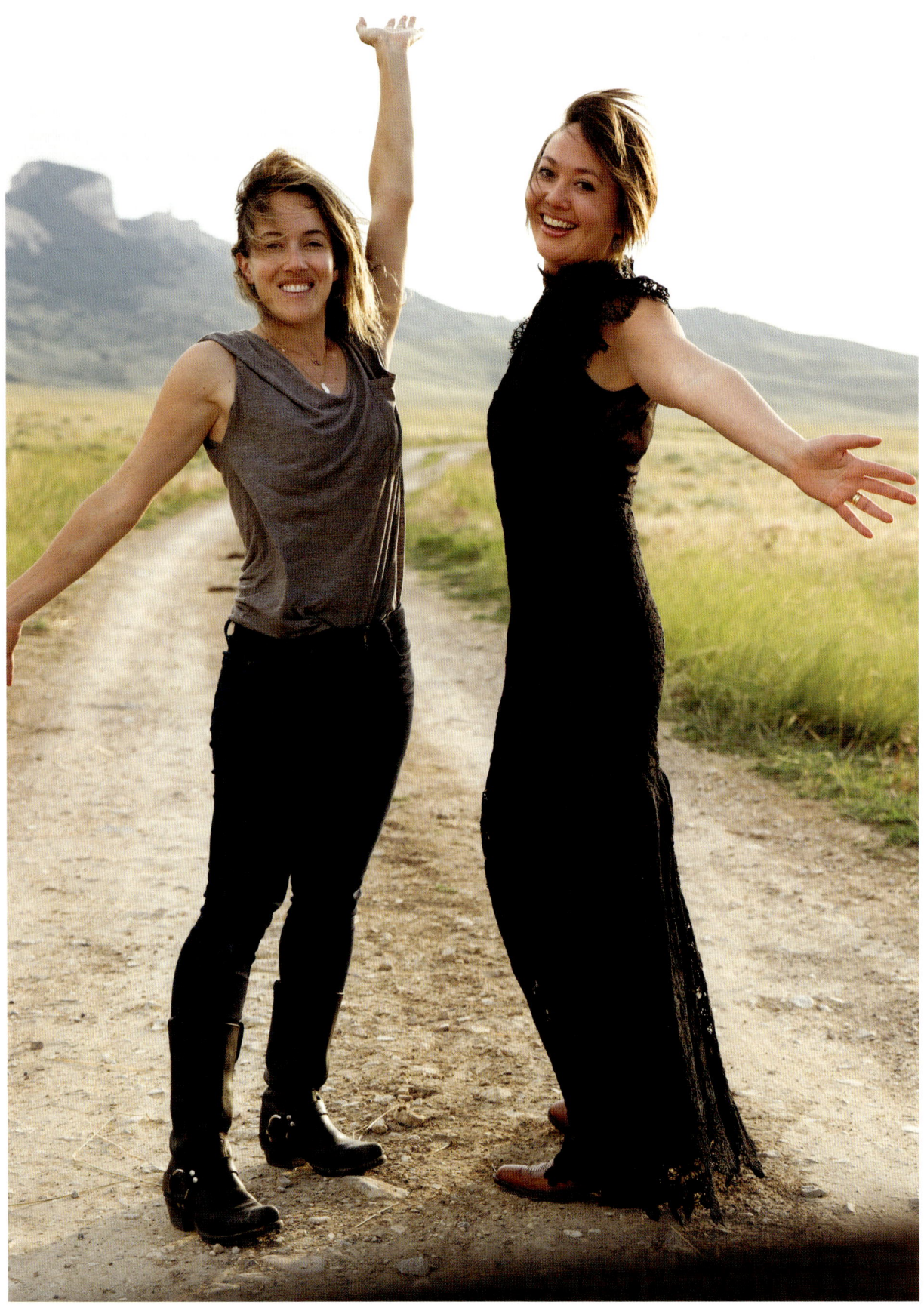

The Journey

From the beginning, I knew I could tell five stories in a year. That felt possible. The scope of this project—photographs, interviews, an exhibit, and, eventually, this book—was always multilayered. But where to start? The thought of finding everyone at once, of piecing together all the moving parts while keeping my commercial studio afloat, was overwhelming. I also wanted to learn how to produce a podcast. I wanted to shoot film for the first time in a professional setting. There were a lot of unknowns, but five stories in a year gave me a clear way forward.

At the center of it all was Wyoming. I wasn't interested in conducting remote interviews or using existing images. I wanted to meet each woman in person, to collaborate and create something new—together. Despite my deep roots here, my knowledge of the state was surprisingly narrow—mostly confined to Park County and Powell, Jackson, and places I'd driven through for road trips or high school sports but had not spent significant time in. Through storytelling, I would step into uncharted territory, just as the women I sought to feature had done in their own lives.

Production often spanned two or three days per subject. Wyoming is vast. Jackson, where I'm based, sits on the northwestern edge of the state. The next town over is a forty-five-minute drive. It's a seven-hour stretch to cross the state one way. A ten-hour round trip to create a story wasn't unusual, but it never felt like a burden. The road provides me with rhythm and time to think. Long drives became part of my creative process, a way to make sense of the swirling ideas and possibilities ahead.

The First Five

The first story found me. I was meeting with a friend who works in development, hoping to get some fundraising advice, when she asked, "Have you heard about a woman painting ten-by-thirty-foot canvases from her ranch in Banner?" That was how I found Neltje.

Word of mouth became the heartbeat of this project. Men and women made recommendations, and a network began to form organically. I also created a nomination form on the project website, inviting the public to send in their own suggestions. I pored over lists from Wyoming women's organizations, looking for stories that felt electric.

The first five women came from these conversations. They were visible. Trailblazers. Women who had broken boundaries in their fields, like Marilyn Kite, Wyoming's first female supreme court justice, and self-made businesswoman Clarene Law, who had forged her own path, defying expectations along the way.

To be a boundary breaker is often to be celebrated. But the lived reality of breaking boundaries can also be painful. Growth isn't easy. It demands risk, discomfort, and courage. These first five women embodied that truth. And in telling their stories, I realized I was breaking my own boundaries too—pushing beyond my comfort zone and trusting the process as it was unfolding.

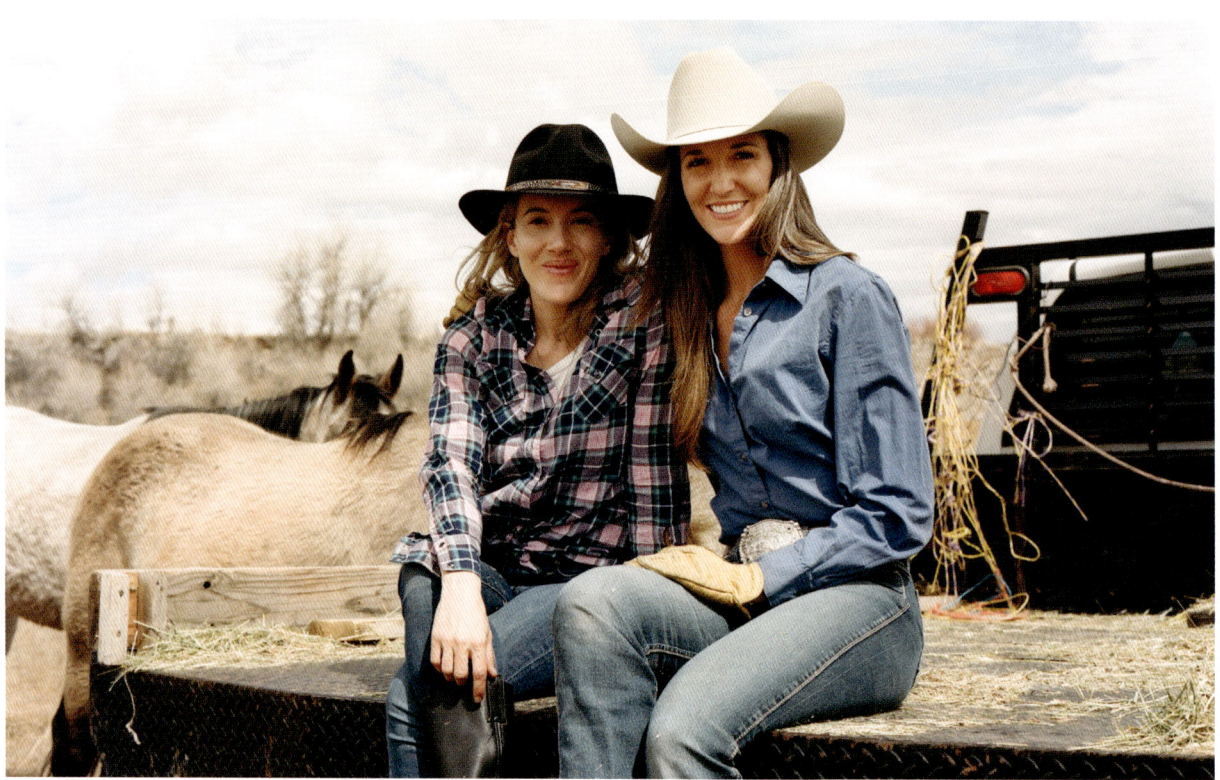

When I launched chapter I in the fall of 2017, I had no concrete plan for chapter II. I had been so laser-focused on producing the first five stories—securing funding, building a website, learning to shoot film, launching the podcast—that I couldn't think beyond them. Much of this project was about being completely present with the creative process. While I did have specific visions and goals, like the exhibit and producing a certain number of profiles, I didn't follow an exact roadmap for how to make it all happen. An incremental, organic unfolding coalesced with hustle, perseverance, and passion to make magic. But once those stories were out in the world, I finally had space to ask: *What's next?*

The answer came through contrast.

If chapter I featured women who were well-known and who lived in Wyoming's cultural or central hubs, chapter II would take me to the state's more rural and industrial areas. I wanted to find the women who weren't necessarily widely recognized but whose impact was deeply felt within their communities. At the same time, a phrase kept circling in my mind: *Filling the void.*

It's an essential part of the creative process. The space between ideas. The unknown. The thing you don't yet see but have to trust is there. Much of the creative process requires facing fear, the constant companion to courage. We often think of a void as lacking aliveness. In reality, it's the opposite. The void is the energy of potential and possibility. It is the nucleus of life.

The void is also representative of Wyoming's vast landscapes, which to some, could appear empty, for lack of structures, people, or, in parts of the state defined by prairie, features like forests and trees. But there is beauty in the supposed emptiness, the seeming nothingness.

That's what I wanted to explore next.

Finding these women required a different kind of search. I knew I wanted to feature a female pilot, but a simple Google search turned up nothing. So, I pulled out a map, found every town with an airport symbol, and started cold-calling. When I got to Upton and spoke to Lori Materi, their airport director, I knew I had found the right person. Each story led to the next.

The Evolution of Chapters

Chapters III, IV, and V came more quickly, just in time to meet my exhibit deadline at the Buffalo Bill Center of the West in October 2019. I wanted to complete twenty-five stories in total. I arrived at twenty-two for the opening, so the final three stories were produced in 2021 after I had my two children. In a full-circle moment, I ended production where my story began—in Powell, my hometown, with Sara Wood, one of my former classmates.

Each chapter became a study in growth—what it takes to show up fully in life.

Breaking Boundaries requires courage: the willingness to go where you haven't been before.

Filling the Void means trusting the unknown: the bravery to discover what potential lives in the spaces you may overlook.

Power explores the importance of dreams, the collective, and standing for what you believe in.

Rising is about creativity, spontaneity, and collaboration.

The Cowgirl State is a culmination: a declaration to claim space and leave your mark.

Each story was an exploration of another unknown. Sometimes that meant geography—where she lived. Other times, it was her industry or background. I wanted the collection of stories to be varied, spanning the familiar and the unexpected, showcasing the full depth of Wyoming women.

Each chapter was a window, an opening, a lesson.

I expected that, by the end, I would have a sense of completion—a clear, defined understanding of the stories I had told. But if anything, this process only showed me how there is always more to uncover.

And in that way, the project never really ends. It expands, shifts, and reveals more.

By breaking boundaries, filling the void, stepping into my own power, embracing reinvention, and ultimately claiming my place in Wyoming, I have been stretched and changed. I've learned that the unknown is never truly empty. It is always full of possibility—if you dare to look.

The Podcast

Amplifying women's voices and stories has always been at the heart of my mission, which is why adding an audio component to this project felt essential. The podcast allowed each woman to tell her story in her own words, bringing a new depth to their narratives. My setup was low-tech but high-quality, and mobile enough that we could record in kitchens, living rooms, bedrooms—wherever the best sound could be found.

Podcasting is a mainstream medium now, but when I launched the first season in 2017, it was still emerging as an art form. I was drawn to its intimacy and its imperfection. Hosts said "like" and "um." They weren't polished, they were real. I thought, *Could I do that too?* The conversational nature made it feel accessible.

Years earlier, while studying photography at Northwest College (2008–2010), I'd worked on a project about generational farming families. I spent hours recording interviews, then painstakingly transcribed and crafted written narratives. I didn't love the postproduction process, but I cherished the conversations— the magic of sitting with someone, listening, and learning. I realized that what I cherished most wasn't just the story itself, but the *voice* telling it. A podcast felt like the natural evolution of that work.

A friend in tech guided me toward travel-friendly microphones that deliver studio-quality sound. I learned to create makeshift recording spaces— sometimes wedged near a bedroom closet— removing clocks and unplugging electronics to eliminate interference. I recorded in GarageBand, monitoring audio through headphones and fine-tuning each session before we began.

Former director of cultural affairs and production at Wyoming Public Media, Micah Schweizer became an invaluable mentor. His most impactful advice? "Listen. Really listen. If you're fully present in the conversation, the next question will come naturally." He also urged me to conduct interviews in the first person—"Tell me about your time in . . ." versus "Tell us . . ."—which created a sense of intimacy, as though the listener were being spoken to directly. Transcribing my early interviews, while tedious, helped me recognize themes and sharpen my instincts as an interviewer.

Dennis Davis, my journalism professor at NWC, gave me an unexpected but necessary piece of permission: to record myself. At first, I had only a mic for my guest. I wasn't sure my voice was necessary. It wasn't until I lost an entire interview with Wyoming's first female supreme court justice, Marilyn Kite—because my voice wasn't recorded—that I realized my mistake. Fortunately, she let me re-record, and from then on, I never questioned whether my voice belonged in the mix.

Editing was another learning curve. I didn't know any audio editors, but I reached out to my friend Leo Bleier, a former Wyoming resident turned Los Angeles reality TV editor. While his work was visual, he helped me master the sound for each podcast track, ensuring that even from Wyoming, these stories resonated universally.

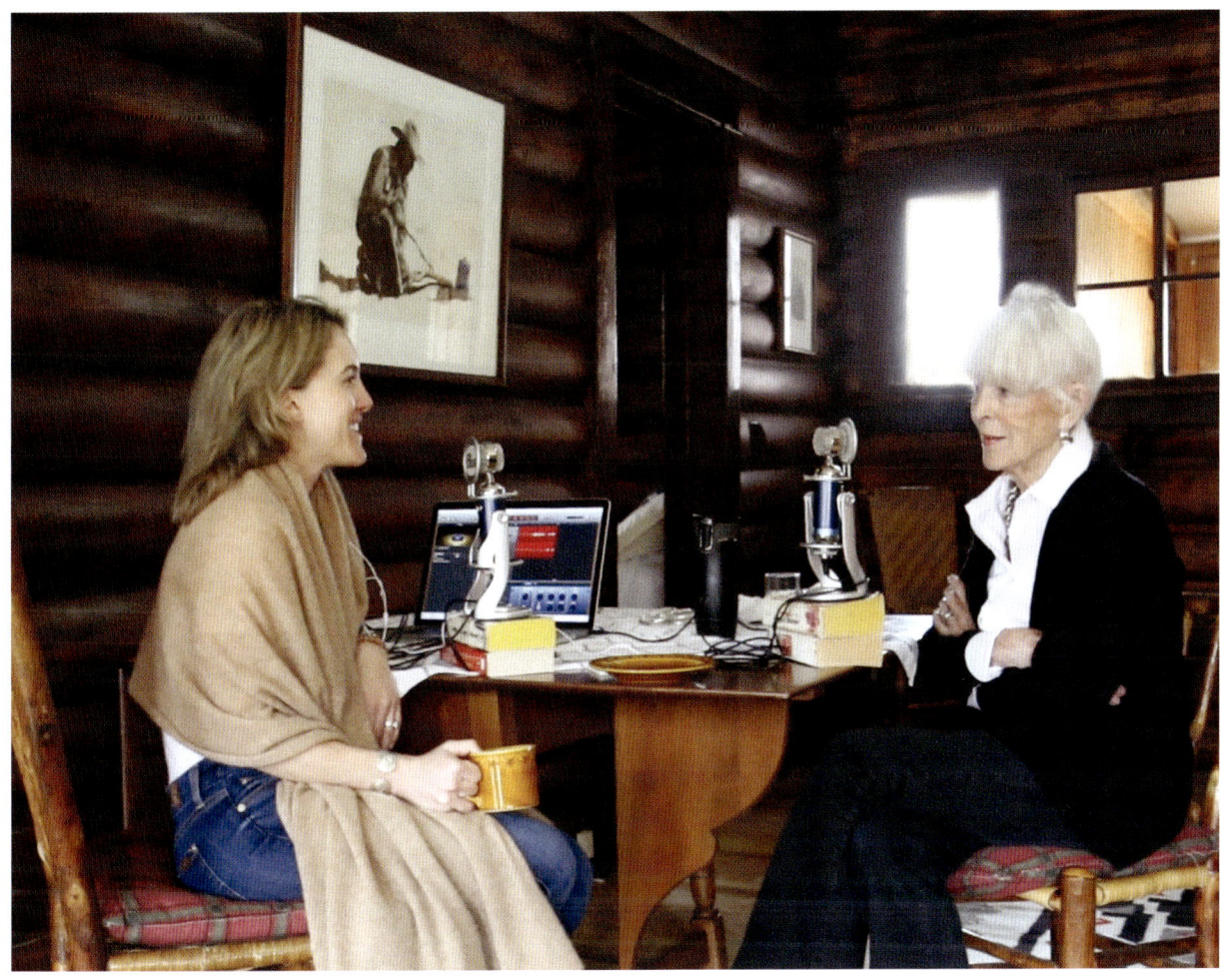

The podcast became my favorite part of the project. The biggest challenge, the steepest learning curve, and the most rewarding element. It stretched my storytelling muscles in a new way, layering sound over image, voice over vision.

It also stretched my *literal* voice. As a dancer and photographer, I had always expressed myself visually, never audibly. At first, I edited myself out of the conversations. Over time, I let more of myself in.

To me, these recordings are absolute treasures. A couple of the women—Neltje, Clarene

Law—have, sadly, since passed, but their voices and stories stay alive. Even though I've listened to them hundreds of times now, I still find new wisdom in their words. Their stories live on, not just in memory, but in their own voices, speaking across time.

You can listen to the *Women in Wyoming* podcast on Spotify, iTunes, and SoundCloud.

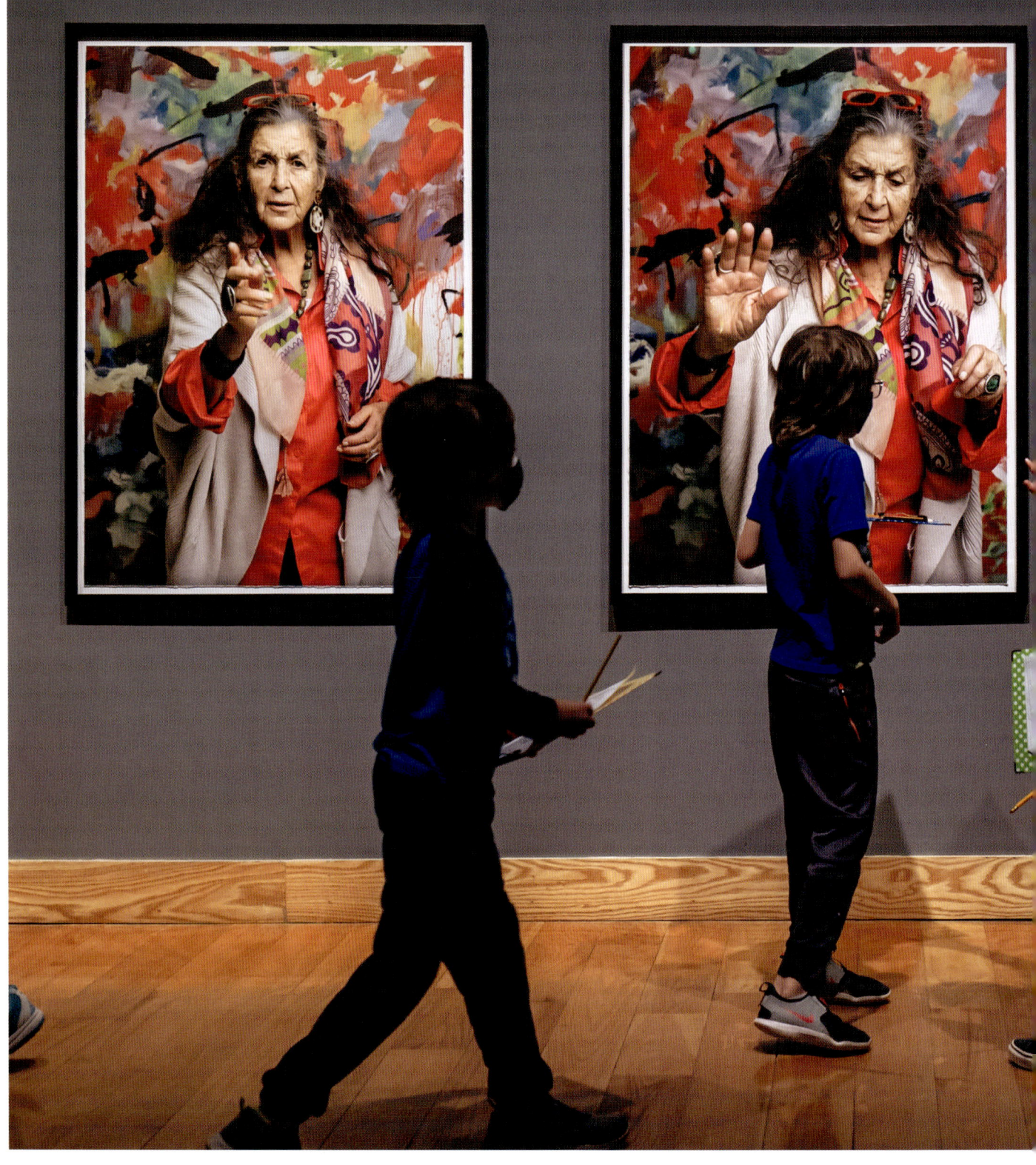

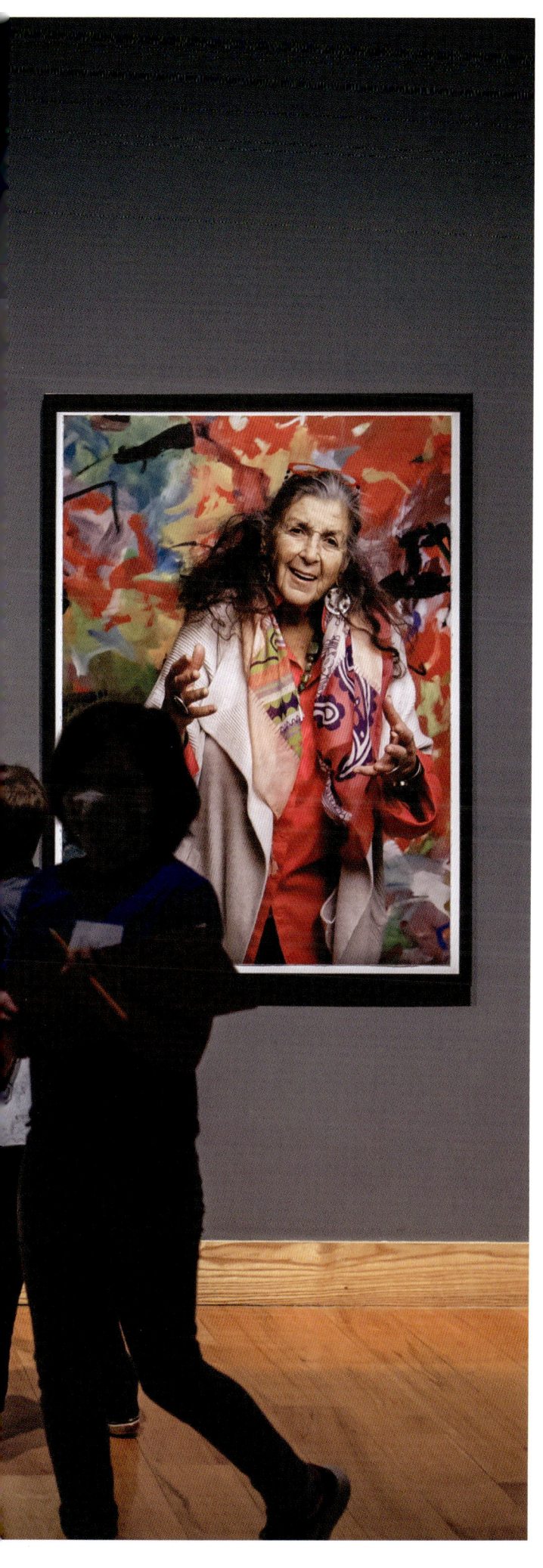

The Exhibit

In the earliest days of the project, before I had shared any stories publicly, I reached out to someone I knew at the Buffalo Bill Center of the West in Cody, hoping to connect with a curator. This Smithsonian-accredited institution, a cultural landmark that houses five museums under one roof, was a cornerstone of my childhood, located twenty minutes from where I grew up.

I had previously created a small exhibit for *Been Here for Generations*, my project about farming families, at the Homesteader Museum in Powell, but the idea of submitting to a major institution felt daunting. I quickly learned that large venues typically require a completed body of work for review, and securing an exhibition slot can take up to two years. I felt it might take me a decade before I would have a complete exhibit to present! I tucked that information away and started production of my project in earnest.

By the fall of 2017, I launched the first five stories from "Chapter I: *Breaking Boundaries*." With a mix of hope and nerves, I sent the curator a link to my website. "Is there any way you would consider an exhibit while I'm still in process?" Her reply was exhilarating: "Can you consider the fall of 2019?"

Suddenly, everything became real. My amazing curators, Rebecca West and Karen Brooks McWhorter, and I were off to the races. I had a deadline, accountability, and a massive opportunity.

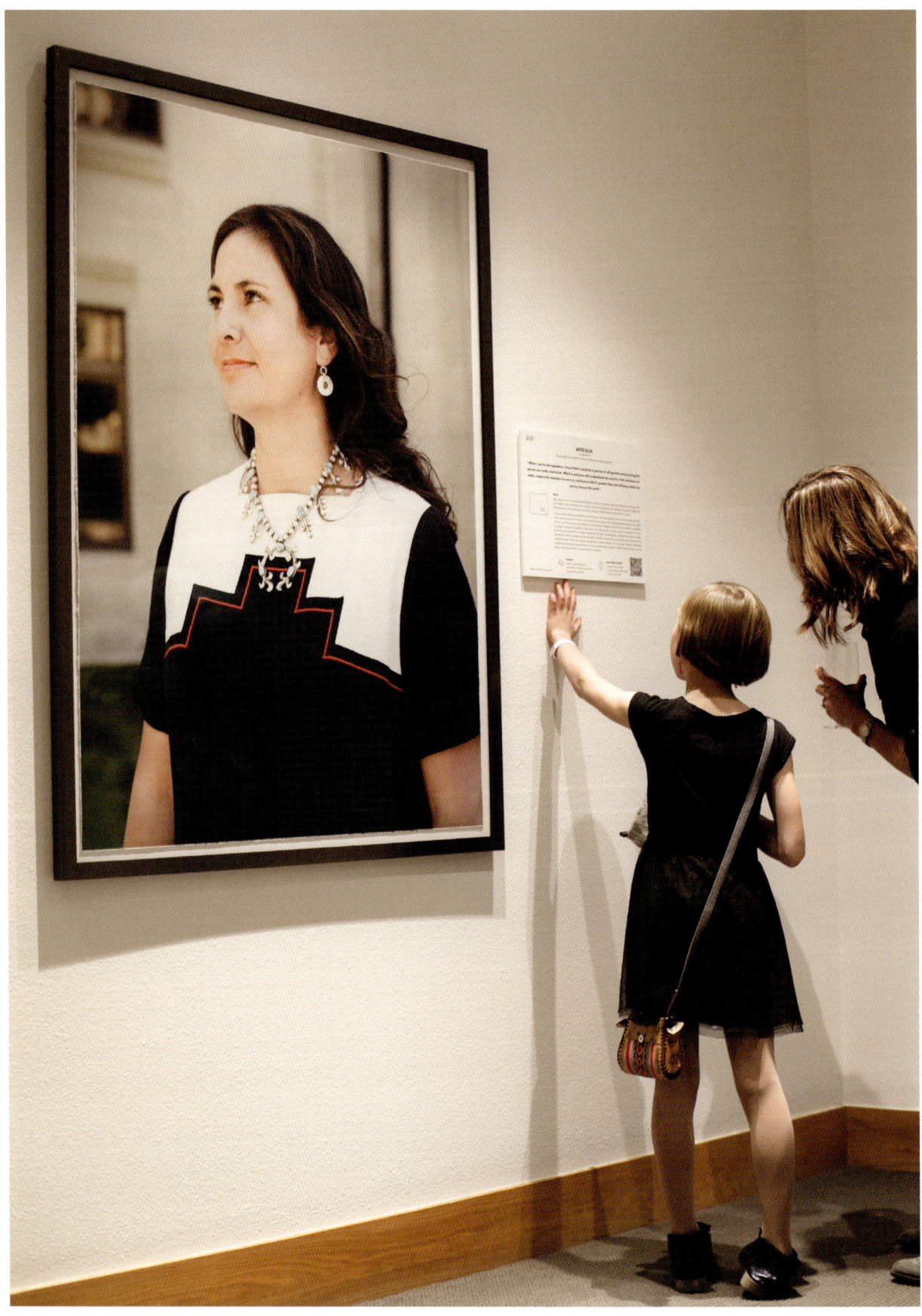

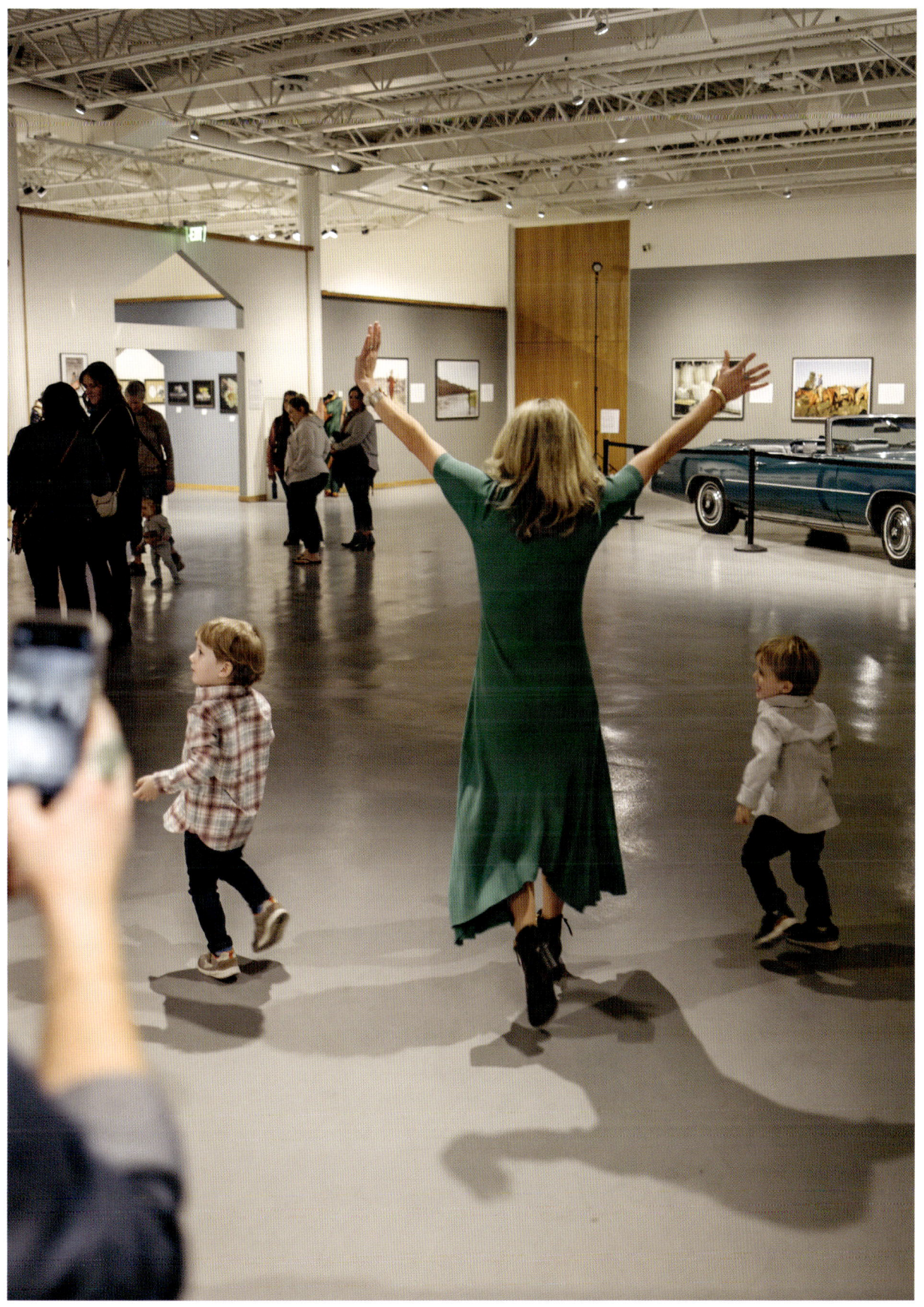

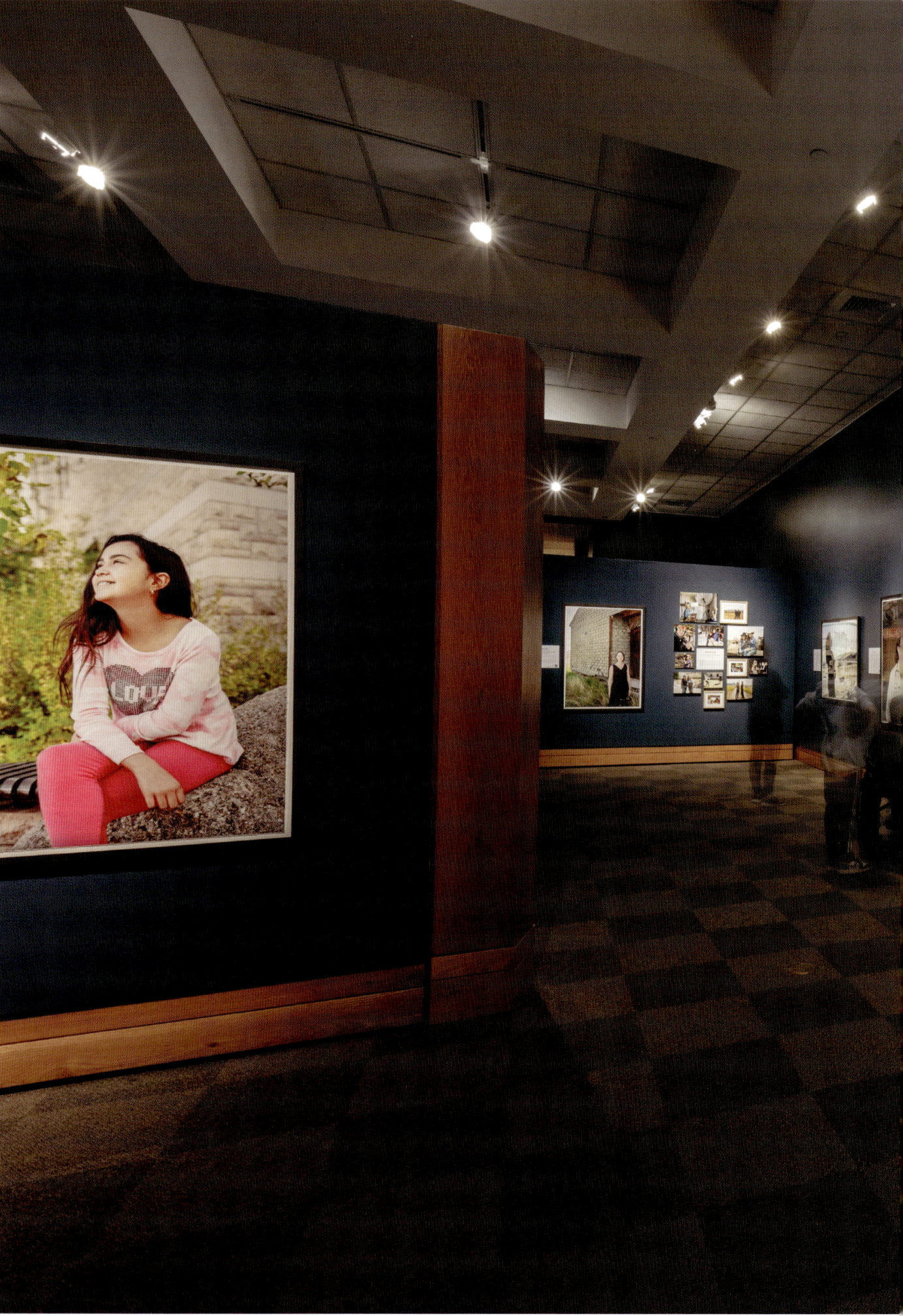

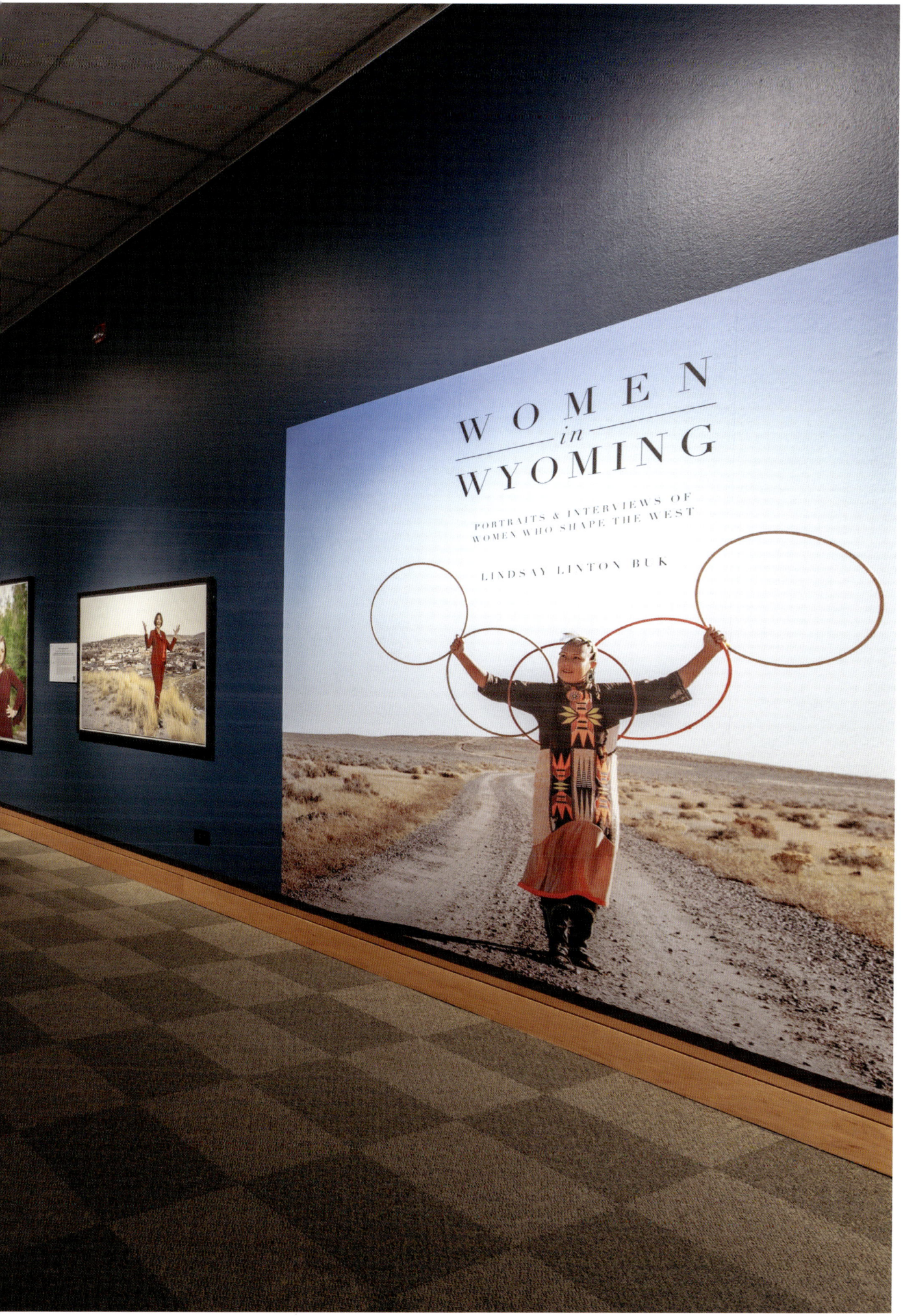

Venues

Since its debut in 2019, the exhibit has toured multiple venues around Wyoming, the country, and the world. It continues to reach new audiences and expand its impact.

- **Buffalo Bill Center of the West, Cody, Wyoming:** October 2019–August 2020
- **University of Wyoming Art Museum, Laramie, Wyoming:** September 2020–July 2021
- **Center for the Arts and Art Association galleries, Jackson, Wyoming:** August–September 2021
- **FotoNostrum Gallery, Barcelona, Spain** (*Julia Margaret Cameron Photography Award, 6th Biennial of Fine Art & Documentary Photography, The Worldwide Photography Gala Awards—Honorable Mention for Mickey Thoman's portrait*): December 2021–January 2022
- **National Cowboy & Western Heritage Museum, Oklahoma City, Oklahoma:** September 2023–January 2024
- **Nicolaysen Art Museum, Casper, Wyoming:** February–April 2024
- **Poppy coworking space, Jackson, Wyoming:** June 2024–January 2025
- **Brinton Museum, Big Horn, Wyoming:** March–July 2025

Each venue offers new opportunities for curation, design, and interaction. As our world grows more fragmented, the exhibit serves as a powerful space for connection—bringing people together through shared experiences and storytelling.

When I first began this project, I didn't envision an exhibit tour. But the project's ongoing evolution reflects exactly what it is about: aliveness, spontaneity, and taking up space. The exhibit is more than just a display of photographs; it is an evolving, living tribute to the women who have shaped Wyoming and beyond. With every new venue, the project continues to grow—not just in physical space, but in the stories it carries and the connections it fosters.

For image information, see page 285.

Exhibit Prints

For the exhibit, select negatives were sent to Lesly Deschler Canossi of Fiber Ink Studio (Beacon, NY) and Duggal Visual Solutions (NYC) for high-resolution drum scanning, creating 100 MB digital files to maintain exceptional print quality at large scales.

The portraits were printed on Hahnemühle bamboo fine-art paper with a hand-torn, deckle edge by Lesly Deschler Canossi. Dana Smith of Fort Frame Gallery (Jackson, WY) handled the mounting and framing, with each framed print measuring 40 by 54 inches in both horizontal and vertical formats. Teton Art Services (Jackson, WY) custom-built fine-art crates for safe transport and provides installation and shipping services when needed.

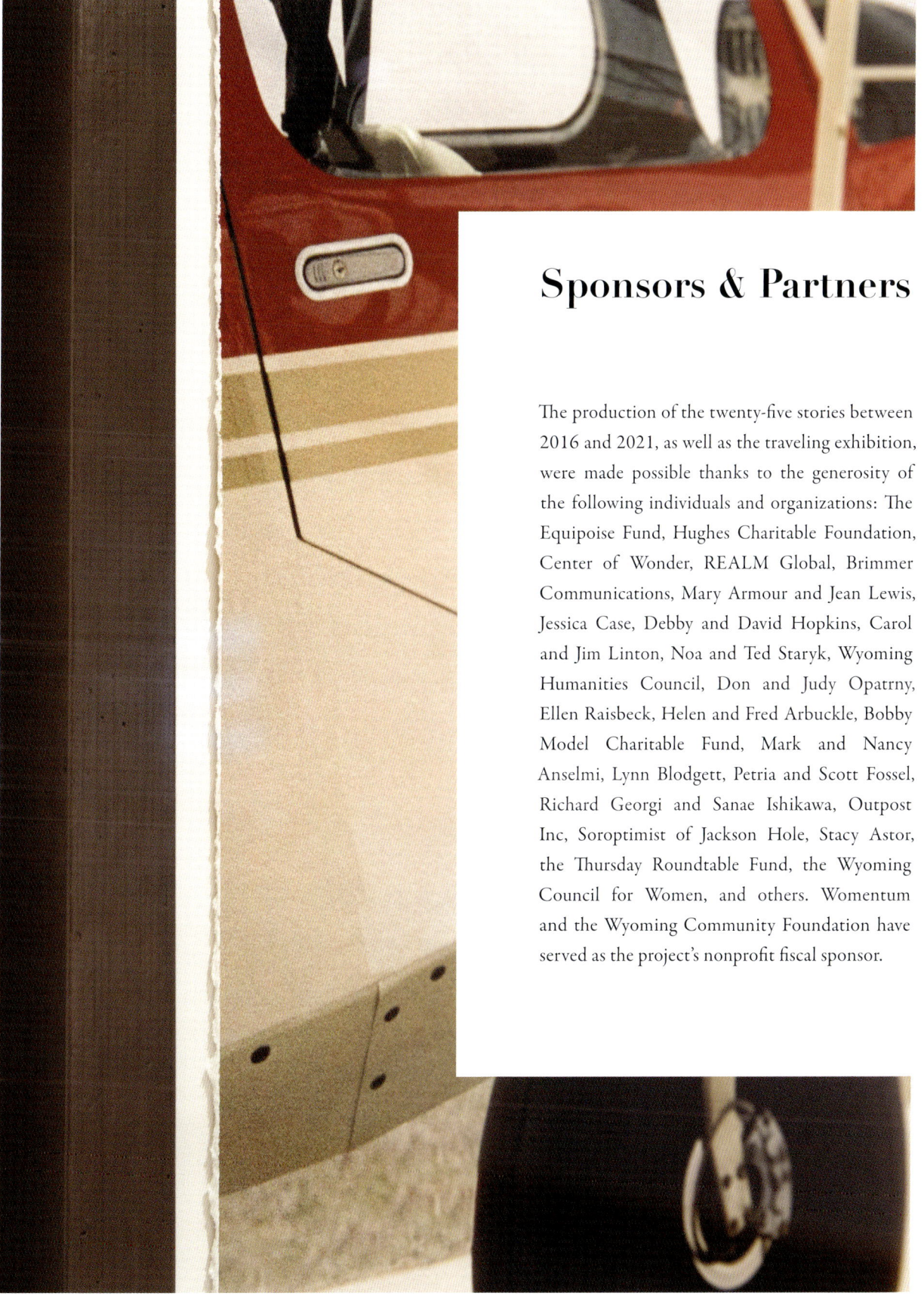

Sponsors & Partners

The production of the twenty-five stories between 2016 and 2021, as well as the traveling exhibition, were made possible thanks to the generosity of the following individuals and organizations: The Equipoise Fund, Hughes Charitable Foundation, Center of Wonder, REALM Global, Brimmer Communications, Mary Armour and Jean Lewis, Jessica Case, Debby and David Hopkins, Carol and Jim Linton, Noa and Ted Staryk, Wyoming Humanities Council, Don and Judy Opatrny, Ellen Raisbeck, Helen and Fred Arbuckle, Bobby Model Charitable Fund, Mark and Nancy Anselmi, Lynn Blodgett, Petria and Scott Fossel, Richard Georgi and Sanae Ishikawa, Outpost Inc, Soroptimist of Jackson Hole, Stacy Astor, the Thursday Roundtable Fund, the Wyoming Council for Women, and others. Womentum and the Wyoming Community Foundation have served as the project's nonprofit fiscal sponsor.

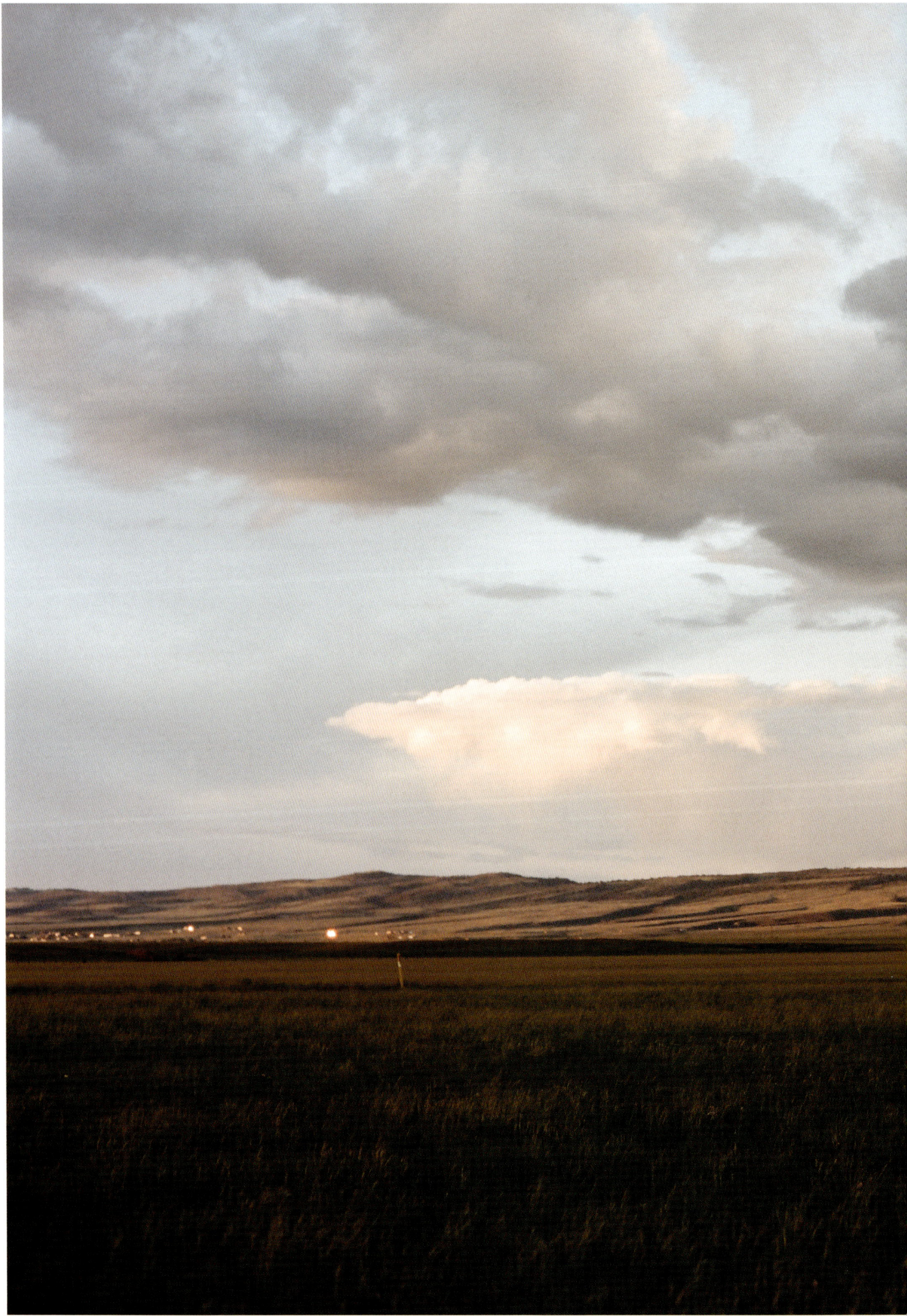

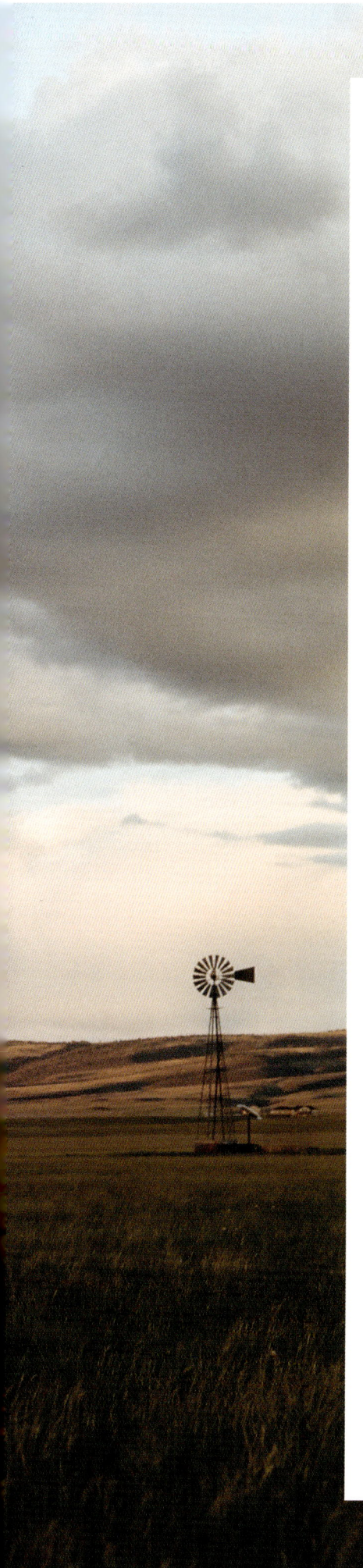

Epilogue

In 2017—when I was still in the midst of putting together what would become chapter I of this book—I presented my project to the ENDOW Council, a new economic initiative created by former Wyoming governor Matt Mead to engage the talent and ambitions of Wyoming people to find solutions toward diversifying the economy. It was my first formal speaking engagement about the project. Production was underway, but stories hadn't been shared yet.

As it is for so many people, public speaking was a huge fear of mine. My nerves would take hold, and I'd choke on my words. Through a cracked voice, I'd eventually find my footing and fake confidence. In advance of the ENDOW engagement, I attended a few sessions at our local Toastmasters chapter to practice and address this barrier.

As I stood before the ENDOW Council at Half Moon Lake Lodge that evening, a group of thirty or so leaders, up-and-coming to established, from all across the state, huddled around me. Standing shoulder to shoulder, the energy between us was electric. My nerves vanished among the supportive crowd. I shared my vision and clips of what I'd produced so far—images and ideas never before seen publicly. The distance that typically separates us in Wyoming—geographic, professional, political—evaporated that evening, cultivating a powerful spirit of possibility.

From that pivotal evening to the launch of chapter I, in the fall of 2017, the energy of the project grew and opportunities multiplied. More speaking engagements, more exposure, and more production ensued throughout the remainder of 2017 and 2018. Then, in 2019, the country celebrated the 150th anniversary of Wyoming recognizing women's right to vote and hold political office. A national spotlight looked to Wyoming and hit upon my project. Features on the Travel Channel and on Forbes.com catapulted my project into nationwide visibility as it became a barometer of women's achievements through a contemporary lens. Serendipitously, the timing aligned with my exhibit launch at the Buffalo Bill Center of

the West in October 2019. It was beyond exciting (and completely unplanned) to meet that
moment. The entire year felt charged around
this celebratory occasion.

The velocity of that moment felt unstoppable—
until the trajectory shifted, and my life followed suit. Following the exhibit debut, my
husband and I excitedly welcomed the birth of
my first son, Hank, in December 2019. Just as
we were emerging from the first foggy months
with a newborn, the world shut down due to
the COVID-19 pandemic. As the world with-
drew, I, too, turned inward, focusing on our
family. My husband and I welcomed our second son, Luke, in June 2021. Quietly, I navigated the profound changes, challenges, and
gifts of motherhood, in addition to the monumental transformations of the world outside. I
completed the final three stories of the project
and focused on touring the exhibit, which I
could do from home. Motherhood invited me
into new moments of surrender and the vitality
of support systems.

Wyoming and the world continue to change at
exponential rates. Some things remain constant,
I've learned. I continue to witness the fierce
devotion of individuals, nonprofits, and organizations committed to improving our state and
embodying the community-mindedness that
makes Wyoming special. As my boys get a *little*
older, I rediscover the part of myself that loves
to create. It's why I wrote this book a number
of years after production. This moment of life
is about exploring the intersection between creativity and motherhood.

I've also learned I can't do it all on my own.
Now that I'm a mom, support, partnership,
and community are essential. My experience
parallels the paradox of Wyoming as the
Cowboy State: We celebrate the cowboy as a
symbol of self-reliance, resilience, and freedom,
yet the reality is far more complex. Rugged
individualism may be romantic, but it can also
be isolating and limiting. If Wyoming is truly
the Equality State, then perhaps our greatest
act of independence and freedom is not standing alone but standing together.

The people who love and work to help people—
that's Wyoming at its best. And that's what
we must champion, not just in our communities but in our policies, our leadership, and
our future.

Once, I believed I could never have a future in
Wyoming. It felt too small, too isolated, too
empty. But through the creation of this project, I've learned that creativity isn't just about
making art—it's about shaping a life, a community, a state, and a state of being. Women
in Wyoming have long embodied this creative
spirit. They've had to. Whether they are building businesses in small towns, advocating for
policy changes, or finding new ways to uplift
one another, they are continually shaping
the future. Wyoming has offered me unique
creative challenges, but more important, it
has shown me what creation really means—
turning possibility into reality, even in the
hardest places. Putting together the traveling
exhibit, which shares the stories with communities around the state, nation, and world;

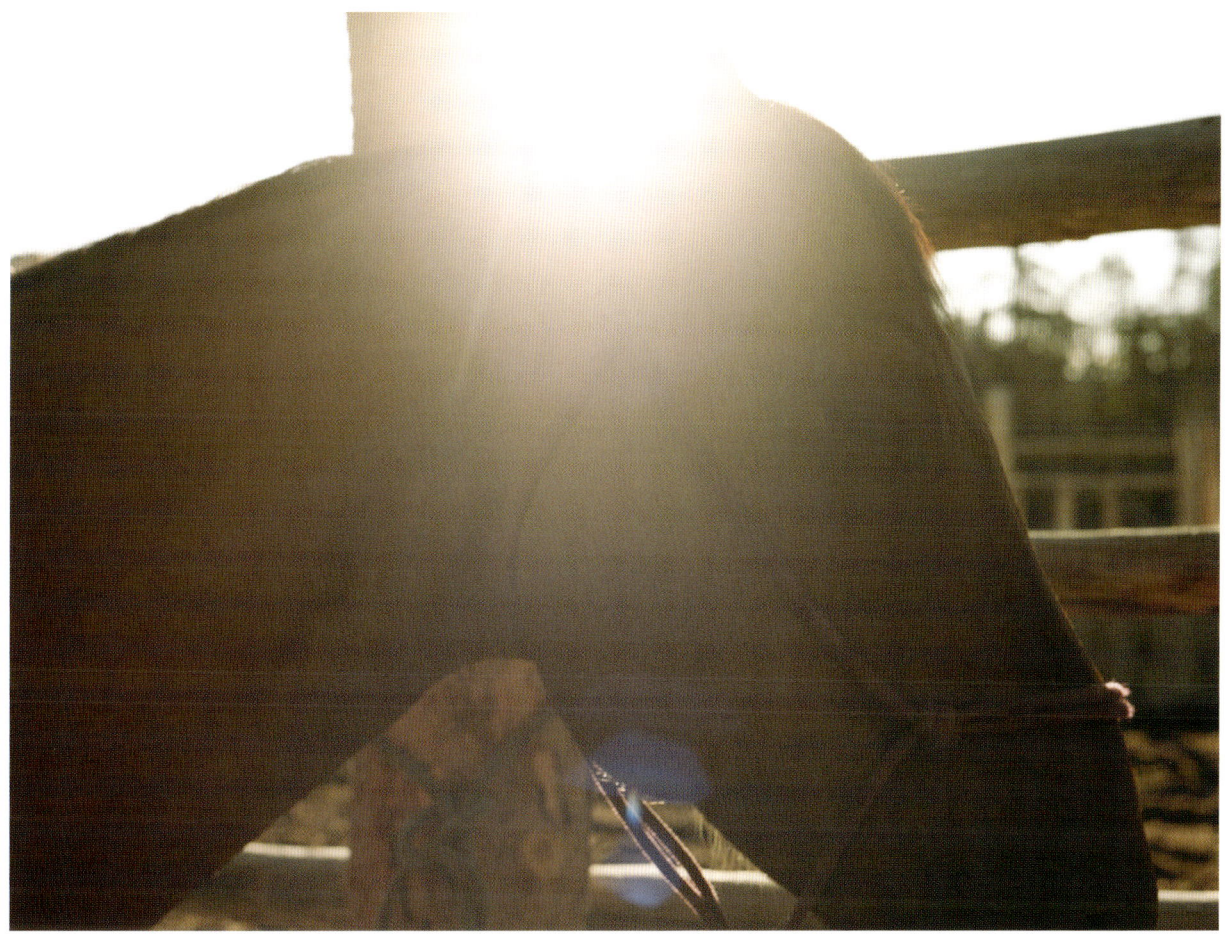

cocreating women's programs with Leadership Wyoming (the Brio Collective); speaking about the project to numerous audiences around the state and country; serving on the advisory board of the Wyoming Women's Foundation; and, of course, building lasting friendships with the women in this project—these opportunities have given me a life in Wyoming that is so rich, connected, and full.

The moment I harnessed to seek out these stories—traveling thousands of miles to meet with strangers who became friends and mentors—has closed. I found the clarity to answer the question that, for so long, dreaming across the expansive spaces of the Bighorn Basin, gripped my attention: *What is possible in Wyoming? Who will I become?* Now I know that life can be a series of never-ending aha moments, reinvention, and evolution, if you dare to explore and discover.

A decade in the making, this book's publication marks ten years from when I officially began work on this project, beginning with producing Neltje's story in December 2016. The book is the final piece of this project, and I sense new questions, new unknowns, and new discoveries on the horizon. Ultimately, these stories and my journey to share them in various mediums represent a much larger metaphor about the endless continuum of life—one that, I hope, is imbued with the expansive spirit of limitless possibility and, ultimately, aliveness.

Acknowledgments

Clarene Law told me, "It'd take everyone in my life to make who I am today." Creating this book is a culminating moment, and it's thanks to everyone in my life who has been a mentor, teacher, supporter, partner, challenger, or friend. The list is endless. Success is a collective effort. I am indebted to the many hands and minds who helped bring this book to life, as well as the many other facets of the project—the podcast, the exhibit, and beyond.

To my Buk boys—Dane, Hank, and Luke. Dane, thank you for your partnership, listening ear, and for supporting me in my creative efforts and dreams. Hank and Luke, thank you for making me a mama, for your silliness and endless energy. I love you guys.

To my parents. My mom, Carol Linton, who first exposed me to art, beauty, photography, travel, and adventure. You've been my right-hand woman for the project from its inception through this book's completion. Thank you for giving me life and continuing to support me in life. To my dad, Jim Linton, you are a beacon of kindness and generosity. Thank you for showing me what it means to love my community and family. I hope I made our Linton ancestors proud. To my Linton and Buk families—your love and support means the world.

A very special thanks to the David & Leslye Hardie Charitable Trust, David and Debby Hopkins Foundation, Mickey Babcock, and Jean Lewis for helping fund the historical research and a part of the creative production of this book.

To my editor, Bridget Watson Payne, for your insight, expertise, organization, and vision. I felt deeply supported in your care. I loved collaborating with you on this project and am eternally grateful you were my editor. Thank you for helping me bring this book to life—it is what I've always envisioned and more. To everyone at the Collective Book Studio—especially Angela Engel, Elisabeth Saake, Rachel Lopez Metzger, and Amy Treadwell—thank you for supporting this body of work and the opportunity to step into authorship. To Brenda Modliszewski, thank you for your fine-tuned eye and attention to detail to ensure this book's accuracy and impact. To Liliana Guia, thank you for designing a gorgeous book!

To Brianne Corcoran, my writing partner, you wizard! You helped me sharpen and connect the dots. Our collaboration helped distill the numerous facets of this project into a clear vision and narrative. You are magical. Thank you, thank you.

To my knowledgeable historical advisor, Jennifer Helton: Your insights, expertise, and research on Wyoming's suffrage story, as well as on the historical women featured, were invaluable contributions to this project. Additional thanks to Kylie Louise McCormick of WyoHistory.org for enthusiastically joining the project toward the end. Your vision, contributions, language updates, and fact-checking strengthened the historical aspects of this book immeasurably. To Morgan Albertson, executive director of History Jackson Hole, thank you for generously sharing your institution's research about women in the Tetons. Kristen Broeder, thank you for your initial investigations into historical photography. Your legwork in that department helped me see that a book about Wyoming's historical women with their accompanying images needed to be an entirely separate project.

Thank you to Beth Venn, executive director of the Neltje Center for Excellence in Creativity and the Arts, and Lucas Watkins, Neltje's studio manager, for adding more detail and depth to Neltje's story. I am grateful to the family of Clarene Law: Charisse Haws, Teresa Meadows, and Steve Meadows, for acting on behalf of your beloved mother to ensure her legacy was accurate. Additional thanks to Laurie Thoman on behalf of Mickey Thoman and Sue Simpson Gallager on behalf of Ann Simpson for helping confirm details and adding extra life to these important women's stories. Thank you to Jean Lewis, Katie Hogarty, and Kerry Lloyd of Climb Wyoming for your assistance in updating Climb's story and for your championing of this project. Thank you to Dr. Cecilia Aragon for your support and assistance in updating WLYC's story, as well as for your long-term encouragement of this project.

To Mandy Fabel, Sara Beck, Carol Linton, and Sarah Jo Sinclair, thank you for carving precious time out of your full lives to be my beta readers. You are dear friends, family, colleagues, mentors, and anchors. Your feedback, suggestions, reflections, and encouragement made this book stronger. Love you all!

Andrea Shallcross, thank you for your generous expertise and attention to detail in professional matters far outside my areas of knowledge. Your industry know-how solidified my confidence and direction.

Thank you to the incomparable Fran Hauser and Bethany Saltman of *Bookbound*: Your expertise, care, and community guided me through so many phases of the publishing process. I'm in awe of you ladies and so grateful to be your student.

To my Northwest College (NWC) family— Gary Bakken, Dennis Davis, Christine Garceau, Jayne Johnson, Jen Litterer-Trevino, Anthony Polvere, Craig Satterlee, and J. L. "Woody" Wooden—I would not be here without your teaching and encouragement. Because of the technical foundation of the photography program, plus the lifelong friendships, camaraderie, and support I found there, I'm fueled to keep discovering. To the administrative team at NWC—Jill Hartmann, Shelby Wetzel, President Lisa Watson, and many others— thank you for championing my work, inviting me to be 2024's commencement speaker, and continuing to support the future of NWC. There are many others in Powell who have been friends and supporters.

To the incredible curators and institutions, as well as their boards and staff, who have supported the exhibit since 2019: Rebecca West and Karen Brooks McWhorter at the Buffalo Bill Center of the West, who took a chance and were the most amazing curators to work with for the first exhibit; Nicole Crawford and team at the University of Wyoming Art Museum; Oona Doherty and Marty Camino at the Center for the Arts gallery and Jennifer Hoffman and Bronwyn Minton at the Art Association gallery in Jackson; Nathan Jones, formerly a curator at the National Cowboy & Western Heritage Museum in Oklahoma City, OK, as well as Gretchen Jeane; Allison Maluchnik and team at the Nicolaysen Art Museum; Heather Smith at Poppy coworking space; Kendra Heimbuck, Barbara McNab, William Lopez, Jochen Wierich, Jacob Ruleaux, Kim Taylor, and team at the Brinton Museum. Each of these institutions and their people work hard to cultivate spaces for communities to gather and connect. Thank you for the opportunity to showcase some of Wyoming's powerful women, and for your support of this body of work. Thank you Tayloe Piggott for hosting a one-night opening for the launch of Chapter I: Breaking Boundaries in 2017—the evening generated excitement for the full exhibit in 2019. To Rowene Weems, thank you for the first shot at creating an exhibit for *Been Here for Generations* at the Homesteader Museum—that experience was invaluable to this project's development.

I am very grateful to Samin Dadelahi and Sarah Chapman at the Wyoming Community Foundation, as well as to the board and staff, for believing in this body of work as my current nonprofit fiscal sponsor. Your leadership goes beyond your position and titles—you exemplify great leadership through collaboration, expertise, and thoughtfulness. The mission of the Wyoming Community Foundation is connecting people who care with causes that matter to build a better Wyoming. Additionally, I am honored to serve as vice chair of the advisory board of the Wyoming Women's Foundation, which invests in the economic self-sufficiency of women and opportunities for girls in Wyoming. Thank you to executive director Rebekah Smith Hazelton for your support of this project and leadership for women and girls in Wyoming, in addition to Associate Director of Policy Micah Richardson for your devotion to advocacy and community.

A warm, heartfelt thanks to my incredible lead sponsors who funded the production of the twenty-five stories between 2016 and 2021, as well as the production of the traveling exhibition. They are Hughes Charitable Foundation, the Equipoise Fund, Center of Wonder, REALM Global, Brimmer Communications, Mary Armour and Jean Lewis, Jessica Case, Debby and David Hopkins, Carol and Jim Linton, Noa and Ted Staryk, Wyoming Humanities Council, Don and Judy Opatrny, Ellen Raisbeck, Helen and Fred Arbuckle, Bobby Model Charitable Fund, Mark and Nancy Anselmi, Lynn Blodgett, Petria and Scott Fossel, Richard Georgi and Sanae Ishikawa, Outpost Inc., Soroptimist of Jackson Hole, Stacy Astor, Bomber Mountain Derby Devils, the Thursday Roundtable Fund, and the Wyoming Council for Women. Thank you for your belief in this vision, and in many cases, your friendship and mentorship in addition to your financial backing.

Between 2016 and 2021, the project partnered with Womentum, a 501c3 organization in Jackson, who served as the project's nonprofit fiscal sponsor. Womentum's mission is to inspire and connect women to thrive as leaders. To Caryn Flanagan, Womentum's executive director at the time of the project's inception, thank you for your belief in this vision. Additional thanks to the many supportive past and present board members of Womentum over the years, including: Ponteir Sackrey, Megan Smith, Leslye Hardie, Kris Shean, Betsy Carlin, Lina Collado, and many others.

Thank you to former Womentum executive director (and fellow author) Samantha Strawbridge for your warm support and mentorship. You helped me cross the finish line with production and shepherd in the creation of this book. Thank you to Womentum's current leadership team, Executive Director Kristen Fox and Program Director Elisabeth Rohrbach, for your continued support. You all truly embody your mission to uplift women in our community. Thank you.

Thank you: Laura Bell, Isabella Beroutsos, Lynn Blodgett, Shari Brownfield, Jason Buk, Pam Cutler, Lyn Dalebout, Greta Eagan, Andrew Eccles, Lindsay Getz, Chantalle LeKrey, Lindsay Love, Julie Ottusch, Whitney Ralli, John Sargent, Casey Sedlack, Erin Taylor, Taylor Timmis, and Bonnie Wan, for acting as a connector, a resource, a cheerleader, a writing partner, or a sounding board for this book's creation.

To the many, many friends, colleagues, journalists, clients, and beyond who have championed me and this project over the years: Tessa Baker, Liz Brimmer, the Brio Collective cohorts, Sandy Buk, Melissa Cassutt, Kristen Czaban, Wyoming state superintendent of public instruction Megan Degenfelder, Rudi Dubois, Lisa Finkelstein, Lydia Heinbockel, Cathy Holman, Molly Hughes, Jessica Jaubert, Kate Johnson, Hailey Morton Levinson, Melissa Lyon, Natalia Macker, Maureen "Mo" Murphy, Peg Ostlund, Tracey Poe, Anita Roman, Joel Saferstein, Lauren Shortt, Jen Simon, Ashleigh Snoozy, Goda Stevens, Melissa Thomasma, Tia Troy, JoAnn True, Jennifer True, Melissa Turley, Kristin Walker, Susan White, Kate Wilson, Ciela Wynter, Irina Zhorov, and countless others—you lift me up. Additional thanks to Dustin Bleizeffer and WyoFile.com for your early publication of these stories.

Finally, to all the women in the project—Neltje, Affie, Marilyn, Nimi, Nina, Clarene, Lynette, Bernie, Dr. Diane, Lori, Megan, Mickey, Rita, the girls and leadership of Wyoming Latina Youth Conference, Dr. Ray and the moms of Climb Wyoming, Aura, Lauren, Rosie, Hillary, Liz, Jill, Jessie, Ann, Jasmine, Marnie, and Sara—it is an honor to stand together. I love you all.

Resources & Citations

All population data throughout the book is from the *U.S. Census 2023*

Introduction

Shape: form, create
Merriam-Webster. (n.d.). "Shape." In *Merriam-Webster.com dictionary*. https://www .merriam-webster.com/dictionary/shape

Across 97,914 square miles
This figure varies depending on the source. 97,914 derives from: State of Wyoming. (n.d.). *About Wyoming*. https://www.wyo.gov/about-wyoming; Wyoming Secretary of State. (n.d.). *State Symbols*. https://sos.wyo.gov/Services/StateInfo_Symbols .aspx

75 percent of grasslands and rangelands
Marin, J. (2023, August 31). *Land Use by State: A Visual Guide*. Acres. https://landvalues.acres.com /land-use-by-state-visual-guide

Wyoming passed one of the nation's first equal pay laws, requiring that teachers be paid on the basis of their qualifications, not their gender. And the state also recognized married women's rights to control their own property and wages. At the time, these freedoms were unheard of across most of the country.
Helton, J. (2019). "So Great an Innovation: Woman Suffrage in Wyoming," in L. Lahlum and M. Rozum (Eds.), *Equality at the Ballot Box* (pp. 33–70). Historical Society Press.

Chapter I: *Breaking Boundaries*
The Road to Neltje
I ascend over 5,000 vertical feet, climbing switch-back after long, stretching switchback.
From the town of Ten Sleep at 4,426 feet to the top of Cloud Peak Skyway Scenic Byway on Powder River Pass at 9,666 feet is a difference of 5,240 vertical feet: Wyoming Office of Tourism. (n.d.). *Ten Sleep*. Travel Wyoming. https: //travelwyoming.com/places-to-go/cities/ ten-sleep

At 9,666 feet above sea level, I reach the road's summit.
Wyoming Office of Tourism. (n.d.). *Cloud Peak Skyway Scenic Byway*. Travel Wyoming. https://travelwyoming.com/listing /cloud-peak-skyway-scenic-byway/292

Marilyn S. Kite
A healthy, functioning, independent democracy is dependent upon a healthy, functioning, independent judicial system.
Kite, M. S. (2007). "Wyoming's Judicial Selection Process: Is It Getting the Job Done?" *Fordham Urban Law Journal*, 34(1), 203.

Wyoming's Judicial System
Wyoming's nomination system begins with an unpaid, volunteer judicial nominating committee comprised of three attorneys elected by members of the Wyoming State Bar and three non-attorney electors of the state who are appointed by the governor. The commission recommends candidates to the governor, who makes the final appointment. Later, the public can vote to retain appointed

judges. Wyoming's system was redesigned in the 1970s to limit political influence from public elections and overreach from the executive branch. While not completely devoid of politics due to the governor's input, and not completely transparent with the independent-yet-private nominating committee, Wyoming's system is a unique one that attempts to maintain separation of powers. As Marilyn urges, "The rights guaranteed by the United States Constitution to the citizens of our country mean little without an independent judiciary to enforce those rights."

Kite, M. S. (2007). "Wyoming's Judicial Selection Process: Is It Getting the Job Done?" *Fordham Urban Law Journal, 34*(1), 203.

Wyoming Women Win the Vote: The Story of Suffrage and Groundbreaking Women of History

Additionally, Wyoming's suffrage law recognized the voting rights of all women citizens, regardless of race.

Helton, J. (2025, February 27). *"Then I breathed freely": Black Women Vote in Wyoming, 1870.* WyoHistory.org. https://www.wyohistory.org /encyclopedia/then-i-breathed-freely-black -women-vote-wyoming-1870

Most women in Wyoming held power and positions of influence unmatched by their fellow American contemporaries.

Helton, J. (2019). "So Great an Innovation: Woman Suffrage in Wyoming," in L. Lahlum and M. Rozum (Eds.), *Equality at the Ballot Box* (pp. 33–70). Historical Society Press.

The legislature also passed one of the nation's first equal pay laws, requiring that teachers be paid on the basis of their qualifications, not their gender.

Helton, J. (2019). "So Great an Innovation: Woman Suffrage in Wyoming," in L. Lahlum

and M. Rozum (Eds.), *Equality at the Ballot Box* (pp. 50, 53). Historical Society Press.

Senator John Fosher, who knew firsthand how much women contributed to their communities, and who may have headed the advocacy of suffragist Amalia Post,

Massie, M. A. (1990). "Reform Is Where You Find It: The Roots of Woman Suffrage in Wyoming." *Annals of Wyoming, 62*(1), 17. Personal account from Jim Allen, great-great-nephew of John Fosher, and former representative for District 33, April 2025.

When Wyoming officially entered the Union, in 1890, it became the first state to guarantee women's freedom and equality.

Kinney, Amy L. (2019). "A Sentiment of Justice: The Woman Suffrage Question and Wyoming Statehood," in L. Lahlum and M. Rozum (Eds.), *Equality at the Ballot Box* (pp. 169–173). Historical Society Press.

First woman in Wyoming to vote: Louisa Swain (1801–1880)

The crowd continued to cheer for her as she walked home.

Helton, J. (2019). "So Great an Innovation: Woman Suffrage in Wyoming," in L. Lahlum and M. Rozum (Eds.), *Equality at the Ballot Box* (p. 57). Historical Society Press.

Indigenous women like the Haudenosaunee (Iroquois), who held enormous power in their societies and had voted for centuries . . .

Wagner, S. R. (2001). *Sisters in Spirit: Haudenosaunee (Iroquois) Influence on Early American Feminists.* Native Voices.

America's first female justice of the peace: Esther Hobart Morris (1814–1902)

Helton, J. (2019). "So Great an Innovation: Woman Suffrage in Wyoming," in L. Lahlum and M. Rozum (Eds.), *Equality at the Ballot Box* (pp. 44–49). Historical Society Press.

National Park Service. (n.d.). *Esther Hobart Morris*. https://www.nps.gov/people/esther -hobart-morris.htm

attending the California Woman Suffrage Association convention in San Francisco in 1872
San Francisco Chronicle (San Francisco, California), Wed, Feb 14, 1872.

Suffragist and one of the first women in the U.S. to serve on a jury: Amalia Post (1826–1897)

Helton, J. (2019). "So Great an Innovation: Woman Suffrage in Wyoming," in L. Lahlum and M. Rozum (Eds.), *Equality at the Ballot Box* (pp. 49, 56–58). Historical Society Press.

Massie, M. A. (1990). "Reform Is Where You Find It: The Roots of Woman Suffrage in Wyoming." *Annals of Wyoming, 62*(1), 17.

America's first female bailiff: Martha Symons Boies Atkinson (1830–1917)

Hein, R. (2016, October 3). *"Those Damn Women": Louise Graf and Women on Wyoming Juries*. WyoHistory.org. https://www.wyohistory .org/encyclopedia/those-damn-women-louise -graf-and-women-wyoming-juries

Laegreid, R. (2019). "Martha Symons Boies Atkinson: First Woman Bailiff," in L. Lahlum and M. Rozum (Eds.), *Equality at the ballot box* (pp. 285–289). Historical Society Press.

Viner, K. (2020, January 23). *Women on the Jury: Wyoming Makes History Again*. WyoHistory.org. https://www.wyohistory.org/encyclopedia /women-jury-wyoming-makes-history-again

America's first female prison chaplain: May Gorslin Preston Slosson, PhD (1858–1943)

Beach, C. (1927). *Women of Wyoming*. C. M. Beach.

One of the prisoners said of her abilities and popularity . . .
Cordova, R. (1902) "A Lady Prison Chaplain." *The Wide World Magazine*, 500–504. https://archive.org/details /wideworldmagazin10londuoft/page/500 /mode/2up?view=theater

Wyoming's first female legislator: Mary Godat Bellamy (1861–1955)

Helton, J. (2024, December 6). *Wyoming's First Woman Legislator*. WyoHistory.org. https://www .wyohistory.org/encyclopedia/mary-godat -bellamy-wyomings-first-woman-legislator

First women in Wyoming to own and publish a newspaper: The Huntington Sisters [Gertrude (1866–1925), Laura (1870–1962), and Carolyn (1879–1904)]

Van Pelt, L. (2015, July 25). *The Lyre Girls*. WyoHistory.org. https://www.wyohistory.org /encyclopedia/lyre-girls-first-women-newspaper -owners-wyoming

One of Wyoming's first female physicians: Dr. Lillian Heath (1865–1962)

Van Pelt, L. (2014, November 8). *Lillian Heath: Wyoming's First Female Physician Packed a Pistol*. WyoHistory.org. https://www.wyohistory.org /encyclopedia/lillian-heath

Wyoming Secretary of State. (n.d.). *Wyoming Women of Note: Dr. Lillian Heath Nelson*. https://sos.wyo.gov/WomenOfNote/WomenOfNote_2020_07.aspx

At sixteen years old, Lillian Heath assisted Dr. Maghee with the medical study of criminal Big Nose George Parrott. Maghee gifted her the top half of the skull, which was used to identify Parrott's remains in the 1950s.

Van Pelt, L. (2024, November 15). *Big Nose George: A Grisly Frontier Tale*. WyoHistory.org. https://www.wyohistory.org/encyclopedia/big-nose-george-grisly-frontier-tale

Influential psychologist: Dr. June Etta Downey (1875–1932)

Hein, R. (2018, February 8). *June Downey: Scientist, Scholar and Poet*. WyoHistory.org. https://www.wyohistory.org/encyclopedia/june-downey-scientist-scholar-and-poet

Historian, geographer, and first female member of the Wyoming State Bar: Dr. Grace Raymond Hebard (1861–1936)

Scharff, V. (2003). *Twenty Thousand Roads: Women, Movement, and the West* (pp. 94–114). University of California Press.

Rancher, justice of the peace, game warden, and politician: Maggie Gillespie (1861–1942)

Beach, C. (1927). *Women of Wyoming*. C. M. Beach.

Wyoming state flag creator: Verna Keays (1893–1982)

McCormick, K. L. (2021, August 31). *The Wyoming State Flag and the Women Who Made It Fly*. WyoHistory.org. https://www.wyohistory.org/encyclopedia/wyoming-state-flag-and-women-who-made-it-fly

Journalist, writer, historian: Agnes Wright Spring (1894–1988)

Flowers, K. M. (2023, March 6). *Agnes Wright Spring: Equality as a Matter of Course*. WyoHistory.org. https://www.wyohistory.org/encyclopedia/agnes-wright-spring-equality-matter-course

Wright Spring, A. (1981). *Near the Greats*. A Platte N' Press Book.

Jackson's all-woman government (1920–1923)

History Jackson Hole. (2020, May 26). *Petticoat Rules: The first women leaders of Jackson 100 years ago*. Buckrail.com. https://buckrail.com/petticoat-rules-the-first-women-leaders-of-jackson-100-years-ago/

Small-town mayor: Lizabeth Wiley (1870–1957)

McCormick, K. L. (2023, May 1). *"It can be done": Mayor Lizabeth Wiley and the KKK*. WyoHistory.org. https://www.wyohistory.org/encyclopedia/it-can-be-done-mayor-lizabeth-wiley-and-kkk

Thrill-seeking journalist, author, and publisher: Caroline Lockhart (1871–1962)

Clayton, J. (2007). *The Cowboy Girl: The Life of Caroline Lockhart*. University of Nebraska Press.

Clayton, J. (2014, November 8). *The Old West's Female Champion: Caroline Lockhart and Wyoming's Cowboy Heritage*. WyoHistory.org. https://www.wyohistory.org/encyclopedia/old-wests-female-champion-caroline-lockhart-and-wyomings-cowboy-heritage

Pargament, E. (2024, July 25). *Caroline Lockhart: 5 Facts about Cody's Western Novelist.* Buffalo Bill Center of the West. https://centerofthewest.org/2024/07/25/caroline-lockhart-5-facts-about-codys-western-novelist

America's first female governor and first female director of the United States Mint: Nellie Tayloe Ross (1876–1977)

Scheer, T. (2005). *Governor Lady: The Life and Times of Nellie Tayloe Ross.* University of Missouri Press.

American photographer, businesswoman, and homemaker: Lora Webb Nichols (1883–1962)

Van Pelt, L. (2014, November 21). *Lora Webb Nichols: An Eye on Early Wyoming.* WyoHistory .org. https://www.wyohistory.org/encyclopedia/lora-webb-nichols-eye-early-wyoming

Wyoming's first female secretary of state: Thyra Thomson (1916–2013)

Wyoming State Archives. (2014, November 17). *Thyra Thomson, Wyoming Secretary of State 1963–1987.* [Oral history interview by Mark Junge, November 1993]. WyoHistory.org. https://www .wyohistory.org/oral-histories/thyra-thomson-wyoming-secretary-state-1963-1987

First Black woman in Wyoming's legislature: Harriet Elizabeth "Liz" Byrd (1926–2015)

Van Pelt, L. (2015, May 24). *Liz Byrd, First Black Woman in Wyoming's Legislature.* WyoHistory .org. https://www.wyohistory.org/encyclopedia/liz-byrd-first-black-woman-wyoming-legislature

Chapter II: *Filling the Void*

Lynette St. Clair

Language is more than words; it is a bridge between generations, carrying stories, customs, and values that define a people.

According to the Linguistic Society of America, of the approximately 7,000 languages spoken today, 50 to 90 percent are at risk of extinction by the end of the twenty-first century. Recognizing the urgent need for preservation, the United Nations declared 2019 the International Year of Indigenous Languages (IY2019), to raise awareness of this crisis and emphasize the vital role languages play in cultural diversity. As languages disappear, so too do the histories, traditions, and worldviews they carry—making their preservation essential for the richness of our shared human experience. https://www.lsadc.org, https://en.iyil2019.org

Riehl, A. (2019, November 8). "Why Are Languages Worth Preserving?" *Sapiens.* https://www.sapiens.org/language/endangered-languages

Dr. Diane Noton Coale

More than 50 percent of health-care providers experience burnout, and for those in isolated areas, the pressure is even greater.

Audis, B., Damayanti, S., Maher, K., et al. (2019, July 9). "The Impact of Burnout Syndrome on Practitioners Working within Rural Healthcare Systems." *American Journal of Emergency Medicine.* https://pubmed.ncbi.nlm.nih.gov/31706660

Megan Grassell

These developing years for girls can be challenging.

Peetz, C. (2023, November 2). "Girls' Self-Confidence Has Plummeted, a New Survey Shows." *Education Week*. https://www.edweek.org/leadership/girls-self-confidence-has-plummeted-a-new-survey-shows/2023/11

Chapter III: *Power*
Mickey Thoman
One-room ranch school
The Thoman Family. "Thoman Ranch School History" (family history document).

Ranching is significant to Wyoming's economy, adding nearly $2.5 billion in revenue, and a lifestyle vital to many communities.
U.S. Department of Agriculture. *Wyoming Agricultural Statistics 2023* (p.5). https://www.nass.usda.gov/Statistics_by_State/Wyoming/Publications/Annual_Statistical_Bulletin/WY-2023-Bulletin.pdf

Climb Wyoming
Single mothers and their children experience the highest rates of poverty among families in Wyoming.
Climb Wyoming. (n.d.). *You Help Build a Stronger Wyoming*. https://climbwyoming.org/about-us/support-climb

Chapter IV: *Rising*
Hillary Walrath
Federal public lands comprise 48 percent of Wyoming.
Wyoming Game and Fish Department. (n.d.). *Access Summary*. https://wgfd.wyo.gov/public-access/access-summary

Chapter V: *The Cowgirl State*
Marnie Peterson
The FDA announced their commitment to phasing out animal testing and exploring new approach methodologies (NAMs), like live animal tissue alternatives.
U.S. Food & Drug Administration. (2025, April 10). *FDA Announces Plan to Phase Out Animal Testing Requirement for Monoclonal Antibodies and Other Drugs*. https://www.fda.gov/news-events/press-announcements/fda-announces-plan-phase-out-animal-testing-requirement-monoclonal-antibodies-and-other-drugs

The Creative Process: The Exhibit
Neltje's triptych at the University of Wyoming Art Museum.
Image credit: Janelle Rose.

Admiring Senator Affie Ellis at the Buffalo Bill Center of the West.
Image credit: Sarah Averill.

Opening night at the Nicolaysen Art Museum; Lindsay, with sons Hank and Luke Buk. Clarene Law's iconic 1976 Cadillac Eldorado and one of Neltje's 10-by-30 foot paintings were featured in this exhibit.
Image credit: Ben Winckler Photography.

The National Cowboy & Western Heritage Museum.
Image credit: Simon Hurst.

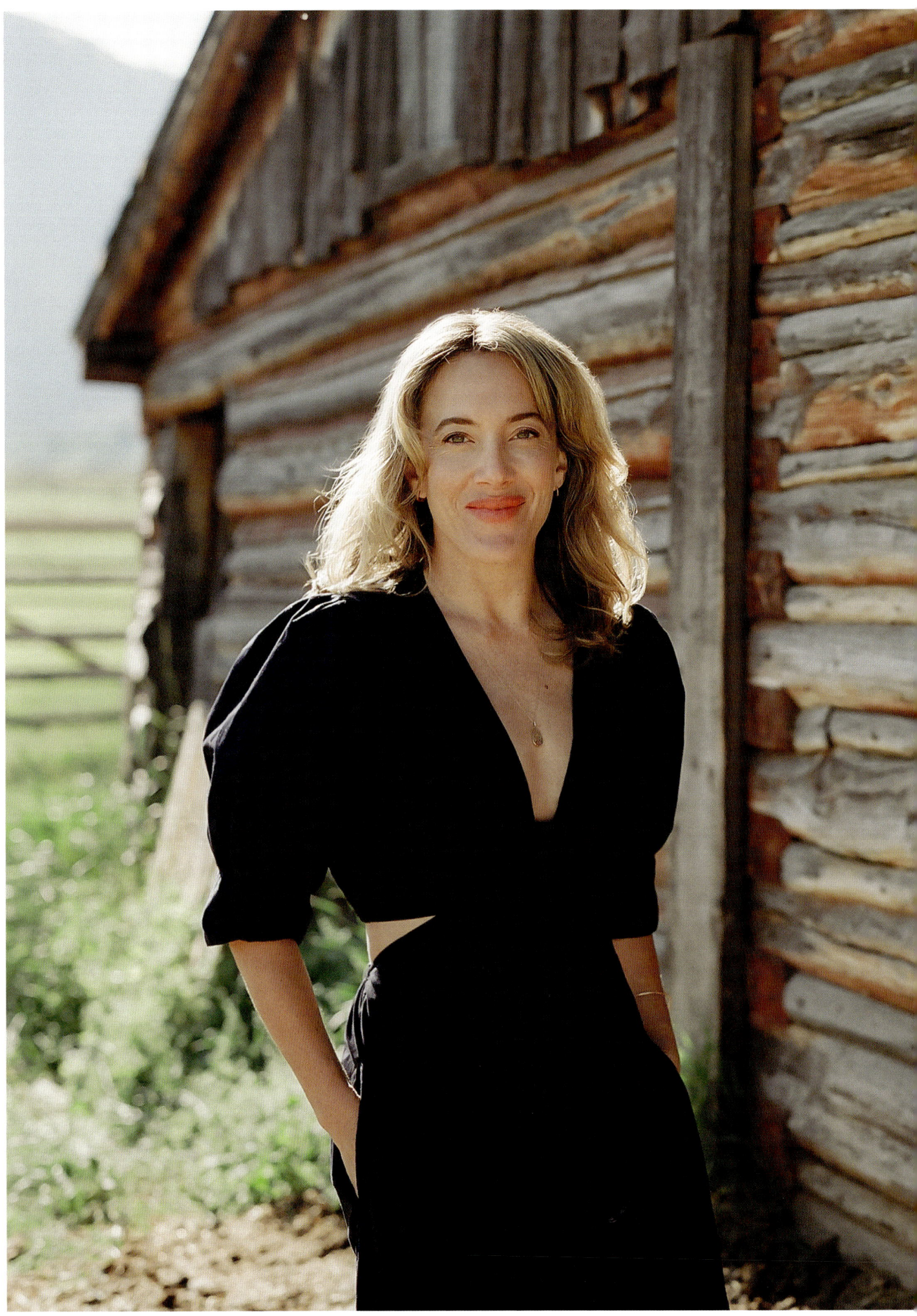

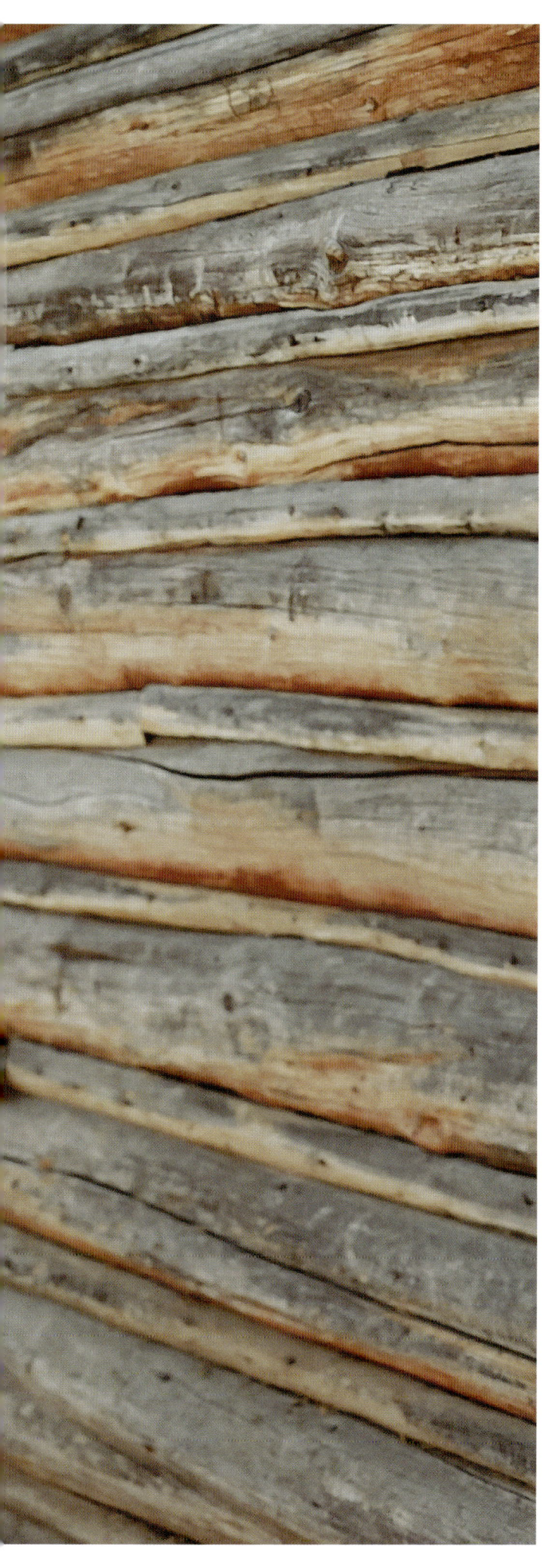

About the Author

Lindsay Linton Buk is an artist, photographer, and fifth-generation Wyoming native—originally from the small farm town of Powell. Lindsay worked as a commercial photographer in New York City and taught photography workshops for Canon before returning to Wyoming, where she founded her photography studio. Her portrait work has appeared in *Outside* and *Southwest* magazines. Her *Women in Wyoming* project has generated national acclaim, with features on Forbes.com and the Travel Channel, among others. In addition to her creative work, Lindsay is passionate about advocacy. She serves as vice chair of the Wyoming Women's Foundation, which works toward economic self-sufficiency and opportunities for girls in Wyoming, and the Wyoming Making History Committee of the Smithsonian American Women's History Museum. She lives in Jackson, Wyoming with her husband and two wild Wyoming boys. You can see more of her work at LintonProductions.com.

Image credit: Carrie Patterson

Library of Congress Cataloging-in-Publication Data available.
ISBN: 978-1-68555-244-2
Ebook ISBN: 978-1-68555-661-7
LCCN: 2025911432

Manufactured in China.

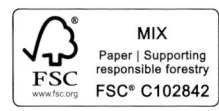

Editor: Bridget Watson Payne
Design: Liliana Guia
10 9 8 7 6 5 4 3 2 1

The Collective Book Studio®
Oakland, California
www.thecollectivebook.studio